PRESENT PAST

PRESENT PAST

Modernity and the Memory Crisis

RICHARD TERDIMAN

Cornell University Press

Ithaca and London

Contents

vi   *Contents*

Preface

This book is about memory: about how the past persists into the present, and about how this singular persistence has been understood in the last two hundred years or so. I begin by offering a frame for understanding the urgency of concern with memory in the modern period. Then I consider a series of texts in which such preoccupation with the mnemonic is central. I center discussion on four writers—Alfred de Musset, Charles Baudelaire, Marcel Proust, and Sigmund Freud—whose reflections on memory in the modern period I claim are exemplary and diagnostic.

Most often we think of memory as a faculty constituting our consciousness and our self-awareness, as the means by which the coherence of our identity and our history is constructed and sustained. Such mnemonic activity is fundamental. But there is another side to memory—memory as a *problem*, as a site and source of cultural disquiet. The figures I discuss in *Present Past* saw unprecedented perturbations in memory's practice and disturbing dangers in its effects. My concern with memory in this book arises in a parallel disquiet. Our present is still not on easy terms with how the past endures, with how it continues to occupy and preoccupy us. From the unending recurrence in national and international affairs of conflicts rooted in seemingly bygone political, religious, or cultural disputes to the involuntary repetition of struggles with psychic trauma surviving from an archaic period of our individual lives, we appear unable to cease contending with a past we might otherwise have thought was gone. But the past does not evaporate. Its persistence is the effect of memory. So although memory salutarily stabilizes our sense of the world, that is not all it does. Intertwined with such beneficent and indispensable effects, the uncanny ambiguity of memory manifests itself in just these sorts of discomfiting survivals.

Concerns with such effects would seem completely illogical if they were not so urgent. About what could we do less than about the past? Why then do we worry about it so insistently and so intricately? Part of the objective of this book is to help to understand why concern about memory arose and became so pressing in the period I examine here. Coupled with that question is another that occupies me centrally in what follows: the relation between *memory* and *theory*. I argue that the intensified reflection about culture's constitution and its processes in post-Revolutionary Europe sought to make sense of disturbances in the realm of memory. I want to understand how the paradigms of memory projected then relate to the period's cultural and social theory.

I call the period that *Present Past* deals with "modernity." The term might seem to have lost any possible precision. But I want to take the chance of this instability to reconceive modernity in relation to the cultural disquiet I term the memory crisis. So in seeking to make sense both of modernity and of the memory crisis, I have sought to avoid preconstituted categories. I want to let these notions inflect each other in the interweaving of the cultural preoccupations on which I focus in the hope that clearer images both of "modernity" and of the "memory crisis" will emerge from this association.

Our ideas about modernity were probably determined most by Baudelaire. In Chapter 4 I discuss his Swan/Sign Poem ("Le Cygne") from *Les Fleurs du mal*, a text that as much as any in the European tradition founded and framed the historical distinction that projects modernity as a temporal and cultural category. "Le Cygne" does so through an intense reflection on the processes of memory—on their mechanisms and on the disturbances to which they are subject. Rooted in this concentration on the realm of the mnemonic, the poem foregrounds the *sign* as modernity's central emblem. Manifestly, it has occupied that role ever since. But we have forgotten Baudelaire's insistent *historicization* of the sign and rewritten it as a timeless entity. In contrast, I want to examine how Baudelaire's centralization of the semiotic in the experience of modernity arose in his understanding of his period's crisis of memory. Thus my reading of Baudelaire's text will claim that a fundamental sense of cultural disturbance links his representations of the mnemonic and the semiotic, and establishes the connection of both to what he named and we know as modernity. This deeply historicized relation between the problem of memory on the one hand and the representation of experience on the other underlies my interpretation of all of the figures I consider in this book.

The length of this book has made it necessary to omit the original French texts of much of the material I quote. Inevitably translations involve compromises, but I have provided the original text whenever the translation could not capture pertinent nuances. Unless otherwise noted, translations are my own, and reference is given to the original to facilitate checking. I quote Freud from the *Standard Edition* (except for texts that do not appear there), interpolating his German wherever the discussion requires this sort of precision. The editions of texts from which I quote will be found in the list of Works Cited.

In a book on memory, acknowledgments are a performance of—and a metacommentary on—the object of analysis. In the spirit of such an instantiation of my topic, I want to remember the people and institutions who assisted me over the years during which this book was in progress.

Let me begin by thanking Michael Schudson. Years ago we discovered a mutual fascination with the functioning of memory in culture; his *Watergate in American Memory* is a splendid fruit of his ingenious concern with the memory problem. Together we taught a joint Literature and Communications course at the University of California, San Diego, where the project of my own book first began to take shape. I'm grateful to the students in that course. My thanks next to Satya Mohanty, whose invitation to write an essay for a special issue of *Diacritics* produced my first attempt to frame the problem I seek to deal with here. Let me express my gratitude to the students in the Literature and the History of Consciousness seminars at the University of California, Santa Cruz, and in the French Department at Stanford University, who sat through my early efforts at the analyses in this book.

My thanks to the colleagues who read and reacted to my manu-

script at various stages. Their criticism was as generous as it was
acute. Let me first name Ross Chambers and Hayden White, whose
engagement with my project, and insight concerning it, were extraordinary. Many other colleagues contributed in crucial ways to
helping me with the development of the book. I thank them here.
From my year at the Stanford Humanities Center, Elizabeth Eisen-
stein, Steven Mailloux, Renato Rosaldo, Constance Sherak, and Katy
Trumpener. Among colleagues at Santa Cruz, Karen Bassi, Dilip
Basu, Harry Berger, Norman O. Brown, David Hoy, John Jordan,
Marsh Leicester, Kristin Ross, Cole Swensen, and Tom Vogler. In
Paris, Françoise Gaillard, Luce Giard, Jacques Le Brun, and Annie
Tardits, whose ongoing generosity has deepened my Francophilia.
And at other institutions, Geoff Batchen, Natalie Zemon Davis, Do-
minick LaCapra, Suzanne Nash, Martha Nussbaum, Michael Roth,
Tadeusz Slawek, Randolph Starn, Don E. Wayne, Nathaniel Wing,
and Andrew Wright. With admirable perseverance Debra Satz urged
me toward a greater clarity, for which I thank her affectionately. I
want to remember Michel de Certeau, whose intelligence and good-
ness over the years we were colleagues inspired my work.

In October 1989 the Loma Prieta earthquake abruptly interrupted
my progress on this book. I would like to express my gratitude to the
friends who helped me so generously—and, amid the aftershocks,
frequently with considerable courage—in the aftermath of the
upheaval: Stephen Harris, David Ingram, David and Rachel Kliger,
Karen McNally, Jon Pettis, Julia Simon-Ingram, Greta Slobin, and
Daniel Terdiman.

Pierre Bourdieu, director of the Centre de Sociologie Européenne
at the École des Hautes Études en Sciences Sociales, invited me to
Paris to do a seminar on my research. I thank him for his generosity
over many years. And I am grateful to Élina Almasy for her assistance in enabling me to publish the lectures I gave at Hautes Études
in *Information pour les Sciences Sociales*.

I am grateful to the Stanford Humanities Center and to Bliss Car-
nochan, for many years its director, for a fellowship that permitted
me a year to devise the overall conception of this project and begin
to work it through. Marta Sutton Weeks generously provided the
funds that made that fellowship possible. And I thank the University

of California for the President's Research Fellowship in the Humanities which gave me a year to finish the book. The Committee on Research and the Humanities Division, University of California, Santa Cruz, granted continuing and generous support for my work.

For the kind and intelligent assistance they gave me in the course of my research, my thanks to the staffs of the Bibliothèque Nationale, Paris; of the libraries of the University of California, Santa Cruz, Berkeley, and San Diego campuses; and of Green Library at Stanford University. Particular gratitude to Laura McClanathan and Mathew Simpson of McHenry Library, UCSC, for their assistance.

For their invitations to present portions of my work in lectures, I thank Yale University; Harvard University; the University of Michigan; Washington University, St. Louis (particularly Julia Simon-Ingram); the University of Southern California (particularly Peggy Kamuf); the University of California, San Diego; Miami University of Ohio (particularly Peter Rose); and New Mexico State University (particularly Mary Wolf).

My thanks to those who helped my project through the stages of its production: particularly, to Betsy Wootten, Barbara Lee, Claire Braz-Valentine, and Marilyn McLeod at UCSC; to Bernhard Kendler, Teresa Jesionowski, Linda Wentworth, and George Whipple of Cornell University Press; and to Andrew Lewis, who edited the manuscript for the Press. I am grateful to Stuart Christie, Dan Duane, and Jon Hunt for help at the proofreading stage.

Portions of Chapters 1 and 2 are extensively revised versions of an article that appeared in *Diacritics*, 15, no. 4 (special issue, on "Marx after Derrida"), Winter 1985 (copyright © The Johns Hopkins University Press). Chapter 3 is a revised version of an essay published in *Representations*, no. 26 (special issue, "Memory and Counter-Memory"), Spring 1989 (copyright © University of California Press). I thank the publishers of these journals for permission to use this material here.

RICHARD TERDIMAN

Santa Cruz, California

Abbreviations

Corr. Marcel Proust, *Correspondance*. Edited by Philip Kolb. 19 vols. to date. Paris: Plon, 1970–

CSB Marcel Proust. *"Contre Sainte-Beuve" précédé de "Pastiches et mélanges" et suivi de "Essais et articles."* Edited by Pierre Clarac and Yves Sandre. Paris: Gallimard-Pléiade, 1971.

JS Marcel Proust. *"Jean Santeuil" précédé de "Les Plaisirs et les jours."* Edited by Pierre Clarac and Yves Sandre. Paris: Gallimard-Pléiade, 1971.

RTP54 Marcel Proust. *A la recherche du temps perdu*. Edited by Pierre Clarac and André Ferré. 3 vols. Paris: Gallimard-Pléiade, 1954.

RTP Marcel Proust. *A la recherche du temps perdu*. Edited by Jean-Yves Tadié. 4 vols. Paris: Gallimard-Pléiade, 1987–89.

SE Sigmund Freud. *The Standard Edition of the Complete Psychological Works*. Translated and edited by James Strachey et al. 24 vols. London: Hogarth Press, 1953–74.

Part One

AN INTRODUCTION
TO MEMORY

1

Historicizing Memory

Memory is not a constantly accessible copy of the different facts of our life, but an oblivion from which, at random moments, present resemblances enable us to resuscitate dead recollections.
—Marcel Proust, *La Prisonnière*, *RTP* 3:3653; *RTP54* 3:146

Hysterics suffer mainly from reminiscences.
—Sigmund Freud and Josef Breuer, *Studies on Hysteria*, *SE* 2:7 (emphasis theirs)

Even memory has a history. Of course every culture remembers its past.[1] But how a culture performs and sustains this recollection is distinctive and diagnostic. This book seeks to understand modernity's relationship with memory and, in particular, some of the stresses that have characterized that relationship.

In a world of change, memory becomes complicated. Any revolution, any rapid alteration of the givens of the present places a society's connection with its history under pressure. But in Europe in the period after the 1789–1815 Revolution, and particularly in France, the uncertainty of relation with the past became especially intense. In this period people experienced the insecurity of their culture's involvement with its past, the perturbation of the link to their own inheritance, as what I want to term a "memory crisis": a

1. For Yuri Lotman and B. A. Uspensky, culture *is* precisely such recollection: "We understand culture as the *nonhereditary memory of the community*" ("On the Semiotic Mechanism of Culture," 213).

3

sense that their past had somehow evaded memory, that recollection
had ceased to integrate with consciousness. In this memory crisis the
very coherence of time and of subjectivity seemed disarticulated.[2]

The abyss in time was widely perceived. In his *Confession d'un
enfant du siècle* (1836) Musset evoked the precariousness of the post-
Revolutionary conjuncture: "All that was is no longer; all that will be
is not yet. Look nowhere else for the secret of our suffering."[3] Musset's plaint may have been characteristically self-dramatizing, but it
expressed a feeling much more widely (if diffusely) experienced in
the hundred years from the publication of his novel through the first
part of our own century.[4]

Of course other societies and other ages have had tense relationships with their pasts.[5] But to writers in what some have termed the
"long nineteenth century"—the period running from 1789 to 1920 or
so—the experience of such stress seemed singularly traumatic, par-

2. A piquant detail recollected in Eugen Weber's *Peasants into Frenchmen: The Modernization of Rural France, 1870–1914* suggests how powerful a perturbation, how fundamental a dividing line the French Revolution continued to represent in popular imagination well into the nineteenth century. Weber recalls that as late as the fin de siècle period,
storytellers in Upper Brittany dated the disappearance of the region's indigenous fairies
from the time of the Revolution (109). For a less fanciful evocation of the *willed* demarca-
tion the Revolution was conceived to symbolize, see Bronislaw Baczko, "Le Calendrier
républicain: Décréter l'éternité," 40. The celebrated conclusion of François-René de Chateaubriand's *Mémoires d'outretombe* (composed in 1841) conveys the sense of rupture
strikingly: "If I compare the two terrestrial globes, the one I knew at the beginning of my
life and the one I now behold at the end of it, I no longer recognize the one in the other"
(4:637).
3. Alfred de Musset, *La Confession d'un enfant du siècle*, ed. Gerard Barrier, 20.
4. This sense of the vacuity, the *inanity* of the present echoes as well in numerous
other texts from the same period. Some examples: from a letter of Gustave Flaubert to
Louis Bouilhet (19 December 1850): "We—all of us—have come along either too early or
too late. We'll have done the most difficult and the least glamorous job: making the transition. To do something that lasts, you need a solid foundation. The future torments us and
the past holds us back. That's why the present escapes us" (*Correspondance*, 1:730; all
reference to Flaubert's correspondence is to this collection). From Charles Baudelaire's
Fusées: "Lost in this ignoble world . . . I'm like an exhausted man whose vision can see of
the past . . . only disillusionment and bitterness, and of the future only a storm in which
there is nothing new, neither instruction nor even suffering" (*Oeuvres complètes*, ed.
Y.-G. Le Dantec and Claude Pichois, 1264). Examples of the topos could be multiplied
indefinitely.
5. For one recent examination of this problem, see Anthony Kemp's *Estrangement of
the Past: A Study in the Origins of Modern Historical Consciousness*. The most systematic
examination of how the past has been understood and managed in France can be found in
Les Lieux de mémoire, edited by Pierre Nora.

ticularly new and dire. As the title of a recent study of the period by David Lowenthal puts it, beginning in the nineteenth century the past began to look like a foreign country.

In *Present Past* I want to consider the determinants and the consequences of this cultural stress. I argue two theses concerning the century that precedes and still informs our own: first, that one of its most powerful perceptions was of a massive disruption of traditional forms of memory, and, second, that within the atmosphere of such disruption, the functioning of memory itself, the institution of memory and thereby of history, became critical preoccupations in the effort to think through what intellectuals were coming to call the "modern." The "long nineteenth century" became a present whose self-conception was framed by a disciplined obsession with the past.

The traces of such a problematic and conflicted recollection are widely visible in the cultural production of this period. Simultaneously, the problem of the past and of the relation to it through memory came to preoccupy social and psychological thinking. Theoretical systems focused on this relationship because it had come to seem unaccountably troubled, because it had developed complications that people felt no one had quite encountered before. The loss of a sense of time's continuous flow and of our unproblematic place within it, the disruption of organic connection with the past evidenced in numerous texts from this period—such representations indicate an epochal rupture, a perception by those who were living within it that the world had decisively changed.

In the second chapter of this introductory section, as an early and still-striking model for the cultural mutations I allude to here, I reconsider Ferdinand Tönnies's classic account of the epochal transition from *Gemeinschaft* to *Gesellschaft*, from forms of social existence based upon traditional family and village structures to new forms rooted in urban existence, in the anonymous market, and in the abstract relations of civil society. Of course the polarity this model posits may be excessively schematic (the same could be said for accounts strongly influenced by Tönnies, such as those of Georg Simmel, Georg Lukács, and Walter Benjamin). But its advantage is that, at a time when the changes it sought to describe still resonated as living memories for the Europeans who had experienced them,

Tönnies's model managed to catch elements of the fundamental shift that played a major part in determining what I am calling the memory crisis.

At the risk of oversimplification, we could put it this way. In traditional societies, in a sense that a number of theorists describing the transition at issue here have sought to frame, objects and people could be said carry their pasts and their meanings openly. The influence of this mode of conceiving the precapitalist past remains strong. For example, in *Peasants into Frenchmen* Eugen Weber approvingly recalls the sociologist Henri Mendras's version of the account: "As . . . Mendras says, the peasant shows what he does or is about to do in forms of behavior that are wholly familiar to his fellows and so are easily interpreted by all of them" (92).[6]

But in the more complex society of post-Revolutionary cities and protocapitalist economies, the interpretation of behavior became notoriously problematic. Whole literary plots—quintessentially those of the detective stories, which many have argued represent the furthest development of the theme of such hermeneutic difficulty in fictions from the period—turn on this newly disquieting lack of transparency. At the same time, the recollection of the past—particularly by that growing segment of the urban population who had grown up far from the cities where they had come to live as adults—obliged people to reconstruct the prehistory of their new environment in the effort to naturalize it. They were involved in an effort of memory that made the very lack of transparency of the past a conscious focus of concern.[7] In the face of these developments, historicizing memory

6. For a moving evocation of the experience of memory in traditional rural societies, see John Berger, *Pig Earth*. Berger confirms the vision of relative *transparency* of meaning in the village setting: "In a village the difference between what is known about a person and what is unknown is slight. . . . Peasants do not *play roles* as urban characters do . . . because the space between what is unknown about a person and what is generally known . . . is too small" (10). See also Françoise Zonabend, *The Enduring Memory: Time and History in a French Village*. This relative transparency of meaning in peasant communities is what gives significance to a story such as that of Martin Guerre, in which such clarity of meaning, and of recollection, was lost. *The Return of Martin Guerre* is a *modern* story in the sense that its interest for those who rediscovered it arises in its singular reenactment and displacement of the modern memory crisis, seen in microcosm, and in an entirely unexpected time and setting. See Natalie Zemon Davis, *The Return of Martin Guerre*. In my discussion of Proust's "Combray" in Chapter 6, I return to consideration of the recollected transparency of "village" meanings.

7. I addressed some aspects of these problems in my analysis of the nineteenth-cen-

means crediting and seeking to account for pervasive perceptions throughout the "long nineteenth century" that the mnemonic faculty had *itself* undergone mysterious and unsettling mutations.[8]

✿✿✿

How could we question the past? What precedes us seems to constitute the frame of our existence, the basis for our self-understanding. Yet however necessary its lineaments may seem to our comprehension of the world, this conception of the "past" is no less contingent than any cultural fact. We say, in a now-familiar formulation, that we *construct* the past. The agent of that construction is what I term "memory." Memory is the modality of our relation to the past.

The object of any study must be distinguished from the remainder of the world's endless flux. Taxonomy is always tempting. But in the case of the diverse, variegated functioning of memory during the modern period, such an exercise in distinction risks providing a false clarity, an illusory resolution, precisely because of the ubiquity and the inherent variability of memory's processes. Rather than a strict definition, this book offers a sequence of designations and exemplification of how during the modern period the past has been made present, and how such construction of the mnemonic realm has been theorized during the "long nineteenth century."

---

tury necessity for "learning the city"; see Richard Terdiman, *Discourse/Counter-Discourse: The Theory and Practice of Symbolic Resistance in Nineteenth-Century France*, chap. 1.

8. There has been an extraordinary amount of research on memory since the beginning of the period I deal with in this book. I ought to suggest how *Present Past* might be distinguished within this field. There are, first of all, three areas of memory research that have almost nothing to do with what follows: (1) the literature on the psychology of recall characterized by Hermann Ebbinghaus's pioneering behaviorist, positivist research (see Friedrich Kittler, *Discourse Networks 1800/1900*, 206–23), or by studies of such phenomena as the reliability of witness recollection (see Elizabeth Loftus, *Eyewitness Testimony*); (2) the studies of the cultural memories of marginalized or stressed groups (for example studies of the memory of the Jews by Bernard Lewis or Jonathan Boyarin); and (3) the theoretical or neurobiological studies of the functioning of memory (see Israel Rosenfield, *The Invention of Memory: A New View of the Brain*; Edward S. Casey, *Remembering: A Phenomenological Study*; Ulric Neisser, ed., *Memory Observed*; and George Johnson, *In the Palaces of Memory: How We Build the World inside Our Heads*). In general, my inquiry does not concern the accuracy or functioning of (principally short-term) memory. I seek to understand *how* memory became a cultural preoccupation beginning after the French Revolution and to demonstrate the informing presence of such a preoccupation in cultural production. This latter concern intends to open into an investigation of the characteristic practices and theorizations of memory in the post-Revolutionary period.

The following might stand as a bare-bones paradigm for memory's activity. *A content of some sort is registered, with whatever fidelity the registering system can manage. Time passes. A representation appears, responsive to the content previously registered.* What has happened is memory. Whenever anything is conserved and reappears in a representation, we are in the presence of a memory effect. Memory thus complicates the rationalist segmentation of chronology into "then" and "now." In memory, the time line becomes tangled and folds back on itself. Such a complication constitutes our lives and defines our experience. The complex of practices and means by which the past invests the present is memory: *memory is the present past.*[9]

But that equation makes memory pretty much coincident with *representation*—with the function by which symbols, or simulacra, or surrogates, come to stand for some absent referent. Of course the referents of memory are always absent. The past is gone. But then, so is virtually everything else. Maybe just as *everything* is representation, *everything* is memory. Yet despite the intertwining of the two problems, there is room for disentangling their respective foci. In what follows, I hope to make clear how much the "crisis of representation" that has so often been said to characterize modernity arises as the flattened form in which the memory crisis was able to appear to a culture intent on coming to terms with its own isolation from history. The crisis of representation can thus be construed as the memory crisis seen *from within* the latter's own cognitive restrictions. Historicizing memory then restores a temporal depth to the notorious and daunting representation problem itself.

But "memory" is so omnipresent, so fundamental to our ability to conceive the world that it might seem impossible to analyze it at all. Memory stabilizes subjects and constitutes the present. It is the name we give to the faculty that sustains continuity in collective and in individual experience. Our evidence for it may be as indirect as

9. With this formulation I seek to make clear that the investment of the present by contents from the past need not be under the conscious control—or even enter the conscious awareness—of any given subject. From Marx to Freud this demotion of active consciousness of the past has been a formative theoretical element. I consider this point in detail in my discussion of Freud in Chapter 8.

Freud's evidence for the unconscious, but it is an essential postulate in our attempt to explain how the world remains minimally coherent, how existence doesn't simply fly apart. Memory functions in every act of perception, in every act of intellection, in every act of language. So even framing the questions one might ask about memory is difficult. We might as well attempt to see vision.

The reappearance of content is the zero-degree of meaning production. Authentically singular instances (if they exist at all) by definition can have no meaning. But any *relation* requires us to hold the terms in question within the same field. The process of such fixation always involves time, and hence inevitably invokes memory. Although the notion of the synchronic might suggest that no memory effect need be present in the supposedly simultaneous perceptions of pictural space or in the seemingly atemporal relations between elements of a conceptual structure, an entire body of analysis—from Kant to perceptual psychology to deconstruction—argues that the notion of simultaneity is always already subverted by the intervention of temporality. Instantaneity is a fiction; even the time of perception takes time.[10] Memory thus underlies the possibility of intelligibility as its precondition. Cognition cannot be divorced from the *re*-cognition of memory: no memory, no meaning.

But how can a faculty so deeply intertwined with the very possibility of *thinking* itself be thought about? How might we get some perspective on this apparently seamless and omnipresent function? My answer here is to historicize it. Seeing the phenomenon of memory as itself *differentiated in time*, as localizable in some internally segmented temporal series, may provide some definition of the problematic that memory establishes. In *Remembering*, Edward S. Casey

---

10. In *The Critique of Pure Reason* Immanuel Kant argued that even the simplest act of perception has a temporal dimension. Any such act—the fundamental form of mediation by which we relate to the extra-individual world—synthesizes immediate presentation on the one hand, and recollection on the other; see Charles M. Sherover, *The Human Perception of Time: The Development of Its Philosophic Meaning*, 112. I return to this pairing of immediate presentation and recollection in my discussion of Freud's theory of memory. At the turn of the century, philosophers of time proffered the notion that all perception involves a displacement or extension in time as though it were a new discovery. William James and Henri Bergson were emphatic on the point; Bergson was the most explicit when in 1896 he announced that "the moment has come to reinstate memory in perception" (*Matière et mèmoire: Essai sur la relation du corps à l'esprit*, 65). See also Stephen Kern, *The Culture of Time and Space 1880–1918*, 42–43; and Casey, *Remembering*, 17.

puts it that, with memory, we are always already "in the thick of
things" (ix). Breaking memory out of such undifferentiated and pervasive flux through periodization may give us a way to get a handle
on memory's ubiquity.[11]

The puzzlement concerning the mnemonic characteristic of the
analyses of it since the Revolution might remind us of a parallel—
and simultaneous—discovery of unexpected depths underlying other
fundamental elements of nineteenth-century life. Consider the be-
musement of the political economists who sought to comprehend the
reality of the everyday objects—the goods, the commodities—whose
exchange increasingly pervaded and defined modernity's emerging
socioeconomy. To paraphrase Marx in *Capital* (1867), at first commodities seem simple, but closer examination discloses that the commodity is rather "a very strange thing, abounding in metaphysical
subtleties and theological niceties" (1:163). This discovery of a "mystical character" (1:164) concealed within the commodity was all the
more surprising because of the commodity's apparent banality. By
the time of *Capital*, commodities were everywhere.[12] How could
they cloak arcana?

The puzzlement attached to the commodity was the same one that
complicated the understanding of memory beginning in the post-
Revolutionary period. The surprise they occasioned was double: not
only did the phenomena in question prove unexpectedly baffling
and elusive but what added to the disquiet that attached to such
mysteries was the scandal of having discovered them, in such seemingly refractory forms, at the very heart of the everyday. Memory
and the commodity seemed linked in a common resistance to analysis—a resistance all the more frustrating because the culture that
began to perceive it so acutely during the first part of the nineteenth
century had made a considerable investment in construing its own

11. If "memory" is everywhere, the repetition of the word itself threatens to clot the
sentences of anyone writing about it. To permit some verbal variety, I use "mnemonic" as
an adjective equivalent to "memory," or as an adjectival noun ("the mnemonic") designating "the memory realm." In this book I do not use "mnemonic" or "mnemonics" to refer to
artificial aids to memory.

12. Indeed, this perfusion of economic and social space by commodities was the point of
the sentence that opens Karl Marx's *Capital: A Critique of Political Economy, Volume 1*:
"The wealth of societies in which the capitalist mode of production prevails appears as an
'immense collection of commodities'" (125).

heightened capacity for analysis as one of its most essential, and most laudable, qualities. But in the face of such self-congratulation, memory and the commodity seemed to thumb their noses at understanding. For the nineteenth century, their fractiousness instantiated the now-familiar paradox that what is closest to us is what is most forgotten.

In a celebrated and evocative sentence from the *Communist Manifesto* (1848) concerning the pervasive transformations, the constant revolutionizing of the bourgeois age, Marx wrote, "All that is solid melts into air."[13] The phenomenon of such deliquescence captures something important both about memory in this period and about the objects—including commodities—to which memory could traditionally count on attaching itself. The image makes it clear that mnemonics and economics are not so disconnected as they might seem.

Memory and *exchange* have been "facts" throughout history, but in the "long nineteenth century" each underwent an epochal reconfiguration.[14] The activities that memory and the exchange of commodities assured in their respective spheres turned out to frame the parts of the world in which they were exercised. Since the twin revolutions—economic and political—of the nineteenth century, it was becoming increasingly clear that the processes that characterize the economic and the mnemonic realms are what make the social world happen for us. Goods move and are transformed in their circulation; memories are displaced and transformed with the passage of time or in the course of an increasingly dense and highly organized process of information exchange. In their admittedly diverse ways, these functions appear to be fundamental parts of what we might term modernity's "operating system." Without them the world would be unrecognizable.

But the connection I have suggested between memory and the commodity reminds us that one of the most powerful reflections on the problematic character of reality in the capitalist period itself turns squarely on memory. Marx had provided a seminal analysis of the fetishism of the commodity in the first volume of *Capital*. Based upon it, Lukács's celebrated "Reification" essay in *History and Class*

13. Karl Marx and Friedrich Engels, *The Communist Manifesto*, 83.
14. On the fundamental quality of such mutation in the economic realm, see Georg Lukács, *History and Class Consciousness: Studies in Marxist Dialectics*, 84.

Consciousness (83–222) theorized the reflexes in consciousness and
in culture of the domination of the socioeconomy by commodities.
Lukács sought to decipher the "imprint on the whole consciousness"
(100) of what is usually called the "commodity form." But we could
better understand it as the commodity process. The point of his account was that this process systematically *gets forgotten*. Pierre
Bourdieu termed this sort of suppression "genesis amnesia."[15]

What this analysis conceives is that commodities determine, and
are reciprocally determined by, a systematic perturbation in the
realm of memory. Essentially, "reification" is a memory disturbance:
the enigma of the commodity is a memory disorder. As interpreted
by Marx, and more systematically developed by Lukács, the theory of commodity fetishism can be seen as a pertinent—indeed a
quintessential—example of just the opacity in mnemonic functioning that was coming to consciousness in the post-Revolutionary
period.

The experience of commodification and the process of reification
cut entities off from their own history. They veil the memory of their
production from their consumers, as from the very people who produced them. The process, in Theodor Adorno's terms, created an
unprecedented and uncanny field of "hollowed-out" objects, available
for investment by any meaning whatsoever, but organically connected with none at all. Moreover, as Benjamin glossed Adorno's
description, the rhythm—we might say the *efficiency*—of such "hol-
lowing-out" of the elements of social and material life increased
ceaselessly over the course of the nineteenth century.[16]

The consequences of this abstraction of commodities from the history of their production, of this isolation of the present from the past,
are considerable. The great Viconian postulate that social existence is
inherently comprehensible, that we know what we have made—a
doctrine to which Marx himself referred approvingly (see *Capital*,
1:493 n.4)—omits a crucial precondition for such epistemological optimism. To understand what we have made, we have to be able
to *remember* it. Because commodities suppress the memory of their
own process, they subvert or violate this fundamental tenet of the
mnemonic economy.

15. Pierre Bourdieu, *Outline of a Theory of Practice*, 79.
16. See Susan Buck-Morss, *The Dialectics of Seeing: Walter Benjamin and the Arcades Project*, 182, citing Adorno and Benjamin.

This subversion of memory is all the more unexpected because normally objects have an intimate relation to remembrance. Through their associations, they play a familiar triggering or anchoring role in the mnemonic process. Indeed, the nineteenth century institutionalized and exploited this connection between memories and objects in the form of a brisk trade in "keepsakes" and "souvenirs."[17] So it is astonishing when somehow the mnemonic potential of the objects fundamental to an entire social formation turns up radically disrupted or disabled. Then the object—in its "metaphysically" enigmatic commodity form—mutates into a privileged icon symbolizing the whole crisis of memory and the sudden opacity of the past.

Adorno expressed this association unmistakably when he wrote in a letter to Benjamin that "every reification is a forgetting."[18] The enigma of the commodity arises from its somehow unexpectedly having gotten implicated at the heart of the memory crisis. Adorno's phrase then reappeared in *Dialectic of Enlightenment* in the analysis of what he and Max Horkheimer ironically term "the price of progress."[19] The centrality of the memory problem in the complex of processes that *produce* modernity under capitalism could hardly be made clearer.[20]

In the post-Revolutionary period, two concrete forms of apprehension, two species of mnemonic dysfunction, came to define the mem-

17. On the period's fascination with souvenirs and their conversion into commodities, see Thomas Richards, *The Commodity Culture of Victorian England: Advertising and Spectacle, 1851–1914*, 218–19 and particularly 222: "The phantasmal mirth of the keepsake had become the cheap phantasmagoria of the commodity." See also Susan Stewart, *On Longing: Narratives of the Miniature, the Gigantic, the Souvenir, the Collection*, xii and particularly 151: "The souvenir is not simply an object appearing out of context, an object from the past incongruously surviving in the present; rather, its function is to envelop the present within the past. Souvenirs are magical objects because of this transformation." Walter Benjamin had important things to say about souvenirs; see Buck-Morss, *Dialectics of Seeing*, 189 (citing Benjamin): "The souvenir [*Andenken*, the withered form of experience] is the complement of the *Erlebnis* [fully realized experience]. In it is deposited the increasing self-alienation of the person who inventories his past as dead possessions." See also Shelley Rice, "Souvenirs."

18. Martin Jay, *Marxism and Totality: The Adventures of a Concept from Lukács to Habermas*, 229.

19. Max Horkheimer and Theodor W. Adorno, *Dialectic of Enlightenment*, 230.

20. In *The Body in Pain: The Making and Unmaking of the World*, Elaine Scarry provides an admirably modulated account of how the agency that creates artifacts can be "forgotten" or pass from the consciousness of those upon whom its agency is projected (see esp. 311–12).

ory crisis. We would have expected that mistrust of memory, that
awareness of its uncertainty, would have dominated preoccupation
with the mnemonic. Chateaubriand expressed this apprehension clearly
in *René*: "What, then, is man whose memory dies so quickly?"[21] For
memory is notoriously and prodigiously fallible; even the most familiar content is imperfectly retained in recollection.[22] And it is true that
during the period of the memory crisis people did worry intricately
about *forgetting*. It seemed to them that their past was only slightly
less uncertain than their future. But at first glance it might appear
surprising that a very different mnemonic problem also occasioned
anxiety. Difficulties increasingly seemed associated not only with forgetting but with its seeming contrary, with a perverse persistence of
recollection. This period was preoccupied by a broad concern with
both of these mnemonic problems. Beginning in the early nineteenth
century, we could say that disquiet about memory crystallized
around the perception of two principal disorders: *too little memory*,
and *too much*.[23]

   Both of these deviations from nominally unproblematic rememoration attracted anxious concern and generated concerted reflection.
The theories of memory I discuss in this book are strongly marked
by, and intricately responsive to, these perplexities. For the memory
crisis did indeed produce theory—a body of efforts to understand the
disturbances troubling the mnemonic realm and to comprehend their
social and cultural consequences. This should not be surprising, for

   21. François-René de Chateaubriand, *René*, 224.
   22. Fully fifty percent of Americans recollect that Lincoln faces to the left on the penny.
Left and right regularly run neck-and-neck in tests of our recollection concerning this most
quotidian of our perceptual objects.
   23. In any case, the doublet of *remembering* and *forgetting* has ceased to be understandable as a simple plus-and-minus binary. As construed in the outflow of the memory
crisis, recollection and forgetting are both generally seen as representations: both meaningful, both interpretable. They stand in no simple or low-order relation to each other.
Indeed, within the discourses that organize our current understanding it is impossible to
conceive of forgetting as nothing more than a failure of inscription, as a simple *absence*.
Any construction of memory as "presence" and forgetting as "absence" collapses the complexity of the dialectic that produces culture out of their complex interplay. Freud made
this point with epochal force, as I will argue in Chapters 7 and 8. See Yosef H.
Yerushalmi, ed., *Usages de l'oubli*, and *Communications* 49, ed. Nicole Lapierre, especially Nicole Lapierre, "Dialectique de la mémoire et de l'oubli," 5–10, and Jonathan
Boyarin, "Un Lieu de l'oubli: Le Lower East Side des juifs," especially 185–86. See also
Umberto Eco, "Un Art d'oublier est-il concevable?"

two distinct but related reasons. First, when elements and processes of culture lose transparency they always draw reflection to themselves (see Terdiman, *Discourse/Counter-Discourse*, 97). But that phenomenon, which frames the culturally situated instrumentality of any theoretical production, couples here with a second, more specific and more focused determination.

For the relation between the processes of memory and of theory is itself particularly intimate—we might almost say inextricable. Memory is a theory machine. And theories are memory machines. Since the French Revolution there has been a special intertwining between the problem of memory and the forms and generation of cultural theory. Our understanding of memory bears both on the impulse to theory and on the specific forms of cultural understanding that have been formative in the modern period. In any case, it is clear that the memory and the theory machines geared up and functioned with special productivity in the nineteenth century. Like so many of the instruments our society has devised to construct and sustain its forms, their output has been rising ever since.

How can we understand this relation between theory and memory? We could say that theories are memory machines because they determine what, in the flux of experience, we apprehend and cognize. Theories organize what we notice, and thereby what we recall. By determining interpretation they act inevitably as schemata for memory. Even those theories most reluctant to credit a relationship between discourse and its referents nonetheless function to model representations and to determine their field of referentiality.

To clarify the relation between memory and theory, consider forgetting. As I observed, the threat of forgetting has formed one principal strand of post-Revolutionary mnemonic disquiet. But forgetting is not a unitary phenomenon, for although sometimes we simply forget, at other times—with whatever embarrassment—we recollect having forgotten. The latter experience understandably spurs efforts to reduce the frequency of the former. Such efforts produce an important cultural technology. We could say that among the things that memory conserves, perhaps what it conserves par excellence are paradigms, protocols, practices, mechanisms, and techniques *for conserving memory itself*. It would not be hard to argue that a cul-

ture's theories do the same: they recall and reproduce the cognitive
and epistemological operations their culture has found important. So
a culture's theories are among its fundamental memory formations.
As such, theories determine how cultures reproduce and represent—how they remember—themselves.

Still, theories handle memory's uncertainties diversely. They too
are profoundly historicized.[24] We could imagine a systematic history
of the mechanisms cultures have devised to palliate memory's fallibility and to maintain mastery of its contents. Unfortunately, we lack
such a history, but in an intriguing and amusing essay, "Trou de
mémoire, image virale," Alain Gauthier and Henri-Pierre Jeudy fantasized establishing a museum of the contrivances that people have
devised to help them recall the past: a collection of remembered
attempts to remember. For example, they projected an archive of all
the handkerchiefs knotted by all the people who feared that they
would fail to recall—not only *what* they were supposed to recall, but
that there was something to recall in the first place.[25] The Museum of
Knotted Handkerchiefs portrays in enlightening caricature a culture
seeking to hold onto itself. In its very extravagance, in the variety of
its contrivances for forestalling oblivion, Gauthier and Jeudy's Museum epitomizes a society's puzzlement in the face of the difficulty of
memory. We could say that theories function like the knots in culture's handkerchief. As their knots come under our fingers they
evoke once again what they sought to remind us to remember. As-
suming we remember to check our theoretical handkerchief for its
knots to begin with, what is called up or called forth will be the
product of a past commitment transformed into the substance of a
memory.

Nothing is more uncertain than the success of such a mechanism.
The epistemological divide between *then* and *now* is such that we
can never guarantee we will recall the necessity of recollection, or
that the past's claim upon the future will be transmitted or honored

24. Frances Yates's classic, *The Art of Memory*, describes the complex of mechanisms
for assuring mnemonic accuracy that functioned from Antiquity to the Renaissance. But
then, as she explains, the traditional *artes memoriae* fell into disuse. The reasons for this
epochal disappearance were no doubt complex, but it seems evident that profound
changes in social organization and hence in the information economy in Europe after the
Renaissance determined a transformed complex of mnemonic needs.

25. Alain Gauthier and Henri-Pierre Jeudy, "Trou de mémoire, image virale," 137.

at all. But we have nothing better to go on than the engagement we have taken in (and with) our history to mortgage the approaching present that at one time was our future to a past that always runs the risk of falling irretrievably out of mind. Hence we theorize.[26]

So a theory functions like our memory of what we know and want to know. Is there a parallel metaconsciousness of memory in the theoretical realm? The question leads us to ask whether theories themselves have the capacity to overcome genesis amnesia and represent the process by which they were themselves devised to marshal the material to which they attend. We could then go on to wonder whether in conceiving such processing, theories understand the social and political determinations of the transformations, the systematic inflections by which the unstructured is structured through them—and whether they recall the history by which such determinations became functional within them. Does a given theory remember what it is while it functions, recollect what it is doing as it organizes the doing of it? No doubt every conceptual paradigm has some opening to such considerations. Yet the centrality and the detail of their recollection of the determinations underlying how they function may provide a useful criterion for distinguishing between different theoretical orientations.

The intimacy between the adumbrations of cultural theory and the paradigms of memory they project or inscribe leads me to consider how the relationship with the past has become focused in several influential paradigms—sociological and psychological with Musset and the romantics and, at a much later and different stage, with Proust; semiotic with Baudelaire; explicitly psychoanalytic and hermeneutic with Freud. In divergent but exemplary ways, the four figures whose relation to the memory crisis occupies me in the later parts of this book sought to understand these difficulties of memory, and to resolve the anxieties that attend them.

Since the twin revolutions of the nineteenth century, European culture has offered just a few dominant paradigms for conceiving the

26. It may be worth speculating that the "predicament of theory" may have more to do with the irreducible uncertainty of the mnemonic realm than current debates framed around this label have suggested. And even that the proliferation of the theoretical enterprise in our own time may reflect the perceived intractability of holding on to anything of our pasts at all.

"memory function"—that systemic, essentially historical metaconsciousness I mentioned earlier. These versions trace a map of the
possibilities by which the mnemonic has been represented and conceptualized in the modern period. Musset, Baudelaire, Proust, and
Freud enable us to see how modern reflection on memory responds
to the polar disorders that focus the memory problem. Their theories
of memory may also help to demonstrate how the enterprise of "theory" has itself been mediated by the memory crisis. Through analysis
of their representations, I want to frame memory and theory not as
reified and separable entities, but as mutually determining instances
of our continuous and intricate negotiation with the past.

The objects with which I deal in this book date roughly from
the century of post-Revolutionary modernism—from 1836 (the date
of Musset's *Confession d'un enfant du siècle*) to 1937 (the date of
Freud's last essays). The texts I consider are quite disparate. I deal
with two extensive bodies of material—Proust's *A la recherche du
temps perdu* and Freud's psychoanalytic works—and with two individual works—a single novel (Musset's *Confession*) and a single
poem (Baudelaire's "Cygne"). These divergences are, in part, adven-
titious, and arose in the chances of any research that seeks to make
sense of a period and a set of problems that offer many more sites for
investigation than can possibly be addressed. But I draw at least this
advantage from what might otherwise seem an incommensurability
in my texts: what I term the memory crisis was a cultural complication of great generality and depth. It can be detected virtually anywhere in the culture that one looks, and its manifestations are visible
both macroscopically and microscopically. The diversity of my objects of investigation attempts to test these hypotheses.

But it is nonetheless true that this book asks metonymies to work
very hard. An individual poem of Baudelaire is made to stand for
larger bodies of texts by its author. Single authors are made to stand
for broad movements in art and culture. Aesthetic and scientific
movements are made to stand for entire societies. Theory is taken as
a cultural practice, which is perhaps the most problematic metonymy of all. Indeed, it may appear that my objective has been to
reexamine a very small number of very familiar figures. It may even
seem that I do this in ignorance of the critique of the construction of
history as a tradition of elite producers of culture—those bearers of

the traditional authority of the canon frequently (and with considerable cogency) identified as dominant, male, white, and dead.

Such a critique has important implications for a book on memory, for it seeks to intervene in the substance of recollection itself.[27] I am sympathetic to it. But in demonstrating that dominant traditions are constructed, contingent, and contestable, it tends to project the notion that such dominance must be contested by exchanging its products for others. I believe that there are alternate ways to pressure hegemony. My own effort has been to examine—treating them as if they were not obvious—the mechanisms by which such hegemonies (in the form of widely influential representations and theories) become constituted and are themselves propagated. I have sought to recall and to attend to the moment of contingency, not the moment of stabilization.

Hegemony is not fundamentally upset when we replace the attributes or contents it has valorized with others. The privilege of any dominant discourse is to "go without saying." Dominant discourses claim to totalize the world of possible utterances—or would, if from within the confidence of hegemony, they felt the need to make claims at all. But of course by their privilege that is what they are exempted from doing to begin with. As I put it elsewhere, "The dominant is the discourse . . . granted the structural privilege of appearing to be unaware of the very question of its own legitimacy" (*Discourse/Counter-Discourse*, 61). On the other side of the line defining the "field of struggle" within any culture, counterdiscourses seek to upset the pretension of the dominant to exhaust the field of possible speech. The privilege of counterdiscourses is the obverse of their limitation: because they have not yet become triumphant or transparent, they have an analytic power and a capacity to resituate perception and comprehension that their dominant antagonists cannot exhibit.

We should note, however, that such discourses of difference and of contestation inherently exercise a mnemonic function. *They recall the dominant's other*; they restore to its flattened, false totalizations the presence of the subjects and the perspectives that it has not been

27. Michel Foucault made this point explicit: "Memory is actually a very important factor in struggle. . . . If one controls people's memory, one controls their dynamism. . . . It is vital to have possession of this memory" ("Film and Popular Memory," 92).

able to subsume and has consequently sought to exclude. Dominance, of course, is itself sustained by memory—but a selective, highly ideologized form of recollection that brackets fully as much as it restores. But although memory sustains hegemony, it also subverts it through its capacity to recollect and to restore the alternative discourses the dominant would simply bleach out and forget. Memory, then, is inherently contestatory.

So in this book I seek to examine how the representations of memory by four writers themselves contested the hegemonies out of which they arose as alternatives. However dominant, dead, white, and male they may seem today—all four ran painfully up against the constructions of the dominant discourse active in their own periods. They paid real prices for their heterodoxy. From this group of figures, each of whom contributed to what we term modernism, and whose experience and activity have helped us to construe contestation as a specific cultural project to begin with, there is still much to learn.

> Before we can understand what history *says* about a society, we have to analyze how history functions within it.
> —Michel de Certeau, *The Writing of History*, 68 (translation modified)

In the nineteenth century the inadequacy of available memory mechanisms to the needs of a transformed society had become critical. The memory crisis arose from this inadequacy. But just a short time *before* the upsurge of concern I identify as the beginning of the crisis, what stressed the nineteenth century so acutely did not seem so problematic. Even a few years before, visions of memory had been more serene. Recall the conclusion of the *Phenomenology of Spirit* (1807). The final problem Hegel considers is *recollection.*[28] Recollection figures the Spirit's triumphant self-absorption at the end of history. This is a mode of self-consciousness characteristic of one of

28. G. W. F. Hegel, *Phenomenology of Spirit*, especially 492–93.

the oldest figures of classical idealism, the identical subject-object. In
it, what we remember is the other made ours—an epiphany reas-
suringly harmonizing self and world, past and present, being and
becoming.[29] Traces of the nineteenth century's mnemonic anxiety
seem very distant from such confident marshaling of memory in the
service of truth. Goethe shared this idealist calm. "I do not recognize
memory in the sense that you mean it," he said. "Whatever we encounter that is great, beautiful, significant need not be remembered
from the outside; need not be hunted up and laid hold of. . . . Rather
. . . it must be woven into the fabric of our inmost self, must become
one with it. . . . There is no past that one is allowed to long for."[30]

But only slightly later in the nineteenth century, reflection on
memory mutated. It began to lament the absence of mnemonic harmony. The tone became one of disquiet, disruption, trouble. Hegel's
confidence in the recuperative power of recollection no longer adequately expressed the complications of memory for Baudelaire's century. No epiphanies resolved the disjunction between the present
and the past. Compare Goethe's sanguine optimism with Baudelaire's
despair about the disappearance of the past. "I ask any thinking person to show me what remains of life," he wrote in "Fusées" (*Oeuvres
complètes*, 1263). For the nineteenth century, and continuing into
our own, the problem of memory foregrounds a painfully divided
structure of consciousness. And the stress attending the mnemonic
increasingly infuses the theoretical paradigms by which we seek an
understanding of experience.

By the nature of the case we can tap the atmosphere of such mnemonic disquiet only episodically. There are of course difficulties with
such a method. It would be satisfying simply to reoccupy the past as
familiar territory. But that's the problem. The project of reproducing
the consciousness of a period runs into just the methodological impossibility that frames and determines the memory crisis itself. *The
past is never present.* It can never be brought back intact. Histori-

29. On this confident evocation of the mnemonic, see Herbert Marcuse, *Eros and Civilization: A Philosophical Inquiry into Freud*, 212; Jay, *Marxism and Totality*, 225–27;
Fredric R. Jameson, *Marxism and Form: Twentieth-Century Dialectical Theories of Literature*, 112–13; and John O'Neill, "Critique and Remembrance," 1–11.

30. *Goethes Gespräche*, 4 November 1823; cited by Ernest G. Schachtel, "On Memory
and Childhood Amnesia," 2.

cism was born out of this very problematic and foundered on it. Yet it would be naive and self-disabling to imagine that because we can not reoccupy the site of a past reality we are thereby prohibited from knowledge about it. The functioning of memory—and the deep paradox within it—mean that our access to *any* reality is subject to the same restraints as our attempt to reconstitute the truth of history, to tell (as Leopold von Ranke put it in a celebrated apothegm) "how it really was."

The "real" historical referents of our discussion will never fit between our pages. In representation, reduction is inevitable. "Reductionism" has had bad press, but we cannot avoid it. Arguably, an effort to understand the functionality of memory in culture is a pertinent place to confess this. For any investigation of the memory function immediately subverts naive or mythic or positivist notions of how past contents of culture are projected beyond themselves into the future that is our own present. Indeed, the problem has only become more intractable in the period since the memory crisis became acute. The flux of reality in the postmodern world has become so inexpressibly dense that even if only such information as could be reduced to digital expression were recorded, all the memories that could accommodate such registration would fill up and overflow in a moment. The past as past is gone without recourse. It then becomes clear that *the most constant element of recollection is forgetting*, discarding the nonretained so that retention, rememoration can occur at all. So what we call the past is always already and irretrievably a profoundly altered or attenuated version of the contents that were potentially available to consciousness when that past was present. Reduction is the essential precondition for representation. Loss is what makes our memory of the past possible at all.

But nostalgia for a totalizing or unproblematic circulation between present and past is none the less seductive. The fantasy of such mnemonic freedom focused the nineteenth century's experience of the epochal disturbance of memory that they believed themselves to have suffered. Musset's *Confession d'un enfant du siècle*, for example, can be understood as an effort to comprehend the stress of the past upon the present. Its celebrated second chapter thematizes the generation of this stress—in both senses of "generation." In his mode of romantic despair, Musset seeks the diagnosis of a cultural crisis.

And he locates this crisis in a systematic perturbation of memory—
specifically, in a bewildering disjunction between older and younger,
between fathers and sons. His text becomes a somber epic of misremembering: "Then these men of the Empire . . . *remembered*
their sons. . . . They inquired where they were. The children were
finishing school . . . , and in their turn they inquired where their
fathers might be. . . . They *remembered* having seen, in dark corners
of their paternal houses, mysterious busts with long marble locks and
Roman inscriptions" (4–6; citation highly excerpted, emphasis mine).
This abyss in time then produces the text's most celebrated sentences: "Behind them a past forever destroyed; before them . . . the
first glow of the future; and between these two worlds . . . something
vague and unsettled . . . separating past and future, but yet neither
the one nor the other: the present" (7). Such rhetoric of an irreme-
diable split in time became common for a significant portion of the
nineteenth century.

When time is out of joint, nothing preoccupies the mind as much
as time. The past invests the present because of its paradoxical inaccessibility. As Gustave Flaubert put it: "I find it impossible to do
anything. I spend my time reviving the past" (to Princess Mathilde,
13 October 1870). Something like the logic of discontinuity, which
has become familiar to us in contemporary theoretical systems, begins to seem the conceptual reflex of this experiential tangle. Already
in certain nineteenth-century texts, what we might term the failure
of diachronicity was experienced as a kind of epistemic rupture—
something akin to a Kuhnian paradigm shift that, in its uncanny familiarity, lets us know the world has changed.

In the conceptual realm, it would seem that nothing is ever given
without first having been taken away. In *Discourse/Counter-Dis-
course*, concerning a parallel crisis in the mechanisms of nineteenth-
century socialization, I argued that "there is no process of institution
in social life without a preceding, and determining, destitution. As
the transparency characterizing areas of social existence not previously experienced as problematical is progressively lost, the effort to
master such areas in their transformed state attempts . . . to reproduce a dying innocence through the concerted mobilization of knowledge" (97). We could comprehend the nineteenth century's preoccupation with history in just this way: as the attempt to master the

crisis of diachronicity, the new and disorienting opacity of the past, by theorizing and retheorizing the relation with time itself.

From Flaubert to Foucault, such a preoccupation has been thought the century's characteristic project. In Flaubert's words, "The *sense of history* is completely new in our world" (to Mlle Leroyer de Chantepie, 18 February 1859) and "The sense of history dates from yesterday, and it may be the best thing about the nineteenth century" (to the Goncourts, 3 July 1860). Foucault puts it this way: "Since it is the mode of being of all that is given us in experience, History has become the unavoidable element in our thought. . . . In the nineteenth century, philosophy was to reside in the gap between history and History, between events and the Origin. . . . This question was to bear down upon philosophy, heavily and tirelessly, from Hegel to Nietzsche and beyond."[31]

Characteristically, Foucault omits the name of Marx. But the nineteenth century's preoccupation with the developmental character of time cannot be divorced from the disruptions of memory which underlay its theoretical concerns and determined their urgency. As was the case with historical materialism, certain of the philosophical or conceptual projects to reintegrate or reconceptualize the relation to the past carried a powerful *enthusiasm* for the very historical dynamism that produced the disjunction with the past that the period seemed perpetually to be lamenting. A myth of progress makes the loss of memory less troubling. But alongside such optimistic readings of history's new forms, there remained a deep perception of the memory crisis as a historical disaster. A funereal image of Musset's powerfully foregrounds this valence: "Make no mistake: the black costume worn by the men of our period is a terrifying symbol" (*Confession*, 11).

For Musset the Revolution had produced these disorienting temporal and mnemonic disjunctions, and determined their psychic costs. Later, as Walter Benjamin argues in his studies of Baudelaire, the sense of loss would arise in part as a result of vertiginous modifications in social space, and in the production of social relations, that characterized the nineteenth century. Both diagnoses agree that it was the experience of history itself that occasioned profound muta-

31. Michel Foucault, *The Order of Things: An Archeology of the Human Sciences*, 219–20.

tions in history's conceptualization. Both are thereby forcefully materialist in their strategies.

✿❀✿

Among the most striking representations of what I am calling the nineteenth century's memory crisis occur in its literary texts. Two loci, evoking two different genres, are particularly significant. The first is the repository of painful reflections on memory that provides one of the thematic lines of force in *Les Fleurs du mal*. For example, the four "Spleen" poems of the first part of *Les Fleurs du mal* evoke, each in a different way, the crisis of recollection. Generally in these texts, in the image of the twin dysfunctions that focus the nineteenth century's mnemonic disquiet, memory is represented either in monstrous hypertrophy or in pitiful underdevelopment. "J'ai plus de souvenirs que si j'avais mille ans" ["I have more memories than if I'd lived a thousand years"] (no. 76) expresses this distortion in one way; "Où coule au lieu de sang l'eau verte du Léthé" ["In which, instead of blood, flow the green waters of Lethe"] (no. 77) expresses it in the other. Both lines signify an exorbitance of memory, its transformation into catastrophe, which may, at bottom, be the primary determinant of Spleen itself.

It is the novel, however, that most organizes itself as a projection of the memory function and its disruptions. Novels are exercises in the process of memory. Of course writers in all periods have turned their imaginations toward the past, but nineteenth-century plots particularly present themselves as the diegesis of history's stress: much more under the sign of a tense exploration of the past's disjunction from the present than under the more traditional guise of rehearsing some consecrated mythology symbolic of the community's consciousness of itself.

Flaubert is exemplary in this regard. Two cases may help to demonstrate his attentiveness to memory as one of the crisis-elements in his representation of nineteenth-century existence. The first confronts dual characterizations of Charles Bovary. The first is apparently innocent, made by the village curé half a dozen or so pages from the beginning of *Madame Bovary*: "The young man had a fine memory."[32] But this seemingly innocent detail collides with another

32. Gustave Flaubert, *Madame Bovary*, 9.

passage almost exactly the same distance from the book's conclusion: "It was a strange thing that Bovary, while he thought continually of Emma, was forgetting her; and he despaired at feeling her image escape from his memory despite the efforts which he was making to hold on to it" (352). Memory's inherent and inescapable fallibility, powerfully inflected by the operation of the subjective factors that will later preoccupy Proust and Freud, here becomes both the *content* and the *means* of Flaubert's narration.

Moreover, we need to take note that just a few lines below the curé's initial admiring characterization of his memory, we are informed how profoundly *unmemorable* poor Charles Bovary is and will remain. As the narrator writes, "Not one of us could recall a single thing about him now" (9). Indeed, at the beginning of the novel this already-dying evocation of the solidarity of collective recollection (through Flaubert's celebrated vanishing narrative "we") stands as a striking sign of the sudden *difficulty* of the past. The curé's praise of Charles's memory may be the *only* positive element the novel attaches to him. So its utter cancellation at the end of the text completes the uncanny emptying process that the narrative operates upon its own mnemonic material—beginning with its progressive erosion of Emma's recollections of Sir Walter Scott and of the entire febrile apparatus of romanticism (38), of La Vaubyessard (58), and so on, which constitute her personal fantasy of the past. Such a process confronts the past and present of the narrative itself under the sign of a deeply diagnostic disjunction. These disorders of the memory function might almost come to seem the fundamental determinant of the rhetoric of irony practiced throughout *Madame Bovary*.

This irony is then radicalized at the conclusion of *L'Éducation sentimentale*, in the excruciating scene in which Frédéric and Deslauriers reminisce—in which, as Flaubert says, they "resumed their life."[33] "And, exhuming their youths, at each phrase, they asked each other: 'Do you remember?'" (426). *L'Éducation* is a text about the impotence of memory, about what has become its grotesque and scandalous vacuity. And with this scene the novel ends, undermining on the level of its themes and its rhetoric the project of its own

33. Gustave Flaubert, *L'Éducation sentimentale*, 425.

diegesis. The concluding evacuation of recollection leaves the narrative empty. It signifies the failure of organic integration of the past into the lived experience of characters, which is one sign of what I have been calling the memory crisis. This crisis then reaches an absurdist paroxysm in *Bouvard et Pécuchet*, in which the accumulative power of memory becomes completely unstrung as the characters pass serenely through a series of disasters, each of which simply vanishes as soon as it occurs.

Cultural theories are readings of how the past invests the present. They read the memory relation. Any culture superposes the layers of knowledge, practice, habit, and perception that compose social existence and experience. Like the economic infrastructure that sustains the social formation, culture is an accumulation—but one that is highly and consequentially organized. It achieves its relative stability, its practical weight, its seeming coherence, through its constant rehearsal and reproduction in individual and social memory. As I argued earlier, the practices of a cultural system (and its theories central among them) both function as a memory and function to ensure memory's stabilization and transmission.

Thus no theory is ever properly synchronic. Theories focus a culture's temporal vectors; they register the flow of its history. They become its "constant capital" (see *Capital, Volume 1*, chap. 8), inheriting their organization and their material from its past, mediating the structure and the substance of its future. A culture's theories, far from appearing as abstract elements in some speculative epistemology, paradoxically come to seem the most *practical* of its practices, for it is they which most centrally inscribe, and are most centrally inscribed within, its sense of time. The practices of a culture, however ahistorical they may appear when we conceive them as stable, self-reproducing structures, record the history of their own production as graphically as nineteenth-century capitalism in England—and the accumulation of its constant capital, its massed productive resources—turned out in Marx's analysis to seem a palimpsest written upon the earlier text of what he termed "primitive accumulation" (*Capital, Volume 1*, part 8).

Any cultural accumulation necessarily registers time, but in periods of stress such as the one that concerns me here, it may come to

seem that a culture's texts do *nothing but*. Consider Alfred de
Vigny's preface (1827) to *Cinq-Mars*: "In recent years (and perhaps as
a result of political developments), Art has borne the impression of
history more strongly than ever before. We all have our eyes turned
to our Chronicles, as if, having once attained maturity in our progress toward greater things, we were pausing a moment to take account of our youth and of its errors. In addition to PRESENT CON-
CERNS it has thus become necessary to attend to MEMORY."[34] This
questioning of memory foregrounds the crisis of diachronicity I have
been emphasizing here. The diachronic is the experience of difference over time, but the mutation of time's difference into disparity,
into abstract otherness, in which the element of relation is eclipsed
and replaced by something like disjunction—such a situation figures
a divorce between past and present in which diachronicity itself is
catastrophically set adrift. Vigny's image of divorce between cultural
youth and maturity carries this meaning.

Musset and Baudelaire saw clearly that this dislocation, so characteristic of the nineteenth century, arose in systemic *institutional*
transformations. The social dislocations produced by the revolutions
of the nineteenth century upset long-consecrated patterns of socialization. It no longer seemed clear who learned or who taught, nor in
what loci, nor to transmit what contents. A fundamental generational
link was profoundly upset. For the nineteenth century, history became the register of this crisis. In the outflow of such disturbance,
our contemporary suspicion about meaning, the familiar crisis of representation to which I referred earlier, might appear as the theoretical reflexes of this epochal change in the patterns of production and
transmission of socially sanctioned sense.

Forms of specifically institutional disorganization may explain
some of the aspects of the memory crisis early in the nineteenth
century, but later on its determinants located themselves at an even
deeper level of the social formation. The key to understanding such
location is to understand why "history" became a focus of consciousness in this period, an object of intense research and preoccupation.

In *The Historical Novel*, Lukács provided one basis for understanding this development:

34. Alfred de Vigny, "Réflexions sur la vérité dans l'Art," 53; emphasis Vigny's.

It was the French Revolution, the revolutionary wars and the rise and fall of Napoleon, which for the first time made history a *mass experience*, and moreover on a European scale. During the decades between 1789 and 1814 each nation of Europe underwent more upheavals than they had previously experienced in centuries. And the quick succession of these upheavals gives them a qualitatively distinct character, it makes their historical character far more visible than would be the case in isolated, individual instances: the masses no longer have the impression of a "natural occurrence."[35]

But the vision of the past as a complication arises at the confluence of forces transforming nineteenth-century life that are even more deeply seated than the political and military upheavals to which Lukács referred. These determinants lie in the realm of production of the social, and they form the background for the remainder of my argument here, for they determine the phenomenon—and the problem—of memory in its distinctively modern form.

The following seem particularly important among the developments determining the reconfiguration of the nineteenth-century experience of memory:

- The leap in the productive power of human labor that resulted from the coming of machines, and the rapid, virtually endless replication and dissemination of objects that machines make possible. For the first time in history, the capitalization and industrial reorganization of production in nineteenth-century Europe permitted the creation of sufficient surplus to make economic development self-sustaining. This alteration of social rhythm underlay significant modifications in the experience and the perception of time for most members of the culture.[36]
- The experience of vertiginous changes in the organization of pol-

35. George Lukács, *The Historical Novel*, 23.
36. Walter Benjamin had striking (if characteristically telegraphic) things to say about the effect of capitalism on memory: "The worlds of memory replace themselves more quickly [in the capitalist period], the mythic in them surfaces more quickly and crassly, [and] a totally different world of memory must be set up even faster against them" (*Passagen-Werk*, in *Gesammelte Schriften*, 5:576; cited in Buck-Morss, *Dialectics of Seeing*, 278).

itics and sociality, in demography and population distribution, in the constitution and organization of the urban environment, in family structure and dynamics, and in what earlier I termed the "institutions of memory" and its associated technologies and practices.

- The increasing institutionalization and stabilization of the analytic tendency in middle-class thought. It was this tendency that made the construction of machines (and of an entire socioeconomy dependent upon them) the object of instrumental reflection. The production process thus ceased simply to be an activity; it became a technique, a *discipline*, with all the consciousness of artifice that the latter term implies. Such a discipline implicitly takes time and hence the relation of the present to the past as its problem.

- The early development of what the Frankfurt School would call the "culture" or "consciousness" industry: the rise of the media, embracing an educational system, an increasingly massified press, and an increasingly programmed collective experience in shopping, in entertainment, in sports, and in national political ceremonial,[37] all of which combined to institutionalize an innovative—and frequently a bewildering—cultural memory.

- The increasing abstraction of psychosocial life, perceived in the widely noticed mutation in everyday experience according to which the objects of concern to individuals were typically *out of sight*, consequently shifting cognitive activity from the immediately perceptual to the mnemonic realm (I return to this issue in Chapter 2).

- A coordinate shift in the mode of conservation (and awareness) of the past, from the activity of live, organic memory to what might be termed artificial or archival memory (in the form of written documents and similar "extra-individual" mechanisms for recollection, themselves increasingly organized and marshaled by institutions, ranging from the educational to the bureaucratic, dedicated to the preservation of the past).

37. See Horkheimer and Adorno, *Dialectic of Enlightenment*; Hans Magnus Enzensberger, *The Consciousness Industry*; and E. J. Hobsbawm and Terence Ranger, eds., *The Invention of Tradition*.

Such developments socialized the citizens of a much broader and more centralized, standardized, normalized socioeconomy to the patterns of general assumption, of communal consciousness, of habituated practice, which alone could enable such a society to function at all. But a simple, if devastating, perception emerged from the experience and from the contemplation of these factors. It was the realization that *nothing* is natural about our memories, that the past—the practices, the habits, the dates and facts and places, the very furniture of our existences—is an artifice, and one susceptible to the most varied and sometimes the most culpable manipulations.

These developments defined a situation of great stress. A social formation depends for its stability on a relatively stable understanding of its past, consequently on a generalized assent to the structures and cultural discourses produced out of that past to regulate the present. In the "long nineteenth century" the response to this stress was necessarily complex, but its outline in the theoretical realm includes one fundamental element: for the nineteenth century, and for better or worse, history increasingly became the discipline of memory.

Positively, history systematized the memory problem. By interrogating it through its own paradigms, it created the preconditions for uncovering the crisis that disconnection with the past inevitably entailed. But though history thereby became guarantor and registrar of the past, its locus when "natural" or "organic" memory became problematic, its sedimentation as "discipline" had a subtle negative resonance. For history simultaneously became the place to which the mnemonic crisis determined by such evacuation could be *displaced*—at the limit, it became the tomb in which it could be concealed. By taking on the function of "preserving" the past, history hid the individual *dispossession* of the past that the texts I cited earlier never ceased lamenting.[38]

Michel de Certeau has provided the clearest theory of the "separation" that intervenes in what he termed the "historiographical operation" (*Writing of History*, part 1). The *experience* of history may be a continuous, developmental process; but *written* history as a practice, as a discipline, presupposes a break between present and past, be-

38. On the paradoxes of this dual valence of the historical, see Foucault, *Order of Things*, 368–70. The "tomb" imagery I utilize here is drawn from and brilliantly explicated by Michel de Certeau, *The Writing of History*, 2.

tween historiography and its object—ultimately, between the dead and the living.[39] In *The Collective Memory*, Maurice Halbwachs provides an account of this separation that articulates it well with the periodization of the memory crisis that concerns me: "General history starts only when tradition ends and social memory is fading or breaking up. So long as a remembrance continues to exist, it is useless to set it down in writing or otherwise fix it in memory. Likewise the need to write the history of a period, a society, or even a person is only aroused when the subject is already too distant in the past to allow for the testimony of those who preserve some remembrance of it."[40]

Seminal work has been done in recent years to strengthen our understanding of the remarkable renewal of historiography in nineteenth-century Europe. But the point of my argument here is to relate the innovations in the period's history-writing, and even more pointedly in the culture's *reflections* on history-writing, to disturbances in the memory function within post-Revolutionary society. I would surely affirm the clear intellectual—and the intensely political—preoccupations that motivated and sustained the "renaissance" of history-writing in nineteenth-century Europe. But parallel to these more overt determinations of history's restoration and disciplinarization, I believe the intensity of the renewed "historical" impulse translates a powerful nineteenth-century perception of the *deprivation* of the past. Underlying the period's celebration of history's new pertinence, I think we can detect a sense of the memory crisis as an historical disaster.

From these developments, which have to a large degree determined our own capacity for memory of the past, an epochal inflection thus needs to be recovered—to be exhumed, to recall Flaubert's word from *L'Éducation* and de Certeau's imagery in *The Writing of History*. What is at stake is nothing less than how a culture imagines the representation of the past to be possible, for the problem of representing the past is really the representation problem itself, seized in its most critical locus in experience.

39. See François Hartog, "L'Évidence de l'histoire," 5. Pierre Nora's introduction to *Les Lieux de mémoire* makes much of the same distinction: "Memory, history, far from being synonymous, appear now to be in fundamental opposition" ("Between Memory and History," 8).

40. Maurice Halbwachs, *The Collective Memory*, 78–79; translation modified.

2

Theorizing Recollection

[Socrates:] I have forgotten to mention your art of memory.
            —Plato, *Lesser Hippias*, 368b

Memory believes before knowing remembers.
            —William Faulkner, *Light in August*, 111

Since the nineteenth century, memory has seemed the mechanism by which ideology materializes itself. Memory had always functioned that way, but now the process by which the reproduction of cultural practices was managed had been sufficiently broken away from the apparent transparency of "natural order" to require some thought—and theory—on its own. Yet just as the role of ideology was coming theoretically clear, its functioning was being automated considerably. This is why what I have been terming "natural" or "organic" memory increasingly appeared a problem in this period. The paradox is worth noticing. At the same time as some were thinking the process through, the nineteenth century was developing systems to ensure that the practices that organize social production and reproduction would be so thoroughly internalized that they could function outside consciousness. Under such conditions, the determinations they exercised could hardly be evaded; but their formation could hardly be recovered. They functioned as a history that virtually *excluded* memory.

In strikingly parallel notions, Bourdieu and Foucault theorized this complex of invisible structures organizing social activity. Bourdieu named the complex determining individual behavior "habitus"; Fou-

Gensis Amnesia

cault spoke of the "discourses" that "order" us—in the strong sense.[1] We know these things without knowing that we know them. The structures organizing us are held in a memory that is effectively locked up. Explaining the notion of "genesis amnesia" to which I referred earlier—and suggesting the pertinence of the investigation of Freud's theory of memory with which this book concludes—Bourdieu puts it this way: "The 'unconscious' is never anything other than the forgetting of history which history itself produces by incorporating the objective structures it produces in the second natures of habitus" (*Outline of a Theory of Practice*, 78–79). This occulting of memory is a mechanism familiar to us in the Freudian theory of neurosis, but we will find traces of a parallel consciousness in a wide variety of theories of social or cultural process. Such representations of the ghostly presence of the past have this in common: that—in the same way that under capitalism Marx had claimed that the power and creativity of the worker seem to pass into the tool—they seek to explain how in the modern period memory appears to reside not in perceiving consciousness but *in the material*: in the practices and institutions of social or psychic life, which function within us, but, strangely, do not seem to require either our participation or our explicit allegiance.[2]

This phenomenon has been central to Marxist analyses of social existence since the nineteenth century. As Fredric Jameson argued some time ago, Lukács's contribution to its theorization was to demonstrate how the blockage of our access to recollection of the past, the loss of the *developmental* memory by which the historical determinants of social life and knowledge might otherwise be revealed, could be understood to *constitute* bourgeois society.[3] More recently, Gerald A. Cohen has systematized analysis of the differential *place* of

1. See Pierre Bourdieu, *Outline of a Theory of Practice*, and Michel Foucault, "The Discourse on Language." I discussed the relation of these theories to the earlier work of Marx and Gramsci and to the contemporary thought of Althusser in my *Discourse/Counter-Discourse: The Theory of Practice of Symbolic Resistance in Nineteenth-Century France*, particularly 41–43.

2. See Karl Marx, *Capital: A Critique of Political Economy*, Volume 1, 548, and my *Discourse/Counter-Discourse*, 293.

3. For Lukács, Jameson argued, what is false or mystified is not the *content* of bourgeois thought but rather its *form* (*Marxism and Form: Twentieth-Century Dialectical Theories of Literature*, 183). A divorce between thought and its historical determinants defines this organized structure of misrecognition.

illusion in precapitalist and capitalist formations.[4] Cohen argues that under capitalism, although certain forms of social relations are perfectly overt (the utilitarianism of human relations, visible in the undisguised adversarial stance pitting capitalist against worker, for example), what becomes occulted are crucial elements of transformative practice—essential *forms of time*. Thus the diachronicity of labor time is transformed into the illusory synchronism of exchange-value (338). *Process* is thus the specific realm of ideological illusion under capitalism. Under such conditions it is no wonder that the past begins to seem an impenetrable problem. Indeed, under such conditions it is uncertain how we ever get from *then* to *now*.[5]

Certain products and materials resume their shape after they have been deformed. Permanent-press slacks keep their crease through wearing and washing; plastic utensils bounce back even when dropped or crushed. This property is termed "materials memory." It seems a process without a subject: it "just happens." This may be a useful notion for understanding the conservative character built into social existence and practice by the sorts of mechanisms Marx and Freud—among many others—have sought to account for. Such a concept would allow us to argue that the knowledge of social process does not disappear, but (like the productivity of the worker reified in the tool) rather it seems to *migrate* into a different place, into a text different from the one we carry in our recollection. Such a memory forcefully produces the past in the present. And refining its own production was one of the primary technologies of the nineteenth century. In turn, its adequate comprehension and theorization has been one of the important projects of our own period. I want to argue that such a "materials memory" functions even *within* signs, and constitutes them as one of the enigmas of our social life. But let me first consider several other loci in which materials memory operates.

The first would be in the practices of "invented tradition" identified by Eric Hobsbawm.[6] Hobsbawm and his collaborators discov-

---

4. See Gerald A. Cohen, *Karl Marx's Theory of History: A Defence*, appendix 1.

5. Freud radicalized this perception of an essential occultation of the past in his theory of an *unconscious* memory—a memory absolute in both its registrations of experience and its unavailability to consciousness. I return to this influential and perplexing paradigm in Chapters 7 and 8.

6. See E. J. Hobsbawm and Terence Ranger, eds., *The Invention of Tradition*.

ered a surprising fact about the ceremonies and rituals that define
the "traditional" pole of nineteenth-century society. An astonishing
number of them were simply created wholesale. Thus the formal
pomp of monarchy (in Britain particularly) turned out to be a com-
paratively recent transformation of an age-old tradition of slovenly
ceremonials (*Invention*, chap. 4). The tartans, kilt, and bagpipe of
Scotland turned out to be, if not pure inventions, then at least conscious cultural impositions around which Highlanders could rally after the Union with England (chap. 2). In France, the most venerable
organized ritual of national celebration—Bastille Day—dates only
from 1880 (271). These practices seem to inhere in our expectations
of the world. Their recency then astonishes us because we have been
induced to forget their greenness. The rapidity with which genesis
amnesia has operated to obscure their origins is an earnest of its
broader mystifying function within modern culture.

Such invented traditions are often the phenomenal forms of a
broader instance that they exist to project and to sustain: the modern
state. Hobsbawm puts it this way: "The state . . . raised unprecedented problems of how to maintain or even establish the obedience,
loyalty and cooperation of its members, or its own legitimacy in their
eyes" (264–65). Invented traditions establish or symbolize the cohe-
sion of such polities, whose existence becomes internalized within
the memories of those subjected to it as if it were a fact beyond
change and independent of memory. Baudelaire put his finger on a
crucial characteristic of the state when he observed ironically of
Napoléon III that his greatest glory was to have demonstrated that
anyone can control a government by taking over the telegraph and
the printing office.[7] For these institutions are metonymies of the
power to regulate social discourses—precisely the discourses that (in
what appears one of the most massive and consequential genesis am-
nesias of all) produce the state as a seemingly timeless entity.[8]

Baudelaire's insight points to the "materials memory" produced in
the forms of the nineteenth century's increasingly powerful information media. I discussed these developments in *Discourse/Counter-*

7. Charles Baudelaire, "Mon coeur mis à nu," in *Oeuvres complètes* (1961), 1286.
8. A more local analogue would be other State interventions in the mnemonic register,
such as the proffered amnesty by which in 1859 Napoléon III sought to take control of the
opposition to his regime, which I consider in Chapter 4.

Discourse, in particular the disorganization of consciousness induced by the practices of the daily newspaper, which is a structured experience of confusion that naturalizes new forms of cultural and perceptual contents: "Newspapers trained their readers in the apprehension of detached, independent, reified, decontextualized 'articles'. . . . [The newspaper] is built by addition of discrete, theoretically disconnected elements which juxtapose themselves only in response to the abstract requirements of 'layout'" (122). I could as well have said that what I termed "newspaper culture" produced a new and more abstract form of memory. Newspaper culture puts the paradigms of natural memory in crisis by excluding the context that makes such memory functional for us.

In his work on Baudelaire, Walter Benjamin suggested that the alterations in space produced by the experience of the modern city induced a parallel sort of abstraction in the consciousness of those who were obliged to function within its limits. In the city, familiar objects are much more frequently out of sight than in older forms of agglomeration. Following Simmel, Benjamin commented upon the predominance of the eye over the ear in urban life as a particular perceptual innovation, and speculated that the social content of the detective story depended upon the "obliteration of the individual's traces in the big-city crowd."[9] He argued that the nineteenth-century city produced a particularly acute experience of disconnection and abstraction.

Such abstraction defeats the associative structure of natural memory and induces in its place a different form of the habitus or technology of recollection that we could call "archival consciousness." Its principle would be the increasingly randomized isolation of the individual *item* of information, to the detriment of its relation to any whole, and the consignment of such information to what earlier I called "extra-individual" mnemonic mechanisms. Such abstraction has been increasingly programmed by the practices of modern socio-economies since the industrial revolution.[10]

9. Walter Benjamin, *Charles Baudelaire: A Lyric Poet in the Era of High Capitalism*, 38, 43. See also Georg Simmel, *Soziologie: Untersuchungen über die Formen der Vergesellschaftung*, 650–65, and Wolfgang Schivelbusch, *The Railway Journey: Trains and Travel in the 19th Century*, 80.
10. Another example may be useful here: the invention and cultural influence of pho-

The mode of institutionalized abstraction (represented by the cognitive practices of the newspaper and the identity photograph, but effective in diverse realms of nineteenth-century experience) foregrounds the fundamental opposition between traditional and modern social organizations—and between the characteristic "mentalities" associated with each—that toward the end of the century Ferdinand Tönnies sought to model. To the representation of opacity and alienation that had emerged in Marx and that was soon to be echoed by Freud, Tönnies counterposed the projection of alternatives—a utopian ideal type that reads the reality of late nineteenth-century sociality. *Gemeinschaft und Gesellschaft*, Tönnies's influential theory of the dichotomy between traditional and modern social forms, appeared in 1887.[11] Unfortunately, it has been more alluded to than read. In the context of my argument concerning the nineteenth-century crisis of memory, Tönnies can help to focus perceptions of a fundamental *difference* between the nineteenth century's problematic experience of memory and the past it imagined it had lost in gaining what we know as modernity.

Perhaps the most striking aspect of how Tönnies's celebrated concepts have been taken up is that the notions of *Gemeinschaft* and *Gesellschaft* have typically had only a loose relationship with the actual details of Tönnies's analysis. The translation of Tönnies's title presents a problem, but not simply the problem of selecting in a given target language appropriate equivalents for the terms of his original. The particular form of *opposition* between the terms must also be translated. Dichotomous systems (of which Tönnies's stands as one of the most familiar) are a typical and comprehensible product of periods of perceived cultural stress: of instability, transition, and the disquiet that precede the internalizations and restabilizations of

tography. Benjamin considered these developments in *Charles Baudelaire* (see particularly 48 and 146–47). He pointed out how important photography proved in organizing the administrative control processes of the modern state. The insight is crucial. It links up with the notion of a constitutive decontextualization of the photographic object, and its pervasive influence in altering the ground of visual memory. On the photograph and its transforming relation to memory, see Michelle Perrot, ed., *From the Fires of Revolution to the Great War*, vol. 4 of *A History of Private Life*, 465.

11. The very title of *Gemeinschaft und Gesellschaft* presents an intricacy worth a second look. To begin with, the Loomis translation appeared in the United States as *Community and Society*, but in England as *Community and Association*.

emergent social or conceptual forms. Such systems counterpose the present's perceived deficiency against an image of the past retained (or reconstructed) in memory. They measure the distance between intensely consequential alternatives—what in the flattening consciousness of crisis are conceived as the characteristics that mark current experience or practice *in their inadequacy or imperfection*. The oppositions they figure are therefore often highly modalized by affects of loss or lamentation.[12]

Vilfredo Pareto captured the abstract structural character of such oppositions in his observation that dichotomous concepts such as Tönnies's could really be translated or represented by *any two* differential symbols (see *Community and Society*, 285 n. 2). This insight registers the degree to which Tönnies's celebrated binary can be taken as an empty structure ready to be recycled or reconstructed, to be filled up with a variety of contents materializing and overdetermining the core antinomy that, in 1887, "community" and "society" were intended to represent. This arbitrariness helps to account for the curious distance between the concepts Tönnies developed and the way tradition has taken them up. But to Pareto's structuralist depiction of how Tönnies's concepts have entered the conceptual lexicon I want to restore the element of historicization: an insistence on the degree to which, in its moment, the opposition Tönnies theorized responded to a *situation*. The urgency in question can be focused in a reading of the nineteenth-century memory crisis.

The history of nineteenth- and early twentieth-century models in social theory reveals a remarkable proliferation of paradigms exhibiting the same fundamental structure as that figured in Tönnies's opposition—a virtual obsession with dichotomy.[13] All of these notions

12. In Chapter 4 I offer an account of a parallel dichotomous paradigm in Baudelaire dividing *then* from *now*, but one much more thoroughly alive to the abstract nature of its internal opposition, and intent upon grounding it in the specifics of the mid-nineteenth-century historical moment and in the determinants of its experiential reality.

13. See John C. McKinney and Charles P. Loomis's introduction to *Community and Society*. They name the following versions of the fundamental dichotomous division defining social forms: "Maine's status society and contract society; Spencer's militant and industrial forms; Ratzenhofer's conquest state and culture state; Wundt's natural and cultural polarity; Durkheim's mechanical and organic solidarity; Cooley's primary and secondary (implicit) groups; MacIver's communal and associational relations; Zimmerman's localistic

must of course be construed as what Max Weber later termed "ideal types." We cannot therefore appropriately imagine mapping such artificial and constructed concepts directly on any history. Yet the very contrivance of the ideal type and of the dichotomous opposition has a particular relevance to the sort of historical situation in which these concepts arose as mechanisms for thinking about reality. The reality itself was new, and it was perceived as replacing an older set of structures in which nothing like the disquiet produced by modern forms of sociality seemed to threaten. The clarity of this imputed difference is what motivated the formation of dichotomous systems to begin with.

However sophisticated its theoretical detail in the work of diverse nineteenth- and early twentieth-century thinkers, this oppositional structure recycles in a more abstract form the stark "abyss in time" that I suggested earlier was a widely perceived reading of the relationship between the post-Revolutionary or modernist present and the vanished traditional past. Eugen Weber's image of the *fin des terroirs*—the loss of traditional village society—can focus the way the structure of oppositions inherent to ideal types transforms itself into a reading of history. In *Peasants into Frenchmen* Weber attempts to navigate the difference between change and fundamental *mutation*—the historical moment at which the pure dichotomies of ideal types can truly be thought to seize the movement of reality. Weber puts it this way: "Societies that had been stable and homogeneous for centuries were coming under several stresses at once. In stable societies, changes—and there is never a time when changes do not take place—affect only details, not the general structure. But the late-nineteenth century rural society of France was no longer stable; and it was gradually becoming less homogeneous. Every blow

---

and cosmopolitan communities; Odum's folk-state pair; Redfield's folk-urban continuum; Sorokin's familistic vs. contractual relations; Becker's sacred and secular societies; as well as such nonpersonalized but common dichotomies as primitive-civilized; literate-nonliterate; and rural vs. urban" (12). Max Weber's typology was more supple, but his notions of the "rationalization" and of the "disenchantment" of the world can be inscribed within the same implicit structure. See also David Frisby, *Fragments of Modernity: Theories of Modernity in the Work of Simmel, Kracauer and Benjamin*, 13, on the relation of Durkheim, Simmel, and Weber to this pattern. Lest it be thought that I see Tönnies as the originator of this general paradigm, I should note that something like it is already present in Adam Ferguson's 1787 *Essay on the History of Civil Society*; see Albert O. Hirschman, *The Passions and the Interests: Political Arguments for Capitalism before Its Triumph*, 120.

against the details of its organization placed its total system more and more at the mercy of modernity."[14]

Traditions had always changed, but now, as Weber observed, they died and were simply not replaced (x). From a slightly different angle, Fernand Braudel noted that the general appearance of markets all over Europe varied little from the sixteenth through the early nineteenth centuries. But then all at once their appearance was modified—by the monetarization and the sudden expansion of trade, by the coming of the canals and railroads, and by a dozen other mutagenic forces.[15]

Such infrastructural changes—which formed the substance of nineteenth-century social history and motivated the institutionalization of diverse "human sciences" in the same period—transfigured the modalities of memory and the experience of the mnemonic realm. Pierre Nora puts it this way: "Consider . . . the irrevocable break [*cette mutilation sans retour*] marked by the disappearance of peasant culture, that quintessential repository of collective memory whose recent vogue as an object of historical study coincided with the apogee of industrial growth."[16] We get an image of this mutation in Eugen Weber's account of the long tradition and sudden disappearance of the *veillée*, the winter-evening gathering of the entire village population in traditional French communities for socializing, shared work and storytelling: "Veillées . . . had a didactic function. . . . Traditional skills were learned by participation. Traditional wisdom was learned in the same way. The talk was full of allusions to the past: the time of the lords, of the Revolution, of the wolves and how they disappeared. The oral culture perpetuated itself by the tales told, the pious legends, the teachings about the supernatural realm, the explanations of nature and of life, the precepts that applied to every sort of situation and that were contained in the formulas, songs, and proverbs repeated over and over again" (*Peasants into Frenchmen*, 414).

14. Eugen Weber, *Peasants into Frenchmen: The Modernization of Rural France, 1870–1914*, 191.

15. See Fernand Braudel, *The Structures of Everyday Life: The Limits of the Possible*, 436–563, and especially *The Wheels of Commerce*. Michel de Certeau theorized a parallel distinction between the changes that allow structures of existence to remain the same ("tactics") and the changes that alter them ("strategies"); see *Practice of Everyday Life*, xix, 36–39.

16. Pierre Nora, "Between Memory and History," 7.

But by the 1880s, even in remote Brittany, the veillées had disappeared. What Weber terms their "didactic function"—what I would rather term their mnemonic function—had been replaced by stories learned from schoolbooks (415). We need to understand the nineteenth-century memory crisis—and the perception of a fissure dividing present from past—against the background of such infrastructural mutations.

So beyond the detail of his taxonomy, Tönnies's system of social polarities can be read as an effort to find a theoretical figure for a profound and disquieting *sense of loss*. To read it in this way runs against the grain of Tönnies's own conscious intentions. For (despite his own socialist sympathies) Tönnies sought to function as a social scientist in the consecrated nineteenth-century model. He maintained that his typology inscribed no differential valuation; he was interested only in facts and in patterns. Nor, he claimed, did he intend that the remapping of his structural polarity as a historical succession (*Gemeinschaft* → *Gesellschaft*) should be taken to imply any subjective assessment. Such a sequencing was meant to refer neither to a myth of progress nor to one of decline. It was just a sequence. Thus when critics accused him of recommending *Gemeinschaft* as good and condemning *Gesellschaft* as bad, Tönnies insisted that his categories were purely structural and descriptive (see *Community and Society*, 2–3 and 284 n. 2).

It is difficult, however, to square such a pretense of objectivity with the language and imagery that animate Tönnies's discussion. In his book's opening pages he explains the contrast between the elements of his model in terms of a progression in individual development: "In Gemeinschaft with one's family, one lives from birth on, bound to it in weal and woe. One goes into Gesellschaft as one goes into a foreign country" (33–34; translation modified). It would be difficult to miss the affective charge in such an image. In particular, the "foreign country" into which we are precipitated in the social formation of *Gesellschaft* unmistakably evokes the dangerous epidemic of "nostalgia" that began in the eighteenth century and continued to cause alarm as late as Tönnies's own period.[17] The "organic" (33) tra-

17. This "nostalgia" has little to do with our wistful contemporary regret for the past, but rather with what physicians of the eighteenth and nineteenth centuries described and

ditions and customs of *Gemeinschaft* Tönnies conceived as fundamentals of existence. He likened them to the relationship between mother and child (37), or between people and the house they live in (42).[18] So their replacement in *Gesellschaft* by the modern experience of individual isolation (65), of rational calculation of value and of utility (76), and of abstraction generally are developments that Tönnies hardly construed neutrally. For him the transparency of relationships between individuals organically linked had an unmistakable appeal; the reifications and alienations of modernity he could describe with scientific objectivity, but never in such a way that the unfavorable burden of their *difference* was entirely purged.

The organic solidarities of *Gemeinschaft* are coordinate with—indeed, might be said to constitute—a whole set of memory practices, an entire mnemonic formation. Tönnies made the point himself in a 1911 addition to his book: "The forms of will such as liking, habit, and *memory* are as essential for and characteristic of Gemeinschaftlike associations as those of deliberation, decision, and concept are of

treated as a full-blown illness precipitated by separating the sufferer from the familiarity and security of home. In 1801, for example, Stendhal suffered a serious attack of this disease, duly diagnosed by his physician; see *Journal*, 12 December 1801, in *Oeuvres intimes*, 1:31–32. Marcel Proust referred to the phenomenon at the opening of *Le Côté de Guermantes* in his gently mocking depiction of the physical and affective decline of Françoise caused by her displacement from home in Combray to Paris, where she had come to live with the narrator's family after the death of Tante Léonie; see *RTP* 2:309 and *RTP54* 2:9. Jean Starobinski described nostalgia in a classic article: "At the end of the eighteenth century people began to be fearful of extended sojourns away from home because they had become conscious of the threat posed by nostalgia. People even died of nostalgia after having read in books that nostalgia is a disease which is frequently mortal" ("The Idea of Nostalgia," 86). See also Michael S. Roth, "Dying of the Past: Medical Studies of Nostalgia in Nineteenth-Century France."

18. In evoking to characterize *Gemeinschaft* the experience of the *house* in which people live, Tönnies tapped into a deep reservoir of memory. The intensity of such a relation has been recognized and referred to since the classical period. Indeed, the *artes memoriae* of antiquity instructed people to "place" images of material they sought to recall in their own houses (see Frances A. Yates, *The Art of Memory*, 6). The phenomenological tradition made much of the intimacy of the individual's relations with his or her house—what Gaston Bachelard called "one of the greatest powers of integration of the thoughts, memories, and dreams of mankind" (*Poetics of Space*; cited in David Harvey, *Condition of Postmodernity: An Enquiry into the Origins of Cultural Change*, 217). Bachelard might have been thinking of Proust's own description of Tante Léonie's house in Combray, which focuses memory (and considerable affect) for his narrator (I return to the narrator's recollection of the house in Chapter 8). See also Edward S. Casey, *Remembering: A Phenomenological Study*, 211, on Heidegger's "topology of Being" and its relation to this theme.

Gesellschaft-like associations" (134; emphasis mine). It would be easy
to project Tönnies's paradigmatic opposition forward toward Benjamin's notion of the decline of what we might term organic experience [*Erfahrung*], or Martin Heidegger's critical account of the modern technological transformation of people and things into a "standing
reserve" [*Bestand*].[19] Many of Tönnies's themes thus foreshadow—
or positively proclaim—familiar modernist and even postmodernist
problematics: mechanical reproducibility, dehumanization, the flattening of time, the bleaching out or dehistoricizing of tradition. What
interests me, however, in the binary paradigm that Tönnies, more
than any other theorist, made available for conceiving modernity is
its own strategic and reductive recollection—or projection—of traditional memory structures and experiences.

We could put it quite simply. *Gemeinschaft* is the paradise of
memory. But as Proust asserted in a celebrated aphorism, the only
paradises are the ones we have lost (*RTP* 4:449; *RTP54* 3:870). Their
distance from our present is always infinite. Essentially, Tönnies
transformed his account of traditional memory into a systematic *nostalgia for memory*. His projection of the memory crisis was to conceive it—displaced into the neutralities of social science—as a longing for what had once been held in recollection but could no longer
be. The dichotomous formalization he devised thus reconceived the
modern experience of memory *as a crisis*; the very form of its polarity figured the mnemonic "abyss in time." This is why Tönnies
himself resisted conceiving of his own model as an historical account:
because the past of *Gemeinschaft* he projected exists in an *irretrievable* space—as far from the modernist present as paradise itself. This
non-negotiable distance defines the physiognomy of the memory
crisis to begin with. The past of *Gemeinschaft* to which Tönnies's
polarity refers as an apparent norm is really *memory on the point of
disappearance*—an exquisitely liminal recollection of recollection,
frozen just as it passes into oblivion.

Structuralist theories, such as Tönnies's, that marginalize or abstract
their historicity render their relation to the memory problem

19. See Walter Benjamin, "Some Motifs in Baudelaire," in *Charles Baudelaire*, 117,
and Martin Heidegger, "The Question Concerning Technology," 17. For these connections, I am indebted to Edward Dimendberg. See his "Film Noir and Urban Space"
(Ph.D. diss., University of California, Santa Cruz, 1992), 26.

opaque. Conversely, by the nature of their attention to temporality and causality, materialist models have had the virtue of foregrounding the intertwining of the conceptual and the mnemonic. The historically demystificatory intention of certain strains of Marxist theory is well known, as I suggested earlier in referring to Lukács's notion of reification. But let us see what happens when *language* itself is brought into this problematic.

M. M. Bakhtin's theory derives its power from an insistence upon recovering the charged and conflictual history of language—of words—even in the face of the generalized decontextualization of social objects and signs that is the reflex of the memory crisis. The effect of Bakhtin's work is to reassert the mediations linking social objects and signs to the cultural system in which their meanings become meaningful. The basis of such a relation is a "materials memory" within the sign analogous to others I considered earlier. The sign itself recalls and signifies its "conditioning" by culture, and such determination is essential to its meaning.[20] What Bakhtin termed "dialogism" enforces the reestablishment of such relations for all cultural objects and ensures the restoration of a fundamental cultural memory at the level of the sign itself.[21]

Dialogism, in other words, is a memory model. It seeks to recall the semantic and social *history* carried by a culture's language, but which tends to be forgotten, to be blanked, in characteristic forms of mystification and amnesia since the revolutions of the nineteenth century. Bakhtin thus argued that "the word in language is half someone else's,"[22] but he did not conceive this shared ownership as a dispossession. He rather thought of it as a liberating *recollection* of the collective condition of possibility of any language, of any social communication.

Bakhtin's reassertion of the social character of cultural existence can help to lay bare what threatens in the developments that have altered the forms of memory's functioning over the period I have been discussing. Increasingly, as is notorious, these more modern forms isolate consciousness in a perpetual, inescapable present that might remind us of the dehistoricized abstractness of Tönnies's *Ge-*

---

20. M. M. Bakhtin, *Marxism and the Philosophy of Language*, 21.

21. This relation has sometimes been termed "intertextuality." Julia Kristeva borrowed the notion of intertextuality from Bakhtin; see her "Mémoire," 44.

22. M. M. Bakhtin, *The Dialogic Imagination: Four Essays*, 293.

sellschaft, in which synchronic and diachronic connection with other social existences becomes unimaginable. Our experience of the prison-house of language then turns out to be a memory problem. It is as if we had forgotten language's—and culture's—realm of freedom.

The introduction of dialogism into my argument recalls that early theorization of this recollecting mechanism belongs to the period in which the memory machine and the theory machine were gearing up. Such efforts to restore our connection and conceive our relation to the past are preoccupations characteristic of the nineteenth century. We find them in the programmatic attempts to institutionalize the discipline of history or discover the psychology of memory. But they are detectable far beyond these areas. In *Discourse/Counter-Discourse* I considered two examples of how we might read the preoccupation with memory in such less obvious loci.

The first of these cases was Flaubert's practice of and reflection on quotation, on what I termed "re/cited" language. "Re/citation" lifts words from the past of someone else's usage and projects them into the present of our own (see *Discourse/Counter-Discourse*, chap. 4). Notoriously in his *Dictionary of Received Ideas*, and more generally throughout his writing, Flaubert imported *others'* speech, in the form of platitudes and banalities, clichés and dominant stupidities— what he termed *bêtise*. The montage of such degraded expression and his own high style produces powerful collisions—but it also reveals how insidiously, despite our best efforts to resist it, the *bêtise* of others contaminates our own expression. In effect Flaubert was exploring the capacity of language that Bakhtin later theorized, to reproduce itself in difference. He was measuring and representing the complex, nearly inextricable intertwining of distance and intimacy, of separation and implication, that occurs when we write or speak the signifiers that come from others, from elsewhere, and from another time. It turned out to be impossible to control the speech we cite, or to mark its difference from our own. We are not free to keep the past *past*—it colonizes our present whether or not we realize its encroachment. In effect Flaubert was examining what happens when we become aware of *language itself* as the primary product and the primary mechanism of memory.

Baudelaire and Mallarmé also contended with these fundamental mnemonic and linguistic structures. Baudelaire made a fetish of the cliché (see *Discourse/Counter-Discourse*, 211), and Mallarmé in his translations meditated on what can be preserved and what resisted of *others'* language. But in *Discourse/Counter-Discourse* I argued that the new genre of the prose poem became the central place where these writers and others sought to explore how language carried the past within itself, and how such alien contents might be managed (chaps. 6 and 7). After mid-century, *prose* increasingly appeared to the avant-garde as the speech of its antagonists, as the instrument of middle-clase production and domination. The prose poem sought to reconquer the instrument of such expression by turning it against its hegemonic exponents, by converting the pedestrian into *art*. The transformation of prose in the prose poem after the middle of the nineteenth century thus projected a fundamental intertextual palimpsest. In effect the new genre projected revolutionizing the language of the bourgeoisie by "re/citing" it. In the prose poem the pervasiveness of nineteenth-century prosaicism in its full instrumental vulgarity and the recollected purity of a prerevolutionary idealization of poetry come together in a practice that we could interpret as an experiment to see how far it might be possible to transform our own memory of language.

These developments were increasingly driven by the gloomy realization that the contents of memory carried a threat. The techniques and developments that insured nineteenth-century intertextuality inscribed a consciousness of social difference and constituted a response to it. Here then is one place where the negative aspect of the mnemonic—the threat of its excess, of *too much* memory—emerges. It is visible as well in the phenomenon of habituation, of Bourdieu's habitus become sovereign, and in the related banalization or *bêtisification* of language experienced by writers beginning in this period. Intellectuals recalled (and were obsessed by) what they experienced as the ridiculous middle-class voices of their fellow citizens.[23] They discovered that they could not suppress the echoes in their own writing of journalism's degraded rhetoric, no matter how strenuously they sought to project its counterdiscourse; they could not fail

23. For example the schoolteacher's "Quos ego" that Flaubert satirized at the opening of *Madame Bovary* (strikingly analyzed by Michael Riffaterre in "Flaubert's Presuppositions").

to remember the power of instrumental language, which—in Mallarmé for example—generated a fantasy projection of a counter-language beyond instrumentality. It was because of these painful memory effects that the concept of social divisions inscribed in language became so powerfully focused in this period.

In such cases, *what is remembered materializes as alienation*, with profound linguistic, rhetorical, and social consequences. Memory is the precondition for any intertextuality, for any dialogism. But beginning in the nineteenth century such intertextualities always produce irony. The perception of memory as a danger awakened in the culture at just the point when the character of memory itself was being profoundly altered. This inchoate sense of the contents of recollection as a *threat* (which attains its most acute and corrosive representation in *A la recherche du temps perdu*, as I will consider in Chapters 5 and 6) is a critical reading of the multiform presence of the past in modern experience.

It might seem paradoxical that a culture whose memory was threatened should have perceived memory as a threat. How can we explain such an apparent misrecognition? In the nineteenth century the determinations of ideology and habituated practice—the contents and mechanisms by which the past is experienced in memory—no longer seemed organic links that instituted the present by tying it to its past. On the contrary, the threat perceived in memory corresponds to the most characteristic danger identified in every radical critique of modern society: routinization, autonomization, instrumentalization, and colonization of consciousness, of the individual, of labor, and of the entire social process. Memory was coming to seem a mechanism of subjection.

At a moment when the progressivism of the nineteenth century was still credible, Jules Michelet wrote with enthusiasm that "every period dreams the next one" (*Avenir! Avenir!*; cited in Benjamin, *Charles Baudelaire*, 159). But later it became clear that this optimistic projection had as its inescapable accompaniment an uncanny dreaming of the present *by the past*: the domination of contemporary reality by a history that is nominally gone, but which persists in the inert contents and forms of memory. In one of his most celebrated sentences Marx evoked this perception: "The tradition of all the dead

generations weighs like a nightmare upon the brain of the living."[24]
The memory crisis carries a generalized perception of this burden.

Sometimes this weight bearing down from the past seems comic.
In the "Machinery" chapter of *Capital*, Marx noted the following perverse effect of such numbskull persistence of memory: "To what an
extent the old forms of the instruments of production influence their
new forms at the beginning is shown . . . perhaps more strikingly
than in any other way by the fact that, before the invention of the
present locomotive, an attempt was made to construct a locomotive
with two feet, which it raised from the ground alternately, like a
horse" (1:505 n. 18). In such a situation, memory seems genially ludi-
crous—almost like a historical Freudian slip. But generally the constraints upon the present imposed by involuntary recollection and
reproduction of the past appear much grimmer. For the period,
Nietzsche became the great theoretician of the cost we incur by having history. The second of his *Unzeitgemässe Betrachtungen*, often
known in English as "The Use and Abuse of History" (1874), powerfully expressed the revolt against retention of the past.[25] Nietzsche
twists Matthew 8:22 into a sarcastic credo for historians: "Let the
dead bury the living" (72). But according to Nietzsche, historians
were not the only ones who faltered under the burden of the past.
Everyone in the nineteenth century suffered from the "malady of
history" (122); everyone's memory was obliged to "revolve . . . un-
wearyingly in a circle" while remaining "too weak and weary to take
even a single leap" outside it (64).

Under such conditions memory seems malignant. In a classic article Hayden White surveyed the impulse to repudiate the historical
"burden of the past" that began in the nineteenth century—an impulse particularly visible in a tradition of literary works that manifest
an explicit and intense hostility toward historical consciousness.[26] The

24. Karl Marx, *The Eighteenth Brumaire of Louis Bonaparte*, 1. See also Jacques Le
Goff, *Histoire et mémoire*, 52.

25. The title of Nietzsche's collection has been rendered as *Unmodern Observations*
(the William Arrowsmith edition) and as *Untimely Meditations* (as translated by R. J. Hollingdale). The second essay, "Vom Nutzen und Nachteil der Historie für das Leben," is
titled "History in the Service and Disservice of Life" in the Arrowsmith edition and "On
the Uses and Disadvantages of History for Life" in the Hollingdale translation, which I cite
here.

26. See Hayden White, "The Burden of History." See also Edward Shils, *Tradition*,

perceived oppression of stereotyped behavior, of preformed ideas, of
prescribed morality produced a reaction characterized by ardent
cries for life, spontaneity, and originality. Edward Shils expressed
the impulse clearly: "Civilization seemed to have gone too far. It had
become heavy with elaborate codes of conduct which had no ratio-
nale other than the fact that they were 'done'; it had become so
drawn into the complex, rule-bound institutions which had grown up
that a great simplification seemed called for. . . . European civilization came under the criticism that it had reached a point where its
traditions were suppressing the physical vitality necessary for its survival" (*Tradition*, 232–33).

In *Ulysses*, James Joyce put this impulse to have done with the
past most succinctly when he had Stephen Dedalus exclaim that
"History . . . is a nightmare from which I am trying to awake."[27] Yet it
strikes with an acerbic—nearly a mad—irony when we realize that
Joyce's urgent call for emancipation from the past *itself* ventriloquizes
the "nightmare" citation from Marx's *Eighteenth Brumaire* that established the topos of such a will to liberation from history for a large
part of the European tradition. That this echo in *Ulysses* is almost
surely unintended only heightens the irony of such a flawless, exemplary reenactment of the involuntary colonization of the present by
the past.

History thus turned adverse. People's relation to it in experience
and in theory became a conceptual leapfrog in two dissimilar movements: the first, a registration of the leviathan density of the practices and discourses that oblige us haplessly to relive the past in the
present; the second, an intense aspiration to negate these practices
and discourses. But by the nature of the problem this negation can
itself only be imagined in the manner devised by the past for its own
overcoming. We have no memory of the future; or rather, we can
remember the future only as a counterdiscourse of the past, regu-
lated by the past in the mode of all such inevitably unidirectional

---

232–33; David Lowenthal, *The Past Is a Foreign Country*, 233; Martin Jay, *Marxism and
Totality: The Adventures of a Concept from Lukács to Habermas*, 233; and Stephen Kern,
The Culture of Time and Space, 1880–1918, 54, 61. At the beginning of *The Burden of the
Past and the English Poet*, Walter Jackson Bate surveyed the tradition of such resistance to
tradition in pre-nineteenth-century Europe (see particularly 3–5).

27. James Joyce, *Ulysses*, 28.

determinations. In the nineteenth century, even utopias turned out
to be memory effects.

It was out of such perceptions that the mechanisms of the ideological began to be identified and theorized in the period of concern to
me here. For writers, *language* became the focus of investigation.
Involuntarily, uncontrollably, language carried the burden of the
past. The perception began to form that a culture's tropes and commonplaces, its figures and its characteristic locutions, were essential
reservoirs and enforcers of its habitus.[28] In discussing the period,
Foucault speaks to the question of language as follows: "Having become a dense and consistent historical reality, language forms the
locus of tradition, of the unspoken habits of thought, of what lies
hidden in a people's mind; it accumulates an ineluctable memory
which does not even know itself as memory. Expressing their
thoughts in words of which they are not the masters, enclosing them
in verbal forms whose historical dimensions they are unaware of,
men believe that their speech is their servant and do not realize they
are submitting themselves to its demands" (*Order of Things*, 297).

Two fundamental attitudes, each of which has had immense influence since they were articulated in the nineteenth century, sought to
subvert this dead weight of the past. Marx theorized lifting it through
its radical supersession in social revolution. Nietzsche projected its
radical obliteration in the consciousness of a new human being with
the strength to *forget* the past. For my purpose here, Nietzsche's
attitude is the more pertinent because it seeks to stage the drama it
projects *within* language itself.

What is developing in Nietzsche is an alternative version of Mallarmé's notion that somehow language can lift itself outside the determinations of history. It later became theorized in Victor Shklov-
sky's concept of *ostranenie*, "making strange," which transcends the
banality of linguistic habit. But in the face of these projected evasions
of the increasingly burdensome inertness of the past in language, we
need to recall how profoundly such strategies were themselves determined by the force of the past and the contents of language that they
sought to nullify. Language turned inward to evade its own "mate-

28. See Terdiman, *Discourse/Counter-Discourse*, chap. 4, and Françoise Gaillard, "A
Little Story about the *bras de fer*; or, How History Is Made."

rials memory." Such a movement of active forgetting positively *radicalized* genesis amnesia, for it was obliged to forget the very past that had induced its need for forgetting. The autonomization, the de-instrumentalization of language characteristic of high modernism, are counterdiscourses seeking to disregard the dominant discourse that situates them in their overdetermined reaction.

For such conceptualizations, the very notion of a dialectic, of an otherness with which one is irreducibly *linked*, is anathema. The Nietzschean attitude, in a kind of hypercontrariety, can only project the other as what one cancels. Thus the past becomes hypostatized as the radical antinomy of the present. At the conclusion of Chapter 1, I argued that the problem of representing the past is really the representation problem itself. In the Nietzschean attitude, the denial of the past and the crisis of representation reveal themselves as coterminous, as the inseparable recto and verso of a historical page that Nietzsche wished once for all to turn. But through this work of denial the determinations of the representation problem emerge into our own theoretical memory.

A profound alteration in the character of reproduction, and hence of representation generally, occurs in the capitalist period. For mass production is *re*-production of a preexisting model whose chronological and epistemological privilege can hardly be doubted. The model is the standard against which its reproduction must be measured; the prototype *is* the type. Being derivative, what follows it (either in the temporal or in the mimetic sense) can hardly avoid appearing somehow inferior, at least in the consciousness of a certain intelligentsia (whose birth as a definable social fragment moreover precisely parallels these developments). To such consciousness, the mass multiples of industrial capitalism appear degraded by just this derivativeness.

In the realm of the aesthetic, this condition of modern production gave rise to Benjamin's widely known reflection on the "aura" that attaches only to originals.[29] This valorization reflects the *de*-valorization of the object in a world in which objects are counted by the trillions. Such a situation was unprecedented in human experience.

29. See Walter Benjamin, "The Work of Art in the Age of Mechanical Reproduction," in *Illuminations*, 221.

And it is easy to imagine how it became the origin of profound imaginative displacements. In the contemporary crisis of representation, the text is denied auratic privilege if it conceives itself as the reproduction of any preexisting object. It can have aura only to the extent we consider it *unique*. In such a conception, then, the text is the memory, the representation, of nothing. It projects itself outside of time, beyond history, free of the mnemonic.[30]

Understanding the historical *situation* of such ideas of liberation will depend on a theory of time: time as the medium of change and transformation, as the mode in which everything is always already in the making, and still uninterruptedly being made anew. For crucially, theories of a sovereign, unique, and undeterminable text project an essential *timelessness*. Such paradigms are isomorphic with the model of linguistic communication—the free and effortless passage of signs in which meanings are exchanged but otherwise nothing changes—stigmatized by Bourdieu and Jean-Claude Passeron, among others. Models like these achieve their systematicity (as did Saussure's) at the price of bracketing temporality and, particularly, the phenomenon of entropy. They conceive time (in Viggo Brøndal's words) as "this great impediment to any rationality."[31] But the consequences of this exclusion of a constitutive register of the social are considerable.

Such a projection of timelessness is a privilege characteristic of dominant discourses in the period since the revolutions of the nineteenth century (see the introduction to my *Discourse/Counter-Discourse*). Under capitalism, as I argued in Chapter 1, the traces of history, of process, of *time*, disappear from the forms of bourgeois thought. The self-confident stability, the apparently untroubled absolutism of ideology in its modern guise, are the rhetorical reflexes of such abstractions. A would-be totalitarianism thus paradoxically becomes the covert model for avant-garde art writing and for all theories that hypostatize a sovereign and indeterminable text. To be sure, such aesthetic and theoretical paradigms conceive themselves

30. I will return to the problem of originality and its relation to the memory question in my discussion of Proust in Chapters 5 and 6.
31. See Pierre Bourdieu and Jean-Claude Passeron, *Reproduction in Education, Society and Culture*, especially 19–23. Brøndal is quoted in Sebastiano Timpanaro, *On Materialism*, 159.

as resolutely counterdiscursive. But despite such a self-conception, both discourses—the dominant (in its confident referential instrumentalism) and its counterdiscursive avant-garde or theoretical antagonist (for which such utilitarianism is the very sign of degradation)—want to conceive a world defined by the untroubled stability and effectiveness of language itself.

Yet if we accept such assumptions, either of unproblematical referentiality or of hermetic *self*-referentiality, it becomes hard to imagine language at all. As I put it elsewhere, "Why have language if there is . . . nothing *different* to say? Why say anything if the linguistic—and by implication the social—field is harmonized in some crystalline oneness? . . . *Language presupposes difference.* It exists only within a 'differential' world" (*Discourse/Counter-Discourse*, 15). But *time* is a fundamental mode of such difference, and time must be central to any representation model.

A succession of synchronies does not produce diachrony.[32] Any transformational account of human structures (and of history par excellence) must be able to conceptualize the *irreversibility* of transformations. Structuralism, Greimas frankly acknowledged, could not. This directionality of time we experience concretely. It appears as the stubborn materiality, the apparent sovereign independence, of the referent of any memory. Such resistance of the historical to the free manipulations of thought uncovers the intrinsic idealism of any logically or mathematically transformational account. For within such paradigms, as Greimas observes, why should the mutation "A → B" not spontaneously reverse itself and thereby *undo history*?

How can we understand the resistance of temporality to our playing it backwards? How can we figure the directionality of time, the fundamental asymmetry of past and future in the modification of systems? Understanding the mnemonic depends upon a model that inscribes the single-ended arrow of temporality. The key to such a model is a theory of *production* as the paradigm for all social transformation—and, as I will argue, for all representation. The outlines of such an account are present in a diverse tradition of theorization both within and outside Marxism, but they were first developed by Marx himself.

---

32. See Algirdas-Julien Greimas, "Structure at histoire."

For Marx the one notion essential to *any* social production—human labor—appears as the sole transhistorical condition of social life: "Labour, then, as the creator of use-values, as useful labour, is a condition of human existence which mediates the metabolism between man and nature, and therefore human life itself" (*Capital*, 1:133). Positing labor as an axiomatic absolute is strategic. It permits Marx to *found* the diachronic, the historical itself, and thereby to suggest a first level of solution to the problem of historical directionality. It is in connection with this discussion of the transhistoricity of labor that Marx gives his most general definition of the concept of production itself: "When man engages in production, he can only proceed as nature does herself, i.e. *he can only change the form of the materials*" (ibid.; emphasis mine). A passage from the *Grundrisse* then expands the discussion of production: "The transformation of the materials by living labour, by the realization of living labour in the material—a transformation which, *as purpose*, determines labour and is its purposeful activation . . .—thus preserves the material in a definite form, and subjugates the transformation of the material to the purpose of labour."[33]

Then, in a particularly evocative and important sentence, Marx draws the essential relation between these conceptions and the question of temporality that is my concern here: "Labour is the living, form-giving fire; *it is the transitoriness of things, their temporality, as their formation by living time*" (ibid.; emphasis mine).[34] Two notions are thus coordinately posited: (1) the determinant of temporal asymmetry, of the directionality and indeed of the concept of time itself, is human labor exercised in the material—the social—world, and (2) such directionality is inscribed and is socially experienced in the subjective purposiveness that animates all labor.

33. Karl Marx, *Grundrisse: Foundations of the Critique of Political Economy*, 360–61; emphasis mine.
34. On these questions, see Carol Gould, *Marx's Social Ontology: Individuality and Community in Marx's Theory of Social Reality*. I am indebted to her treatment. In his account of Marx's relation to scientific theory in the second half of the nineteenth century, Anson Rabinbach (following the work of Agnes Heller) suggests that Marx's early conception of labor as the quintessential human activity (for example in the *Economic and Philosophical Manuscripts*) was superseded in the late 1850s by a "mature" view of labor as a "burdensome necessity" (*The Human Motor: Energy, Fatigue, and the Origins of Modernity*, 72); however the passages from the *Grundrisse* and from *Capital* cited here makes it difficult to sustain this distinction cleanly.

Neither the results of such purposiveness in the social world nor the transformations it dictates can be reversed by some arithmetical change of sign. Because purposiveness is conditioned by perception of concrete conditions in relation to which it is deployed, because it is contingent on these conditions but is in no way rigidly or univocally "deducible from" them, it necessarily plays itself out in time and cannot be abstracted from temporality. No negation, no inversion could ever undo earlier transformations. The various factitious "Restorations" that history has produced stand as evidence of the emptiness of such a notion.[35]

Human choices and actions are never linked to their determinants or to their effects with the simplicity of deductive logic. This is what necessitates the inclusion of an asymmetrical time dimension in writing their history. In certain Idealist systems, reversibility might be conceivable (though not for Hegel, as his celebrated dictum about the Owl of Minerva demonstrates). But reversibility is excluded in Marx's system, in which terms are never synchronous, never in simple formal relationship with one another. This is why Marxian determination is always dialectical, never mechanical. The complex burden of the empirical and the conjunctural always intervenes to create and assure the "play" within the linkages of the system that is the locus for human freedom, the site for the purposeful production of history.

Recognizing the potentiality of this freedom conceives the determinants of temporality from the side of their production. But like Minerva's owl, memory and history see them from their other side. We will inevitably be disappointed if we attempt to ask historical questions about the future, or try to recollect what is to be,[36] for if we can understand social history, such understanding can be constructed only as an a posteriori, as a contingent series based upon what has already occurred. History depends upon the patterns of actualization of potentialities in prior moments of social reality, and of these potentialities we always find more than one. The existence of multiple, conflicting possibilities is given in the very notion of contradiction

35. For an empirical confirmation of this theoretical point, see Robert A. Kann, *The Problem of Restoration.*

36. This is so despite Lewis Namier's celebrated conundrum, that historians "imagine the past and remember the future." See Lowenthal, *The Past Is a Foreign Country,* 234.

requiring resolution by labor, and experienced as the dialectic between desire, work, and purposiveness and the elements in the social world that resist them.[37]

Because history is directional, certain operations of understanding are possible only retrospectively, toward the past: *in memory*. Just as we have no recollection of the future, the directional asymmetry of time is not subject to elision and cannot be overcome in thought. For in it lies the possibility of altering what lies *outside* thought, the materiality of social life. Whereas certain structuralist and poststructuralist models posit the multidirectional play of thought as a sort of mathematical projection of freedom, they lose thereby the possibility of figuring the conditions for purposive activity in the social world, for creating that which cannot be undone by a simple change of Mind.[38]

So for Marx, reality is segmented into past/present/future by human labor mediating human production. The source of the *difference* that produces the pastness of the past is the labor of material transformation itself. And this version of difference counterposes itself against any theoretical effort to erase the directionality of time—particularly structuralist systems more or less directly influenced by Saussure, in which abstract difference appears not as *contradictory* (in the sense of the dialectic) but as antinomic, synchronic, logical, and empty.

I will suggest shortly how this dialectical difference about "difference" can inform a theory of memory and of representation consistent with the Marxian dialectic itself. But (in what may seem an unanticipated convergence) let me first sketch how the foregoing argument opens a passage between the paradigms of Marx and Jacques Derrida. Both agree that the relation of logical identity ($A = A$) is without pertinence in the social world. There, in the irreducible dimension of time, nothing remains steady at all.[39] As the transhistorical essences and changeless qualities of predialectical metaphysics

37. Concerning these issues, see Ernesto Laclau and Chantal Mouffe, *Hegemony and Socialist Strategy: Towards a Radical Democratic Politics*. They would substitute the notion of "antagonism" for the Hegelian or Marxian "contradiction."

38. On this problem, see Richard Terdiman, "On the Dialectics of Postdialectical Thinking."

39. See Scott Meikle, "Dialectical Contradiction and Necessity," 9.

give way to the Hegelian, the Marxian, and eventually to the Derridean postulations of a human world of ceaseless change, the necessity of a new paradigm for understanding relations between the elements of this social world and the systems they comprise asserts itself more and more strongly. Indeed, the irrelevance of the laws of traditional logic to such systems (including cancellation of the law of difference, $A = not\ not\text{-}A$) may be one of the factors that give rise to the appearance within Derrideanism of a kind of ludic anarchy.

Derrida might respond that efforts to stem such disseminations, to freeze the play of *différance,* can be no more legitimate than the attempts by earlier, specifically anti-Marxist thinkers to stabilize the ceaseless movement of social contradiction in the name of some proper and decorous notion of Law and Order. The exercise of such authority always implies that somebody possesses a club—or at least the power to determine where the movement will *stop.*[40] But to return to the relation between dialectics and deconstruction, whatever their internal resistances to each other, the inscription within these otherwise disparate theoretical paradigms of time as uncontrollable agent of change, the consequent irreducible non-self-identity of nature and of language, constitute an inter-paradigmatic link that needs to be explored further.[41]

In the interim, I want to suggest that memory might productively be conceived in terms of the dialectical model relating time and transformation that emerges in Marx's theory of labor. For memory conceived as pure reproduction (as in the historically important notion of the *ars memoriae* of antiquity) engages us in an infinite regress. Classical mnemonists and rhetoricians sought identical reproduction of already constituted texts. What they memorized and performed were effectively lists, and what they sought was fidelity. Such practices project a world in which stasis is normalized, and in which change is noise, derogation, or a fault in transcription.[42]

40. This issue is central to my discussion of Freud's "mnemo-analytic" hermeneutics in Chapter 8.
41. Concerning non-self-identity, see Suzanne Gearhart, "Philosophy *Before* Literature: Deconstruction, Historicity, and the Work of Paul de Man," 78.
42. The ideal form of such memory reproduces predetermined contents in a predefined order. It seeks to sustain content against the universal tendency of remembered material to drift entropically. Such a model depends upon a mechanism of *registration.* It incorporates what Israel Rosenfield described as "a myth that has probably dominated thought

But the original *constitution* of such lists—or of any figuration of the world—is the real problem a theory of memory must elucidate. It cannot be enough to account for the retention of the old, or what in this book I am terming *reproduction*. Such retention tends toward defeat of the transformative effects of social time. The process of such reproduction is surely interesting, but it omits the moment at which—the more fundamental process by which—that which is to be conserved is itself given being: the moment of *representation* by which outward reality becomes figurable.

Because our reality exists only in the present, we are obliged to represent our experiences. The problem of natural recollection thus can hardly be exhausted by the theory of the *ars memoriae*. Frances Yates makes the point herself when, at the conclusion of her book, she traces the art of memory past the point at which the influence of the classical mnemonic systems waned. It turned, she said, "from a method of memorising the encyclopaedia of knowledge, of reflecting the world in memory, to an aid for investigating the encyclopaedia and the world *with the object of discovering new knowledge*" (368– 69; emphasis mine). In my terms here, memory passed beyond the reproduction model and frankly declared itself as *representation*.

In *The Domestication of the Savage Mind*, Jack Goody explored the prehistory of writing as a memory device. His investigation permits a way out of the regress of which I spoke. He makes the point that when you "write something down," you do not simply codify what is already there. Whatever the form of knowing that precedes its recording, the form produced in the text is inevitably new—the very image, etymologically speaking, of a "literary creation."[43] The representations of memory thus cannot be conceived (or depreciated)

---

ever since human beings began to write about themselves: namely, that we can accurately remember people, places, and things because images of them have been imprinted and permanently stored in our brains" (*The Invention of Memory: A New View of the Brain*, 3). The locus classicus of such mechanisms is Plato's projection of a wax block capable of recording impressions as if from a seal ring (*Thaeatetus*, 191). The connection of such a model with the classical "art of memory" is explicit in Cicero's *De Oratore* (see Yates, *Art of Memory*, 2). It is well known (in part through Derrida's discussion in "Freud and the Scene of Writing") that Freud contrived a revised version of the wax-tablet in one of his most highly developed memory models; see Sigmund Freud, "Note upon the 'Mystic Writing Pad'," *SE* 19:227–34.

43. Jack Goody, *The Domestication of the Savage Mind*, 116.

as the real in some derivative or residue form. *They are the form
that the real transformed by our work upon it takes in consciousness.*
The work of theory since the nineteenth century has been to comprehend this fundamental process by which reality is made knowable
for us.

The notion of memory as *representation*—with all the contingency
and uncertainty that the word implies—will be essential to the
analyses to follow. The essential element of memory is the unforesee-
able *productivity* of its representations. Thus the contrary of memory
as a theoretical system is the crystalline abstraction of logic. This is so
because, however much a logic may transform its material, in a deep
sense such a system can produce nothing *new*. Everything that can
be generated out of it, everything it implies, is already present. A
logic refers to nothing beyond itself and contains its world inside the
system it comprises. Such a logic thus slips back into self-identity,
into tautology. It cuts nowhere into the external world we can recall—which is the only one we can change. The certainty of the postulates of logic is paid for at the cost of their disconnection from the
mode in which our lives are lived. Its truths are unassailable precisely to the extent that nothing in the world has any grip on them.
They are true because they *represent* nothing.[44]

By refusing the determinations of the referential, such systems remind one of Nietzsche's antirepresentational aestheticism,[45] and of
the autonomous artistic texts whose privilege has been the preoccupation of certain thinkers since Mallarmé and the nineteenth-century avant-garde. In contrast to these paradigms, a historical, authentically productive dialectic seems a promising model of human
memory. The Hegelian version of such a structure already contained
major elements fundamental to representation of the past. In figuring

44. A remarkable passage cited by Yates from one of Descartes's early works reveals
how intense the opposition between logical-deductive and empirical-mnemonic systems
can become. Descartes projected a system in which memory would be entirely superseded
by reducing all knowledge to logical propositions. "Since all can be reduced to one it is
obviously not necessary to remember all the sciences. . . . This is the true art of memory"
(*Cogitationes privatae*, 1619–21; cited in *The Art of Memory*, 373–74). See also Le Goff,
Histoire et mémoire, 154, and Michel Beaujour, "*Memoria* à la Renaissance," 110.

45. See Allan Megill, *Prophets of Extremity: Nietzsche, Heidegger, Foucault, Derrida,*
194.

a reality outside itself, consciousness both posits and negates its referent. But unlike the final synthesis of Recollection that Hegel projects at the conclusion of the *Phenomenology*, this process can never be totalized. The purpose of conserving—of remembering—what is overcome in the process of the dialectic is to prevent *either* of its terms from being transformed into the *only* term. Any slippage into self-identity produces one of two polar hypostatizations: either of the *present*, of the "text" (in an abstracting and self-referential idealism), or of the *past*, of the "referent" (in a detached and inert materialism). Each of these reifications freezes the dialectical process. Sustaining the tension between the terms is crucial in order to inhibit cancellation of their contradictory energy; otherwise, the productivity of the system comes to an end, stopping time and purging memory of its representational capacity.

The Hegelian paradigm (thus rewritten) thereby permits the active relation of consciousness to material reality. But in the next movement of its own historical and conceptual development, Marx identifies the source of its fundamental dynamism: the transformative capacity of human labor. Then the last element of the system's idealism, of its formal self-reflexivity, is emptied out of the dialectic. Its referentiality, its opening to the social world, becomes comprehensible. In such a paradigm, nothing happens by itself; everything is made; and making is as endless as the flow of time itself. A model of memory adequate to the complications of modern social existence would need to integrate these same determinations.

Derrida's poststructuralist angle on the dialectic helps to foreground what is distinctive in this paradigm precisely because he seeks its critique from a standpoint outside it. In his reflection on the preface in his own preface to *Dissemination*, Derrida discusses the distinction between the pre-logical, historical character of a prefatory text such as the one with which Hegel opens the *Phenomenology*, and the "philosophical" (that is, trans- or metahistorical) intentionality of the *Phenomenology* itself. Because of its explicit consciousness of time, because of its overt inscription of *différance*, Derrida (against Hegel) would privilege the preface. And he recognizes the force of a parallel perception in Marx, expressed in the history of Marx's own text, in the history of his reading of Hegel and of his rereading of his own earlier production. For Derrida notes that it is precisely in the celebrated 1873 "Afterword" to the second edition of *Capital*—subsequent, in other words, to the text's initial appearance and to a short but decisive history of its misunderstanding by the critics whom Marx contests in his "Afterword"—that Marx made his most trenchant attempt to situate his own thought on the dialectic in relation to—and *after*—Hegel's. This textual sequence thereby produces (as a kind of metonymic exemplum) a local history, a *recollection*, of the development of the theory of history itself.

In the "Afterword" Marx deploys two figures by which his relation to Hegel might be represented: one *logical* (evoking movements of reversal or overturning), the other *historical* (evoking the temporal displacements of posteriority). The text, the "Afterword," thus seeks to do two things at once. First, it attempts to reverse certain misapprehensions (notably of a Marxian apriorism and idealism that had been mistakenly suggested by the deductive structure Marx had employed to present his thought in *Capital*). And second, it seeks to develop (in time and in conceptual penetration) the historical consequentiality of Marx's differences with Hegel. Derrida points to the fact that this series of textual displacements and differences around the concept of the dialectic is itself a historical enactment. For these texts are authentic material events, not just a series of philosophical positions staked out within the abstract field of possible speculative paradigms. This is why Derrida makes a point of limiting himself to what he calls "'textual' indications": "We have now arrived at the point where the relation between the 'text' . . . and the 'real' is being played out."[46] In this chain of textual and conceptual displacements, in its ambiguous *hors*-textual relation to the texts preceding it, the "Afterword" in *Capital* thus becomes a powerful figure for the irreducibly *historical* character of thought. Theme and form become asymptotic, for Marx's nominal subject here (his reconceptualization, his rewriting of the Hegelian dialectic) is figured in the very form of the text itself, which would be incomprehensible outside of its historically determined posterity to Hegel.

It would not seem to strain Derrida's reflection to argue that for him difference *is* history, figured (as Derrida himself writes it, commenting upon the "postscriptural" character of Marx's rewriting of

46. Jacques Derrida, *Dissemination*, 32–33.

Hegelian logic) as the "force of historical nonreturn resistant to any circular recomprehension within . . . the Logos" (*Dissemination*, 34–35; translation modified). In connection with this particularly dense Derridean phrase, we might recall Greimas's insight about the irreversibility of time and the necessity of modeling its constraint. In any case, what has intervened in the passage from text to text that Marx and Derrida both enact and reflect upon is not just abstract distinction, but a consequential and irreversible development, a *productivity*. This perception foregrounds the transformative character of social memory, which I argued was contingent upon such productive diachrony and is analogous with it. Furthermore, it entails the dialectic's inherent historical limitlessness.

Despite this, however, there is within Derrida an intense resistance to the notion of a dialectical history. Thus in *Dissemination*, in the preface particularly, Derrida seems to have taken great pains to distinguish the movement of his own thought—for example, the irrepressible displacements of dissemination itself—from what might have appeared analogous forms in Marx. The section of Derrida's preface that immediately precedes his discussion of Marx's rectification of Hegel emphasizes the necessity of supplementing the triad of what Derrida terms traditional "ontotheology" (25). One senses the dialectic's characteristic triad lurking behind this designation (see Megill, *Prophets of Extremity*, 272–74). This tetradic supplement to the dialectical triad would seem to function not so much to transcend or sublate it as purely and simply to explode it. By virtue of its very positioning in the text of his own preface, Derrida's disseminating supplement to Hegel cannot fail to frame—and could be taken as an effort to transcend—Marx's own conceptual "postscript" to Hegelianism, which Derrida goes on immediately in his own preface to discuss. So at the opening of *Dissemination* Derrida effectively puts himself in the paradoxical position of writing a preface to Marx. Though Derrida's preoccupation here would seem to be the textual character of history, or the historical character of texts, *this* textual order disrupts nominal temporality. Here Derrida precedes Marx.

Derrida's resistance to, or suspicion of, Marx is based on the grounds of a finalism within the dialectic. He construes such a teleology as a servitude that (like the weight of the past itself that Nietzsche stigmatized) might illegitimately constrain the play of signs and

concepts. Such a constraint would then force them into some sort
of derivative, ultimately deductive relation with the propositions to
which they are inevitably subsequent, and by which Derrida fears
they might turn out eventually to be bound (see Terdiman, "On the
Dialectics of Postdialectical Thinking"). Then human freedom would
turn out to be no more than an illusion, "history" no more than the
playing out of a predetermined script—a text already written. Futu-
rity would empty out, because (as in deductive logic) its content
would turn out to have been already fully present in the past. The
paradigm of *différance* would then collapse into an inert synchronism.

But however telling a critique this may be of the apriorism of
Hegel's thought in its fully developed "philosophical" phase, it seems
foreign to Marx. Derrida considers the point in "La Différance," in
the course of a discussion of Saussure's notion of the sign. He wants
to distinguish the tendency in Saussure toward a static, analytic tax-
onomizing of the system of *langue* from the real play of difference in
human language. He points out that the apparently "systemic" differences, which were the object of Saussure's theorizing, are social *effects* and cannot be adequately conceived in the absence of a notion
of their inevitably social *production*. To this point, Derrida would
seem to be arguing for the rehabilitation of diachronicity in the face
of Saussure's temptations toward synchronism. The movement of this
implied critique would thus precisely parallel Marx's effort in the
"Afterword" to *Capital* to elucidate his own difference from Hegelian
idealism and apriorism (*Capital*, 1:100–102). For both Marx and
Derrida, it would seem that the fundamental alternative to the ideal-
izing abstraction of the paradigms against which they counterpose
their own must be conceived along the lines of a model both *materialist* (because it depends on the concrete elements that occupy the
field of their theories' concerns, but at the same time are relatively
independent of its control) and *historical* (because these elements
preexist the operation of the theory, and become the indispensable
preconditions for any transformations it describes). But Derrida's
treatment of this reintroduction of the social dimension of time, of
the liberating power of human process, is curiously grudging and
ambiguous: "If the word 'history' did not entail in itself the motif of a
final repression of difference, one could say that only differences can

be from the outset and thoroughly 'historical.'"[47] Here, as in the preface to *Dissemination*, Derrida is implicitly seeking to differentiate his own thinking from that of Marx.

But if the Marxian dialectical process is limitless, then any ultimate repression of difference such as Derrida attributes to its supposed finalism would amount to a reification, that is, to a violation of its fundamental dynamic. Let us not forget Adorno's insight concerning reification's link to the memory problem: "All reification is a forgetting."[48] In such a forgetting, the crucial tension between the dialectic's paired dynamics of conservation and overcoming is unstrung by an unbalancing of the terms, and with it the dynamism of time that drives the process of history itself.

The dialectic must always both remember (conserve) and overcome (transform) its referent. Along the lines of the memory model I sketched earlier, this is the process of representation itself, engaged in a fundamental historical dimension. Such a process bears within it the potential for unconstrainable production of the new, which suggestively resembles Derridean *différance* and dissemination. Conversely, any failure of the tension between the two dynamics of the dialectic leads to one or another of the contrary situations I outlined. One hypostatizes an independent *consciousness* (an amnesic idealism of the text and its free play, which—in Adorno's terms—willfully and reductively "forgets" its contingency). The other projects a sovereign *referent* (a reifying, inert materialism whose effect is to deny freedom, initiative, or creativity to human activity). It would appear that Derrida attributes the latter distortion to Marx, but intermittently demonstrates the temptation to commit the former one himself.

Derrida's suspicion of a rigidifying finalism inherent in the dialectic has analogues in assaults on it by other theorists, including certain celebrated ones. Inevitably, these attacks on history are based on forgetting or distorting the memory function. Thus in his polemic with Jean-Paul Sartre, Claude Lévi-Strauss stigmatized what he considered a simplistic evolutionism inherent in dialectical reason, guilty of conceiving culture as a single line of development. But as Sebastiano Timpanaro observed, such an argument is designed to oppose

47. Jacques Derrida, "La Différance," 12.
48. Max Horkheimer and Theodor W. Adorno, *Dialectic of Enlightenment*, 230.

all historical development not reducible to "physical procreation":
"Since the *Signorie* were not sexually engendered by the *Comuni*,
nor bourgeois society by feudal society, nor was Lenin the son of
Marx or Engels in the material sense, one would have to conclude
that there is no derivational relationship between the one and the
other" (*On Materialism*, 180).

It would be an extraordinary logic, indeed, that could see only
biology as instituting relation. The determinations exercised by the
past on the present are, on the contrary, extraordinarily diverse.
They take the form of a generalized dialogism linking any present
and its past, a relation constituted by the "invented traditions," the
ideological weights, the semiotic resistances, the neurotic replica-
tions—all the various components of what I termed the "materials
memory" functioning in any period. The cultural accumulation of
these recollections by which the past invests the present are the preconditions and the elements for any social life; the principal among
them preoccupy the conceptual models that the remainder of this
book will seek to examine.

But Lévi-Strauss's biological *reductio* has had offspring of its own,
which still object to the implicit totalitarianism of *any* unified line of
development, whether historical or genealogical. To avoid such constraint, they are driven to seek theoretical grounds for evading *any*
determination at all. By rejecting the totalizing control of any dominant language or meaning system, they insist upon a liberatory space
for difference within the social or textual whole. We can observe this
argument variously in Foucault, in Jean-François Lyotard, in Derrida, as earlier it was central to Nietzsche, to Flaubert, or to Mallarmé. It opens the world of language and the social to disseminated
and incessant subversion. But the temptations of the stochastic, of a
theoretical anarchy, are clear in such conceptions. In their stress
upon the limitless and liberatory play of chance, they overreact against
determination altogether and land in a theoretically unmanageable
indeterminacy that sets all understanding of social existence adrift.

Thus in *The Postmodern Condition* Lyotard speaks of his "incredulity concerning metanarratives."[49] He conceives metanarrative as a

---

49. Jean-François Lyotard, *The Postmodern Condition: A Report on Knowledge*, xxiv;
translation modified.

preexisting text that determines the texts it regulates. Lyotard means to undermine sovereign representations, preestablished, universal laws for resolving difference. He wants to preserve the space of alterity; indeed, this is what *The Differend* is all about. But we need to recall that the production and reproduction of such alterity is the most characteristic and continuous product of the dialectical process itself. In time, alterity means *change*, and that is what the dialectic *does*. Lyotard's insistence on difference recalls the multiform, incessant, and brilliantly inventive subversion by nineteenth-century counterdiscourses of the dominant discourses of that period. The poststructuralist suspicion of hegemonizing totalities thus has prestigious genealogical and ideological roots, but there is an important distinction between projections of salutary conflict over meaning and the celebration of no determinable meaning at all. One might usefully conceive the poststructuralist aporia as a place not just of undecidability, but, in a very Bakhtinian spirit, as a place of *struggle*.

✿☙❧

> Our entire contemporary social system has little by little begun to lose its capacity to retain its own past.
> —Fredric Jameson, "Postmodernism and Consumer Society," 125

> The new arose out of the old to a greater extent than has generally been appreciated.
> —Albert O. Hirschman, *The Passions and the Interests*, 4

Since the revolutions of the nineteenth century the referent of discourse has increasingly been produced as "strange" within the atmosphere of generalized befuddlement about the previously naturalized functions of our social life. Such a sense of confusion is one reflex of what I have been calling the memory crisis. As a result of these disorienting developments, the referent has come to *stand out*: what used to seem a *thing* reveals itself to be a *reification* whose mystifying solidity once it is plumbed and probed turns up porous and destabilized. It is consequently no wonder that when certain strains of contemporary theory contemplate the *how* of meaning, they collapse into its contrary, a fundamental suspicion concerning signification itself.

Such suspicion cannot be divorced from the crisis of memory. As the Faulkner epigraph to this chapter suggests, the problem of cognition is no problem at all—as long as organic and naturalized belief in inherited meanings remains secure. But when, in the complex of developments that make up the memory crisis, such belief falters, then signification turns labyrinthine and refractory. That is when theory begins appealing to the paradoxical stability of what I might term "representational nihilism," to the notion that our meanings are constructed freely and cannot be referentially constrained. Yet the cost of resisting closure through simply setting meaning adrift is considerable. Signification itself diffuses and is in danger of disappearing. In this perspective our contemporary suspicion about meaning, the familiar crisis of representation, appears as theoretical reflexes of the same changes in the patterns of production and transmission of socially agreed sense that determined the memory crisis. It might seem surprising that a crisis already a hundred and fifty years in the bottle has not yet been resolved. It has not, but it has shifted.

Today the meaning-crisis no longer (as in the past century) reflects an uncertainty about how social values and significations can be transmitted in a world turned topsy-turvy by revolutionary change. Rather, contemporary suspicion concerning meaning might be seen as translating a resistance to envelopment in the meanings that under an increasingly hegemonic contemporary capitalism are all too densely and all too successfully programmed and reproduced for all of us. It is not only Europe that is contemplating the institution of a single market. Our own flirtation with a "New World Order" threatens to place us all in the same economic—and discursive—space. Since the nineteenth century, alienation from the agencies that administer such production and reproduction has been the most notorious fact about the social fraction we term the intelligentsia. In the face of the meaning-crisis that preoccupies us today, Flaubert's withering scorn for the bourgeoisie, his proto-deconstruction of *their* meanings in his *Dictionary of Received Ideas* and throughout his work, take on the character of a premonition. We can read his concerted heterodoxy as an early form of the effort to evade domination by the institutional mechanisms producing signification—to avoid becoming part of *their* memory. More recently, the prolongation of this effort has seemed to require a virtual dissolution of the concept of meaning itself, as the meanings propagated within our society penetrate its cultural infrastructure and increasingly defy evasion.

Deconstruction of these mechanisms remains the primary critical task. It seems clear that among their diverse resources, strains of poststructuralism make themselves available for pursuing the work of ideological critique that began in the nineteenth-century realization that *nothing* in social life is self-evident, that everything is artifice. Michael Ryan puts this helpfully:

> Political criticism is a necessary consequence of the interaction of deconstructive philosophy and Marxist literary theory, for what that interaction shows is that discursive operations in texts cannot be declared an other to a real presence of substance in society; social life is itself constituted as a network of representations, relations and discursive practices. . . . In addition, social structure and activity is an agonistic texture of relations, not, as conservatives claim, an organic or natural process, nor, as liberals claim, a happy multiplicity that somehow attains unity. There is no unity or natural meaning or truth to those conflicted social relations; they consist of scissions without closure or determinacy, an unstable relation of force between contending parties.[50]

The analytical strain in middle-class thought to which I have referred, and which has enabled bourgeois production from its first triumphant phase, can operate in *this* factory too. From Marx and Flaubert to Foucault and Derrida, the culpable contingency, the insidious usurpations of dominant and would-be dominant social discourses have thus been exposed to a powerful critique.

Such demystification is fundamentally a task of *remembering*. It is not surprising that, in its vocation for ideological critique, deconstruction has its own reading of what I have termed the "materials memory" of the word. Deconstruction argues for a *radical* contextualization of language use: this in one sense is what the dissemina-

---

50. Michael Ryan, "The Marxism-Deconstruction Debate in Literary Theory," 32.

tion of meaning means. For deconstruction, as for all paradigms that theorize the internal relationality of language systems and of their social functioning, no utterance is unambiguously positive; every speech act contains a negative moment that is the deconstructive accompaniment of its positive assertions. As what Barbara Johnson described as a "teasing out of the warring forces of signification,"[51] deconstruction aims to detect the unspoken multivocality of any word and thereby to *reactivate the memory* of its place in a network not just linguistic but, much more radically, socialized and historicized. In the word, the traces it carries forward with it reach back like a recollection of all the labor that has produced and sustained its difference, of all the struggles that have necessitated and engendered speech acts to begin with. Deconstruction constructs the memory whose potentiality is the silent obverse of every act of language, and thus of every social act. And in doing so it remembers and re-presents a century and a half of efforts to forestall the fundamental deculturation of memory itself.

Such memory must be the fundamental form of demystification. For the everyday experience of memory—simultaneously distancing its referent and calling back to mind that which is not present— enacts a displacement that brings the entire problem of representation into focus. Representation as rememoration foregrounds the fact that experience *is* always *other* than it *was*: inevitably and constitutively *historical*. Such a construction situates memory as the most consistent agent of the transformations by which the referential world is made into a universe of signs.

Since the memory crisis of the nineteenth century, cultural objects have carried the enigma of the past and of its determinations as a particularly stressful and mystified content. They bear these problematic meanings in the form of time become palpable, of the labor that determines it become material: as representations of the movement that, in separating the present from the past, produces the present as the past's representation. Discourses of domination, in their effort to stabilize the flux of social life and veil the violence by which such order is established, ceaselessly attempt to erase the *dif-*

51. Barbara Johnson, *The Critical Difference: Essays in the Contemporary Rhetoric of Reading*, 5.

ference that marks this flow of time, but memory—of events, of institutions, of language itself—preserves such difference. Our theory must strive to recollect this intimate and elemental form of our history, for it is from such differences that our world is ceaselessly being constructed, and their recovery provides the basis on which it can be understood.

Part Two

THE AMBIGUITIES
OF REMINISCENCE:
TWO NINETEENTH-CENTURY
REPRESENTATIONS

3

The Mnemonics of
Musset's *Confession*

Let's not talk about the past.
——Alfred de Musset, *Confession d'un enfant du
siècle*, 313

Self-understanding . . . of our epoch's struggles and desires . . . is a *confession*, and nothing else. To have its sins
forgiven, mankind only needs to declare them for what
they are.
——Karl Marx, letter to Arnold Ruge, September 1843,
The Letters of Karl Marx, 32

In confession the sinner tells what he knows; in analysis
the neurotic has to tell more.
——Sigmund Freud, "The Question of Lay Analysis,"
(1926), *SE*, 20:189

In Musset's *Confession d'un enfant du siècle*, memory is more than
a medium. It is the source of the most intense dissonance within
the text, the site of an archetypal catastrophe. Memory organizes the
Confession on every level. But having constructed the novel, memory undoes it from top to bottom.[1]

---

1. Alfred de Musset (1810–57) published the *Confession d'un enfant du siècle* in 1836.
He was already known as the author of *Un spectacle dans un fauteuil* (written in 1832), *Les
Caprices de Marianne, Fantasio*, and *Lorenzaccio* (1833), *On ne badine pas avec l'amour*
(1834), and a number of important poems. The *Confession* is manifestly a recollection and
representation by Musset of his liaison with George Sand. They met in 1833, and their
love affair ended disastrously in 1835. Musset's use of their correspondence from the period of the love affair (he asked George to lend him his letters while he was composing the

Confession is a quintessential form of mnemonic performance, but its functioning cannot be dissociated from some deep paradoxes.[2] What is its significance in the age of Europe's de-theologization? By troping the traditional rite, Musset drew attention to transformations in the relationship between the present and the past which preoccupied the protomodernity of the early nineteenth century. This transformation is readable in what we might conceive as a displacement of the ethical. Confession has always been a conduct of ethics; yet a reading of Musset's *Confession* in search of its moral meaning might very well come up empty—unless we admit that the transcendental function of traditional confession is replaced in the novel by something combining avowal and *prise de conscience*, the transformative coming-to-consciousness that functions like an internally generated epiphany. I suggest that the theater of confession on whose stage Musset's protagonist performs is a kind of chamber theater, a kind of minimalist psychodrama set over against the cosmogony of a waning Catholicism.

We might conceive confession as a subset of autobiography—but particularly the autobiography of sin, of error, of transgression. Its practices of avowal are governed by liturgical, juridical, and—in the modern period—psychological or psychoanalytic rituals that despite their evident diversity have as their common purpose some form of individual or social purification (see Hahn, "Contribution à la sociologie de la confession," 54). In essence they are designed to free the

_____

novel) is well known. See Claude Duchet's preface to Maurice Allem's edition of Musset's *Confession d'un enfant du siècle*, ii. One could make the case that the Musset-Sand liaison was the most "written" love affair of the nineteenth century. In addition to the *Confession* in which Musset memorialized it, three other novels took it as their subject: George Sand's *Elle et lui*, Paul de Musset's *Lui et elle*, and Louise Colet's *Lui*. (Colet became Musset's mistress in 1852. Her text, which also fictionalized her relationship with Flaubert, has recently appeared in English: *Lui, A View of Him*.) On the tetralogy commemorating the Sand-Musset liaison, see Duchet, "Preface," i n. 1.

   2. On the general phenomenon of confession, see Aloïs Hahn, "Contribution à la sociologie de la confession et autres formes institutionalisées d'aveu: Autothématisation et processus de civilisation." So intimate is the relation between the ritual of confession and the faculty of memory that, in a curious philological confirmation, we find it inscribed in a nearly forgotten usage in Catholicism. The Church traditionally called the site of a martyr's remains a "confession." This word was taken as the equivalent of the Latin term for such a monument: a *memoria*. See Charles G. Herbermann et al., *The Catholic Encyclopedia*, 4:214, s.v. "confession," and Jacques Le Goff, *Histoire et mémoire*, 135. The resonances of these two familiar terms intertwine in this antique mnemonic observance.

future from the past. Thus, as in the performance of the Mass itself, absolution *takes away* sin, and thereby rewrites the penitent's history. Consequently, the past that is the referent of confession is always an "inauthentic" one—or is made to become so. It is narrated not in the service of memorialization, but of erasure. Thus if confession is a species of autobiography, it is one that significantly subverts its genus.[3]

Moreover, confession is a performative, intensely instrumental text, unlike the autobiographical discourse of which at first glance it appears as only a subsidiary type. As performed in confession, the act of memory is stressed by an emotional tension that does not necessarily accompany ordinary autobiography—namely, the therapeutic anxiety that underlies the desire for shriving to begin with. This tension is a precondition of the confessional act, for confession exists to achieve the result—absolution—that will obliterate it and disable the maleficence of the past. Or to put it differently, confession is an act of memory that seeks to neutralize memory: in confession one remembers *in order to forget*. Since this peculiar form of autobiography depends upon annulling the past—the life it recounts—the condition of confession's existence is that the object of its narration cease to exist. Confession undoes the subjectivity that is both the source and the referent of its own articulation. In that sense the confessional artifact consumes not only itself but its maker.

Yet when a confession takes the form of a consciously literary text, written for publication and willed into circulation by its author, its impermanence is transformed, indeed overturned. Inevitably, the sacramental model undergoes some form of tropological displace-

3. The role of the Christian confessional text as a model for modern autobiographical discourse has long been speculated upon. See Jacques Voisine's introduction to his edition of Jean-Jacques Rousseau's *Confessions*, v–ix; Hahn, "Contribution à la sociologie de la confession," 54 n. 2; and Daniel J. Selden, "'Dark Similitudes': Saint Augustine and *The Confessions of J. J. Rousseau*." In Michelle Perrot, ed., *From the Fires of Revolution to the Great War*, vol. 4 of *A History of Private Life*, Alain Corbin clarifies the alterations in nineteenth-century confessional practice—contingent in part upon the long process of rigidification in Church attitudes that began with the Council of Trent, in part upon an increasing secular attention to introspection and self-analysis throughout French society (see 497–98). The result, as Corbin writes, was that "the nineteenth century is regarded as the golden age of the confessional" (549). However diffusely, such developments bear upon Musset's text.

ment in the self-conscious literary "confession."[4] As a result, the confessional text ironizes the genre that forms its intertextual referent.
By virtue of such symbolic labor, *form* becomes one of its intense
preoccupations. The tension between the ritual of liturgical confession and the symbolic activity of literary confession thus complicates
the apparently simple process of remembrance that defines confession to begin with. Musset's novel subverts representations of such
mnemonic simplicity in a radical way. The practice of confession refracted through its literary cognate begins to take on an uncanny
complexity. By the end of his novel, Musset has reconceived the
mnemonics of confession as a catastrophe. His novel becomes a key
text in the registration and representation of the memory crisis.

Such an outcome might seem unexpected. As I have suggested, in
principle confession is highly ritualized and intensely instrumental.
Its complexities might at first appear contained by such ritualization.
Furthermore, confessions represent themselves as a means toward
a predetermined result, the conquest of a dialectic of *time*. They
narrate the process by which a defective past is transformed into an
integral present. But even as this dialectic defines their form and
mediates their thematic organization, it also adds another complication, another dialogic overlay, which in their process of remembrance
and of narrativization literary confessions can never entirely forget.
Inevitably, they are preoccupied by their performative efficacy, and
this preoccupation rivets attention upon the relation between past
and present. Confession, we might say, is the most intensely self-
reflexive of all the arts of memory.

Literary confession, then, tropes its sacramental intertext. Yet to understand the effect such tropology or displacement produces, we
need to consider *La Confession d'un enfant du siècle* first of all in the
image of a traditional sacramental confession. One point is striking at
the outset. As he sets out to acknowledge his sins, the penitent who
confronts us in Musset's novel appears distinctly paralyzed. Personal
stock-taking—what the Church terms internal avowal ("aveu inté-
rieur")—traditionally preceded and facilitated the act of liturgical

---

4. Selden provides a helpful discussion of literary confession in Musset's most promi-
nent predecessors in the genre, Augustine and Rousseau. See "'Dark Similitudes.'"

confession itself (see Hahn, "Contribution à la sociologie de la confession," 54). Such an individual practice implied that once in the confessional the penitent's narrative, in effect already having been rehearsed, would flow freely. But in confronting his transgressions Musset's protagonist seems unable to begin the narrative process that ought to mediate their erasure. He delays this process by a pair of false starts that comprise the text's first two chapters. It is striking that *La Confession d'un enfant du siècle* is celebrated as much for these nominally liminal texts as for the more properly penitential narrative they precede and defer.

Each of these unexpected exordia displaces and upsets the relation between the first-person speaker in the text and the personal responsibility for his own memory and his own past which the ritual of confession presupposes. This traditional assumption of responsibility—both sacramental and analytical—by the penitent is crucial to understanding the complex relation between Musset's text and its generic and theological relatives. The Augustinian confession, for example, is rooted in the Johannine doctrine of the Logos, according to which signs point unerringly to their (ultimately theological) referents. Such a metaphysics guarantees both the adequacy of language to its representational task and the accountability of the subject producing such representation.[5]

But from the beginning, Musset's *Confession* unstrings the sacramental ritual upon which it draws. It purports to lay out the basis for the text's existence and its bearing. But in its initial sentence the novel decisively desubjectifies its own first-person narrator and distances him from the material of his own text: "To write the story [*histoire*] of one's life, one must first have lived; therefore it is not mine which I write."[6] Several issues circulate in this sentence, which, in its repetition and its chiasmic crossing of terms, seems

---

5. On Augustine and traditional Catholic doctrine of representation, see John Freccero, "The Fig Tree and the Laurel: Petrarch's Poetics," 35–37, and Selden, "'Dark Similitudes.'" On the necessity of responsible admission of transgression ("aveu"), see Michel Foucault, *Histoire de la sexualité, I: La volonté de savoir*, 71–98, and Martine Reid, "La Confession selon Musset."

6. I am quoting Gérard Barrier's edition of Musset, *La Confession d'un enfant du siècle* here and henceforth in the body of my text. Barrier's edition reproduces the text of the original 1836 edition, which is more complete than the 1840 re-publication. Translations are my own.

determined to undermine its articulation and its articulator simultaneously. The conceit in the sentence is fundamentally ambiguous.
The narrator who denies having lived might be stigmatizing some as-
yet-unknown force that has prevented him from authentic participation in his own existence. Or he might be making the quite different
point that a history ("l'histoire de sa vie") can only be written when it
is over. The former meaning without doubt refers to a preoccupation
insistently thematized in the text, a certain paralyzing dispossession
of the self, what Pierre Barbéris has termed "absence à soi-même."[7]
This is surely the primary signification here, but the alternative
meaning, playing on the polysemy of "histoire," functions effectively
as well, for it implies what I want to claim will be a crucial distinction
between two kinds of retrospective narration: "history," which lays
an implicit claim to objectivity, authority, dispassion, and to the consequent possibility of totalization, and a more subjective and *im*-per-
fect or untotalizable form of personal memory, of which the *Confession* itself, along with many other identifiably "romantic" texts,
stands as exemplification.[8] This distinction between objectifiable *history* and subjective *reminiscence* (a distinction mirrored in the increasing disciplinary segregation essential to the professionalization
of "history" in the early nineteenth century) in turn suggests a symbolic complex within which the memory function, already evoked by
the confessional form, is further problematized.

A second ambiguity within the opening chapter concerns the instrumental quality that the text claims for itself. This claim evokes

7. Pierre Barbéris, *Balzac et le mal du siècle*, 1:806.
8. There is thus a striking difference of vision between the "unfinished" character of
Octave's story in the *Confession*, about which no explicit "lessons" are or can ever finally
be drawn, and the seemingly parallel experience of Frédéric Moreau in Gustave Flaubert's
Éducation sentimentale. The celebrated concluding chapter of *L'Éducation* (to use Flaubert's own term) "resumes" and closes the life of Frédéric and his generation in a way that
would be impossible in Musset's textual system. (This difference is coherent with and takes
root in the characteristic choice of first-person narration by Musset, and third-person by
Flaubert.) In Frédéric's concluding evocation of "the best time we ever had," something
like an acceptance of the past, through its (however ironic) summary and totalization,
occurs in a way which Musset seems specifically to refuse. Barbéris makes a parallel point;
see *Balzac et le mal du siècle*, 1:111 n. 1. Martine Reid argues for more closure to Musset's
text than I see. She emphasizes the return to third-person narration in the epilogue (part
5, chap. 7), and examines the suggestion that the conclusion thematizes Octave's passage
into a decisively new phase of his life; see Reid, "La Confession selon Musset," 55, 70.
This reading is more optimistic than seems justified to me.

the pragmatic or performative character essential to confession. Immediately following the opening sentence, which I have already quoted, Musset's narrator likens himself to a wounded person with a gangrenous limb, and his narrative to the surgery that will remove it. Through the graphic image of the amputation, the *Confession*'s purpose is figured as therapeutic. We might understand the image in the following way: despite the pain such dismemberment must inevitably cause, the process of confession will expel and distance it from the self that is its subject and its source. The narrative is thus imagined to function curatively, like the surgeon's saw and scalpel, to heal the patient by eliminating the disease that, having been produced in and by the body, now threatens to annihilate it.

But if we follow the logic of the figure, we will want to ask an obvious question. Who is the patient? The text wavers on this critical point. Musset begins by stating categorically, "If I was the only sufferer, I would say nothing; but since there are many others who suffer from the same illness, I write for them" (19). The *Confession* thus seems to take a collective, almost an epidemiological point of view toward the disease that preoccupies it—a point of view implied from the very outset by its title. For the phrase *"enfant du siècle"* refers us to the realm of a generalized sociology, a kind of cultural critique that subverts the notion of a confession as a quintessentially *personal* and subjective text.[9]

But having insisted upon the socially diagnostic and collectively therapeutic purpose of the narrative, Musset's narrator then abruptly revises his perspective: "But even if no one else pays any attention, I will still have drawn benefit from my words and better cured myself." This deeply ambiguous position, wavering between individual and collective, between personal and social, proves crucial throughout the *Confession* by virtue of its very lack of resolution. By foregrounding an unsettled relation similar to that between the emerging discourses of psychology and of sociology, this ambiguity becomes the central problem the text seeks to solve.

The second element of the strange double exordium of the *Confession*, Musset's extraordinary second chapter, is much the more cele-

9. Concerning the origin and range of meaning of the phrase "enfant du siècle" and of the associated "mal du siècle," see Barbéris, *Balzac et le mal du siècle*, 1:31 n. 1, and Duchet's introduction to *La Confession*, ix–xvii.

brated.[10] I want to reconsider it now in light of the thematic and conceptual complexes to which I have already referred. In chapter 2, the tension between the personal and the social is *explicitly* the issue. The remainder of the *Confession* might be read as a quintessential example of romantic personal lyricism, of the performance of a stagy, self-dramatizing ego, but the second chapter diverges sharply in tone and bearing. It generalizes the familiar melodramatic subjectivism of romanticism and projects it upon an epochal historical conjuncture. I suggested that in its opening sentence chapter 1 called into question the relation of the confessional narrative in the text to "history," but here, in the first words of chapter 2, we are instantly and unexpectedly propelled into history itself: "During the Revolutionary wars . . ." (20). The second chapter then goes on to root in the historical crisis of the preceding generation—that is, in the French Revolution—the personal crisis of Musset's own demographic cohort, the "pale, ardent, and nervous generation" (20) who were the offspring of Napoleon's soldiers. As I suggested in my opening chapter, this younger generation experienced its relation to the Revolution as a profound crisis of memory, a crisis that took the form of an excruciating disjunction from their own past. For Musset's contemporaries, the present appeared as an incomprehensible aporia—as "an unidentifiable vague and floating something [*je ne sais quoi*] separating past and future while being neither one," or as a historical moment "neither night nor day; half mummy and half fetus" (25).

But the present is always the locus of memory. For memory, whatever its retrospective referent, is inevitably performed *now*. Musset's conception of an empty present thus upsets the economy of human time. The evacuation of contemporaneity simultaneously unhinges the past and confounds recollection, hence the "somber epic of misremembering" of the *Confession*'s second chapter and the global sense of mourning (28) and of loss (37) that Musset claimed characterized the mood of his own period.

In terms of the polarity posited in the novel's first chapter—on one side a subjective, personal vision, and on the other a collective,

10. Musset published the second chapter of the *Confession* ("Fragment d'un livre à publier") separately in September 1835, four months before the book appeared in its entirety.

social perspective—the second chapter is the site of a discursive crisis. In the conflict of this self-divided text a question arises—what I term the problematic of *the past's representation in the present*. The formula is deliberately ambiguous, turning on multiple meanings of "representation." I mean to interrogate on the one hand the mechanisms by which the present "represents"—that is to say, depicts or interprets—the past and, on the other, the mechanisms by which the past is "represented in"—that is, occupies or invests—the present.

The former of these dynamics is the basis for Musset's nominal project of confessional autobiography, the means by which recollection of the past might heal and absolve the present. Like sacramental confession, this project presupposes control of the processes by which the past is represented. But the latter dynamic decisively subverts such mastery. It refers to a daunting reversal of discursive control, and tends toward the pole of "dispossession" of the present by the past that Musset evokes in the mnemonic dystopia of his second chapter.

Alfred de Musset has a peculiar position in the canon. He is named in the pantheon of nineteenth-century writers. Yet with the exception of a few anthology poems and one or two plays, he is hardly read at all. In particular, though *La Confession d'un enfant du siècle* gave the history of criticism a name for subjectivity's disquiet in the early post-Revolutionary period, the novel itself has mostly been ignored because of the overpowering predominance of the great realist fictions of Musset's period—the novels of Stendhal and Balzac in particular. That they have put in Musset in shadow is somewhat paradoxical. The realists built their fictions upon accounts of the connections, the mediations, between self and society, between inner and outer reality, between subjective and objective understandings of the world in the formative period of post-Revolutionary modernity. But Musset's novel uncovers how deeply *uncertain* these connections were. If Balzac and Stendhal's great achievement was to have asserted the intensity of relation between history and individual consciousness, Musset's was to have foregrounded—in the very hesitations of his account of the power of such a connection—its extraordinary intricacy and difficulty.

In this sense realism is a simpler paradigm—more decided, less ambiguous and groping. Musset never demonstrates the clarity of assertion that makes Balzac and Stendhal, however diverse they may be, such extraordinarily good reads. With them we always feel we are in the hands of an intelligence that knows how the world works and how to describe it. And the scale of their achievement in having done so in a world so unprecedented surely justifies the admiration in which they have been held.

But Musset is interesting because, though the paradigms of early realism were available to him, he shows nothing like the same assurance that the real can be possessed in language. He is passionately on the side of subjectivity, an attitude in which he conforms to the romantic identity through which he is regularly characterized. In Musset, the realist balance and equilibrium that both satisfy and fascinate us in Stendhal and Balzac is destabilized. And to that extent its problem is deepened.

What was at issue in the period—both in the realists and in Musset—is the problem of determinations. What accounts for behavior? what sense can be made of experience? Oversimplifying considerably, we might hazard the following distinction. In the realists, determinations emerge principally in the realm of the social, but in Musset it is in *time* that we must seek the explanation of what happens in the world. More specifically, Musset's *Confession* asks which moment in the temporal flux of experience—*past* or *present*—controls representation. The answer to this question—whether the present or the past—determines which among the narrative systems Musset's text proffers at its opening will control the material of the narrative to follow. Personal subjectivity, the individual perspective controlling depiction, obviously must dominate the representation of the past *by* the present. This mode expresses itself in the familiar romantic strains of mnemonic absorption in the seductive labyrinths of remembrance. But in the contrary representation of the past *in* the present, history menacingly usurps contemporaneity. This is the disease of *too much memory* that I described in Chapter 1. Under such conditions, individual subjectivity is overwhelmed by the persistence of the past and comes to seem dominated, indeed possessed by it. Consequently, in this mode, expression turns distant and analytical, even (as in Musset's second chapter) powerfully ironic.

This point might be put in terms of the discourses of familiar disciplines. On the one hand, in cases that foreground subjective and contemporary narrative control, the discourse of *individual psychology* appears as the model for textualization. This is the mode of "reminiscence." On the other hand, the contrasting paradigm, in which the determination of the past predominates, produces an early version of the discourse of *history*, of the determination of social existence by the dynamic force of what has been—a structure powerfully suggested by Musset in the *Confession*'s second chapter. In Musset's text these two modes of discourse coexist awkwardly—so ungracefully (as in the formal division between the first two chapters and the remainder of the novel) that the text appears to need to segregate them absolutely. Yet beneath such appearances the problematic subtending this apparent antagonism is fundamentally and productively dialectical, evoking a flow of determinations both temporally and conceptually bidirectional. Beyond the opposition symbolized by the ungainly divided structure of the *Confession*, a project of discursive synthesis is slowly beginning to be thought through and worked out.

The sequential structure of Musset's text and the apparent disjunctive ordering of chapters 1 and 2 in relation to the remainder of the *Confession* might then be taken as the early stage of an epochal project—the development of a fully historicized and socialized account of personality and behavior. To be sure, within the *Confession* such an account figures as not more than a potentiality. The unresolved impulses in Musset's text toward an explanatory discourse that might synthesize the paradigms of "psychology" and "history"—the personal and the collective, subjectivity and objectivity—fundamentally threaten its coherence. For the text can certainly not reconcile them within itself. In response to the threat of its dispersion, therefore, the *Confession* seems to separate out its unreconciled tensions in a primitive segregation. The tale thus proceeds by a narrative parataxis that juxtaposes—without the slightest comment or explanation—the two divergent and even antagonistic paradigms it has marshaled to make sense of its material.

This unarticulated confrontation—of the material of chapter 2 on the one hand, and Octave's confession on the other—challenges us to make sense of its border. What does it mean for these two unreconciled discourses to butt against each other in the *Confession*? The text's two strains of retrospection seem to call for resolution in some synthesis that they project over their own horizon. Such a synthesis would pass beyond parataxis into something resembling the hypotaxis of explanation. Such a synthesis is finally projected in the *Confession*—if only on a profoundly displaced level of the text's symbolic meaning. This project of imaginary resolution alludes, as if proleptically, to an emergent mode of the mnemonic whose early definition is one of the text's most fruitful dynamics. Seen in this way, Musset's novel becomes conceivable as the sign of a deeply unsettled preoccupation with the functioning of memory in the early nineteenth century. Beyond the theme of difficult or disturbed reminiscence that the *Confession* develops in its narrative, the hybrid text itself stands as an exemplary case in the diagnosis and the playing-out of the memory crisis.

The *Confession* is obsessed with memory. Musset's narrative reads the mnemonic crisis everywhere. The perturbation of reminiscence represented in chapter 2 is unmistakable. But once the story moves from the second (or "historical") chapter to Octave's confessional tale itself, the voice that had framed the analytical perspective visible in chapter 2 disappears within the first-person protagonist. Under these altered conditions of narration, mnemonic disturbance is *performed* rather than explicitly thematized. Important signs of the text's fixation on the crisis of memory are thus displaced in ways we need to elucidate.

To be sure, explicit motifs of recollection and forgetting remain constant in the portion of the text (through the end of part 2) that recounts Octave's experience after he discovers how his Parisian mistress has betrayed him—the discovery that he says inaugurated his experience of the *mal du siècle* (38). One example of such attention to the phenomenon of memory can stand for many others. After a considerable hiatus in which he has avoided contact with anyone connected with the woman who deceived him so painfully, Octave unexpectedly meets one of her friends. This encounter instantly resurrects his sense of loss and revives all the pain it caused him: "I stared at her hands, her clothes; each of her gestures went straight to my heart; *our entire past was written in them*" (66–67; emphasis mine). In Musset's period the motif was—and no doubt still appears to us—

a sentimental commonplace: suffering triggered abruptly by a somber memory; the perverse persistence of unhappy recollection.[11] The
past appears as an ineradicable inscription that, when read in the
present, displaces the immediacy of experience and co-opts contemporaneity.

Octave's second romance, the tragic liaison with Brigitte Pierson,
reiterates and radically dilates this painful play of remembering and
forgetting. The memory thematic dominates this longest and most
consequential portion of the text and intervenes most intensely at the
most significant moments in its narrative development. For example,
following Octave's declaration of love, Brigitte's reaction foregrounds
the theme of memory's functioning. She orders Octave to stop seeing
her: "It would be useless for you to try to *forget* your moment of
weakness; what has happened between us can neither be *repeated*
nor entirely *forgotten*" (165; emphasis mine). After a time, however,
Brigitte suspends her prohibition and allows Octave to return. He
describes the situation thus: "What had occurred [between us] did
not come up. She seemed *not to want to remember it*, nor did I want
to speak about it" (171; emphasis mine).

Musset perceives and represents an adversarial, "ideological" component determining the play of memory in a love affair. Memory
effects become a battlefield in erotic relations. The tension between
women and men had already been foregrounded in chapter 2: "All at
once, in an unprecedented way, in every salon in Paris, the men
retreated to one side of the room and the women to the other; and
thus, the women dressed in white as if they had just become engaged, the men in black as if they had just been orphaned, they
began to scrutinize each other with deep suspicion" (28).

---

11. Such experiences might remind us of the commonplace romantic connection between the act of reminiscence and a particular site or monument charged with the capacity
to stimulate it—for example, the "monument" to which Musset ironically refers in his
poem "Souvenir" (1841). Just as the *Confession*, "Souvenir" refers to his love affair with
George Sand. At one point in the novel the continuation of such suffering occasions a
moment that confirms the distinction between "reminiscence" and "history" that forms an
important (if latent) structure in the text. In an effort to obliterate his present pain, Octave
attempts to lose himself in the study of the past. In an involuntary play on the word, the
text describes this impulse as follows: "Je me jetais dans l'histoire" ["I threw myself into
history"] (75)—thereby confirming the characteristic of this mode of relation to memory,
its flattening of affect and its displacement of subjectivity in exchange for the analytical
distance that forms its cognitive—and sometimes its emotional—advantage.

Now, in the case of Octave and Brigitte, such suspicion takes the form of a subtle struggle over the control of memory and forgetting. In one characteristic scene, Octave has been vaunting the memory of his amours in Paris, comparing Brigitte cruelly to the demi-mondaines he knew there. Brigitte conceives the extravagant notion of making herself up to resemble the women she imagines Octave has loved before her. Her impulse translates an apprehension that, compared to them, she may appear to him unattractive: "'Do I suit your taste?' she asked. 'Am I pretty enough to make you *forget* the thought of other loves?'" (205; emphasis mine). But her gambit to recolonize Octave's memory aborts painfully. On Brigitte's side the strain of the travesty breaks through in an involuntary shudder (205); on Octave's the experience resurrects an excruciating sense of guilt: "'Take off those flowers, take off that dress. *Don't remind me* that I'm nothing but a prodigal son; *I'm only too aware of the past*'" (206; emphasis mine).

The thematic complex based on this play of remembering and forgetting, particularly upon the alternating persistence and imperma-nence of emotions and on the lovers' more or less conscious attempts to manipulate or control them, pervades the novel. This complex represents a fundamental element in the *Confession*'s representation and its interrogation of memory. To be sure, scenes like these give the impression of being set pieces in the theater of nineteenth-cen-tury passion, bravura combats of the same imperious subjectivity that romantic writing sought to define and depict. But precisely because the treatment of this theme in the novel is rooted in the portrayal of *conscious* behavior, in the willed struggle of individual intentions and competing desires, the fundamental paradoxes of subjectivity— and hence of the constitution of such subjectivity in the processes of memory—tend to escape its conceptual grasp. For the most pro-found contradictions inherent in the functioning of memory surface when its representations *exceed* a subject's willed control.

This is the secret bearing of Musset's *Confession*. The confessional structure of this text insistently refers us beyond itself to a set of deeper paradoxes; and the contradictions to which these interrupted dynamics point stress the *Confession* profoundly. The exploration of these deeper paradoxes constitutes the text's most consequential ele-ment.

Everyone in this novel has an end in mind. The novel stages the clashes of competing subjectivities, the struggles of contending egos. The means of reaching their objectives is language. Martine Reid has noted the density of reported speech and conversation, and the co-ordinate paucity of description, that characterize Musset's text (see Reid, "La Confession selon Musset," 55, 57). Indeed, it sometimes appears that all the characters in the *Confession* do is talk: as if the mode of expression learned in the confessional had proliferated to fill the entire space of discourse, as if penitential speech had become the model for language in general. In the migration from the realm of the sacramental to that of the quotidian, a covert complicity, a scandalous fit between the discursive paradigm from which the novel draws its title and the structures of behavior that it depicts is made visible.

What links these seemingly disparate communicative modes and intentional acts is the analytic impulse characteristic of middle-class consciousness—a structure of consciousness whose functionality in the period of social and economic transformation immediately following the July 1830 revolution was particularly consequential. This capacity may have been born of the need to optimize production, but its paradigms lent themselves as well to comprehending the production of the self.[12] The *Confession* contributes to such an analytic discourse, for which understanding individual behavior becomes the fundamental concern of representation.

The textual complex to which I want to turn now distinguishes itself from the one I have been considering in terms of the category of intentionality. The competition between Octave and Brigitte for control of recollection and representation, as we saw, takes place within a frame in which each lover's speech always refers outward, as an effect to be induced in the interlocutor. In these interpersonal structures the control by each self of its *own* consciousness, its *own* intentionality—and hence of the competence of its own memory—is never called into doubt. The effects that I want now to consider possess no such cognitive privilege. They remain confined within the complications of a single consciousness; and they invoke paradigms

---

12. Richard Terdiman, *Discourse/Counter-Discourse: The Theory and Practice of Symbolic Resistance in Nineteenth-Century France*, 90.

not of the manipulation of others' emotions or experiences, but of the
problematic comprehension of *one's own*. Here is where I would
claim Musset's interrogation of memory is at its most acute and demonstrates its most striking originality.

In the *Confession* recollection and its representation are obligatory
and urgent. Octave's first words in the text reflect precisely this: "J'ai
à raconter . . ." ["I have to tell . . ."] (32). The formula recurs chillingly at a crucial turning point later in the text—after the first time
Brigitte and Octave make love, and immediately following the lyrical
invocation to the "eternal angel" of happy nights of passion that
closes part 3: "J'ai à raconter maintenant ce qui advint de mon
amour" ["Now I have to tell what happened to my love"] (187). This
repetition of the narration's—the confession's—opening warns that
something somber is soon to befall this passion. Thus part 4 of the
Confession begins with a sharp rhetorical reversal, a plunge from the
heights of part 3's erotic happiness that is threateningly signaled by
the repetition of Octave's original exordium.

The introductory formula that Octave invokes reemphasizes the
ritual injunction to anamnesis, to remember and to retell, inherent
in the paradigm of confession itself. It does so first when he begins
his narration, and again on the threshold of the most guilt-ridden
part of his story. But Octave's words do not seem designed to inspire
confidence. They suggest what *must* be done ("J'ai à raconter . . .") in
such a way that the will—and perhaps even the capacity—to *do it*
seems subtly put in doubt. They counterpose the necessity of recollection against the uncertainty of the mnemonic performance they
summon up.

This uncertainty does not simply reside in "bad memory," in some
troublesome insufficiency of recollection. The tension communicated
by Octave's preparatory phrases registers something deeper. Given
its fictional structure and its enunciative situation, everything the
Confession represents arises in memory. Memory alone provides the
matter of this text. But the *Confession* subverts the transparency of
its own medium. The interrogation of its own cognitive and representational basis begins with its opening sentence. And in the course
of its narration and analysis, the grounding of representation in memory eventually undermines itself and emerges as a scandal. What the
Confession then confesses is the darker side of its own modality, the

somber implication of memory in the production of individual unhappiness. Memory has always been figured as a mediator of our guilt,
but in turning the mnemonic faculty upon itself, the *Confession* reconceives memory as the determinant of our sins.

Once again, the notion of *determination* is central. Musset's representation of memory turns on locating the power of our history to
dominate and even to shatter our present. In consequence the solidity of what we term the "present" simply collapses—and with it the
notions of individual coherence, autonomy, or self-control predicated
on it. Such a subversion of the stability of the present was foreshadowed in chapter 2's bizarre figuration of contemporaneity as an
empty space between past and future, but here the consequences of
such a reconception of reality are projected on the innermost experience of the individual ego.

In this representation Musset upsets the structures that had sustained the familiar romantic hypostasis of the individual. Confession
might seem to centralize the self; yet in Musset's rewriting of the
genre, the imagery of a sovereign, Promethean subjectivity diffuses,
disintegrates, and gives way to something like a proto-Freudian disquiet concerning the ego's contradictions, its fundamental non-self-
identity, and the paradoxical self-destructiveness of the behavior it
adopts to realize its desires. This destabilization of the image of the
individual generalizes the text's initial suspicion concerning the (au-
thorial) subject, expressed in the opening lines of chapter 1. But this
thematic return to the beginning does not indicate some organic closure or harmonious recontainment of the text's own self-questioning.
Rather, it radicalizes the *Confession*'s pursuit of this process, which
cannot ever "conclude" or be totalized.

There is no need to exaggerate the originality of the paradigm Musset devised to represent the conflicted psychology of the self. He did
not invent a new discourse from whole cloth: the *Confession d'un
enfant du siècle* does not mark the sudden appearance of a new mode
of analysis. To begin with, a concern with memory's persistence and
with the survival of childhood experience into adulthood had been
preoccupations at least since Rousseau's own *Confessions* and Chateaubriand's *Mémoires d'outre-tombe*. Musset's depiction of such effects is consistent with such earlier thematics. But his *Confession*

diverges in the *expression* memory is given in his text. Memory functions in Musset in ways familiar from earlier protoromantic and romantic explorations of the past's baneful presence in adult experience, but what is new is how he represents such material in his
novel. Musset may be the first writer to have foregrounded the *collective* and *transferential* character of our relation to the past—a
structure Freud later formalized as the heart of psychoanalysis.

But it remains true that Musset followed a tradition that had been
seeking for a long time to identify the determinants of our behavior.
Inevitably, his text shows the evidence of its own determination by
the discourses of the past. The romantics anticipated his preoccupation with memory and childhood, but much of his novel's analytical
structure derives from the French Enlightenment, which looked to
the realms of politics and of ideology to identify what bound individuals and limited their freedom. As the historical, political, and sociological excursus of the *Confession*'s celebrated second chapter reminds us, speculation concerning these latter areas of social existence
had been crucial in reflection on the Revolution and its aftermath.
Not surprisingly, memory of this conceptual complex conditioned
Musset's figuration of the subjection of an *individual* present by the
past.

It was thus natural for him to frame his analysis in terms of the
problematic of *liberté* that, since the generation that produced the
Revolution itself, had defined efforts to think through the contradictions of social life. In the Enlightenment and post-Revolutionary
analysis of the factors that seemed to distance individuals from their
own freedom, Musset found a language in which their *self*-alienation
might be conceived.

What I am suggesting is that, even after the politics in which it
had first been rooted had been closed off by the end of the Revolutionary period itself (as chapter 2 of the *Confession* so powerfully
argues), the problematic of freedom that Musset's generation had inherited was still unresolved. Musset's forebears were inspired by the
Enlightenment concern to identify—and to revolutionize—the factors that limited the freedom of human beings. We might say that
the effort to theorize these determinants proceeded through two major phases. The first, pre-Revolutionary moment located in the society of estates, in the fixed hierarchy of absolutist monarchy and he-

reditary aristocracy, a fundamental structure of restriction that the Revolution strove to eliminate. But it became clear that, however radical, such liberating political change did not exhaust the constraints on social existence whose identification appeared so urgent throughout this period.

So, in a second phase, whose definition was the work of the first half of the nineteenth century, a pervasive set of deeper infrastructural constraints was detected and theorized. Their locus was the constitution not of the State, but of the individual subject as social actor. In this way the theory of ideology emerged as a crucial field of knowledge within the "liberal" societies of Musset's century. According to the insights developed in this analytical field, not only armies but *schools*, not only policemen, judges, and jails but *language itself*, turned out to have a powerful capacity to determine and limit social behavior. And they did so all the more mystifyingly because they were not *experienced* as structures of oppression.[13]

But though Musset's analytical means derived from those which had arisen in the investigation of political and ideological constraints upon individual freedom, in the *Confession* he detected a third site and began to theorize a third discourse of behavioral determination. It would be absurd to argue that Musset invented depth psychology. My assertion here is more modest. I want to suggest that in the *Confession* he provided a coherent representation and developed the beginnings of a systematic theory of neurosis. His interrogation of memory was the key to these developments.

Musset's account of the disquiet around memory was thus influenced by, and in turn displaced or reconceived, certain older thematic tensions. The central of these counterposed the motifs of freedom and subjection to the discourses of the past. In the *Confession*, this conflict transfers and reinscribes *within* the realm of the psychological the political instance that dominated social imagination in the period after the French Revolution. In this context, the repetitive— indeed, virtually obsessive—preoccupation of the *Confession* with *liberté* begins to make sense. The concept of freedom central to the

13. These notions derive from the work of Antonio Gramsci and Louis Althusser. I discuss their contribution to its development and to the theory of ideology in *Discourse/ Counter-Discourse*, particularly in the introduction, 41–43, 52. I return to the problem in discussing Freud's theory of memory in Chapter 7.

novel emerges from the realm of ahistorical and indeterminate generality to take its place in the conjunctural economy of the text. The unresolved divergence between the nascent "psychological" and "historical" discourses whose articulations I earlier sought to distinguish within it played a crucial role in the definition of this theme.

In the *Confession*'s second chapter, "liberté" (which Musset claimed had intensely preoccupied his generation after 1815) refers so repeatedly and so forcefully to the period and the ideals of the Revolution that the celebrated republican slogan seems to have been transformed by history into a mnemonic devised specifically to remind Musset's present of a crucial loss: "For them [the children of the generation who had made the Revolution] there was something in the word 'liberté' that made their hearts beat faster, at once like a distant and terrible memory and like a cherished and even more distant hope" (24).

But the nineteenth century reserved an exemplary lesson for those whose aspirations formed around the ideal of *liberté*. Musset conveys the chilling effect of this lesson on the young people of his own generation: "They trembled with excitement when they heard the word *liberté*; but returning home they saw three baskets being carried to the cemetery at Clamart: it was three young men who had said *liberté* too loudly" (24). The reference was transparent in 1836. Though the number of victims had been discreetly modified, the passage recalls the four "Sergents de La Rochelle" executed in September 1822 after a revolt in that city had challenged Villèle's Ultra-Royalist government. The La Rochelle rising, along with similar movements in Belfort, Saumur, and Colmar, had been brutally repressed.[14] More globally, however, the entire Bourbon Restoration is conceived here as a warning for any in Musset's generation who might have been tempted to revive the old revolutionary catchword *liberté* as a program for political action.

Yet the most fundamental determinant of the demoralization evidenced in the second chapter of Musset's *Confession* was the July Revolution itself. For (as is now a historiographical commonplace) this product of the long-repressed libertarian aspirations of the post-Revolutionary generation ended up ironizing such reformist desires

14. See Jacques Droz, *Europe between Revolutions, 1815–1848*, 106–7.

completely. The political and ideological production of the pervasive sense of despair under the July Monarchy has been exhaustively studied by Pierre Barbéris.[15] But there is no more effective evocation of it than the *Confession*'s second chapter.

As if to demonstrate the sense conveyed there that politics was simply exhausted after 1830, in the body of Octave's confession the notion of *liberté* mutates radically to take on a deep *psychological* resonance. What on the scale of history had appeared as the aspiration for freedom—from traditional feudal exactions, from aristocratic privilege, or from a closed and oppressive of political system—here, under the influence of the paradigm transformation I have already traced, became converted into an intense impulse to *freedom from the psyche's own past*.

The following schema seeks to make sense of the metamorphosis of the theme of *liberté* from part to part within Musset's text, and of the coordinate transformation of discursive elements that define its influence. The *Confession d'un enfant du siècle* is composed of three major structural segments, whose rhetorical and conceptual relations to one another determine how each portion of the text "remembers" and represents what precedes it, how it links to its own past.

Chapter 2, the explicitly sociohistorical diagnosis, was clearly intended to serve as a macrocosmic frame for the remainder of the text consisting of Octave's account of his disastrous amours. This historical frame relates to the personal narrative it was designed to introduce in the mode of a metadiscourse or of a metonymy—standing as explanation to that which is to be explained, or at least as general to particular. In the economy of the *Confession*, history is conceived as generating a complex of interpersonal and social structures (accounted for in chapter 2), which, upon the transformation of narrative paradigm at the beginning of Octave's own first-person narrative in chapter 3, then manifest themselves in the form of personal disasters in

---

15. See Pierre Barbéris, *Balzac et le mal du siècle*, vol. 2, chap. 7 ("Balzac et l'École Romantique en 1830); chap. 8 ("L'école du désenchantement, I: Mésaventures d'une révolution"); and chap. 9 ("L'école du désenchantement, II: *La Peau de chagrin*"). The term *désenchantement* appears in the *Confession* itself (31), carrying with it in 1836 a dense cultural history that registers the fate of political desire in Musset's period. See Barbéris, *Balzac et le mal du siècle*, 2:1417.

individual lives. The effects of unrestrained individualism, the coordinate impulse of interpersonal suspicion poisoning human relations
in the post-Revolutionary period (particularly the instrumentalization
of relations between men and women) then become exemplified in
Octave's story.

But this story, Octave's "confession" proper, in turn divides into
two parts. The first is the account of his Parisian mistress's betrayal;
the second of his liaison with Brigitte Pierson. But here the figural
connection between the successive love affairs is no longer metonymic.
Rather, it wavers uncertainly between metaphor (the second story is
like the first) and tautology (the second uncontrollably *repeats* the
first).

What account can be derived from Musset's text of the mediations
linking Octave's two love affairs to the cultural crisis evoked in chapter 2? And how did Musset construe the link between the two love
affairs? The mediations between the sociohistorical and psychological
instances remain virtually untheorized and opaque—the text (as I
have already suggested) satisfying itself with the paratactic juxtaposi-
tion of the two divergent discourses that confront each other at the
beginning of part 1. However, the mediations between the two successive love affairs are of the greatest interest and are treated in the
text with striking sophistication.

Coordinately, the problematic of *liberté* transforms itself across the
three segments of the *Confession*. In chapter 2, its resonances remain political, though they are already mediated by memory in the
form of intense recollection of an ideal of freedom whose distance
from contemporary experience marks the abyss between past and
present that unhinges contemporaneity. In the succeeding segment,
Octave's Parisian love affair, the horizon of *liberté* inflects. Now freedom begins to be defined in characteristically post-Revolutionary
subjective terms: as projection of an individual autonomy no longer
consciously linked to any particular sociopolitical constraint. Thus
Octave's celebratory self-definition: "I had no profession, no occupa-
tion. . . . My sole ideal, along with love, was independence. From
puberty on, I was powerfully devoted to it. . . . Thus I was free by
my own will" (48–49).[16]

16. The resonances here clearly recall Rousseau, with whose *Confessions* Musset was
familiar despite the contempt he expressed for the work; see his letter to Franz Liszt,

In this second portion of the narrative, *liberté* is conceived as freedom from the recollection of desire and betrayal, from Octave's intense and implacable "memories of the flesh and of the blood" (52). The conceptual slippage seems a natural one, for in *this* existence the most pertinent constraint limiting freedom emanates not from the politico-economic but from the *mnemonic* realm. Thus we witness Octave himself feverishly fantasizing liberation from the demon of remembrance: "Ghosts, ghosts, will you never release me?" (76).

But in the novel's third segment, the narration of Octave's love affair with Brigitte Pierson, the problematic of *liberté* projects a horizon much more striking and specific. Now in the face of extraordinary happiness the text expresses an aspiration for release from the compulsion to repeat the systematic distrust that in Octave has constituted itself as the psyche's memory of the love relationship. This representational and psychological complex, which I compared with a more contemporary notion of neurosis, deserves careful consideration.

The dynamic dominating Octave's love affair with Brigitte is conceived within the *Confession* as a memory disorder. We have already considered the formula that expresses Octave's mnemonic compulsion at the opening of his narrative. But it is worth quoting the entire sentence, for it defines Octave's story as the narrative of an *illness*: "I have to tell [*J'ai à raconter*] how I first contracted the *maladie du siècle*" (38). Octave's account of discovering his Parisian mistress's betrayal follows immediately, but the phrase "maladie du siècle" then returns to mark the text's first experience of the paradigm of baneful repetition that defines this novel's singular economy of time. The expression arises to describe Octave's discovery that a woman with whom he finds himself in a cabaret—the first prostitute he had ever spoken with, as he tells us—"fatally" resembles the mistress who has betrayed him (83). He represents his encounter with this

---

26 June 1836, reprinted in the Allem edition of the *Confession*, xxxvi–xxxvii. Musset's father had written an enthusiastic study of Rousseau, which in 1823 had gotten him fired from his administrative position in the government; see Pierre Gastinel, *Le Romantisme d'Alfred de Musset*, 4 n. 4. Musset's contempt for Rousseau notwithstanding, the extravagant scene (dropped by Musset from the 1840 edition) in which Octave strips off his clothes in a paroxysmic celebration of his freedom (49) clearly recalls Rousseau's epigraph to the *Confessions*: "Intus, et in cute" ("from within, and naked").

doppelgänger as so alarming, as so dire, that it evokes a fear of death. Yet there is something fundamentally improper or distorted in this characterization, for this is not an experience of destruction but of duplication, not a projection of the self's annihilation but rather of an inappropriate resurrection. And the experience of such an un- welcome return of his own history seems even more dreadful to him because he discovers he has no other name for such reappearance than the opaque "maladie du siècle."

The peculiar affective disorder that we associate with Musset's text thus arises in the discovery of an unanticipated, inappropriate, and terrifying reproduction of the past in the present—in an uncanny and malignant effect of memory. Just as this affliction has already mutated in the course of the story, as the narrative continues it will come to identify an even more involuntary mode of recollection of the past, a catastrophization of memory that destroys Octave's ability to love and, ultimately, Brigitte's ability to love him. This memory disorder will eventually be understood to determine the corrosively instrumental mode of relation between people that I have argued characterizes very diverse modes of discourse and representation in Musset's text.

The greatest portion of the *Confession* is written as Octave's first- person account. Thus within the text there is no voice to provide a privileged judgment of the meaning of the tale. But Brigitte comes close to seeming Musset's surrogate as the moral and emotional au- thority in this text. Hers is the most sensitive and the most conscious analytical voice within the *Confession*. Consequently, it is Brigitte who explains the mechanism by which memory becomes a malady, who elucidates the logic by which the past returns to devastate the present. Particularly, it is Brigitte who rationalizes the trope that links the narration and the structure of Octave's first love affair to his love affair with her.

Brigitte thus plays a crucial metanarrative role in the *Confession*. She stands above the action recounted by Octave and *makes sense* of his behavior in a way he is never able to do, which of course compli- cates her role in the text. Because she must articulate the theory and take part in the praxis of the *Confession*, she mediates the emer- gence of its meaning both synchronically and diachronically, both as analyst and as participant. Her relation to Octave is also composite.

She is his mistress, and there is no doubt whatever of the strength of
her passion, but doubling this erotic link there are clear indications
of parental, even of sacerdotal or therapeutic resonances in her relation to him.[17] He meets her immediately following the death of his
father; she is older and has been married. In the village she ministers
to the sick with a nurturing devotion that clearly resembles the calm-
ing protection she later offers her lover. Indeed, Octave's own self-
characterization as "enfant" frames and potentiates all of these figural
manifestations of Brigitte's multiform and ambiguous role.

In the case of Brigitte there is thus an intriguing crossing of lines
and modes of relation. Because of it, her function in the *Confession*
uncannily disseminates. She resists containment in any of the familiar structural cells designating conventional narrative units. This
complex interpenetration of "inside" and "outside," of implication in
the action counterposed against analysis of it, defines an interesting
and richly enigmatic actantial position. Musset's representation of
this position places Brigitte Pierson *within* Octave's process of memory. With this structure, the novel projects the paradigm of a more
fully realized mnemonic—one which, if it is not the product of an
explicitly collective instance of memory in the mode argued by
Maurice Halbwachs, at least establishes remembrance as indissolubly
transferential and dialogic. Brigitte thus figures as a characteristically
modern form of interlocutor—a form for whose more systematic definition we are indebted to Freud.[18]

Read against this narrative and analytical paradigm, the text's final
transformation of the problematic of *liberté* expresses its significance.
Octave is conscious of a disabling obscurity in the analysis he has
conducted of his self-constitution. But in solitude he has no insight
into its etiology. He frames his perplexity in a series of evocative,
melodramatic questions: "By what path, O Providence, have you led

17. Compare his overtly protoconfessional "I could not resist telling her everything I
had in my heart" (154).
18. See Maurice Halbwachs, *The Collective Memory*. The relationship between dialogism and recollection is an ancient and important theme. Edward S. Casey puts it this
way: "Plato's doctrine of recollection . . . shows considerable affinity with Freud's view of
memory. Much as abreactive recollection becomes possible only through dialogical confrontation in psychotherapy, philosophical recollection or *anamnesis* arises after a process
of dialectical cross-examination (*elenchus*)" (*Remembering: A Phenomenological Study*,
302). I will consider the transferential paradigm in greater detail in Chapter 7.

me to disaster?" (158). Or: "'Oh God!' I said to myself with a terrible
sadness, 'is the past a ghost? Can it escape from its grave? Oh, misery, am I doomed never to be able to love?'" (192). Or, most poi-
gnant and most consequential of all, in the course of his anguished
conversation with himself in part 5: "'But why do I suffer?' 'Think
only of your father's example, and of doing what's right.' 'But why am
I unable to do that? why does evil attract me?' 'Get down on your
knees, confess; if you believe in evil, it has already been committed.'
'If I've committed evil, is it my fault? Why has the good abandoned
me?'" (268).

But the insight Octave is able to achieve through *self*-analysis
proves impotent: "In the evenings I sat on my bed and said to myself, 'Well, let me think this through.' Then I put my head between
my hands, and cried out, 'I can't!' but the next day I began all over
again." (261). Octave's questions situate themselves squarely within
the paradigms for comprehending generative process that I argued
were forming in the wake of the middle-class socioeconomic ascent
following the 1830 revolution. But if an answer to his questions implies an analysis of the source of his affliction, then it is clear that
Octave has no answer at all. Brigitte is the actor and the analyst who
brings forth the response to Octave's perplexity. She mediates the
emergence of the text's most striking insight concerning the source of
constraints on individual *liberté*. According to her diagnosis, *persistence of memory* is what restricts freedom. Octave's irrationally repetitive behavior has its determinations in the past.

Brigitte thereby unpacks the text's suggestion (implicit in the very
unintelligibility of its structure) that its three segments somehow *repeat* one another, that they all tell versions of the same tale. It is far
from obvious how the sociohistorical crisis of the second chapter can
be comprehended as a macroscopic analogue of the personal disasters
that befall Octave in two successive love affairs, or how the liaison
with a notorious coquette in the corrosive atmosphere of Paris might
be understood as prefiguring the fate of his passion for a decent and
devoted woman in the peace of the countryside. But the logic of the
Confession's diegesis is causal, not paradigmatic, and the causality it
projects is rooted in a startling and scandalous irrationality. What
turns out to link these deeply disparate narratives is that, through a
logic of the inappropriate whose revelation provides the text's most

interesting intuition concerning our ability to account for our behavior, each segment determines the conduct of those which succeed it. The past devours the present; diachronicity is rewritten as destiny. Memory is the modality of this malignant but seemingly inescapable logic.

Brigitte rationalizes this irrationality. She realizes the deranged domination of the mnemonic:

> "Don't think," she told me, "that I misunderstand your heart, or that I reproach you for the suffering you cause me. It is not your fault, my love, that you lack the strength to forget your past life; you fell in love with me sincerely, and even if I die of your love I will never regret the day I gave myself to you. You thought you would be reborn and that in my arms you would forget the memory of the women who hurt you so badly [*et que tu oublierais dans mes bras le souvenir des femmes qui t'ont perdu*]. You believed it yourself, and both of us were fooled. Oh my child, you bear in your heart a wound which will not heal." (216)

The past of the *Confession* is thus conceived in the image of a trauma. And the mechanism of its projection into the present seems consistent with more contemporary models of the neurotic repetition of personal history. This is the darker side of memory: the catastrophe by which time turns lunatic and begins to flow uncontrollably in reverse.

I want to force my analogy between the structuration of memory in the *Confession* and the formation of neurosis in psychoanalysis one step further. Earlier, I suggested a comparison between the cognitive and emotional role that Brigitte Pierson plays in uncovering the mechanism of Octave's irrationality and the parallel relation of an analyst to an analysand. The divergences are evident, of course—but they disable the analogy mostly from Brigitte's side. She involves herself emotionally with Octave in a way no analyst could ethically countenance. But from the point of view of Octave, the forms of transference he experiences in relation to Brigitte may not be so different from those that might have been generated in an authentic analytic setting. And the forms of understanding at which Brigitte arrives bear close affinity with those an authentic analyst would seek to achieve.

There is however one clear difference. The trauma Brigitte un-
earths—Octave's painful experience of betrayal at the hands of his
Parisian mistress—is an injury of late adolescence. A Freudian would
look further back in Octave's family history. So we might ask whether,
in the structure of recollection I have sought to explicate here, the
Confession bears a memory of *earlier* traumas that could have poten-
tiated, not only Octave's irrational and destructive behavior with Brigitte, but even the preceding Parisian injury that in her analysis
emerges as its determinant.

The *Confession* responds to such a question—indeed, so readily
that we might imagine that Musset's text had somehow uncannily
anticipated it. To be sure, the novel's answer comes to us displaced.
But such displacement is the very stuff of which depth-psychological
analysis is constructed. What (following Brigitte's analysis within the
text) I have termed the "trauma" in Octave's life—the explicit, Parisian injury—is insufficiently archaic to satisfy analytical curiosity. Let
us therefore investigate family history in search of the infantile
wound that might be taken, according to this paradigm, as the source
of later irrationalities. What traces of such history are available in the
text?

Octave's mother is virtually absent.[19] In a suggestive denegation of
the parental, Octave rather speaks of nature as his dear mother (51).
And whatever maternal resonances Brigitte may have had for him,
they necessarily have no relevance (except insofar as they suggest a
structure of unsatisfied need) to the sort of archaic personal history
we are seeking. As for Octave's father, he is hardly less of a shadow.
In part 1, chapter 3, we fleetingly hear of him urging Octave, around
the time of puberty, to choose a profession (48). He does not appear
alive again in the text. But after he dies Octave spends some time
reacquainting himself with his father. Part 3, chapter 2, is largely
taken up with that effort. What emerges is an impossible idealization:
the portrayal of saint, revered by his servants and by the people of
his village, in death romanticized so intensely by his son that Octave
decides to replicate the habits and daily schedule of his father in the

19. Martine Reid has collected references to the maternal thematic in the novel: the
prostitute Marco's playful address to Octave as "bambino mio" (123), Brigitte's "I want to
be your mother" (219). See Reid, "La Confession selon Musset," 65.

period of mourning after his death.[20] In short, the explicit portrayal of his parents gives us no indication whatever of the source of any infantile injury.

Yet in another sense the celebrated second chapter of the novel speaks of nothing else. I have argued at some length that the relationship between this material and Octave's own history is problematic for the novel. At this point, it may at last be possible to make sense of this enigmatic quality itself. If one were seeking to discover how the sociological crisis of chapter 2 might project itself on the screen of infantile subjectivity, the matter recounted there *outside* the bounds of Octave's first-person narration is deeply suggestive. What it figures is a story of an incomprehensible and terrifying absence of the father. The second chapter's opening sentence is justly celebrated and evocative: "During the Napoleonic Wars, while their husbands and brothers were in Germany, anxious mothers brought into the world an ardent, pale, and nervous generation" (20).

The search for the archaic sources of an *individual* trauma has led us back to the structures of *collective* recollection with which the *Confession* so enigmatically and so strikingly begins. Now these structures become readable. It is almost as if, in the fleeting moments of the text cast in the third person, in which it allows itself the intervention of a metanarrative vision whose stance exceeds the subjective scope of Octave's confessional material, an answer floats up out of memory—but a memory whose source has shifted, so that just as in the analytic situation, we can never really know whether it reproduces a real structure, or simply constructs it. But in the memory of this collective past the *Confession* seems to offer an answer to the question of Octave's behavior that transcends and absorbs within itself—in the guise almost of an authoritative therapist extending

20. This idealization of the father has, however, an unresolved and uncanny obverse in the nightmare-like anecdote Octave offers to figure the effect of discovering his Parisian mistress's duplicity: "It was as if in a forest I was seeing an innocent child whose throat bandits wanted to cut; he escapes, screaming, into his father's arms; he throws his arms around his neck, hides under his coat, pleads to be saved; and his father draws a glowing sword; *he is himself one of the bandits, and cuts the child's throat*" (65; emphasis mine). Alternative strategies of idealization or denegation seem to define Octave's mode of relation to the memory of his parents. The deformations they induce might be taken as a measure of the anxiety inherent in the relation as he has experienced it.

more local insights—Brigitte's analytical speculations about how Octave's past has destroyed his present.

This is the structure by which the past colonizes the present and
supplants it—its desires, its intentions, its very identity as the moment
when the future is determined afresh. Memory in this pathological
mode reproduces bygone patterns that in their perverse persistence
deconstruct the very notion of the self and of contemporaneity and
constrain us to accept that, far from being contained within the realm
of the archaic, they define and dominate the present. But this displacement of our subjectivity, the sense that the past is *living us*,
then refers us back, in a vertiginous regression, to the initial sentence of the *Confession*—"Pour écrire l'histoire de sa vie, il faut
d'abord avoir vécu." In this sentence a paradoxical defect of living, an
absence of the narrating self to itself, was uncannily thematized and
foretold. Thus the *vécu* turns up vacuous in Musset's text; thus the
confession radically subverts the basis for its own articulation. For
what could be authentically confessed if not that which has been
lived, and who could confess it if not the individual whose experience it authentically was? But if living has somehow been disabled,
then what remains for the penitent to narrate? And if the self has
been colonized by some alien determination that it cannot even perceive as a source of pathology, what might it mean to talk of an individual at all?

This disconcerting reversal of past and present, this deconstruction
of the orders of time and of subjectivity, this paradox around the very
notion of representation, turns out to be the peril inherent in the
interrogation of memory. It is a danger in which interrogation finds
itself reinscribed within the object of its investigation and perversely
controlled by it. A sovereign and maleficent power seems to displace
the nominally independent consciousness of its narrator in precisely
the same way that the obsessive reprise of transgression fills the entire space of the text. The subversive power of such processes is
decisive, for their result is to block the therapeutic abreactions or
extinction of past contents (and the consequent restoration of psychic
health) that the paradigm of confession had inscribed as the text's
horizon.

In the peculiar form and rhetoric of this text, in its transformation
of the generic paradigm to which it refers, Brigitte's insight into how

Octave's own experience inhabits him, in the doubling and framing of these protoanalytic revelations by the sociopsychological speculations of chapter 2, what is narrated in the *Confession* is a mnemonic disaster, a catastrophe inherent in memory. Romantic personal lyricism and subjectivism thus recalls from its own memory a fracture that undoes its fundamental conception of individuals and of their history. Musset's restaging of anamnesis unexpectedly rewrites the very possibility of remembering or representing the past. In the *Confession* our relation to this past and to its constitution of our present is transformed into something approaching the haunted mnemonics of modernity.

4

Baudelaire's "Le Cygne": Memory, History, and the Sign

Les cygnes comprennent les signes.
[Swans understand signs.]
  —Victor Hugo, *Les Misérables* (1862), 5249

Twenty times I've convinced myself I don't care about politics any more.
  —Charles Baudelaire to Nadar (Félix Tournachon),
  16 May 1859, in Baudelaire, *Correspondance*, 1:578

M emory signifies loss. The memory crisis of post-Revolutionary Europe manifested itself in feelings of exile, anxiety, and displacement. This complex of feelings needs analysis—both as a set of metaphors rooted in the materiality of nineteenth-century social life and as a mechanism arising in language itself.

The memory of loss has a *content* and a *form*: an empirical referent and a semiotic medium. In this chapter I seek to understand the mnemonics of such dispossession by examining the form and content of its representation in Baudelaire's "Le Cygne" (1859), which I take as an exemplary and powerful text on the connection between loss and memory and as the representation of a conjuncture in which this connection took on a particularly intense pertinence. I argue that the relationship between the experience of dispossession "Le Cygne" thematizes and the poem's reflection on the sign was intensely determined by Second Empire history.

A concept and a practice of the sign, closely paralleling what today we believe is theoretically essential about it, is active within *Les*

Baudelaire's "Le Cygne"

Fleurs du mal—most notably within "Le Cygne." In "Le Cygne
Baudelairian sign speaks clearly in its own name, and speaks its
name clearly. Why is it there? What broke Baudelaire's preoccupation
with signs out of the flux of experience? Yuri Lotman and B. A. Uspensky suggested two decades ago that periods of social change are characterized by an increasingly urgent consciousness of the coded nature of
social life.[1] Such a notion has been implicit in my argument from the
outset. Now I want to claim that conceptualization of the "sign" in Baudelaire was determined by experiences of history in the same register
as those that took form in the memory crisis. This conviction will lead
me to examine aspects of Second Empire culture and experience in
relation to the sorts of perplexities concerning language out of which
what we might call "semiotic consciousness" precipitates.

How is loss refracted as a phenomenon of language? Baudelaire's
"Swan" (*cygne*) has long been conceived as a founding reflection on
the sign (*signe*). Such a connection is more than an accident of hom-
onymy. In his intensely intertextual sonnet "Le vierge, le vivace et le
bel aujourd'hui" (1885), Mallarmé laid Baudelaire's wordplay between the semiotic and the ornithological absolutely bare. Yet to take
it seriously in "Le Cygne," I need to disengage Baudelaire's poem
from Mallarmé's. Under the influence of Mallarmé's reconception of
the material of "Le Cygne" in his later sonnet—thus through a version of aesthetic formalism much more powerfully settled and univocal than is appropriate for understanding Baudelaire himself—critics
have understood the *swan/sign* pun they share to authorize a concept
of the sign celebrating the autonomy of the aesthetic, the limitlessness of language's productive power, the freeing of the semiotic from
the constraints of the historical. Against such conceptualizations, I
want to assert the *historicity* of Baudelaire's notion of the aesthetic
and the semiotic. My argument turns on the play and the place of
memory in the constitution of semiosis itself.

The stakes in this controversy over the mnemonic and the semiotic
begin to be visible in the fact that 1859, the year of "Le Cygne," was
also the year of Napoléon III's offer of amnesty to opponents of his
regime. The word "amnesty" is significant. In effect it pulls in two
directions. Through the *-mne* root it recalls the process of memory

1. Yuri M. Lotman and B. A. Uspensky, "On the Semiotic Mechanism of Culture,"
211–12.

within its own signifier, but it simultaneously suspends this recollection with the privitive *a-* that begins the word. Amnesty thus attempts to induce a State-mediated *amnesia*, to upset the process of rememoration, the story told about the past, the very substance of signification itself. Such a gambit aims to disrupt the linkages of signifier and signified that are sustained in social memory. As I attempt to understand the interplay between the mnemonic and the historical in Baudelaire, I want to remember this moment of memory's deeply conjunctural historicization.[2]

We imagine that memory recollects and restores. Its representations promise conservation and continuity in the face of time's entropic drift. But anamnesis is not so simple. The process of memory carries an uncanny danger, which emerges in the paradigm of dispossession that organizes Baudelaire's poem. For the exiles of "Le Cygne," for the dispossessed, memory stages not recovery but *deficiency*. Its representations make an absence present. Or rather, memory figures the inauthenticity of presentness, the traumatic persistence of an irreversible experience of loss. This is history under the sign of disaster. How might we understand this history of loss, this mnemonics of dispossession in "Le Cygne"?

There is a long tradition of belief in the integrative function of rememoration, in its unifying capacity. In a classic essay, Jean-Pierre Vernant retraced the social history of memory in Greek society and underlined how the progressive development of the memory function was a precondition not only for understanding the individual and collective past, but for conceiving such notions to begin with. The general bearing of such a view is that memory creates the unity necessary to ensure that a heterogeneous organism has an identity at all.[3]

2. In August 1859, Victor Hugo was no doubt the opponent of the regime whom Napoléon III most sought to appease with his offer of amnesty. Hugo had remained in self-imposed—but powerfully vocal—exile since the coup d'état that founded the Second Empire in 1852. The facts are widely known (see Richard Terdiman, "1852," and Richard Burton, *The Context of Baudelaire's "Le Cygne,"* 14–17). Hugo refused the emperor's gambit, a fact to which Baudelaire's poem makes indirect reference. The *mode* by which Hugo expressed his scorn is worth noting. He ridiculed the amnesty offer by depreciating its *signifier*, terming it "la chose appelée amnistie" (this so-called amnesty). See the notes to the Claude Pichois edition of Baudelaire's *Oeuvres complètes*, 1:1005. On amnesty, see Nicole Loraux, "De l'amnistie et de son contraire," and Louis Joinet, "L'Amnistie: Le Droit à la mémoire entre pardon et oubli."

3. Jean-Pierre Vernant, "Aspects mythiques de la mémoire et du temps," in *Mythe et pensée chez les grecs: Études de psychologie historique,* 1:80–123, especially 80–81. Much

Baudelaire was notoriously preoccupied by memory. In the cours
of his attempt to think through its complications, he seems at times
to have accepted such an affirmative conception of the mnemonic.
He began writing about memory as early as the *Salon de 1846*, but
probably his most positive statement on memory's behalf is found in
"Un Mangeur d'opium" in "Les Paradis artificiels"—a text composed
in 1858–59, thus nearly contemporary with "Le Cygne."[4] In "Un
Mangeur d'opium," following Thomas De Quincey, Baudelaire considered the metaphor that likens memory to a *palimpsest* (451).[5] In
reworking DeQuincey's figure, however, Baudelaire introduced an
important distinction. He pointed out that a palimpsest manuscript
may superpose radically disparate texts—a Greek tragedy, a monas-
tic legend, a chivalric romance. But for Baudelaire memory worked
differently. "The divine palimpsest created by God which is our incommensurable memory," he claimed, mysteriously suspends the
chaos of random contiguity: "In memory . . . temperament necessarily creates a harmony between the most diverse elements. However incoherent a given existence may be, its human unity is not
thereby disturbed. If one were to reawaken them simultaneously, all
the echoes of memory would form a concert, perhaps pleasant, perhaps disagreeable, but logical and without dissonance" (451).

The metaphorical substrate for inscription—memory—thus *rewrites* the text that it makes available for rereading. In inscribing, it
simultaneously transforms. The point is crucial: the texts of memory
are not *copies* but *representations*. They are always already overwrit-
ten *by the process of writing itself.*[6]

---

closer in time to Baudelaire, John Locke founded his notion of the unity and persistence of
personal identity on the unifying function of memory; see *Essay Concerning Human Understanding*, book 2, chap. 27. Denis Diderot argued vigorously in favor of memory as the
guarantor of individuality in *Le Rêve de d'Alembert*, 270–73, 341. On Kant's parallel
views, see Theodor Adorno, *Negative Dialectics*, 154; on Husserl's, see Edward S. Casey,
Remembering: A Phenomenological Study, 41.

4. Concerning the *Salon de 1846*, see Michael Fried, "Painting Memories: On the
Containment of the Post in Baudelaire and Manet," 512–13. Concerning the date of "Un
Mangeur d'opium," see the Notice, in *Oeuvres complètes*, 1:1361.

5. Unless otherwise specified, quotations from Baudelaire are from the Y.-G. Le
Dantec and Claude Pichois edition of *Oeuvres complètes*.

6. See Chapter 2. Baudelaire's observation concerning the uncanny harmonization of
disparity in memory's multilayered palimpsest could be read as a version, or a prospective
suggestion, of a figure that Freud devised for describing the process of "condensation" in
the interpretation of dreams: "projecting two images on to a single [photographic] plate
. . ." (*The Interpretation of Dreams* [1900], SE 4:293).

Another Baudelaire essay whose genesis is nearly contemporary, "Le Peintre de la vie moderne," includes an entire section ("L'Art mnémonique") that directly evokes the problem of memory under consideration here. The text was begun in 1859 (see *Oeuvres complètes*, ed. Pichois, 2:1416). In it, Baudelaire attempted to analyze the process of composition by which the artist Constantin Guys sought to render or represent contemporaneity. Baudelaire conceived this process in the image of a dialectic between the synthesizing and recuperative power of memory, and an unmediated kinesis by which the perceptions of the eye are instantaneously captured by the movements of the hand in the moment of their formation: "Thus, two things are demonstrated in the execution of M. G[uys]: first is the vigor [*contention*] of a resurrectionist and evocative memory, a memory that says to everything: 'Lazarus, arise!'; the second is a fieriness, an intoxication of the pencil or of the brush, that almost seems mad. It is the fear of not going fast enough, of allowing the phantom to escape before its synthesis has been extracted and captured" (1168).

In this notion, Baudelaire's account of memory is complicated significantly. He conceives memory here both as the means by which a resurrection of experience is made possible, and simultaneously as a mediation that inhibits its integral translation.[7] This complication parallels the one in the De Quincey commentary. Again Baudelaire figures memory not as a passive repository of data, but as its active interpreter and critic. Again memory does not reproduce, it *represents*. This destabilization of the relation between memory and the "objective" contents of the past will be critical for reading "Le Cygne," and particularly for understanding what I term the poem's mnemonics of dispossession.

In these texts, Baudelaire seems to be reaching toward a concept of memory that decouples signifying medium from signified representation. This effort was by no means gratuitous. Baudelaire's preoccupation with memory around the time of "Le Cygne" is part of his conception of an intensely historicized and deeply consequential disturbance in the sign.

Recent scholarship on "Le Cygne" has argued conclusively that the

----

7. Paul de Man has provided an acute discussion of this passage and of the conceptual tension at its heart; see "Literary History and Literary Modernity," 158.

poem must be read in its conjuncture. Baudelaire's themes and signifiers cannot be adequately comprehended outside their specific historical situation.[8] Conceiving them as evocations of some abstract
transhistorical dilemma distorts their referentiality severely. Yet such
a vision of "Le Cygne" runs entirely against the grain of Baudelaire's
own professed aesthetic. In a series of powerful and influential essays
from the period of "Le Cygne" itself, Baudelaire argued for a radically *de*-historicizing conception of art. His position in those essays
has virtually defined the reading protocols of modernism. The transcendental understanding of the Swan/Sign play—implicit in Mallarmé, explicit in most post-Mallarméan criticism—thus puts into
practice Baudelaire's own formalizing aesthetic. So critics have
tended to understand Baudelaire's themes "outside of history"—and
they have done so with great productivity. Consequently, a historically conscious criticism is urging us to read Baudelaire against himself and against a powerful critical tradition. I will return to the implications of such a perverse or subversive reading, and to the
conflict within Baudelaire's work that it brings to light.

❀❀❀

> Peu de gens devineront combien il a fallu être triste pour
> entreprendre de resusciter Carthage!
> [Few people will guess how sad one had to be to want to
> resuscitate Carthage.]
> —Gustave Flaubert, letter to Ernest Feydeau,
> 29–30 November 1859; *Correspondance* 3:59.

What needs to be addressed at this point, however, is the specific
content and the conjunctural reference of the complex of themes out
of which "Le Cygne" constructs what I called its "mnemonics of dispossession." What in 1859 was topical, what was resonant, in the
experience of *loss*?

In an essay on the "Tableaux parisiens" section of *Les Fleurs du*

8. In his "Du temps des 'Chats' au temps du 'Cygne,'" Ross Chambers summarizes the
contributions of a number of critics whose interpretations point toward this historicizing
conclusion. More recently, Chambers has himself provided a brilliant interpretation of "Le
Cygne," which has powerfully informed my own analysis: "Mémoire et mélancolie," chap.
6 of *Mélancolie et opposition: Les Débuts du modernisme en France.*

mal, Ross Chambers remarks acutely that relatively few of the poems
in that portion of the collection are set in Paris at all.[9] But "Le
Cygne" is emphatically among these. The poem evokes a specific
Paris *quartier*—the Carrousel, between the Louvre and the Tuileries palaces—whose resonances at the moment of the poem's composition were particularly rich and consequential.[10] But "Le Cygne"
makes it clear that this evocation occurred under the sign of the irretrievable. The Carrousel remembered in "Le Cygne" in 1859 had
been abruptly razed in 1852. Indeed, its demolition was the first, the
founding, act in the transformations that remade Paris under the Second Empire.

Baudelaire's midcentury poem about loss thus calls us to an examination of the dynamics of mutation, displacement, and spoliation in
early Second Empire Paris. We need to understand what was at
stake in the thematic of dispossession that structures "Le Cygne."
Such an analysis will depend upon reconstructing elements of the
political economy, the demography, the urban topography and geography of the period.

"The past is devoured by the present"—this notion, quoted from
Edouard Fournier's 1853 *Paris démoli: Mosaïque de ruines*,[11] became
a commonplace of the period. The intensity of the transformation to
which it refers was unprecedented. David Pinkney offers a simple
observation that frames the generation of what I term the mnemonics
of dispossession: "Parts of cities, even entire new cities like Versailles, Karlsruhe, or Saint-Petersburg, had been planned and built,
but no one before [Napoléon III] had attempted to refashion an entire city."[12] Walter Benjamin had put the point more bluntly in "The
Paris of the Second Empire in Baudelaire": "Along with the growth
of the big cities there developed the means of razing them to the
ground."[13]

----

9. Ross Chambers, "Are Baudelaire's 'Tableaux Parisiens' about Paris?" 97.

10. The poem's own term for the district is "faubourg." The Carrousel *quartier* was
known as the "faubourg du Doyenné"; see F. W. Leakey, "The Originality of Baudelaire's
'Le Cygne': Genesis as Structure and Theme," 54 n. 4.

11. Three years later, Théophile Gautier expropriated Fournier's subtitle and recycled
it as the title of his own essay on the transformations of the city in *Paris et les parisiens au
XIXe siècle* (see Shelley Rice, "Souvenirs," 157).

12. David H. Pinkney, *Napoleon III and the Rebuilding of Paris*, 4.

13. Walter Benjamin, *Charles Baudelaire: A Lyric Poet in the Era of High Capitalism*,
85.

The scale of the changes Parisians had to accommodate during this period can be evoked only through the most meager metonyms. Statistics (already firmly established as part of the innovative discourse by which the culture was organizing its own mutation and seeking to come to terms with it) can provide some basis for understanding the experience of vertigo, of the "immense Newness that swamps us from all sides," to which so many voices around midcentury refer.[14] Examples of this complaint can be found everywhere in the period. The capital was changing extraordinarily fast. Toward the end of his life Michelet (born in 1798) contrasted "the *French* Paris of five hundred thousand souls which existed when I was born" with "the strange *European* Paris of two and a half million which exists today."[15] This summary demography becomes even more arresting if we analyze it more closely. Consider the period evoked in "Le Cygne" itself. In Paris (the Département de la Seine) in the decade between 1846 and 1856, the population grew by 184,767. But of these new Parisians, however, fully 181,637 (or 98.3 percent of the increase) were added in the second half of the ten-year period in question—that is, between 1852 and 1856. In other words, growth between 1846 and 1851 totaled 0.33 percent of the Paris population; but in the first five years of the Second Empire, between 1852 and 1856, it represented an astonishing 13.49 percent, the highest rate of growth in the history of the city.[16]

The agent (and symbolic villain) of these Second Empire transformations of the city was the prefect, Baron Haussmann, who presided over the process that later came to be called Haussmannization.[17] But

14. The quotation is from a letter from Flaubert to Louis Bouilhet, 19 December 1850, in *Correspondance*, 1:730. The social history of statistics in France is beginning to be written. See *La Statistique en France à l'époque napoléonienne*.

15. Cited in Pierre Citron, *La Poésie de Paris dans la Littérature française de Rousseau à Baudelaire*, 2:265. Michelet's undated text is from an unpublished manuscript in the Bibliothèque Historique de la Ville de Paris.

16. The figures are quoted or adapted from Jeanne Gaillard, *Paris, La Ville 1852–1870*, 190–91. Gaillard provides a partial breakdown by district, which further suggests the displacements around the Carrousel itself (35, 192). Briefly, the population of the Tuileries *quartier* was actually *smaller* in 1856 than it had been in 1800, after having grown steadily from 1800 to 1848. This indicates the suddenness and the magnitude of the population drop once the clearance of the Carrousel began.

17. On "Hausmannization," see T. J. Clark, *The Painting of Modern Life: Paris in the Art of Manet and His Followers*, 30, 34. In "The Housing Question," Friedrich Engels put it more laconically. Speaking of "the practice . . . of turning the working-class districts of our big cities into rubble," he wrote: "That method is called 'Haussmann'" (607–8).

Haussmann had not razed the Carrousel. Prior to his tenure, Jean-Jacques Berger had served Napoléon III as préfet de la Seine. Only ten days after the coup d'état Louis-Napoléon decreed the demolition of the Carrousel and appropriated twenty-six million francs for completion of the project. The Doyenné quarter was razed in 1852 under Berger's supervision, beginning a process of Imperial urbanism that lasted two decades and created modern Paris.[18] The photographer Henri Le Secq recorded the demolition in a brilliantly evocative image.[19]

In the face of such rapid and consequential changes, nostalgia is an easily comprehensible reflex. Such nostalgia in the early Second Empire led to widespread efforts to record the elements of the Parisian past whose disappearance was mandated or threatened. Such memorializing efforts were undertaken not only by opponents of the transformations over which Haussmann presided from 1853 to 1870, but even by Haussmann himself: "The Prefect felt strongly that the old streets and buildings, as well as their destruction and rebuilding, should be documented as part of the city's historic records. . . . For this purpose he hired archivists whose association took the official name of City Council Permanent Subcommittee on Historic Works in 1865. These archivists, in turn, advised [the photographer] Marville, who became the official 'Photographe de la ville de Paris.'"[20]

Contemporary attitudes toward the remaking of the city diverged

18. See Eugenia Parry Janis, "Demolition Picturesque: Photographs of Paris in 1852 and 1853 by Henri Le Secq," 33, and Pinkney, *Napoleon III*, 51–52, 80. The original Carrousel project predated the Second Empire. The plan to fill in the break between the Louvre and the Tuileries palaces by constructing a gallery along the new Rue de Rivoli had been devised and begun by Napoléon I. By 1815, however, the new construction had only advanced as far as the Rue de Rohan, and a gap of nearly 250 meters remained. Continuation of the work had been decided by the Republican government in 1849. Their objective was to demolish the slums between the Louvre and the Tuileries and build modern housing for the working population there. But when the Second Republic was overthrown in December 1851, Louis Napoléon modified the project crucially. Gaillard notes the irony of the resurrection of the Republican government's clearance project by Louis-Napoléon for motives completely different from those which had presided over its earlier conception: "The Republican government wanted low-cost housing for workers; Napoléon III gave them the grandiose edifices of the Rue de Rivoli instead" (*Paris*, 24).

19. See Janis, "Demolition Picturesque," 61 n. 4 and figure 7, and Pinkney, *Napoleon III*, plate 12.

20. Shelley Rice, "Parisian Views," 12. On other conservation and archival efforts, see Rice, "Parisian Views"; Janis, "Demolition Picturesque," and Paul Rabinow, *French Modern: Norms and Forms of the Social Environment*, 78.

sharply. To understand them, we could best begin where the demolitions themselves started, with the Carrousel itself and with the
Quartier du Doyenné that surrounded it. A number of critics have
attempted to elucidate what we might term the social geography of
this isolated little Paris neighborhood, which disappeared in 1852.
Much of the critical attention has focused on the squalor of the area.[21]
Critics have tended to recall Balzac's derisive description of the quarter in *La Cousine Bette*. In that novel the sordid Madame Marneffe
lived on the Rue du Doyenné, her residence presumably chosen in
metonymic congruence with the insalubriousness of the district itself. But an entire generation had passed since *La Cousine Bette*
appeared in 1838. The resonances of the Doyenné quarter for Baudelaire diverge significantly from those in Balzac's earlier references
to it.[22]

Of course, Baudelaire's fondness for the Doyenné slum might be
nothing more than the wistfulness of someone no longer able to find
in the terrain of the present the familiar referents of memory. But
since "Le Cygne" is the only poem among Baudelaire's "Tableaux
parisiens" whose action is located in a definite site in Paris (see Citron, *La Poésie de Paris*, 2:358), it would seem likely that the poet's
nostalgia was bound to more specific contents. And indeed, Baudelaire had quite personal associations with the Doyenné. By his time
the quarter had become a well-known hangout of the nascent coun-
terculture, of the Bohème—specifically, of that strain of artistic bohemians who styled themselves the "Noctambules." Dissident artists
frequented the area: Gautier, Esquiros, Champfleury, Privat d'An-
glemont, Alfred Delvau, Fournier. All of them knew each other, and
all wrote about Paris. A number had memorialized the particular and
distinctive flavor of the old Carrousel (Citron, *La Poésie de Paris*,
2:308–12). Two themes recur in their depictions: the curious, almost
pastoral isolation of the area despite its location in the heart of the
city, and the variegated character of the local inhabitants and mer-

21. Helpful discussions of the Carrousel will be found in Burton, *The Context of Baudelaire's "Le Cygne*," 32–35, and Lowry Nelson, Jr., "Baudelaire and Virgil: A Reading of
'Le Cygne,'" esp. 338.
22. In *La Cousine Bette*, Balzac called for the razing and renewal of the Doyenné quarter; the difference between his own attitude and Baudelaire's could hardly be more explicit. See *La Cousine Bette*, in *La Comédie humaine*, 5:27–28.

chants, including (as Champfleury wrote in 1861) "art dealers, used book sellers, prestidigitators, bird merchants of the most varied kinds. . . . All of the arts had come together in that square, which was frequented by museum-goers, poets, and simple strollers" (quoted by Citron, 2:312). The content of the loss evoked by Baudelaire in "Le Cygne" thus begins to clarify itself. The Carrousel was where a group of artists who had made a strategic investment in representing themselves as figuratively homeless in Paris *felt at home.* For this segment of the nascent avant-garde, the razing of the *quartier* was a symbolic eviction—an exile.

Pierre Citron describes the instability of the living situations of these members of the Bohème (2:310–11). Their poverty and their bachelorhood made them habitual itinerants, frequent solitary walkers. Indeed, we might locate here the material basis of (or preconditions for) that distinctive relation to urban reality that Baudelaire was to figure and celebrate in the person of the *flâneur.*[23] In any case, this contextualization of the Carrousel may help to elucidate an element in the poem that has not drawn the attention of critics: the unexpected auroral setting of Baudelaire's recollected walk across the old Carrousel, "à l'heure où sous les cieux / Froids et clairs le Travail s'éveille" ["at the hour when under skies / cold and clear Labor stirs awake"]. What could the poet have been doing there at the crack of dawn? Read against the background of the Noctambules and their affection for the Doyenné, the situation of the poet in relation to the waking city begins to make sense. This relation is one not of participation but of *distinction.* Unlike the workers just bestirring themselves, Baudelaire, we might imagine, has been up all night and, as the conventional city begins its workaday routine, is himself on his way to bed.

In this sense of distinction in "Le Cygne" we can thus read a complex story of class. A sense of simultaneous proximity and distance in relation to the poor, the disadvantaged, and the working class is intensely thematic in Baudelaire after 1848. It is inseparable from his sense of alienation from the bourgeoisie whose parallel difference from the proletariat was experienced by a number of avant-garde

23. On the habits of the bohemians, see Michelle Perrot, ed., *From the Fires of Revolution to the Great War*, vol. 4 of *A History of Private Life*, 250. For more on the constitution of the *flùneur*, see Rice, "Parisian Views," 9. The analysis of the *flùneur* by Walter Benjamin is well known; see *Charles Baudelaire*, 35–66.

artists as a trap they urgently contrived to evade. These writers and painters sought to disown their middle-class social origins—but *without* consenting to fusion with the workers whose class figured the only alternative to the increasingly dominant bourgeoisie itself.[24] This dynamic of class association and dissociation required a complex imaginative ballet. Some of its complications become perceptible in the next phase of an attempt to contextualize the Carrousel. For even if Baudelaire experienced the demolition of the Doyenné quarter as a personal expulsion from a geographic and socio-symbolic area of the capital in which he had been able to feel relatively comfortable, the more macroscopic refashioning of the city dictated by Napoléon III was politically and economically overcoded in ways that he could hardly ignore.

Consider an anecdote told by Maxime Du Camp. Du Camp asked a Second Empire *nouveau riche* how he had made his fortune. The man replied succinctly that he had been expropriated.[25] The point of the jest becomes clear when we consider the mechanism by which Haussmann managed the clearance of poor *quartiers* and the opening of new boulevards. The State was empowered to condemn any property whose demolition was required under the Emperor's urban renewal plan, but it paid generous compensation for the buildings razed. In 1858, a year before "Le Cygne," a new law dramatically increased the profits to expropriated owners. The consequences of demolition were thus very different depending upon your position in the social scale. When a poor quarter like the Doyenné was razed, the inhabitants lost their lodgings—but the landlords made out like bandits.[26]

Most analyses of the Second Empire transformations of the city observe that they were motivated by a desire to prevent any repeat

24. See Richard Terdiman, *Discourse/Counter-Discourse: The Theory and Practice of Symbolic Resistance in Nineteenth-Century France*, 315–18.

25. The anecdote is found in Sigfried Giedion, *Space, Time, and Architecture: The Growth of a New Tradition*, 767.

26. In practice the process was more complex than this. Frequently, only part of a property had to be demolished. Any portion not taken for the opening of a new street could then be resold, with its value increased by proximity to the newly created artery. See Gaillard, *Paris*, 28, and Paul Rabinow, *French Modern*, 83. Rabinow recalls Maurice Halbwachs's seminal thesis, *Les Expropriations et le prix des terrains à Paris de 1860 à 1900*. Halbwachs demonstrated with devastating clarity how Second Empire demolitions and constructions increased the inequality between rich and poor (in Rabinow, *French Modern*, 262).

of proletarian insurrection. And there is no doubt that such claims are well founded.[27] But although such considerations may help account for the design of wide boulevards across which it would be difficult to throw up barricades, much of the logic behind the transformation of Paris lay beyond any narrow logic of counterinsurgency, in the realm of a more macroscopic political economy of the urban space. Ever since the June Days of 1848 and the expulsion from Paris of the revolutionary National Workshops, each succeeding national government had followed a policy of limiting the presence of workers in Paris.[28] Napoléon III was devising and putting into practice a pattern still familiar today: urban renewal means working-class removal. The process excluded the poor. Thus Alain Corbin has characterized Haussmannization as a "social dichotomy of purification"—as the division of Paris between "foul" and "fragrant," that is, between poor and rich. The symbolic charge thus laid on the poor was clear to Baudelaire and the avant-garde.[29]

For Baudelaire, the abstract sympathy for the disadvantaged that we can read in "Le Cygne" permitted living out a hostility to dominant power while simultaneously avoiding the danger of contamination by the underclass. The poor, those who in "Les Veuves" Baudelaire termed "les éclopés de la vie" (life's wounded) (245), offered themselves as a figure for his personal disenchantment and his sense of dispossession. Poets, he wrote in the same text, "feel themselves irresistibly attracted by whatever is weak, ruined, aggrieved, orphaned" (245). Once the inhabitants of the Carrousel quarter—both the bohemians and the simply indigent—had been evicted in 1852, then the knowledge that fortunes had been made out of their misfortune became the focus for a particularly intense form of Baudelairian *ressentiment*. Political economy itself thus comes to serve as a figure for the alienation and exile that "Le Cygne" so insistently textualizes. In this sense the Carrousel might be taken as a privileged site of disadvantage.

27. Clark, *The Painting of Modern Life*, provides a good discussion of and documentation for this claim (39). See also Giedion, *Space, Time, and Architecture*, 740.

28. Thus in 1857 when Napoléon III learned that the Western Railway was planning to move its workshops (and hence a large number of relatively well organized and well educated railroad workers) into Paris, he wrote himself to his minister of finance, to order him to act without delay to prevent this from happening. See Gaillard, *Paris*, 54–55.

29. Alain Corbin, *The Foul and the Fragrant: Odor and the French Social Imagination*, 134. See also Gaillard, *Paris*, 22, and Janis, "Demolition Picturesque," 38.

But the mnemonics of dispossession in "Le Cygne" reaches beyond the understanding of the Doyenné quarter in countercultural imagination. The locution "Paris change!" (Paris is changing) that begins the second part of "Le Cygne" is as resonant an utterance as any in *Les Fleurs du mal*. Its minimalist narrative subverts transhistorical aesthetics—even Baudelaire's own. It leads us to ask what value was attributed by midcentury dissident culture to the notion of *change* itself—particularly, to the early results of the urbanism whose very name was a characteristic product of the period.[30]

Sigfried Giedion frames the problem in a refreshingly straightforward assertion: "Haussmann," he writes, "created the great nineteenth-century city" (*Space, Time, and Architecture*, 762). But "Le Cygne" was written early in the period of the city's transformation. In 1859, Haussmann had been préfet for only six years; Napoléon III had been emperor for only seven. The "creation of the modern city" was still in its opening stages—as was the complex adjustment required of Second Empire culture to the developments it determined. There are advantages to such periods of incipience. The stresses attributable to processes of accommodation such as those which strained Second Empire society are easier to seize early in a period of transformation. In such moments memory of the "time before" is still active; the ideological density of developing reality has not yet obscured the contingency of this new reality and rendered its structures opaque (see Terdiman, *Discourse/Counter-Discourse*, 108). In 1859 "change" itself still *seemed* like change, it had not yet become routinized or transparent. The aggressive refashioning of the city still possessed its transformative force—even its virulence. In the moment of "Le Cygne," the remaking of the city had not yet demolished the memory of the city it remade. It still figured a dialectic, not an ontology. It was still a struggle and hence it generated a narrative— one whose conclusion was not yet foregone in 1859.[31]

In choosing the scene for his evocation of these transformations,

30. See Françoise Choay, *The Modern City: Planning in the 19th Century*, 7.
31. Gaillard recalls Pierre Citron's remark that for the ten years prior to publication of Baudelaire's "Tableaux parisiens," Paris had hardly been taken as a subject by poets at all. We could speculate that this silence was the result of a general uncertainty, in the early stages of the transformation of the capital, about how it might be textualized to begin with. See Gaillard, *Paris*, 561.

Baudelaire picked a site that had disappeared before Haussmann even took office. Berger had managed the demolition of the Doyenné. But by 1859 Berger was gone and Haussmann was in control. Baudelaire's mnemonics of dispossession conflates the two prefects and represents the new Carrousel as a pure Haussmannian production. To understand this thematic in the poem, we need to establish the projection of Haussmann himself active in the imagination of those who formed his opposition at the moment of "Le Cygne."

The primary element framing the symbolic conflict over the city's transformation was *regularity*. In this period of its passing, the old Paris was conceived by Haussmann's antagonists as randomly charming, haphazard, and disparate. For them, Haussmann had violently undone this familiar and appealing character. And it was true that "to regularize" was a key element in the prefect's administrative vocabulary (Choay, *The Modern City*, 15). In response Victor Fournel satirized Haussmann as "the Attila of the straight line."[32] Théophile Gautier's judgment in 1854 was characteristic, and its reference to memory anticipates Baudelaire's own preoccupation: "'Alignment' has split in half a number of memories [*plus d'un souvenir*] that it would have been pleasing to hold on to."[33] But the locus classicus of opposition to the administered rationalization of the city was a poem of Victor Hugo's, repeatedly cited by adversaries of the regime:

> . . . plus de rues
> Anarchiques . . .
> plus de caprice . . .
> Alignement! tel est le mot d'ordre actuel. . . .
> Ce vieux Paris n'est plus qu'une rue éternelle
> Qui s'étire, élégante et belle comme l'I,
> En disant: Rivoli! Rivoli! Rivoli![34]

32. Victor Fournel, *Paris nouveau et Paris futur*; cited in Choay, *Modern City*, 15. Rice reminds us of Hugo's sarcastic observation in *Les Misérables* that even the new Paris sewer system essential to Haussmann's reconstruction of the city was "neat, cold, straight, correct" ("Souvenirs," 165).

33. Gautier's text was originally published in *Le Moniteur universel*, 21 January 1854; a year later it appeared as the preface to the second edition of Fournier's *Paris démoli*. See Janis, "Demolition Picturesque," 39.

34. Victor Hugo, "Les 'Embellissements' de Paris" (1869), cited in Burton, *The Context of Baudelaire's "Le Cygne,"* 39. "Rivoli" is a reference to the new artery on the north edge of the Carrousel reconstruction itself. The avenue was finished in 1858, a year before "Le

[No more anarchic streets, no more caprice. Alignment! this is today's watchword. . . . The old Paris is nothing more than an eternal street which stretches out, elegant and beautiful as an "I" saying, Rivoli! Rivoli! Rivoli!]

With the force of Imperial decree behind him, Haussmann thus
instituted, and was perceived as instituting, the expulsion of the poor
and the creation and segregation of distinct social—that is, class—
zones.[35] Haussmann termed himself—with evident pride—an *artiste
démolisseur* (see Benjamin, *Charles Baudelaire*, 174–75). But we
must be clear about the range of his demolitions. The process of
alignment and regularization he directed always operated in a class-
discriminatory way.

Against this background the socially specific markers of the Carrousel
in "Le Cygne" take on a particularly intense resonance. Consider the
recollected confusion of objects in the poem's third stanza—"Je ne
vois qu'en esprit tout ce camp de baraques, / Ces tas de chapiteaux
ébauchés et de fûts" ["Only in imagination can I still see this whole
shanty camp, / These piles of unfinished sculptures and barrels"]. In
its political and symbolic content the description becomes readable
as an inverted image, as a counterdiscourse, of Second Empire "regularization." It valorizes disorder as the contrary of an established
order conceived as intolerably oppressive.

But the consequences of the Haussmannian refashioning of the city
are even more striking on the level of ideology and of the transformed structures of perception that they constituted as everyday

---

Cygne." The Imperial justification for the Carrousel project was that it was necessary to
complete the Rue de Rivoli and extend the Louvre toward the Tuileries Palace. The mo-
notonous regularity of the buildings that Haussmann had designed to border the Rue de
Rivoli became a subject for aesthetic protest and parody. But beyond any such architectural controversy the political resonances of the creation of the Rue de Rivoli—like the
sociological resonances of the Carrousel clearance before it—need to be specified precisely. The underlying purpose of the project was to obliterate what those in power perceived as the squalid and dangerous enclave of the Doyenné, just as Balzac had depicted it
in *La Cousine Bette*. This was the area which Mercier had contemptuously termed the
"citrouille." See Gaillard, *Paris*, 32.
    35. For a summary of critiques of Haussmann's policies, see Burton, *The Context of
Baudelaire's "Le Cygne,"* 36. See also Rice, "Parisian Views," 9, and Clark, *The Painting of
Modern Life*, 43–46 and 276 n. 55.

experience for Parisians. Of course Paris had been changing incrementally for many years. In 1836 Musset was already framing the theme: "We live on debris, as if the end of the world was coming."[36] But the acceleration and above all the *rationalization* and *centralization* of change once Haussmann became préfet in 1853 gave a focus to this awareness that had been absent before. This complex of perceptions of displacement, loss, and transformation materializes as an *experience of history*, and it is this experience of history that made Baudelaire's sudden thematization of memory comprehensible.

The issue was timely. The amalgam of nostalgia, anxiety, and contestation that characterizes "Le Cygne" repeated itself through broad segments of the culture. Just a year after "Le Cygne" Edmond and Jules de Goncourt gave a particularly acute analysis of the mutation of Paris life:

> Our Paris, the Paris in which we were born, the Paris of the manners of 1830 to 1848, is disappearing. And it is not just disappearing materially but also morally. Social life is beginning to undergo a great change. I can see women, children, husbands and wives, whole families in this café. Home life is dying. Life is threatening to become public. The club for the upper classes, the café for lower—this is what society and the common people are coming to. All this makes one feel like a stranger in one's spiritual homeland. We are strangers to what is coming and to what is here, as for example these new boulevards which have nothing of Balzac's world about them but make one think of London or some Babylon of the future. It is dumb to live in a time of change [*Il est bête de venir ainsi dans un temps en construction*]; the soul feels as uncomfortable as a man who moves into a new house before the plaster is dry.[37]

The site of the Goncourts' reflections was a café on the newly constructed Boulevard de Strasbourg, which Haussmann had just created to connect the Ile de la Cité and the Gare de l'Est. Their

36. Alfred de Musset, *La Confession d'un enfant du siècle* (1836), 105.

37. Edmond de Goncourt and Jules de Goncourt, *Journal: Mémoires de la vie littéraire*, 1:835; cited in Clark, *The Painting of Modern Life*, 34 and 273 n. 16. Clark gives a broad selection of reactions to the transformations of the city around this time (30–36). The translation of this passage is adapted from *Pages from the Goncourt Journal*, trans. Robert Baldick, 53.

analysis thus arises and is situated in an unprecedented Parisian landscape, an urban topography that had not even been imagined a decade before. The experience of a scandalous estrangement, of an uncanny dispossession in the heart of the familiar—these are the crucial notes in this contemporary diagnosis of the cultural resonances produced by the transformation of Paris. Moreover the curious expression that concludes the Goncourt text—"moving into a new house before the plaster is dry"—was not simply a metaphor the Goncourts came up with to characterize the awkwardness of the accommodations required of Parisians by the city's transformations. "Essuyer les plâtres" referred to something specific and symbolically charged. In the Paris of Haussmannization, almost-completed buildings were left to prostitutes for a short time until the plaster had dried enough to permit final finishing work. The middle class moved in when the hookers left (see Corbin, *The Foul and the Fragrant*, 25). The image of the new Paris, tacky and incomplete, the site of a new middle class of proprietors who seemed virtually to blend with the prostitutes who had anticipated them in their lodgings, pins down with considerable intensity how highly overcoded were these transformations of the city's urban and social fabric.

Haussmann's opponents were not alone in perceiving a connection between urban topography and the character of social existence in the city. Haussmann himself believed strongly in such relations. He and his planners foresaw that their alteration of the city would change more than its geography. They consciously sought to alter the habits and the perceptions of Parisians through the same mutations that produced new districts, boulevards, and *places*. They thus gave careful attention not only to the economics or the topography of their constructions, but to their *ideology*. They were concerned with symmetry, perspective, and their perceptual effects (see Giedion, *Space, Time, and Architecture*, 745–54). Haussmann's constructions make clear his implicit belief in the *symbolic expressiveness* of the urban fabric. His disposition of space was intended to communicate, was meant to determine perception. However contrary their reactions to the transformations of the city, Hugo, the Goncourts, Baudelaire, and their contemporaries were correct to read in these transformations of the city Haussmann's intention to create in Paris not only new streets and spaces, but new *meanings*. A reading of "Le Cygne" in terms of the poem's consciousness of the sign gains pertinence in such a conjuncture.

The results of such transformed meanings can be seen clearly in Jeanne Gaillard's discussion of what the Goncourts might have termed the "moral" consequences of Haussmannization:

> Under the Second Empire, the State exploited the general alter-ation that was occurring in Paris to *permanently modify the rela-tionship between the residents and their city*, to change the very essence of the notion of urban citizenship: they strove to contain Parisians rather than fostering active community.
>
> The collective aspirations which nevertheless continued to mani-fest themselves, first in alimentary practices, but in habits of dress and of leisure, thus remained unresponded to. . . . So much the worse for simple people who expected everything from the City. They would attempt to alter their relation to the collectivity, first in the Paris Commune, and after the Commune through the mech-anism of municipal socialism. (*Paris*, 231–32; emphasis Gaillard's)

As Gaillard suggests, the response of the Commune to the Second Empire gives striking evidence of how Imperial transformations were experienced and understood. By separating individuals and classes from each other Haussmann had produced a sense of exile among the disadvantaged—indeed, had forcefully focused the perception of *dis-advantage* itself as a social and cultural construct. The Commune's seizure of power demystified such exile; the underclass took posses-sion against their dispossession. In this sense the Commune provides a retrospective interpretation of the Imperial regime. The utopian aspirations to which the Communards sought to give political form in 1871 map the distortions and oppressions that marginalized citizens of the Second Empire experienced under the regime they finally overthrew. In this sense, the powerful desublimation of politics that occurred in 1871 clarifies and confirms the sublimated political intu-ition that, in the figures of dispossession in "Le Cygne," we can read in Baudelaire in 1859.

Let us therefore examine examples of the Haussmannian restruc-turing to which one might attribute ideological effects of the sort texts like "Le Cygne" contested. Consider the segregation of the Im-perial regime's administrative functions on the Ile de la Cité. Haussmann achieved this by demolishing a collection of slum dwellings west of Notre-Dame similar to those which had been razed in the Carrousel just prior to his taking office. The result was to create not only a new *quartier*, but a new *type* of *quartier*: a specifically "official" district, containing the Préfecture de police, a military barracks, the Palais de justice, the Tribunal de commerce, the Conciergerie prison, the central hospital—a district, in other words, from which the Paris populace itself was systematically excluded.[38] These administrative buildings were protected from mass political action by the river and could be isolated from uprisings by guarding the bridges. Democratic tradition required that the locus of State power remain within Paris rather than moving outside the capital, for example, to Versailles. Although nominally respecting this tradition, Haussmann's administrative quarter effectively separated the site of power from the people who were ruled by it.[39]

The ideological result of such segregation was expressed as early as 1864 by Auguste Cochin. He observed that after Haussmann's refashioning of the city, the population of Paris were no longer *citizens*, only *inhabitants*.[40] The model of such segregation was also applied to the isolation of the old working-class districts. The Faubourg Saint-Antoine and the other popular *quartiers* were effectively marooned by the new boulevards cut through by Haussmann (see Clark, *The Painting of Modern Life*, 46). The resistance of the disadvantaged to their exclusion and isolation may have been intense, but in the aggregate it was futile.[41]

38. T. J. Clark observes that the Préfecture de police was built with "glee" on the site of Eugène Suë's notorious thieves' kitchen; see *The Painting of Modern Life*, 50.

39. Gaillard, *Paris*, 33; see also Pinkney, *Napoléon III*, 87. I have already mentioned the effects of this eviction of the people from the center: a precipitous decline in the census of residents living in the districts there. In many of them the total population was lower in 1856 than it had been in 1800 (Gaillard, 35). In the case of the Cité, the population declined from 14,000 in 1850 to only a few hundred twenty years later (Pinkney, 87–88).

40. Auguste Cochin, *Paris, sa population, son industrie*; quoted in Burton, *The Context of Baudelaire's "Le Cygne,"* 41. The same point is made by Françoise Choay, cited in Gaillard, *Paris*, 3. On the forced evictions and displacements of the poor, see also Clark, *The Painting of Modern Life*, 45. He recalls Haussmann's own observation that rents in central Paris doubled between 1851 and 1857. What the demolitions themselves failed to do, economic factors thus ensured.

41. See Gaillard, *Paris*, 207. The effects of such geographic isolation of the working class in Second Empire Paris are notoriously a theme of Emile Zola's *Assommoir*.

What of the *representational* effects of the new urban structures? With Haussmann, macroscopic effects of urban *scale* for the first time begin to intrude upon perception. Haussmann's "cannonshot boulevards" (Giedion's term)—some of them three miles long—produced perspectives that could be conceived abstractly, but never directly perceived by the senses (*Space, Time, and Architecture*, 739). In some cases the linear arteries that the préfet drove through the jumble of an essentially medieval city sought to emphasize the grandiosity of a monument. The Avenue de l'Opéra created a perspective for Garnier's wedding-cake opera house, not completed until 1874; the Étoile valorized the Arc de Triomphe, which had been finished in 1836 (see Pinkney, *Napoleon III*, 86–87 and 217). But most of the new boulevards simply dwarfed and distorted the neighborhoods through whose hearts they were driven. Shelley Rice puts these effects well: "Those who lived through the transformation of Paris were . . . living through an era of multiple and shifting perspectives, a time when confrontation between human experience and the artificial range of large-scale visual spaces was causing vistas to break down, objects to lose their solidity, and people to redefine not only their habits and lifestyles but also their very perceptions of their physical selves within the environment" ("Parisian Views," 10).

Opponents of the regime and of its refashioning of the city felt that in the new Paris it was impossible for a resident to experience harmonious association with the urban space. The new city seemed vast beyond any conceivable emotional investment, determined by obscure forces impossible to control or even to influence (see Gaillard, *Paris*, 3 and 231–32). In *The Modern City*, Françoise Choay echoes these claims: "Following the loss of partial conscious control and of implicit subconscious control [by Parisians of their own milieux], those experiencing the urban phenomenon came to consider it as something alien. They no longer felt inside the process . . . ; they remained outside, observing the transformation with the eye of a spectator" (9; translation modified).

Choay's concept of the city is of considerable interest. She frames it as a semiotic system, in terms of the perception of competence or control available to those functioning within its code:

Until the Industrial Revolution, the urban complex may have been a semiotic system, whose elements were related synchronically within context of rules and a code practiced by inhabitant and planner alike. By virtue of its relationship with all the other social systems (political power, learning, economy, religion), the urban system asserted itself as one of communication and information. In other words, the citizen in the process of inhabiting his city is integrated into the structure of a given society at a specific moment in time, and every plan that might exist corresponds implicitly to that structure which it both institutes and controls. . . .

The Industrial Revolution brought about a radical transformation. . . . The city dweller . . . was unable to assimilate this urban revolution in terms of any previous process. . . . He was now confronted with a spatial order devoid of its traditional richness of meaning. It had become monosemantic in the sense that its organization derived solely from the economic cause of its high demographic concentration. (*The Modern City*, 7–8)

In effect, Choay's theory translates Tönnies's distinction between *Gemeinschaft* and *Gesellschaft* into Saussurian terms. Her model is strikingly congruent with the perceptions of dispossession and disorientation felt by Baudelaire and his avant-garde contemporaries.

These perceptions of the new Paris help to explain the uncanny sense of *exile at home* that preoccupied so many of these figures—as if the city were a language that had mutated so rapidly that even its native locutors discovered they could no longer speak it. As the familiar semiotics of the city was thus forcibly displaced, the signifiers that came to compose its new and unfamiliar language were perceived as artificial, inauthentic, or counterfeit. The Paris refashioned by Haussmann began to feel like a space of bogus signifiers. His opponents saw a city in which styles, forms, and functions were unintelligibly garbled and promiscuously confused, undistinguished and undistinguishable. One of the centerpieces of the new Imperial architecture, the extension of the Louvre along the edge of the "renewed" Carrousel itself, was criticized along precisely these lines: "Our new Louvre is excessive and ridiculous, gigantic but not great."[42]

42. Louis Veuillot, *Les Odeurs de Paris* (1867), 183; cited in Burton, *The Context of Baudelaire's "Le Cygne,"* 49.

The new Louvre was inaugurated in 1857. Two years later it appeared in "Le Cygne," scornfully denied the authenticity of its definite article, disdainfully devalorized as "*ce* Louvre" [*that* Louvre].[43]

A notion of such architectural and functional inauthenticity had been forming well before Haussmann took office, for example in Hugo's bitingly sarcastic celebration of the new urban architecture in *Notre-Dame de Paris* (1831):

> We can never be sufficiently amazed at a monument which can equally well be a royal palace, a house of commons, a town hall, a college, a riding school, an academy, an entrepôt, a tribunal, a museum, a barracks, a sepulchre, a temple, a theatre. For the time being it is a Stock Exchange. . . .
>
> Without doubt these are quite superb monuments. Add to them a quantity of handsome streets, amusing and varied like the Rue de Rivoli, and I do not despair that Paris, seen from a balloon, should one day present that richness of line, that opulence of detail, that diversity of aspect, that hint of the grandiose in the simple and the unexpected in the beautiful, which characterizes a checkerboard.[44]

But after Louis-Napoléon's seizure of power, the pertinence of such a rhetoric increased considerably over what it had been under Louis-Philippe. As T. J. Clark points out (*The Painting of Modern Life*, 33), Second Empire pamphleteers liked to take Hugo's satirical tour de force as an emblem for their own attacks on the new city Haussmann was creating. In the hands of Haussmann's critics, the trope of an indiscriminate garbling of signifiers and signifieds was the same one Hugo had employed under the July Monarchy. But during the Second Empire the urban referent offered even less resistance to the figure because the scale of Haussmann's reconstructions was so much more extensive and their political and ideological bearing so much more naked than any previous efforts to refashion the city. Here is a typical broadside, describing Haussmann's newly con-

43. The "new" Louvre, designed by Louis Visconti, was begun on 25 July 1852 and was inaugurated in the presence of the emperor on 14 August 1857. That ceremony was thus a recent memory at the time Baudelaire wrote "Le Cygne."

44. Victor Hugo, *Notre-Dame de Paris, 1482* (1967), 157–58; cited and translated in Clark, *The Painting of Modern Life*, 32.

structed mansions—presumably built for the regime's newly structed rich—on the Rue de Rivoli: "This bronze is really tin, this gold is painted on. These palaces are like theater sets: it's best to see them from a distance."[45]

As this contemptuous rhetoric evolved, three linked metaphors came to dominate its corrosive imagery: *merchandising*, *theater*, and *prostitution*. These were figures drawn from the everyday reality of Second Empire Paris, available for representing a world in which nothing corresponded to the falsified appearance of its surface. At the guilty center of the new ersatz Imperial reality stood the Emperor Napoléon himself, instantly seen beginning in 1852 by a broad group of critics—ranging from Marx on the left to Alexis de Tocqueville on the right—as a debased forgery, a knockoff, of his illustrious uncle.[46] As the discourse of critique formed around his regime, it seized upon the fundamental *underdetermination* of Imperial reality: on an absence of positive content or political principle, on a constant and mystifying surplus of signifier over signified. The Second Empire seemed founded upon a programmatic politics of sham.

The Haussmannian city could then serve as a figure for a deeper perception about Second Empire reality: the notion that such "reality" was itself increasingly tenuous, was slipping away under the pressure of appearance, image, and manipulated belief. The representations readable in Haussmann's urbanism seemed homologous with an impulse toward the simulated and the spurious, toward mystification and inauthenticity. Phoniness propagated. In 1862 the one-time Noctambule Alfred Delvau castigated the modes of public display encouraged in the Second Empire bourgeoisie by the existence of the new boulevards: "Their luxury is entirely on the surface, all their riches are on display, all their seductions are for sale, all their pleasures are walking the street."[47] For the regime's critics, the practices of such vulgarity, arising in an increasing disconnection between signifiers and the realities to which they pointed, served as a metonym for the Second Empire's conversion of reality into a depth-

45. Fournel, *Paris nouveau et Paris futur*; cited in Burton, *The Context of Baudelaire's "Le Cygne,"* 44.

46. See Richard Terdiman, "1848" and "1852."

47. Alfred Delvau, *Les Dessous de Paris*, 134; cited in Burton, *The Context of Baudelaire's "Le Cygne,"* 43.

less and inauthentic image. The increasingly liberated play of these urban, political, and social signifiers—far from inducing some proto-poststructuralist enthusiasm—scandalized critics of the Imperial regime. They conceived the freedom of signs in the Second Empire as a contemptible wantonness. The increasingly unstable semiotization of the city and the culture was represented as a field of systematic and culpable falsity.

But this indiscriminate instability of ideological and material signifiers in nineteenth-century urban space was the condition of possibility for critical consciousness of the semiotic phenomenon itself. What was new and urgent in Haussmann's Paris was an atmosphere of *trouble around the sign.* Such semiotic disquiet stimulated intense interrogation and incited anxious analysis. Particularly, in the case that concerns me here, the scandal of disarticulated signs that preoccupied cultural imagination in Second Empire Paris is what made it possible to write "Le Cygne." Indeed, the uncanny phenomenon of semiotic lability was what made the word play of Baudelaire's title readable to begin with.

⚜⚜⚜

> The slightest alteration in the relation between man and
> signifier . . . changes the whole course of history by mod-
> ifying the moorings that anchor his being.
> —Jacques Lacan, "The Agency of the Letter
> in the Unconscious," in *Écrits,* 174

The notion of the sign may be transhistorical, but a culture's preoccupation with its perplexities is overdetermined by its own internal stresses—by a complex of needs generated within a specific history of cultural practices and material tensions. The precipitation of the sign problem was conjuncturally produced. In that sense, the Second Empire is the moment not only of "Le Cygne" but of the sign itself.

The pertinence and the urgency of the sign problem became focused in the atmosphere of signifying instability mediated by the Second Empire's transformations. As I have argued, such transformations determined alterations not only of urban topography, but of more symbolic structures. At the same time, the *complication* of urban reality was increasing as population grew, as political relations and processes became more intricate, as economic activity became more highly differentiated, as the circulation and distribution of goods and messages become more pervasive (see Terdiman, *Discourse/Counter-Discourse*, chap. 2). In such a situation, signs disengaged themselves from the background that once had seemed to absorb or camouflage them. They interposed themselves as an uncanny presence between consciousness and the increasingly problematic realities of urban existence, in the mode of a seemingly perverse intermediary whose increasing intricacy determined a complex of new cognitive concepts and a tangled network of new cultural practices.

Even in the hard-headed realm of economics, signs were becoming refractory. The extension of credit necessary to the economic expansion of Second Empire society posed a conceptual—one might almost say a *psychological*—problem for those involved in administering it. As in the more strictly linguistic realm, this was the period when the signifiers of fiduciary and scriptural wealth began increasingly to distance themselves from the palpable referent—specie, cash money—upon which they were notionally founded and for which they had been supposed to stand. Homologous with the semiotic uncertainties within which Baudelaire was trying to navigate, we could understand the period's confusions and crises concerning the mechanisms of credit as a perplexity about signs.

Symbolic instruments of credit—uncannily abstract or ghostly signifiers of property—were proliferating in the period. The Comptoir d'Escompte had instituted the use of personal checks in 1848. Paper money, discounted bills, loans on securities, letters of credit were all available mechanisms by the early years of Napoléon III's reign. Just after the coup d'état in 1852 the Pereire brothers founded the Crédit mobilier, and almost immediately won the emperor's support for their enterprise.[48] But despite these mechanisms—or because of

48. It was the Crédit mobilier that largely financed Haussmann's reconstruction of Paris, but the depression of 1857–58 strained the institution considerably, and precipitated widespread fears of a crash. It nearly became insolvent in 1867, and survived only when the government persuaded the Banque de France to maintain its liquidity. The Crédit mobilier lasted until the end of the Empire—significantly, Haussmann himself became its head after the emperor dismissed him as préfet. Finally, it was dissolved and reorganized after the Commune. On these developments, see Gaillard, *Paris*, 387–88; Rondo Cameron, *France and the Economic Development of Europe*, chap. 7; and David Harvey,

them—France during the Second Empire experienced a chronic crisis of economic confidence, attributable to a lack of trust in the increasingly mystifying instruments of credit, which seemed so distant from "real" wealth. In this immediately consequential realm too, it was becoming apparent that signs were far from simple.[49]

One of the names for the moment of this problematization—diagnostic in Baudelaire's lexicon—is "modernity." "Modernity" is a reflex of ambivalence in the face of the transformations of the world. For Baudelaire and for many who follow him, the concept of modernity is an attempt to evade or to disable contradictions inherent in the experience of modern life itself. But the concept carries with it a paradox that has had unfortunate consequences for our understanding of the cultural system—"modernism"—of which "modernity" offers an analysis. No notion could be more historically determined (or determinist) than "modernity." The concept situates itself in a tense relation defined by its assertion of difference from traditional culture. But the very strategy of such denegation requires modernists to deny such contingency, such bound relation to the past. To put this another way, the notion of modernity was constituted as a process to blank out its own constitution as a process to begin with.[50] But such suppression leaves traces. Particularly, the desire to conceive the modern as transcending all temporality, all anteriority, as instituting an absolute present, collides with the complex of conjunctural suspicion about the present itself which the first part of this chapter sought to depict.

Paul de Man framed the stakes in the "modernism" dispute clearly: "Modernity exists in the form of a desire to wipe out whatever came earlier, in the hope of reaching at last a point that could be called a true present, a point of origin that marks a new departure" ("Literary

Consciousness and the Urban Experience: Studies in the History and Theory of Capitalist Urbanization, chap. 3, especially section 2.

49. The semiotics of money has been widely examined. See Jean-Joseph Goux, *Economie et symbolique and Les Monnayeurs du langage*; Ferruccio Rossi-Landi, *Linguistics and Economics*; Marc Shell, *The Economy of Literature*; Harvey, *Consciousness and the Urban Experience*, especially chap. 1; and Terdiman, *Discourse/Counter-Discourse*, especially 114.

50. The contradictions of "modernity" are at the center of Paul de Man's "Literary History and Literary Modernity." See also Clark, *The Painting of Modern Life*, 10–14, and Terdiman, *Discourse/Counter-Discourse*, part 3.

History and Literary Modernity," 148). But as de Man explain
desire for transcendence, for an origin beyond contingency, rapidly
subverts itself: "As soon as modernism becomes conscious of its own
strategies . . . it discovers itself to be . . . part of a generative scheme
that extends far back into the past. . . . Considered as a principle of
life, modernity becomes a principle of origination and turns at once
into a generative power that is itself historical" (150). The impulse to
transcend contingency paradoxically produces the contrary of the result desired, and reinscribes at the heart of its own paradigm the
conjunctural determination it had sought to escape.

We can read such a conflict clearly in Baudelaire. He was preoccupied with the "modern" when he was writing "Le Cygne."[51] The
complications in his conceptualization are revealing. He hesitated
between conflicting paradigms for imagining the experience of time
and, particularly, of cultural activity. At the heart of his writing in
1859, Baudelaire seemed to waver between a vision of time and of
art as transcendent and absolute, and a contradictory sense of their
intense determination by historical conjuncture. This consequence of
his search for a stable anchor for aesthetic activity in a period seemingly so antithetical to aesthetic impulses is striking. His effort de-
vises a powerful tactic for suppressing anteriority, for evading the
complications of the historical and the political. And then it bares
and subverts the tactic itself.

Baudelaire begins by essentializing the presentness of the present:
"Le plaisir que nous retirons de la représentation du présent tient
non-seulement à la beauté dont il peut être revêtu, mais aussi à sa
qualité essentielle de présent" ["The pleasure we draw from the representation of the present arises not only in the beauty which may
accompany it, but also in its essential quality of *present*"] ("Le
Peintre de la vie moderne," 1153). But in "Le Cygne," written at the
same time, Baudelaire negates precisely this move. Rather than absolutizing the present, he radically empties it. Through the mnemonics of dispossession, he constructs a model by which the present—and by extension all immediate social and cultural reality—is

51. Baudelaire's essay on Constantin Guys, "Le Peintre de la vie moderne," written
between 1858 and 1860, offers the most striking evidence of his concern with the issue at
that time. For discussion of the precise date of this essay, see *Oeuvres complètes*, ed.
Pichois, 2:1418.

displaced or even suppressed. Such reality sheds its appearance of transcendence and mutates into an intense reinscription of history. Contemporaneity is then vertiginously rewritten as a relic of the past, as a simulacrum. The divorce between *now* and *then* that any formalism projects in its refusal of extra-aesthetic determination is transformed into a disquieting investment of the present by contents from the past that finally bleach out presentness entirely.

This Baudelairian conflict over the "modern" is homologous with another whose traces were essential in 1859: the effort to frame and solidify the paradigm of "L'Art pour l'art."[52] The formalizing, desocializing, dehistoricizing dynamic we associate with this doctrine had begun to be worked out as early as Gautier's 1832 preface to *Albertus*,[53] and was more fully elaborated in the preface to his *Mademoiselle de Maupin* (1836). But the theory of a poetry radically divorced from political, social, and moral questions was given its canonical form by Baudelaire himself in the very year of "Le Cygne," in his 1859 essay on Gautier (675–700). There, in a celebrated dictum, Baudelaire insisted that "la Poésie . . . n'a pas d'autre but qu'Elle-même" ["Poetry has no other aim than Itself"] (685). For Baudelaire's poetry and for an entire subsequent literary tradition, such a pristine and transcendent formalism, prescribing and celebrating the insulation and isolation of the aesthetic, has been taken as sovereign.

Baudelaire's 1859 essay on Gautier thus consecrates the formalist impulse, but "Le Cygne" simultaneously subverts it. Not only does the poem violate the essay's proscription of the political and the social, but—more subversively still—it narrates the process by which the desocialized and depoliticized ontology glorified in the Gautier piece became ascribed as the ideal of poetry in the first place. The poem undoes the essay, and with it the doctrine the essay had sought to stabilize.

In this perspective, the figurative story of "Le Cygne" is simple. Nineteenth-century formalism sought to suppress, sought actively

52. In an example of the intertextual impulse whose pervasion of "Le Cygne" will occupy my discussion, we should note that the phrase "L'Art pour l'art" seems to have been coined by Victor Hugo himself. See Philippe Van Tieghem, *Les Grandes Doctrines littéraires en France*, 236.

53. Théophile Gautier, *Poésies complètes*, 1:81–84.

and purposely to *forget*, the existence of the political and the conjunctural that it functioned to hold at a distance (see de Man, "Literary History and Literary Modernity," 157). But the intensity of the memories of the political and the social represented in "Le Cygne" sustains precisely the relation with sociopolitical contents that formalist aesthetics had been devised to banish. In "Le Cygne" the romantic topos of poetic exile and the parallel Parnassian absolutization of aesthetic transcendence are forcefully reconceived as historical *productions*.

I interrogate Baudelaire's aesthetics not to fault him for inconsistency, but to show how his inconsistencies are symptomatic of the cultural disquiet that I have been attempting to portray. Absolutizing the present (the characteristic gesture of modernism) and absolutizing the cultural object (the effect of nineteenth-century formalism) are moves that seek to undo the instability of the sign. But for Second Empire culture such instability inevitably carries the mark of the conjunctural, of history. It is the *differentia specifica* that defines this period. So it should come as no surprise that Baudelaire, while forcefully asserting the aesthetic ideology that denies the links between a text and its social determinations, at the same time (though always in a different register) powerfully subverted precisely this position.

So an irrepressible *otherness* of signs, an irreducible *unruliness* of language, might paradoxically come to seem the lone unambiguous signifier in Baudelaire's culture. It means that the culture's own uneasiness about its constitution has come to consciousness and must be addressed on the level of the elements of consciousness itself: on the level of language. In the face of the anxieties such a task generates, one can easily understand a nostalgia for the recovery of an unproblematic relation to the real—the desire, the need to prevent the disaggregation of the past or reliably stabilize the present. This is the retrospective, elegiac atmosphere that dominates "Le Cygne." But under Napoléon III's regime, in Haussmann's Paris, like urban geography itself, language declines to be stable, refuses to settle down and serve as the docile carrier of unambiguous meanings. Second Empire culture *has* no unambiguous meanings for language to carry: at the limit its meaning is that *meaning can mean anything*. The pun in Baudelaire's title instantiates and profits from this slippage.

Under such circumstances language separates itself from its locutors and comes to face them as an adversary. Writing becomes an
intricate and risky sport:

> Je vais m'exercer seul à ma fantasque escrime,
> Flairant dans tous les coins les hasards de la rime,
> Trébuchant sur les mots comme sur les pavés. . . .
>   "Le Soleil" (79)

[I go practicing solo my fantastic swordsmanship / Sniffing out
chances of rhyme at every street corner / Tripping on words like
cobblestones.]

Then exile and dispossession—the mood of "Le Cygne" and of so
much cultural expression after midcentury—become comprehensible
as effects of a newly perceived density and indocility of language. A
faith in referentiality was fundamental to the cultural assumptions of
Balzac, Hugo, or Stendhal only a short period before Baudelaire.
That is why we associate the thematization of history with that so-
called realist generation. Such a confidence remained basic to middle-class economic activity, as it did to the process of Haussmannization itself. But suddenly, for avant-garde consciousness, it no longer
seemed sustainable.

"Le Cygne" is constituted in the outflow of such developments and
such perceptions. From its opening words the poem is structured by
the systematic withdrawal of the referential. The text narrates an archetypal semiotics of bereavement. The poem's practice of the sign
represents the new situation of semiosis under the conditions of the
modern social and economic formation that Napoléon III and his regime were instituting in France after midcentury (see Terdiman,
"1852").

"Le Cygne" thematizes these developments in the figure of memory. *To remember is always to be separated.* In the poem, that separation, analogous to the scission in the sign, becomes the subject
of a series of explicit evocations of loss. The poem memorializes
the elements whose passing has produced an intense experience of
mourning. Mnemonics and semiotics thus metaphorize each other in
"Le Cygne." For as it comes into focus in the period of the Second
Empire, the logic of signs affirms that *the signified is always absent.*

Under the sign of semiotics, history becomes conceivable as the continual creation of new absences. This would be a fair characterization of the thematics of "Le Cygne" itself. What the poem manifests is that the semiotic arises in an irreducible displacement—that "distance" which separates, which in effect exiles, all signs from their referents (indeed, in whose absence we would have no need or use for signs to begin with). It represents this displacement as an uprooting determined by political or social expatriation. The semiotic complex through which Baudelaire figures exile in this poem thus really establishes a zero-degree *politics of the sign.*

Today the perspective on language and on the sign that takes form in "Le Cygne" seems familiar to us. We have grown accustomed to the notion (to quote Maurice Blanchot's influential version) that a word "is not the expression of a thing, but of its absence. . . . The word makes things disappear and asserts the impression of a universal lack [*manque universel*], and even of its own absence [*manque*]."[54] But in "Le Cygne" in 1859 such a representation of semiosis broke new ground.

I have argued elsewhere that new intellectual or conceptual instruments tend to arise when the sort of "lack" that Blanchot refers to in this passage takes form in social experience (see Terdiman, *Discourse/Counter-Discourse*, 97). But of such lacks, the absence constituting semiosis forms an elemental case. The deficiency it puts in play overarches other instantiations because it arises in the material of signification itself. Through this rehistoricization of the elements of the language of "Le Cygne," it becomes possible to understand on the basis of what concrete experiences of displacement and dispossession Baudelaire, in this founding text for modern understandings of the semiotic, materializes a haunting image of the sign.

"Le Cygne" creates a figure in which the sign and the sociohistorical are made to represent and codetermine each other. What is at issue in the poem is the formation of a vision of language and the past

54. Maurice Blanchot, "Le Paradoxe d'Aytré," 1580. No doubt consciously, Blanchot echoes Mallarmé's celebrated evocation of the poetic (or semiotic) flower as "l'absente de tous bouquets" ("Crise de vers," in Stéphane Mallarmé, *Oeuvres complètes*, 360). For a more recent expression of the same position, compare the assertion by Ernesto Laclau and Chantal Mouffe: "The sign is the name of a split, of an impossible suture between signifier and signified" (*Hegemony and Socialist Strategy: Towards a Radical Democratic Politics*, 113 and n. 22).

that might adequately comprehend realities in both of these realms—
realities that the developments of the early Second Empire brought
powerfully into focus. On the horizon of Baudelaire's conception is a
strikingly sophisticated notion of the *interdependence* of conceptual
and historical structures.

In his 1964 essay "Nietzsche, Freud, Marx," Michel Foucault detected vivid—indeed, somewhat startling—emotional resonances in
the semiotic developments in question here. One would not necessarily have expected to attribute affective resonances to the dry
mechanism of semiosis itself, but Foucault claimed that beginning in
the nineteenth century, signs became "malevolent": "There is in the
sign an ambiguous and even suspect means of willing evil."[55] "Le
Cygne" offers an interpretation of this development—a development
about whose tonality Baudelaire and Foucault seem in agreement.
But how could we conceive such malevolence arising in the apparently neutral and abstract processes of semiosis? We find a clue in an
article by Michel de Certeau. In it, de Certeau considers a curious
convergence between *belief* and *desire*. He observes that they have
an element in common: the disappearance of their object does not
diminish them. On the contrary, upon such disappearance belief and
desire turn "violent." For de Certeau, writing—or semiosis, as we
might generalize his insight—is motivated by just this sort of impas-
sioned relationship with something lost.[56] In this perspective, a
bereavement determines all expression. Writing always confirms a
rupture. Texts are always written from exile. Language is always
shipwrecked, eternally marooned like the forgotten sailors lost on
their island with whom Baudelaire movingly ends the litany of the
dispossessed in "Le Cygne." Beginning from such a conclusion it becomes possible to reread the poem from its opening.

"Le Cygne" plays the game of signs with deadly seriousness. The
poem starts with a memorable apostrophe, but an apostrophe to
someone irretrievably lost. The materialization of such a figure in
thought thus resonates with a constitutive desperation; the intensity
of such a relationship with the irretrievable could hardly be greater.

55. Michel Foucault, "Nietzsche, Freud, Marx," 191.
56. Michel de Certeau, "Le Corps et les musiques de l'esprit," 12.

The first words of any text are almost completely underdetermined: one might have started anywhere and said anything; yet for well over a century readers have found the beginning of "Le Cygne" astounding. "Andromaque, je pense à vous. . . . " The form of this address is unexpected; but its *force* seems to come from nowhere imaginable. Reading the line today we may still wonder at the startling materialization of Andromache in the heart of nineteenth-century Paris.[57]

A simple condition makes sense of Andromache's irruption in such an implausible setting. In a world of loss, everything is equally distant; what's gone is beyond degree, is simply *gone*. The signified is always absent. In the calculus of emotion, to be sure, absence is susceptible to significant modulation. We master this truth early on, in our own equivalent of the experiences that Freud examined in the "Fort-Da" game (see *Beyond the Pleasure Principle*, [1920], SE 18: 14–17). But semiosis appears fixated in a stage *before* the psyche learned to believe that what is invisible is not necessarily lost. Signs admit of no degrees: the distance between any signifier and its signified has no scalar dimension and is not negotiable. All such distances are identical and, in a sense, infinite.[58] In the mode thus defined by the lability of signs, the materialization of Andromache at dawn in the streets of central Paris one day in the early Second Empire is no

57. It is worth noting that Andromache's *femaleness* coheres with nineteenth-century projections of the imaginary division of gender. In particular, the role of recollection, of the preservation of memories, was regularly attributed to women. Although we might say this has been true since the Greeks made Mnemosyne a goddess, there is clear evidence for a particularly strong association between women and memory in the nineteenth century. See Perrot, ed., *From the Fires of Revolution*, particularly 19 and 263. The startling effect of the opening of "Le Cygne" depends upon two major factors. First, it would seem hard to conceive of anyone more likely to fetch up in the prosaic and flattened *imaginaire* of the Second Empire metropolis than the widow of Hector. Second, the form of the utterance with which the poem begins conflates two irreconcilable identities. On the one hand, Andromache cannot hear her name invoked because she is foreign to the real world of its utterance. On the other hand, through a kind of knowing paralogism, Baudelaire's reader is obliged to assume the role of the phrase's receiver (on the distinction between "receiver" and "addressee," see Gerald Prince, *A Dictionary of Narratology*, s.v. "receiver"). In effect the first five words of "Le Cygne" constrain readers to negotiate the distance between their own contemporary identities and the imagined reality of a Trojan princess. This impossible displacement then becomes a paradigm for all the others thematized in the poem.

58. Indeed this is precisely what the sign's theoretical arbitrariness means. As Ferdinand Saussure acknowledged, the relationship between signifier and signified is in principle unreasonable (*Course in General Linguistics*, 73). See also Terence Hawkes, *Structuralism and Semiotics*, 25.

less probable than *anyone's appearance in language, anywhere, at any time.*

What then strikes us as the paradox of "Le Cygne" is a disorienting cohabitation within the text of the profoundly conjunctural and the utterly incongruous. Such coexistence forcefully tests the arbitrariness of the semiotic. "Le Cygne," like the sign, systematically subverts propriety. To be sure, the poem is anchored in the reality of early Second Empire Paris and cannot be adequately comprehended outside such localization. I argued precisely this in the first part of this chapter. But my historical argument concluded with a paradox: that such a sociohistorical localization uncannily undermines its own apparent stability. For in reality Second Empire "reality" *figured itself as unreal.* Nothing in the period seemed sufficiently settled or principled to undo the aura of sham, counterfeit, and infinitely negotiable mobility by which this society appeared to live, to conduct its affairs, and to construct its meanings. The generalized experience of loss and dispossession by which the regime's antagonists conceptualized their existence was the reflex of such wanton mutability. By thematizing this experience of loss, "Le Cygne" materializes the logic of its period's own simultaneous self-definition and self-subversion. It narrates its own paradox.

So although "Le Cygne" is firmly anchored in the conjunctural, at the same time it is a text awash in language appropriated from other times and other texts. *Its propriety is the improper.* We might say that, like the unexpectedly mobile Andromache, the language-fragments that materialize within "Le Cygne" can turn up anywhere, but for now they turn up *here.* With them "Le Cygne" both thematizes and practices a radical semioticity.

What I termed the poem's "mnemonics of dispossession" is crucial to this interpretation. On the level of narrative, "Le Cygne" takes its substance from memories of the banished and the dispossessed: Victor Hugo, to whom the poem is dedicated (who for the entire period of the Second Empire daily contemplated his exile from a few kilometers off the French coast); Andromache (mourning the dead Hector in Buthrotum after the fall of Troy); Ovid (whose conflict with the Emperor Augustus was as intense, and whose exile as painful, as Hugo's under Napoléon III); the swan captive far from "son beau lac natal"; the "négresse" grieving for Africa; the shipwrecked sailors;

and so on.[59] In the common experience of the poem's radically heterogeneous cast of characters, the distance between home and exile is established as a powerful figure of the semiotic relation. The memory of mourning becomes the sign of the sign.

These painful experiences come to representation in "Le Cygne" through a dense network of intertextualities, through a clustering of borrowed—*exiled*—texts. *Nothing* in the poem gives itself out as the product of immediate experience or perception. *Everything* is already semiotized, already textualized—the remembered elements most centrally and most diagnostically of all. Everything in the poem thereby exists in a double displacement: both that of the internal distance that constitutes the sign, and that of a more discursive form of transfer. This latter is the movement of intertextuality by which a text "comes over" from another locus (whether from a book or from a memory) to occupy the "alien place" that, in "Le Cygne," turns out to be the space of the present and of textuality itself.[60]

The complex clarifies something fundamental in the constitution of "Le Cygne." Intertextuality is always and by essence tropological. Its process is the practice of the improper. So by a paradox that Baudelaire exploits with brilliant persistence and density in "Le Cygne," the exiled texts that proliferate everywhere in the poem are made at home there precisely by virtue of their constitutive impropriety.[61]

59. Concerning Ovid, the reference in "Le Cygne" ("comme l'homme d'Ovide") is to the Latin poet's description of man's upright countenance, given him by the gods so that he might worship them (*Metamorphoses* 1:84–86). In the period around 1859, however, Baudelaire made a number of references to Ovid, specifically to aspects of his exile. Two are worth mentioning here: a passage in the "Salon de 1859" describing Delacroix's representation of the poet in his *Ovide chez les Sythes* (1052–53), and the reference to "Ovide / Chassé du paradis latin" in "Horreur sympathique" (first published in October 1860; 73).

60. I refer to the description of metaphor in Cicero's *De Oratore*, itself borrowed (in what is beginning to seem a vertiginous reduplication of the intertextual) from Aristotle: "eis quae transferuntur et quasi alieno in loco collocantur" ["those (words) which are transferred and placed, as it were, in an alien place"] (cited in Margaret W. Ferguson, "St. Augustine's Region of Unlikeness: The Crossing of Exile and Language," 842. Ferguson offers rich reflections on the classical topos of figuring a text's reflection on its own linguistic mode through a thematization of exile.

61. This impropriety (to be understood both in its ontological and its economic resonances) still fascinated Baudelaire two years after "Le Cygne" when he sketched the unfinished prefaces for the 1861 edition of *Les Fleurs du mal*. One might say he was still reveling in his robberies. Scandalously, he projected foregrounding the intertextual plagiarisms [*plagiats*] that composed his collection, including, as he put it, "Virgile (tout le morceau d'*Andromaque*)" (187). One of the most consequential and resonant of these "pla-

The impropriety of semiosis equally determines the oddly baffling structure of "Le Cygne." The poem is organized so as not to appear organized. It never lets its narrative narrate. Any impression of high-order structure in the poem, determined by the mastery of a forma-tive consciousness, would have reintroduced—by the back door—the metanarrative security, the confident control of the elements of representation, that is precisely what the framing fiction of "Le Cygne" contradicts. The poem then produces its effect by recording the unpredictable and erratic traces of a consciousness under stress, of a memory in crisis. This consciousness is defined precisely by its mnemonic lability, by its anxious *vulnerability to recollection.* Mem-ories, however incongruous, however disparate, simply keep flood-ing in. Indeed, this permeability to the improper is one way of un-derstanding the poem's fixation on dispossession to begin with. To paraphrase Paul de Man's characterization of the trope, there seems to be no limit to what associations can get away with.[62]

The poem thus presents itself as a peculiar aggregation of dis-persed elements. These heteroclite relics emerge unpredictably from the haphazard repositories of consciousness and culture, from the "storehouse of images and signs" about which Baudelaire was writing in his contemporary "Salon de 1859" (1044). Their irruption exploits the disorienting propensity of memory to countenance the most ec-centric associations and linkages. As Umberto Eco put it in an essay on memory and forgetting, "anything can be the sign of anything."[63]

Traditional aesthetic criteria dispose us to value organicity and clear narrative plotting, but these are impossible within "Le Cygne." This is a *Second Empire* text, written under the reign of what its opponents consistently figured as political and semiotic illegitimacy.

---

giarized" elements in *Les Fleurs du mal* occurs within "Le Cygne" itself: Baudelaire's near-quotation, in his description of the "négresse" in the poem, of his *own* lines from "A une malabaraise," written eighteen years earlier in 1841 (156–57). This *self*-piracy might seem the limiting case of the systematic and shameless reappropriation of texts that "Le Cygne" practices. Proust acutely caught Baudelaire's reminiscences—or robberies—of Hugo, Gautier, Sully Prudhomme, Racine, Sainte-Beuve, Nerval and others; he consid-ered them a constitutive part of Baudelaire's style. See *"Contre Saint-Beuve," précédé de "Pastiches et mélanges," et suivi de "Essais et articles,"* 258–59.

62. Paul de Man, *Allegories of Reading: Figural Language in Rousseau, Nietzsche, Rilke, and Proust,* 62.

63. Umberto Eco, "Un Art d'oublier est-il concevable?" 130.

The poem's stance of mnemonic retrospection represents its own period as postlapsarian, as the aftermath of the loss of precisely the unity and the plenitude that might have made more conventional textual harmonies possible. Consequently, this is the text of an indeterminate and unpredictable heterogeneity, of an assemblage of *disjecta membra*. It is built according to the practice of a bricolage whose very principle—"le bric-à-brac confus"—is strikingly and approvingly figured within the text itself.[64] So the poem's story is that it has no story to tell. For what diegesis is possible within a mnemonics of general dispossession? From the first astonishing evocation of Andromache, the unrationalizable and irreducible displacement inherent in the sign is figured in the form of "Le Cygne" itself. Of course that is how memory works. In the mode of anamnesis, anything can suggest anything. So in "Le Cygne," intertextualities replicate and proliferate. The mnemonics of dispossession opens the text to limitless relation, and hence to the limitless migration of *other* texts. In a poetico-social world in which the bounds of the *proper* have shrunk to invisibility, alterity finds its element.

In the face of what may seem an unlimited poststructuralist drift, I need to acknowledge that certain overdeterminations of the mnemonic and textual process in "Le Cygne" are nonetheless important. They define the consciousness that performs the recollection enacted in the poem. Baudelaire was a writer, and writing preoccupied him. It should come as no surprise that much of the material recollected in "Le Cygne" evokes specifically literary, even high-cultural referents. In particular, Baudelaire was intent on figuring himself as an alienated artist, as a writer *in opposition*. Consequently, the content of "Le Cygne" coheres with a stance of estrangement, heterodoxy, and dissent. Successive instantiations of classical and contemporary resistance to authority thus frame and focus the critique of Second Empire sham politics and counterfeit culture that "Le Cygne" establishes as its project. Beginning with the dedication of the poem to one of the regime's most notorious antagonists, these traditions are brought to bear. In a period experienced as illegitimate and oppres-

---

64. Ferguson, "Saint Augustine's Region of Unlikeness," 863–64, clarifies the linkage in classical literature between the depiction of confusion and the state of exile. This association constitutes another of the poem's proliferating intertextualities—one previously unnoticed by critics, and maybe even by Baudelaire himself.

sive, examples of the cruelty of authority and of resistance to its malevolence resonated with particular force. So the poem's recollection
and textualization of such instantiations function to fertilize—and to
politicize—the successive connections that organize it.

Scholars have painstakingly identified the intertextual references
and relations—both erudite and everyday—that function within "Le
Cygne."[65] In the image of the Second Empire itself, the text seems
defined by their promiscuity. In the consciousness of its opponents,
this dynamic of irreducible referentiality provided an ironic specificity to a regime defined by the vacuity of its ruling signifiers. Thus
"Napoléon III" recalls "Napoléon I"; thus in its usurpation of the uncle's prestige the *Second* Empire parodically evokes the spuriousness
and the posteriority of the nephew's Imperial pretensions.[66]

And then, as we must not forget, this is a *swan* poem. In a poetic
text the signifier "cygne" proclaims its own intense derivativeness.
"Le Cygne" cannot shake off memory of the melodramatic and endlessly retextualized fable of the swan song that flickers on its edge,
even if it seems nowhere quite appropriate to the specific material of
the text itself.[67] But such apparent inappropriateness is no impediment to the most insistent referentiality. Memory regularly retrieves
unsuitable material; the malapropos is its element. So the vintage
mytheme of the swan attaches itself inexorably to this text and becomes a part of the proliferating dialogism that it sustains.

In general, however, the references functioning in "Le Cygne" cohere on clear thematic levels with the overall preoccupations of the
poem. Thus Andromache's resonances: a fallen and banished princess

65. Probably the most complete catalogue and account can be found in Burton, *The
Context of Baudelaire's "Le Cygne."*
66. Cf. Baudelaire's "Another Bonaparte! for shame!" in "Fusées," 1274. See also Terdiman, "1852."
67. The fable of the swan song has a brilliant and prestigious history. It was credited by
Plato, Aristotle, Euripides, Cicero, Seneca, Martial, and many others. Moreover, Plato's
claim in the *Phaedo* that the soul of Apollo had passed into a swan led to an independent
legend that identified the swan particularly with poets. Whence (with considerable consequence for a poem retextualizing the *Aeneid*) Virgil's familiar appellation, "the Swan of
Mantua." On these cultural resonances, see, for example, *Brewer's Dictionary of Phrase
and Fable*, s.v. "swan." For a contemporary evocation of the motif—considered in an
ironic spirit we might compare to Baudelaire's own in "Le Cygne"—compare this passage
from *Madame Bovary* (1857) describing Emma's adolescent literary tastes: "She would
meander along Lamartinian paths, listening . . . to all the songs of dying swans" (part 1,
chap. 6).

whose life in exile appears a debased parody of her former existence, an endless and impotent rehearsal of the dead. Andromache is reduced to simulacrum (as Virgil put it in the *Aeneid*, to seeming a "slave of a slave").[68] This frame of exile contains the whole extended series of figures populating "Le Cygne," to whose common resemblance I referred earlier: in addition to Andromache, Hugo, Ovid, the "négresse," the swan itself, the poet as dispossessed urban *flâneur* or Noctambule, and, more distantly, Virgil's Aeneas, who is Andromache's interlocutor in book 3 of the *Aeneid* and at the time of their encounter is himself experiencing the pain of his own exile.[69]

On a different level, the experience of exile, of the displacement of *place* itself, becomes inscribed in a notional expatriation by which the identities of cities are transferred along a chain that descends to Second Empire Paris. We might image this sequence thus: Troy → Andromache's "little Troy" in Buthrotum ("parva Troia") → Rome (Aeneas's destination and destiny; referent of Ovid's exile) → "vieux Paris" (locus of the Old Carrousel and the Old Louvre) → Second Empire Paris ("nouveau Carrousel," "ce Louvre," etc.). The string of cities seems to figure an abyssal displacement—the image of an unremitting expatriation paralleling the peregrinations of the poem's successive exiles. Such a pattern looks like a carefully figured analogon of the movement of semiosis itself—and, particularly, of the dissemination that seems to propel language from signifier to signifier without ever producing the moment of plenitude that could arrest the semiotic chain or allow the stabilization of meaning. We could put it that under the peculiar conditions of modernity from Baudelaire's time forward, the mnemonic of dispossession in "Le Cygne" figures a *semiotics of signs themselves*.

What I have been calling semiotic "displacement" is sometimes

68. See Burton, *The Context of Baudelaire's "Le Cygne,"* 56, and Nelson, "Baudelaire and Virgil," 333. In "Souvenirs," Shelley Rice argues strikingly that the "cult of tombs" originally conceived in the French Revolution—and (though Rice does not suggest this connection) vividly anticipated by Andromache's memorial rituals for Hector at Buthrotum—enacted a means to "assure the perpetuity" of culture at a moment when its stability seemed broadly threatened. The tomb cult, as Rice observes, had become an important tradition by the time of Haussmann (161).

69. The parallel between Aeneas and Andromache (thematic in the *Aeneid*) depends upon their common destiny of establishing simulacra of Troy far from their original home: Andromache's miniature replica in Buthrotum, and Aeneas's Rome.

seen as no more than an innocent technical given. From such a perspective, the sort of affective investment in the mechanisms of semiosis observable in Baudelaire (or later in Foucault) necessarily appears misdirected. From the same point of view, the notion seems scandalous that the displacements of the semiotic might be analogized to the expatriations produced as a result of a specific urban transformation (for example, the razing of the old Carrousel), or a historical upheaval (for example, the Trojan War that exiled Andromache), or a political trauma (for example, the 2 Décembre coup that did the same to Victor Hugo). And it might seem equally scandalous to have suggested that the impulse to literary formalism in Baudelaire's period might have been determined by the sense of dispossession arising in developments on the order of Haussmann's reconstruction of Paris. But I have sought to claim just these sorts of impropriety, just these sorts of provocation, for "Le Cygne."

My argument has insisted upon the implication of any sign in the dynamic of change that determines our representation of social reality. Particularly after the midcentury revolutions, Baudelaire conceived such change under the sign of melancholy: as an unhappy distance that figured the loss of the past. "Le Cygne" textualizes the sorts of painful displacements that represent politics and sociality as an inevitable site of such melancholy. That is how in this poem the historical and the social become the site of exile. The memory crisis takes form here as a constitutive and systematic nostalgia.

But memory is a fundamental model for all representation. This is what accounts for a general agreement in the critical tradition that "Le Cygne," formed as a reflection on such representation through memory, expresses something elemental in Baudelaire's conception of the world. In effect, "Le Cygne" interrogates the very possibility of expression itself. In the atmosphere of loss at midcentury, the nostalgia that establishes the poem's atmosphere is projected onto the very material of signification, onto the sign itself, in the form of a meditation on the mechanism of all meaning-production.

The drama of "Le Cygne" makes it clear that the painful relations of the historical and the social render the reality and the contingency of the semiotic relation visible to begin with. To those in power, signs may appear transparent. But for Baudelaire, suffering the sense of dispossession that he figures in his poem, the losses, the displacements that signs represent are comprehensible as a kind of virtual narrative, as memories of bereavement and banishment. Semiosis here becomes intensely historicized, intensely political. In such a critical conjuncture, the sign seems almost disoriented and frantic out of its element, seems almost to struggle like the swan whose story Baudelaire memorializes in "Le Cygne."

Part Three

THE VICISSITUDES
OF RECOLLECTION:
TWO TWENTIETH-CENTURY
THEORIES

5

Hypermnesia—Memory in Proust
I. Determinations

Approfondir des idées (Nietzsche, philosophie) est moins
grande qu'approfondir des réminiscences.

[Studying ideas (Nietzsche, philosophy) is not as great as
studying memories.]
—Marcel Proust, *Le Carnet de 1908*, 101

Memory in Proust: even raising the subject again might seem a
provocation. Nothing in French literature since the Revolution
has been more exhaustively analyzed, more unremittingly *haggled*,
than memory in *A la recherche du temps perdu*.[1] What more could
possibly be said about it?

Proustian memory has become the sort of habit Proust warned us
against: so familiar that it escapes definition, so celebrated that it has

---

1. See Christie McDonald's intelligent discussion in *The Proustian Fabric: Associations of Memory*, and Kevin Newmark's essay "Ingesting the Mummy: Proust's Allegory of Memory." Their perspectives diverge considerably from my own. Paul Ricoeur has provided a remarkable analysis of time and memory in the *Recherche*; see *Time and Narrative*, 2:130–52. References to *A la recherche du temps perdu* are by volume and page number to the new four-volume Pléiade edition (1987–89), produced under the general editorship of Jean-Yves Tadié (referenced as *RTP*), and to the three-volume Pléiade edition (1954), edited by Pierre Clarac and André Ferré (*RTP54*). I will also refer to the Pléiade editions of *Jean Santeuil* (referenced as *JS*) and *Contre Sainte-Beuve* (*CSB*). Citations from Proust's correspondence are taken from Philip Kolb's edition: *Correspondance* (referenced as *Corr.*). Translations from Proust are my own, but I have benefited from consulting the translation of *Remembrance of Things Past* by C. K. Scott Moncrieff, as revised by Terence Kilmartin (New York: Random House, 1981). Generally, in my translations from the *Recherche* I have chosen accuracy over elegance, and stayed as close as possible to the rhythm and language of Proust's text.

lost its critical edge. Because of its visibility we can no longer see it. The theory of "involuntary memory" with which the *Recherche* concludes has been embalmed by criticism. It has taken on the lifelessness of a consecrated monument. For more than seventy years, scholars have rehearsed Proust's salvationist notion of the mnemonic to the point that by now the accumulated discourse about the *madeleine*, about the Guermantes matinée, and about the aesthetic epiphany to which Proust's novel eventually leads his narrator has come to seem endless—and endlessly, relentlessly, repetitive. Why has discussion of Proustian memory produced so little insight? The answer depends on an interplay between the expectations Proust's novel establishes, the ideological stresses it seeks to manage, the demands it makes on its readers, and the character of the critical practices it has so forcefully contributed to determining.

Proust's *Recherche* is a quest narrative. His story points ceaselessly to its conclusion. Such a paradigm sets up a powerful—but potentially a risky—expectation. Proust holds out the novel's final revelation of *mémoire involontaire* as the end of searching. He systematically underlines its centrality, methodically prefigures its content, and then, to conclude his book, exhaustively explicates its significance.[2] It is obvious that Proust intends the theory of memory as his novel's culmination: as its answer. Yet for many readers, including some of those who most admire Proust, the revelation at the end of the *Recherche* falls flat. For them, *Le Temps retrouvé*—specifically the Guermantes matinée and its earnest doctrinal aftermath—constitutes a failed climax. Here is one witness to such a judgment: "You remember how Proust, at the end of that great novel, having convinced the reader with the full sophistication of his genius that he is going to produce an apocalypse, brings out with pathetic faith, as a fact of absolute value, that sometimes when you are living in one place you are reminded of living in another place, and this, since you are now apparently living in two places, means that you are outside time, in the only state of beatitude he can imagine. In any one place (atmosphere, mental climate) life is intolerable; in any two it is an

2. On the novel's systematic prefigurations or "prerevelations" of the meaning and the importance of involuntary memory, see Richard Terdiman, *The Dialectics of Isolation: Self and Society in the French Novel from the Realists to Proust*, 120–25.

ecstasy." Thus William Empson in 1930.[3] Yet it is striking how little Empson's caricature of *Le Temps retrouvé* subverts his esteem for the novel it concludes. This may seem surprising when one considers that Empson discards what the novel says is most important about itself; yet this has been a frequent critical tack with regard to judgment of the book's finale, and more generally concerning the extended disquisitions on memory found throughout the *Recherche*. Such a tactic safeguards our opinion of the whole novel by sacrificing judgment of one portion of it—albeit one to which Proust attached great importance.

So Empson disowns the novel's final flourish without significant damage to his appreciation of the *Recherche*. Perhaps his distance from the Proustian critical establishment made it easier for him to do so. In a larger sense, however, his tactic reproduces the aesthetic with which Proust himself has always been associated. Instead of crediting the discursive or doctrinal pretensions of the *Recherche*, Empson values its "fictive," "imaginative," or "novelistic" texture. He thus recirculates the crucial tenet of modernist aesthetics that I began looking at in Chapter 4. This principle hypostatizes a realm of the "purely literary" and privileges it over any other form of discourse.

Expressions of this notion are familiar. They range from Baudelaire's "Poetry . . . has no other aim [*but*] than Itself"[4] to Proust's own "A work where there are theories is like an article with the price tag still attached" (*RTP* 4:461; *RTP54* 3:882). For such an aesthetic, the sole instrumentality of imaginative works is to be noninstrumen-

---

3. *Seven Types of Ambiguity*, 131. Such assessments of the novel's concluding revelation have been frequent in Proust criticism. Another example can be found in Gilles Deleuze's influential *Proust and Signs* (1964): "What constitutes the unity of *In Search of Lost Time*? We know, at least, what does not. It is not recollection, memory, even involuntary memory" (3). For other examples of similar negative opinions, among many possible, see Clive Bell, *Proust* (1929), 51; Rebecca West, *The Court and the Castle: Some Treatments of a Recurrent Theme* (1957), 231; Leo Bersani, *Marcel Proust: The Fictions of Life and Art*, 18; Esther Salaman, "A Collection of Moments," 49–50; Randolph Splitter, *Proust's "Recherche": A Psychoanalytic Interpretation* (1981); Malcolm Bowie, *Freud, Proust, and Lacan: Theory as Fiction* (1987), 71; Vincent Descombes, *Proust: Philosophie du roman* (1987), 31; Antoine Compagnon, *Proust entre deux siècles* (1989), 50; and Richard E. Goodkin, *Around Proust* (1991), 6–7.

4. Charles Baudelaire, "Théophile Gautier," in *Oeuvres complètes*, ed. Y.-G. Le Dantec and Claude Pichois, 685.

tal.[5] Consequently, literature must not be caught up in the controversies and conflicts of everyday activity or utilitarian production; it
must transcend implication in the quotidian and in the prosaic.
Therein lies its distinction and the warrant of its dignity. Such a programmatic repression of the material, the practical, and the external
has permitted critics to sacrifice Proust's extended disquisitions on
the technology of memory to the advantage of a purified, "aesthet-
icized" vision of Proustian novelistic form.

But despite Proust's own articulation of this purist aesthetic within
the *Recherche*, his text is perversely inconsistent concerning it. His
novel has a powerful stake in elucidating the apparatus of the mnemonic, and it does so with earnest insistence. As is obvious, as every
reader of Proust has known since *Du côté de chez Swann* appeared in
1913, and as every introduction to *A la recherche du temps perdu*
has faithfully repeated ever since, the problem of memory is an obsession—both narrative and intricately doctrinal—within the novel.
Memory is the object of the quest upon which the *Recherche*
launches its narrator, and toward which it propels its readers' expectations. And to the extent that (as the narrator concludes) "all the
materials of my literary work are my past life" (*RTP* 4:478; *RTP54*
3:899), memory is inevitably the key to Proust's production process
as well.

This is not news. The *Recherche* begins with a concerted exercise
of memory; it proceeds through recurrent experiences of recollecting
the past; and it accompanies its narrative with elaborately argued
speculations on the centrality of the mnemonic, as upon its difficulties. In *La Fugitive (Albertine disparue)*, 2500 pages into this

5. On the invention of the "purely literary" and the instrumentalization of noninstru-
mentality, see Richard Terdiman, *Discourse/Counter-Discourse: The Theory and Practice
of Symbolic Resistance in Nineteenth-Century France*, part 3, particularly 308. On the
relation between modernist doctrines in literature and contemporaneous theses in philosophy, see Descombes, *Proust*, 15–16. Descombes is caustic concerning Proust's uncritical
adoption of philosophical attitudes fashionable in his period: "Proust the *theoretician* mo-
bilizes the theses of the philosophy of mind [*philosophie de l'esprit*] of his time in the
service of the dogma which he defends in literature." Among the hackneyed elements of
reigning philosophical idealism that Descombes judges Proust credulously to have repeated like "luminous truths" are belief in the privilege of private languages, the myth of
interiority and subjectivity, the doctrine of the quasi-impossibility of communication, and
the theory of art as unique expression of the self. I will return to these issues when I
discuss *Contre Sainte-Beuve*.

novel of mnemonic obsession, the narrator informs us he has been searching for the past without realizing it.[6] But by this point his anti-instrumental naïveté has worn through to the point of overt disin-genuousness. Memory is the enigma this fiction sets out to unravel and the instrument it offers for doing so. And when in *Le Temps retrouvé* the novel at last unfolds its idiosyncratic solution to the memory problem, Proust's seemingly endless text reaches its own horizon, and it stops.

But for all the consequentiality given to it by the quest structure of the *Recherche*, the theory of memory that Proust finally expounds at the end of the novel has been judged a disappointment. This disap-pointment itself is worth a closer look. The sense of anticlimax many feel at the moment that, following Empson, we could term the novel's failed apocalypse creates an embarrassment. Proust asks so much of the revelation in *Le Temps retrouvé* that his novel seems defenseless when the epiphany fizzles. And because the conclusion misfires, the larger phenomenon of memory in Proust—despite the quantity of ink spilled over it—seems to transform itself into an aes-thetic inconvenience. Perhaps this is why most writing about mem-ory in the *Recherche* turns humdrum when it confronts the need to

6. "Le passé à la recherche duquel j'étais sans le savoir" (*RTP* 4:135; *RTP54* 3:555). The problem of naming Proust's penultimate volume continues—indeed, it has only gotten more complicated. The current Pléiade edition reestablishes *Albertine disparue*, the title under which the volume was originally published after Proust's death. Conversely, the 1954 Pléiade editors decided to substitute *La Fugitive*, which Proust had chosen, then abandoned because another novel (by Tagore, now virtually forgotten) had already ap-peared with the same title. See *RTP54* 1:xxiv-xxv, 3:1094; and *RTP* 4:1033–38. In June 1986, the missing copy of the typescript used by Gallimard to establish the first edition of the volume after Proust's death turned up in the archives of Proust's niece Suzy Mante-Proust. This appears to have been the final state of the manuscript of this volume corrected by Proust. An edition of the recovered typescript with Proust's corrections was published in 1987 by Nathalie Mauriac and Étienne Wolff. In Proust's own handwriting the title *Albertine disparue* appears at the beginning of the typescript (165), thus appar-ently settling the question of what he wished the volume to be called. Yet even this resolution is not conclusive. There seems no doubt that Proust felt obliged to choose an alternative title because *La Fugitive* had been preempted by the Tagore volume. *Albertine disparue* was clearly the alternative he selected under the circumstances; however, there is considerably more doubt that, absent Tagore, he would have deviated from his original choice of *La Fugitive*, which so clearly formed a set with the preceding *Prisonnière*. McDonald discusses the problem of the diverse editions of the novel's sixth volume in *The Proustian Fabric*, 150–53.

make sense of Proust's psychological, aesthetic, and ethical claims, beyond simply reiterating what they claim about themselves. Instead of confronting the *problem* of memory in *A la recherche du temps perdu*, scholars have typically busied themselves peeling yet one more time the onion of Proust's own reflections on the mnemonic. This suspension of critical judgment that occurs as soon as the *substance* of Proust's relation to the memory problem surfaces has much to do with the sort of relation Proust's text structures with its readers.

Proust has always attracted an uncommon—even an uncanny—commitment, something like the analogue on the affective level of the sheer persistence required of us to negotiate a text as long and as demanding as the *Recherche*. Having come so far with Proust, it's as if we simply do not want to abandon him at the end. We are a disinclined to engage with the disappointment of Proust's mnemonic revelation, to interrogate the *meaning* of such a palpable mismatch between promise and performance at the conclusion both of the quest and of the *Recherche*. By "looking the other way" we preserve our high opinion of Proust, but betray our reluctance to search for the critical sense in something that, on the whole, doesn't appear to make much sense at all. The result is that the superstructure of the novel's arcane and circumstantial reflections on memory, on its varieties, its arduousness, its soteriological or salvationist potentialities—the whole overdrawn intensity of Proust's doctrinal preoccupations—becomes uncomfortably problematic and tends to drop out of critical discussion.[7]

Despite what Proust urges us to believe at the novel's conclusion, his theory of memory, and its involuntary variety in particular, is unlikely to strike readers as the key to life. But we need to better understand the sources and the consequences of the novel's mnemonic fixation. Proust articulated the substance of his theories concerning memory quite clearly himself, and his commentators have rehearsed them ever since. To this there seems nothing to add. There is no point in ventriloquizing yet another time what the *Re-*

---

7. Concerning the "salvationist" promise of involuntary memory, about which I will have much to say in what follows, it bears noting that the figure is not mine, but Proust's: "But it is sometimes at the moment when everything seems lost that the word arrives which may save us [*qui peut nous sauver*]" (*RTP* 4:445; *RTP54* 3:866).

cherche claims to reveal about memory. We need rather to establish the *stakes* of the mnemonic for Proust. Perhaps the perspective of a study on modernity's memory crisis may make it possible to gain greater clarity concerning the *question* whose answer is the ponderous substance and structure of Proustian memory theory. Such a perspective may help us to identify and to analyze the three-thousand-page problem Proust's celebrated revelation was meant to resolve. To do this, however, will require stepping outside the closure of Proust's own self-understanding.

It is a commonplace that *critical* judgment can only be exercised from such an external vantage.[8] But it often seems as if Proust disables criticism in advance by the intensity and range of his self-reflection. The intricacy and inventiveness of his powers of analysis are so overwhelming that they can seem to saturate understanding, to leave no space whatever for difference.[9] The *Recherche* may be the longest book of modern times; it is certainly one of the most self-aware. In the face of its unprecedented intensity and extension, it sometimes seems that, whatever criticism prepares to argue concerning it, Proust has been there first and has already exhausted the possibilities for further discourse. Then he can seem not only his own best critic, but the only critic his novel has room for.

Nevertheless, the eccentricity of Proust's preoccupation with memory diffuses significantly when it is seen from the perspective of the memory crisis that has occupied me in this book. Of course it might appear that Proust is out of place in a study organized around the

8. This notion, whose formulation he identified with Marx, Nietzsche, and Freud, was developed by Paul Ricoeur as his concept of "suspicion"; see *Freud and Philosophy: An Essay on Interpretation*, 32–34. It will be important in my discussions of Proust and Freud here. One of its earliest and most striking formulations is found in Karl Marx and Friedrich Engels, *The German Ideology*: "Whilst in ordinary life every shopkeeper is very well able to distinguish between what somebody professes to be and what he really is, our historians have not yet won even this trivial insight. They take every epoch at its word and believe that everything it says and imagines about itself is true" (67).

9. Though she was speaking not about writing Proust criticism but about her own fiction, Virginia Woolf's reaction to Proust's ability to overwhelm catches what I am trying to get at here—something between his striking aptitude to seduce readers and his remarkable capacity to overpower them. She compares the *Recherche* with *Mrs. Dalloway* on which she was working at the time: "I wonder if this time I have achieved something? Well, nothing anyhow compared with Proust, in whom I am embedded now. . . . He will, I suppose, both influence me and make me out of temper with every sentence of my own" (8 April 1925, *A Writer's Diary*, 71).

hypothesis of a memory crisis, since if such a crisis existed at all, Proust would seem decisively to have solved it. His own vision of the mnemonic realm is notoriously triumphalist. If we remain within the terms the novel proposes we accept, *A la recherche du temps perdu* would be understood to have liquidated sometime around 1922 the century-long perplexity concerning memory that I have been seeking to analyze.

But locating Proust within a wider cultural fixation upon the mnemonic helps to denaturalize or displace his own seemingly sovereign self-understanding. It enables us to reinterpret the triumphalism of his novel's conclusion. In fact, it is palpable that the *Recherche* is rather a novel of prolonged and urgent anxiety. Critical resituation of its concern with memory is needed to restore the atmosphere of intense disquiet that the conclusion of the novel more brackets than resolves. Then both Proust's long obsession with memory and his sudden eradication of its difficulties lose their carefully sustained singularity and their finality. The closure of his "originality" opens up and the idiosyncrasy of his theory can be remapped in the perspective of a broader cultural apprehension concerning the disturbing presence of the past.

I want therefore to credit the anxiety about the memory problem reflected in Proust's protracted wrestling with its mysteries, while maintaining distance concerning the theoretical or doctrinal resolution by which he intended to manage these contradictions. My vision of memory in Proust will consequently be far less celebratory than the one the novel provides in the aftermath of the Guermantes matinée: a more skeptical conception, but one which seeks to respond to the same anxieties that produced the theory of involuntary memory in the *Recherche*. I want to pull Proust's seemingly eccentric solution back into the memory problem that preoccupied his culture, and force a sense in his connection to the memory crisis.

Proust wanted a conclusion that resolved things, and the structure of his book points insistently toward it. But this result goes against the grain of his novel. Until the end the *Recherche* is never single-voiced; the contradictions and dissonances that stress it define it far more than any of the local solutions upon which the text may appear to settle from time to time. Indeed, though its structure points toward resolution for such an extraordinarily protracted period, it seems reasonable to speculate that the novel's unprecedented extension arises in the very inaccessibility of such resolution. Why else would Proust have written such a long narrative?

No epiphany can then erase the proportions in which the concerns of the *Recherche* are distributed—2800 pages of anxiety set against 200 of salvation. Manifestly, the resolution that appears to sweep away the problems inherent in memory at the end of the book can hardly abrogate the much more lengthy, intense, and systematic agitation concerning the past and our relation to it. Proust's concluding tribute to memory cannot efface the unparalleled anxiety that in the *Recherche* is indissolubly and unremittingly linked to the experience of recollection.

I want to consider this *disquieting* side of Proustian memory in what follows. No one has caught it more powerfully than Samuel Beckett at the beginning of his brilliant 1931 study of the *Recherche*: "There is no escape from yesterday because yesterday has deformed us."[10] What looms in this anxiety is clear intuition of our domination by the past, of a perverse and ultimately incomprehensible control of what *is* by what *is no longer*. Proust called this paradox memory's "strange contradiction": "the painful synthesis of survival and annihilation" (*RTP* 3:157, cf. 3:156; *RTP54* 2:760, 759). This is the perplexity that involuntary memory was meant to undo; in it arises the *malevolence* of the mnemonic realm that Proust's revelation was supposed to suppress. To examine this contradiction and its difficulties, we must speculate on the sources of the danger, indeed the virulence, that Proust detected and represented in the experience of memory and, beyond these, on the relation of this affective complex to other sources of cultural anxiety characteristic of Proust's period. To specify the tactics—expressive and ideological—by which Proust sought to master these stresses or defend against them, we must appeal to the history of this mnemonic disquiet.

Consider the following passage:

> The author of the present book is a sensitive and sickly young man who spends his life among his family and two or three friends. . . .

10. Samuel Beckett, *Proust*, 2.

A space of a few feet where it is a bit warmer than elsewhere is his whole universe. The mantel of the fireplace is his heaven; the hearth is his horizon.

Of the world outside he has seen only what can be seen through the window, and he has not wanted to see any more than that. He belongs to no political tendency. . . .

He prefers sitting to standing, and lying down to sitting. That way one is already used to it when death arrives to lie us down forever. He writes in order to have a pretext for doing nothing, and does nothing under the pretext of writing.

In this evocation of the literary artist's withdrawal we can almost see Proust's *chambre de liège*, the celebrated cork-lined room that in a single image seized modernism's defensiveness about the extra-aesthetic world. However, the withdrawal depicted here is not Proust's on the Boulevard Haussmann, but rather Théophile Gautier's in his preface to *Albertus*, a collection of poems that Gautier published in 1832, nearly forty years before Proust was born.[11] Gautier has uncannily anticipated an entire somatic and psychological *attitude* of modernism: artistically indisposed, recumbent, disengaged—and distinctly paranoid concerning the menace of the world outside the writer's bedchamber. What links Gautier's text to Proust's is the common intent to evade domination by outside forces beyond one's choosing or beneath one's dignity: to slip free of external determination by resolutely barricading oneself.

The effort to suppress extra-artistic determination generalizes an image of "freedom" that for a whole tradition of writers became the ideal for all experience. Such a project constitutes the most characteristic—and probably the most intense—fantasy of modernism. In the Gautier text, it is an attitude still in the process of formation.[12] By

11. Théophile Gautier, *Albertus ou L'Ame et le péché*, in *Poésies complètes*, 1:81; translation mine. I thank Ross Chambers for introducing me to the Gautier text. The atmosphere of Proust's famous bedroom has not been better depicted than by Percy Adlon in his extraordinary film *Céleste* (1981), loosely based upon Céleste Albaret's *Monsieur Proust*. The cork-lined room does not itself appear in Proust's *Recherche*, but from the opening sentence of the novel the recumbent narrator describes himself in an attitude we could easily assimilate to Proust's mode of existence in his real bedroom, or to Gautier's imagined posture in the *Albertus* preface.

12. One could also detect elements of it in Alfred de Musset's nearly contemporary *La Confession d'un enfant du siècle*—particularly in the strange structural segregation of the

Baudelaire's time, only a quarter century later, remembrance of its production was already disappearing over the horizon, though still detectable despite its increasing mystification. Modernism was beginning to be unable to see beyond its own projections of transcendence. But from Baudelaire to Proust this ideological complex had had another half-century to develop and to stabilize itself. To recover it in Proust will require some forceful critical and biographical archaeology.

One way to get at the presence of this internalized fantasy in Proust is to consider the following passage from the *Recherche* in relation to the Gautier quotation above. It comes in the course of his narrator's first trip to Balbec, as part of an extended account of the Grand-Hôtel there. The narrator is describing the brightly lit dining room of the hotel. The dining room strikes him as a vast aquarium in which the diners are swimming. Then, in the middle of the figure, an unexpected and uncharacteristic reflection—the parenthesis in the passage below—occurs:

> Les sources électriques faisant sourdre à flots la lumière dans la grande salle à manger, celle-ci devenait comme un immense et merveilleux aquarium devant la paroi de verre duquel la population ouvrière de Balbec, les pêcheurs et aussi les familles de petits bourgeois, invisibles dans l'ombre, s'écrasaient au vitrage pour apercevoir, lentement balancée dans les remous d'or, la vie luxueuse de ces gens, aussi extraordinaire pour les pauvres que celle de poissons et de mollusques étranges *(une grande question sociale, de savoir si la paroi de verre protégera toujours le festin des bêtes merveilleuses et si les gens obscurs qui regardent avidement dans la nuit ne viendront pas les cueillir dans leur aquarium et les manger).* (*RTP* 2: 41–42, *RTP54* 1:681; emphasis mine).

> [With the electric lamps flooding the dining room with light, it seemed like an immense and wonderful aquarium against whose glass partition the working population of Balbec, the fishermen and the shopkeepers' families, invisible in the darkness outside, pressed up against the panes to watch the luxurious life of the diners floating gently upon the golden eddies inside, as extraordin-

"historical" and the "psychological" fields or regions in the novel, upon which I commented in Chapter 3.

ary to the poor people outside as the lives of strange fishes or mollusks (*an important social question, this: whether the glass partition will always protect the banquets of these strange creatures and whether the ordinary people who watch them avidly in the night will not some day break in to pluck them from their aquarium and gulp them down*).]

The passage is surprising—particularly its exceedingly un-Proustian reference to the "social question" whose exclusion is essential to modernist aestheticism. The parenthesis is so unusual that a note in the new Pléiade edition endeavors to justify it. The editors explain that it was added to the text of *A l'ombre des jeunes filles en fleurs* after 1914, and they speculate that it was motivated by what they delicately term the "threats of revolution which were occasionally perceptible toward the end of the War" (*RTP* 2:1358).[13]

It remains that in this passage Proust's narrator for a moment unexpectedly registers the underclass and the threat that they embody. The fictive author of Gautier's *Albertus* perceived the world outside

---

13. This is not the only passage in the *Recherche* that invokes the sorts of social realities that ordinarily Proust's aesthetic bracketed systematically. In *Le Côté de Guermantes* we find an extended passage that begins: "Ce qui me faisait de la peine, c'était d'apprendre que presque toutes les maisons étaient habitées par des gens malheureux." ["What troubled me was to learn that almost every house was occupied by some unhappy (or *poor*) person"] (*RTP* 2:667; *RTP54* 2:372). One might also consider the baffling declaration of egalitarianism by Proust's narrator—and particularly its reference to the revolutionary Terror—in *La Prisonnière*. As in the Balbec passage under discussion here, the text occurs in a parenthesis. The narrator is speaking of Charlus as a "grand seigneur" and of his ingrained assumption of aristocratic preeminence: "a great nobleman (to whom [however] superiority over commoners was no more essentially inherent than it was in the case of any of his terrified ancestors forced to appear before the Revolutionary tribunal)" (*RTP* 3:820; *RTP54* 3:317). Finally, a contrivance much like the window structure at issue here is present in two memorable scenes in the *Recherche* in which the narrator witnesses scenes of Charlus's homosexuality: the first in *Sodome et Gomorrhe I*, in which through the fanlight between their room and his the narrator overhears Charlus and Jupien's lovemaking (*RTP* 3:6–11; *RTP54* 604–9); the second in *Le Temps retrouvé* in which through an uncurtained window in the corridor of Jupien's hotel he observes Charlus's flagellation by one of the employees (*RTP* 4:394; *RTP54* 3:815–16). These scenes have been extensively commented upon. It may not have been sufficiently noted, however, how much they reproduce the *inter-class* tension that functions in the window scenes already considered. Specifically, for his pleasures the baron requires being beaten by men drawn from the working class, and whom Jupien represents to him as dangerous criminals—thereby reenacting the traditional identification analyzed by Louis Chevalier in *Laboring Classes and Dangerous Classes in Paris during the First Half of the Nineteenth Century*, with all its provocative social and erotic resonances.

through a similar window, and sought its protection from a similar danger. In both texts, the window divides the *social* world in two. It sections off the degradation and the danger of external "real life" from an interior realm of elevated beings and aspirations. But in neither case can the separation prevent awareness of disagreeable realities, or even the intrusion of perilous ones. In particular, though Gautier expresses a sovereign nonengagement with the unengaging world outside his window, the world refuses him this luxury. Rather, *it shoots at him*. I obscured this energetic response on the part of a disdained external reality by truncating the passage when I quoted it earlier. Describing the poet in his bedroom, the sentence I omitted (following "He belongs to no political tendency") is however unmistakably clear: "He only notices revolutions when bullets smash through his windows" (1:81). However carefully barricaded, even the founding hero of *L'Art pour l'Art* cannot contrive to abrogate history completely.[14]

If we return to Proust's narrator in his privileged aquarium in Balbec, it becomes possible to unpack the image of the Grand-Hôtel window somewhat further. No doubt the most pertinent literary analogue of Proust's imagery and, beyond it, of the atmosphere in which the "social question" unexpectedly jumps into the frame of an elegant dining room window is Baudelaire's prose poem "Les Yeux des pauvres." There is no reason to believe that Proust had this text in mind when he was composing his fantasy on the Grand-Hôtel dining room, but he surely knew it.

"Les Yeux des pauvres" offers a third case of an artist contemplating the real world through a window—or rather a third example of a window serving an all-too-fragile barrier between the social and the aesthetic worlds. In case of "Les Yeux des pauvres" it is the window of a café on one of Baron Haussmann's newly built boulevards, in which Baudelaire's narrator and his mistress are dining. The lovers abruptly and uncomfortably become aware of a family of beggars

14. On the production of nineteenth-century aestheticism as a reaction against Fourierist and Saint-Simonian programs to enlist art in the effort to improve the condition of the disadvantaged, and on the phases and development of *L'Art pour l'Art* in general, see most accessibly Philippe Van Tieghem, *Les Grandes Doctrines littéraires en France*, 235–42. The phrase "l'art pour l'art" appears to have been Hugo's (1829), but the notion has long been particularly associated with Gautier.

pressing themselves against the glass and observing them. Under the
pressure of such scrutiny by the underclass, Baudelaire's upperclass
couple begin to quarrel—a quarrel that we could construe as an interpersonal displacement of the social tension from which these three
windows cannot entirely protect the artists who seek insulation behind them.[15]

We can read modernism through these windows. They allow seeing the modernist formation from *outside* its most strategic ideological closure. In each of these imagined situations, the elements of an
excluded world suddenly turn up visible on the other side of the
partition that was supposed to have segregated them out of mind.
What sense can we make of this iterated image? In particular, why
are these moments at a window so alarming, so uncannily *charged*?

No doubt none of these texts refers specifically to any of the
others. But the contrivance of the window offers each of these
writers a way of materializing the tension between a fantasy of security and an all-too-pertinent reality of threat: between the elements
of the world that the increasingly programmatic attitudes of modernism sought to bracket and the purified realm in which such bracketing could succeed only if it remained completely seamless and unde-
tectable. As is already visible in Proust's own contradictory phrase
"paroi de verre," these transparent partitions, these divisions that do
not divide, make a paradox manifest. A window is something like an

---

15. See Charles Baudelaire, *Oeuvres complètes*, ed. Claude Pichois, 1:317–19, and Terdiman, *Discourse/Counter-Discourse*, 317. On Proust's acquaintance with these texts, see
René de Chantal, *Marcel Proust, Critique littéraire*, 439–41. Proust had read Baudelaire's
Petits poèmes en prose as early as 1892. For a fourth case in which an artist confronts the
political and material world through a window—perhaps the most fully realized of such
engagements in any of these texts—see Stéphane Mallarmé's prose poem "Conflit" (1895),
in *Oeuvres complètes*, 355–60. I analyzed this text in *Discourse/Counter-Discourse*, 323–
28. Two moments in *Madame Bovary* (1857) evoke similar structures. At the ball at La
Vaubyessard, in the euphoria of her introduction to the "beau monde," Emma has an
arresting and unwelcome vision of a world more closely linked to her own origins and to
the determinants of her unhappiness: "Mme Bovary turned her head and perceived in the
garden [of the chateau], pressed against the window panes, the faces of the peasants who
were peering in" (part 1, chap. 8). Finally, in a mode of considerably more complex irony,
which powerfully deconstructs the image and the privilege it seems to grant to those
looking *out* of the window over those whose subaltern lives are contemplated through it,
we would need to consider the devastating "Comices agricoles" (part 2, chap. 8), in the
course of which, under the pretext of watching the humble award ceremony being conducted below through the window of the "salle des délibérations" in the Yonville Mairie,
Emma and Rodolphe play out their melodramatic seduction scene.

architectural oxymoron, a kind of self-subverting structure in relation to which the stable separations of the world are problematized and upset. It allows an indiscriminant mingling of inside and outside, of proper and improper. And lest we forget, it can always be smashed when something *real* is projected against it. Its very brittleness is an acute reminder of the sort of menace it frames and simultaneously seeks to forestall in each of the passages I have considered.

What becomes visible through these windows, then, is the return of a very pertinent and consequential repressed. To constitute itself, modernism *required* exclusion of specific aspects of the material, practical, political world. But these window scenes upset the exclusions and make their mechanism and their contents visible. They thus recover a relation that modernism suppresses; they rewrite the world of modernist autonomy and self-absorption as a realm of anxiety, apprehension, and subterranean dependency.[16]

Gautier, Baudelaire, Flaubert, Mallarmé, Proust: in France these were the protagonists and theoreticians of modernism in its evolving stages. They are hardly interchangeable figures, but on the crucial subterranean point of the determination of the aesthetic realm by dynamics from outside it, their consonance is striking. And whereas passages like the ones I have alluded to reveal considerable clarity on the part of the originators themselves concerning the exclusions modernism mandates, most commentary on the modernist autonomy of the aesthetic has flattened the asperities and effaced the complications that these uncannily parallel images of a window onto the real oblige us to recognize.

One further point. The figures obscurely perceptible on the other side of the Grand-Hôtel dining room's glass envelope—"invisible in the darkness"—are specters of a reality considerably more threatening (if more distant) than the locals who assemble of an evening to

16. With his accustomed perspicacity Walter Benjamin made a parallel point in his essay on Proust, using the more traditional language of Hegelian Marxist criticism. Concerning the "upper ten thousand," the flower of the French privileged class, Benjamin wrote that the self-conception of this group required the exclusion from its world of "everything that has a part in production, or at least demands that this part be gracefully and bashfully concealed behind the kind of manner that is sported by the polished professionals of consumption" ("The Image of Proust," 209). Benjamin goes on to argue that Proust "turns his whole limitless art into a veil for this one most vital mystery of his class: the economic aspect" (210). I return to Benjamin's reflections on Proust in Chapter 6.

gape at the Parisian upper crust. Proust's post-1914 interpolation, in other words, clarifies a social *danger* that can hardly be said to have been self-evident in the innocuous curiosity of Balbec's fishermen and tradespeople. The local shopkeepers and fisherfolk are stand-ins. Brilliantly lit from within the dining room, Proust's *paroi de verre* mostly throws the images of the diners back upon themselves. Yet the window eerily superimposes upon their elegant and reassuring reflections the image of figures both visually and socially more obscure. The gawking villagers are hardly a threat to the tranquillity of the rich, but they put the threat in mind. What they recall is a danger on the edge of awareness—one they might not themselves even conceive, but one that *history* imagines on their behalf, and that recollection pulls into the present.

Such restorations of a repressed potentiality constitute structures of memory.[17] They materialize something that consciousness wanted to forget—indeed, something it sought actively to suppress. Restoration is achieved, as the Pléiade note suggests, by reinterpreting the content of a displaced or weakened image of the threat and making it mean more than it had meant to.[18] The projection of these figures onto the surface of the dining room window in the Grand-Hôtel thus functions much like the "screen memories" that Freud theorized in 1899: images by which the unconscious replaces intolerable recollections with less menacing substitutes that have the advantage of blocking access to the contents they overwrite. But in analysis—for which the demystificatory parenthesis in Proust's text stands as analogue— these structures of replacement (what Freud would term "substitute formations") are detectable in the very intensity of the cathexis that has inexplicably attached to them.[19]

17. Indeed, they are precisely homologous with the paradigm of Freudian repression, and of the symmetrical restoration of past contents in therapy, that I will consider in Chapter 7.

18. The threat of revolution perceptible here appears nowhere else in the *Recherche*. In Proust's novel the term "revolution" applies only to innovations in the aesthetic realm. But the menace of what the *Manifesto* called the "spectre of Communism" haunted Proust's own memory in a particularly biographical way. He was born during the Paris Commune in 1871, a fact he repeatedly recalled and for which he regularly blamed his life-long ill health, attributing it to his mother's anxiety during the Siege of Paris and the revolution that followed, and to the privations which she suffered while pregnant with him. See George D. Painter, *Marcel Proust: A Biography*, 1:4.

19. See Sigmund Freud, "Screen Memories" (1899), *SE* 3:303–22. Such a structure of

From Proust's Balbec at the height of Belle Époque euphoria, the threat of revolution can seem invisible, but uncannily and unbidden it materializes nonetheless through the faculty around which so much of Proust's fascination and anxiety turns—through memory. The memory active here subverts the programmatic repressions of modernism. It restores the image of the world enveloping—and determining—the aesthetic, yet normally imperceptible from within its protective enclosure. But note how far the results of its operation stand from the salvationist productions of *mémoire involontaire*. Perhaps we will be obliged to conclude that *the latter is a screen memory as well*.

The stress upon memory in *A la recherche du temps perdu* comes increasingly into focus: *Memory as transcendence. Or memory as repression*. This contradiction accounts for the dynamic that drives Proust's novel. The scene in the Grand-Hôtel dining room destabilizes an aesthetic structure in which Proust's investment is manifestly intense. However fleetingly, the passage enables us to perceive and to assess the fantasy that constitutes modernism. This fantasy dreams a privileged subject's autonomy, projects a hypostatized independence and an untrammeled capacity for self-realization, but then from the edge of consciousness memory draws back the elements of existence that subvert this fabrication. It restores the anxious reality of contingency that the modernist fantasy had sought to block.

The project of such exclusion can be read in other loci as well. It might seem that I have forced Proust's brief post-1914 parenthetical

---

substitution consequently helps to explain the eerie charge borne by all of these images in which writers encounter the dispossessed. On "substitute formations," see Freud, "The Unconscious" (1915), *SE* 14:193; "Repression" (1915), *SE* 14:154; and "Overview of the Transference Neuroses" (1915), 7. Serge Doubrovsky raises the issue of "screen memories," but in a different connection from the one I consider here; see *Writing and Fantasy in Proust: La Place de la Madeleine*, 5–8. Doubrovsky's psychoanalytic perspective leads him to a general demystificatory rereading of Proust. His unwillingness to take Proust's own self-assessment at face value is salutary. But though his critique is remarkably ingenious in its detail, its psychoanalytic foundation entails a familiar pattern of schematisms. In it, certain contents are ineluctably transformed, through however complex a series of "substitute formations," into the predictable Freudian operators of the Oedipus, and associated structures. In Chapters 7 and 8, I consider Timpanaro's critique of Freud's mode of reasoning. Timpanaro targets psychoanalytic tendentiousness particularly. His strictures are particularly pertinent to Doubrovsky's mode of analysis.

addition to the description of the Grand-Hôtel dining room to arrive at my interpretation, but this analysis of the aquarium image in *A l'ombre des jeunes filles en fleurs* coheres with more macroscopic elements in the development of Proust's own project. For the archaeology that will uncover these traces, *Contre Sainte-Beuve* has particular importance. In 1908 or 1909, Proust began working on a project in cultural history and theory whose objective was to challenge the method of the nineteenth century's most influential professional critic, Charles–Augustin Sainte-Beuve. Proust never published this material, and it is unclear whether he would have chosen the title under which it has come to be known (see *CSB* 829). But since its initial publication in 1954, there has been no doubt about the intimate relation between this idiosyncratic critical project and the novelistic material upon which Proust was simultaneously working and which shortly became *A la recherche du temps perdu*.

Twenty years ago *Contre Sainte-Beuve* was accorded separate publication in the Pléiade collection (1971), but today the editors of the new Pléiade edition of the *Recherche* have drawn this material back into the orbit of the novel itself. They are explicit in judging that the writing from this period organized around the attack on Sainte-Beuve and his method must be considered nothing less than "a first version" of the final novel (*RTP* 1:xl and n. 3).[20] But beyond their coincidence in time and their coextension in the school notebooks that Proust began using for his sketches around this period, what connects these two writing projects, seemingly so incommensurable?

Sainte-Beuve died in 1869, two years before Proust's birth. In the decade before World War I he was not at the top of most people's critical agenda. Proust himself acknowledges that Sainte-Beuve doesn't seem an important subject for discussion (*CSB* 216), but Proust nonetheless put considerable energy into taking him on. What made Sainte-Beuve worth demolishing? I think that an important motivation in *both* of the projects Proust began focusing upon around 1909—however diverse their expression—arose in his efforts to in-

20. A detailed philological and chronological account of the connections linking the *Contre Sainte-Beuve* material to the *Recherche* will be found in the article by Claudine Quémar, "Autour de trois 'avant-textes' de l' 'Ouverture' de la *Recherche*: Nouvelles approches des problèmes du *Contre Sainte-Beuve*." See also Luzius Keller, *L'Episode de la madeleine dans les cahiers de brouillon de Marcel Proust*, 8–9.

ternalize and stabilize the ideological commitments of modernism that I argued define important aspects of *A la recherche du temps perdu*. Specifically, the intellectual engagement in *Contre Sainte-Beuve* amounts to an extended polemic against *determinism*. This commitment explains its subterranean affiliation with Proust's novel.

Three recent studies of Proust, which have appeared in close proximity, help us to clarify the stakes in this polemic: Anne Henry's *Marcel Proust: Théories pour une esthétique* (1983), Vincent Descombes's *Proust: Philosophie du roman* (1987), and Antoine Compagnon's *Proust entre deux siècles* (1989). Leaving aside divergences in their weighting or interpretation of detail, these critics clarify Proust's relation to the received doctrines (ultimately drawn from Schelling and Schopenhauer) central to the reigning post-Kantian idealism of his period. Proust's introduction to this body of doctrine no doubt began with Alphonse Darlu, who taught him letters and philosophy at the Lycée Condorcet (and whom he portrayed as M. Beulier in *Jean Santeuil*).[21] The details of the arguments that divided the French philosophical community (subjective vs. objective idealism, etc.) in the period of Proust's late adolescence and early adulthood are not pertinent to my analysis here, nor is the identification of specific sources from which he may have drawn the positions he adopted at that period. But it *is* important that Proust maintained them for the rest of his life. As Descombes puts it, Proust spoke a philosophical language perfectly familiar to his generation (*Proust*, 35), and moreover did so in a generally uncritical way. The stakes in his polemic against Sainte-Beuve can be located in the commitments Proust adopted from this now more or less forgotten tradition.

Contre Sainte-Beuve begins this way: "Chaque jour j'attache moins de prix à l'intelligence" (211; cf. alternate versions on 216; see also *Le Carnet de 1908*, 71). But what specifically does Proust mean by the "intelligence" that every day he values less and less? As Proust uses the term, "intelligence" is the rationalist, utilitarian analytical faculty.

21. In Proust's *Carnet de 1908*, Darlu is the sole person whose influence on him Proust acknowledges (101). Anne Henry argues that the influence of his specific positions on Proust has been exaggerated. She provides the most detailed account of the French philosophical landscape in the 1880s and 1890s. See *Marcel Proust: Théories pour une esthétique*, 76–97.

It is the source and the mechanism of instrumental activity. Consequently, in Proust's somewhat fevered construction it figures a force inimical to poetry; it dries up the soul. "Intelligence" cannot illuminate mysteries, but only corrode their wonder. It cannot comprehend authentic creativity, but only the pedestrian reproduction of more or less successfully disguised commonplaces. Manifestly, the "intelligence" that Proust stigmatizes isn't very smart.

In attacking Sainte-Beuve, Proust is resisting the influence of what broadly we could call nineteenth-century positivist scientism (or "science positive"; see *CSB* 832 n. 5). One could make a strong case that despite the rhetoric directed against Sainte-Beuve, the real object of Proust's critique was rather the philosopher Hippolyte Taine. Indeed, Taine provides Proust his entry into the argument against Sainte-Beuve to begin with, as one night in the narrator's bedroom he and his mother debate Taine's 1869 eulogy of Sainte-Beuve (see *CSB* 218 and 220 n. 3). Essentially, Sainte-Beuve and Taine held that cultural production can be adequately explained by the material elements of culture itself. Taine's celebrated theory of race, milieu, and moment is just one formulaic manifestation of the more general notion that *all* activities of human beings are mediated, in however complex a way, by other activities in comparable registers, and hence are comprehensible in terms of them. Such a theory cannot abstract any area of human behavior from the determining mediations of others less exalted. Therefore it cannot admit the sort of partition—even a semitransparent one—between the activities of everyday life on the one hand and the productions of the soul that Proust (and along with him Gautier, Baudelaire, Mallarmé, and Flaubert) had striven to isolate and protect in their respective "window" scenes on the other.

What is at stake in Proust's polemic against Sainte-Beuve is thus an attempt to strengthen the solidity, the impermeability of the partition between the quotidian and the aesthetic—to stabilize the ideological assumptions of aesthetic modernism. Sainte-Beuve receives the force of Proust's critique not because he made silly judgments concerning Stendhal (though he did; see *CSB* 221–23 and 578), but because his theory subverted what was for Proust and other avant-garde writers the essential frontier between art and other human activities. Like Taine and an entire analytic tradition more or less consciously following out the insights of the developing nineteenth-century concept of ideology, Sainte-Beuve believed it was possible to *explain* literature. Manifestly, Proust had committed himself from the period of his school days to a polar conception, in which art must be maintained absolutely discontinuous with the remainder of life. Proust's notion of the work of art figures an ultimate discontinuity.

The nodal point of the aesthetic complex Proust thus defends in assailing Sainte-Beuve is the nineteenth-century notion of "genius." It plays a considerable role in the *Recherche*. Genius focuses the conceptualization of discontinuity that has been at issue in the diverse expressions of Proust's aesthetic commitments that I have been examining. Genius is a nonpareil that defies analysis and resists relation with anything else. It posits a realm of human activity that in its singularity becomes theoretically opaque. In this projection the innovations of the genius are ontologically disjunctive: incomprehensible, irreducible, absolute.[22]

Positivism subverts such conceptions. Its epistemology claimed to provide nothing less than complete understanding of social and cultural objects. Taine directly challenged the heart of the creation mystery by asserting that *all* human phenomena (even including the productions of genius) were comprehensible in terms of objectifiable categories such as race, milieu, and moment. To the progeny of the romantic generation it must have appeared that the last margins of the artistic arcanum were thus threatened by scientism.[23] In the polemic that evolved around this question at midcentury and after,

22. Compare in England Carlyle's characterization of the genius: "Whence he came, whither he is bound, by what ways he arrived, by what he might be furthered on his course, no one asks. He is an accident in society" (quoted by Raymond Williams, *Culture and Society 1780–1950*, 84).

23. In *Le Côté de Guermantes*, Proust had some fun contradicting Taine's celebrated thesis. First the narrator, then (unconsciously echoing him) Saint-Loup, sententiously declare that sociological "milieu" means nothing, that only "intellectual" milieu has any determinative force over individuals. The involuntary repetition by characters from such different social strata of course slyly instantiates the very point of the assertion; see *RTP* 2:404, 417; *RTP54* 2:106, 119. Whereas Taine is generally conceived of as a positivist, René Wellek has sought to demonstrate the inaccuracy of the characterization. For Wellek, at least in his aesthetic thought, Taine was a pure Hegelian. But Hegel was not less certain than Taine that aesthetic objects could be fully analyzed and understood. See Wellek, *A History of Modern Criticism* 4:27, 36, and his *Concepts of Criticism*, 43. For a recent assessment of Taine, and particularly of his Hegelian side, see Patrizia Lombardo, "Hippolyte Taine between Art and Science." See also McDonald, *Proustian Fabric*, 63, 82.

Taine consequently became the surreptitious (or the explicit) adversary of the partisans of genius theory. Even Sainte-Beuve himself had reservations about whether *everything* in culture could be accounted for by a method such as Taine's. Sainte-Beuve recognized that many considered it marked by a culpable and reductive materialism. In 1864, in a review of Emile Deschanel's *Essai de critique naturelle*, he recognized the force of the positivist viewpoint, but persisted in a crucial reservation: "However careful we are in analyzing and explaining the meaning of works, their origins, their roots, in examining the character of authors' individual talents and demonstrating their links to their progenitors [*parents*] and to their contexts [*alentours*], there will always remain a certain unexplained, unexplainable aspect, which consists of the individual contribution of genius."[24] For his part, Flaubert wrote directly to Taine to criticize his theory: "First there's milieu, then race (which you can define less clearly than milieu), but then comes *the genius of each individual, which you cannot define at all.*"[25]

We could then understand Proust's *Contre Sainte-Beuve* as the most intense and focused moment in this antipositivist polemic—even if Proust's perfervid engagement in it came at a moment when, for many, the doctrinal struggle must have seemed a generation out of phase. But Proust never published this material, confining himself in the *Recherche* to a series of critical skirmishes with Sainte-Beuve dispersed over the novel's entire length. We could think of his somewhat overwrought argument with nineteenth-century positivism around 1908 or 1909 as a conceptual and ideological ground-clearing operation. In effect, *Contre Sainte-Beuve* casts out the demon of determination that Proust reacted against in Sainte-Beuve himself and, through him, in Taine. The work seeks to define and to open a space for the indeterminate innovations of genius, for an unanalyzable freedom of creation. In the *Recherche*, in figures like Vinteuil, Bergotte, and Elstir, Proust then recirculates this image of the genius's incommensurable, unconstrainable power.

24. It hardly seems necessary to mention that Proust does not refer to this discussion, which would have diffused the focus of his polemic against Sainte-Beuve. It occurs in the *Lundi* of 7 November 1864, in Charles-Augustin Saint-Beuve, *Nouveaux Lundis*, 9:70.

25. Emphasis mine. "Il y a le milieu, d'abord, puis la race (que vous pouvez moins préciser que le milieu), puis l'*ingenium* de chaque individu, que vous ne pouvez pas définir" (Letter to Taine [10 November 1868], in *Correspondance*, 3:822).

This construction leads to an absolute autonomization of the work of art. Such a move is manifestly congruent with the representations of *A la recherche du temps perdu* on both thematic and doctrinal levels. Proust's insistence on the nullity of social life and on the discontinuity that divides artistic activity from quotidian existence is the reflex and the fictional figuration of the antideterminist theory of culture that Proust directed so strenuously against Sainte-Beuve, but Proust's representation of artistic activity leaves such activity in an uncomfortable (if predictable) fix. Since nothing comprehensible produced it, the work of art finds itself in the awkward position of being theoretically incomprehensible when somehow it has finally come into being. Like the commodity whose fetishism Marx first detected, the work of art enters the world stripped of its own prehistory. It appears like an aerolith from the heavens. How then can it ever be assimilated, much less explained or understood? Proust addresses this conundrum with his notion that the work itself—that genius itself—generates the structures of understanding that will allow it to be apprehended and valued. But inevitably this takes time:

> Ce temps du reste qu'il faut à un individu . . . pour pénétrer une oeuvre un peu profonde, n'est que le raccourci et comme le symbole des années, des siècles parfois, qui s'écoulent avant que le public puisse aimer un chef-d'oeuvre vraiment nouveau. . . . Les faux jugements . . . ne sont pas évitables. Ce qui est cause qu'une oeuvre de génie est difficilement admirée tout de suite, c'est que celui qui l'a écrite est extraordinaire, que peu de gens lui ressemblent. C'est son oeuvre elle-même qui, en fécondant les rares esprits capables de le comprendre, les fera croître et multiplier. . . . Il faut que l'oeuvre . . . crée elle-même sa postérité. (*RTP* 1:521–22; *RTP54* 1:531–32).

> [Moreover the time required for an individual to penetrate a profound work is only the reduction and, one might say, the symbol of the years, sometimes the centuries, which must pass before the public can appreciate a truly new masterpiece. . . . Incorrect opinions concerning it are unavoidable. . . . What makes a work of genius difficult to appreciate immediately is the fact that the person who wrote it is extraordinary, that few people resemble him or her. It is the work itself which, by fertilizing the rare minds able to comprehend it, will cause them to grow and multiply. . . . The work . . . has to create its own posterity.]

Of course Proust was not a professional philosopher.[26] So it might seem quibbling to observe that his image of the art work leads to a troubling paradox. But these contradictions and perplexities help to locate the stresses that Proust's aesthetic had been unable to resolve. Following those in the nineteenth century who resisted conceptions of cultural objects based upon extra-aesthetic determination, Proust produced a model whose object is manifestly to magnify and to isolate the aesthetic. So complete was his success that in his version, art stands in the same singular position as does the deity in certain theologies: determining everything, determined by nothing. It has no specifiable antecedent and is subject to no comprehensible mediations. Yet mysteriously it produces its posterity. Art has become the unmoved mover.[27] In Proust's projection the aesthetic evades inscription in any external discourse. But this is as much as to say that the aesthetic *transcends memory*. Without recourse to some form of scholasticism, it is hard to imagine how this sort of unidirectional transcendence might make sense. Why would Proust have produced a theory of aesthetic activity so vulnerable to accusations of incoherence or mystification? And why would he have pushed such a shaky theory with such sovereign and protracted insistence?

I think Proust was pressed to the construction of such a vulnerable model for the activity that occupied his life by the need to forestall the conception that stands over against his own view. I conceive his aesthetic as intensely counterdiscursive. Through its insistence we can discern the adversary it supposes and begin to understand why Proust perceived it as a threat. In the context of the ideological struggle that animated *Contre Sainte-Beuve* at just the moment when the *Recherche* itself was coming into being, the effect of such a construction is to play Taine—or determination—back against Proust.

   To explain a text at all, there must always be a *hors-texte*, an *other* of the text's own expression. The text can neither speak nor silence

26. Descombes, who is, bluntly dismisses Proust's aesthetic doctrines as "impossible constructions" (*Proust*, 65).
27. This autogenic fantasy and Proust's intense preoccupation with "originality" is a fundamental theme throughout Doubrovsky's *Writing and Fantasy in Proust*; see particularly 31–37 and 105–9.

it. *Interpretation* is its bearer; *criticism* is what makes such knowledge functional. A notion of overdrawn "insistence" such as the one in Proust's aesthetic theory thus draws a text beyond itself—typically by evoking categories like *absent presence* or *absent cause*.[28] Such displacements and retriangulations—exceeding and subverting the closures of an autonomous and autogenic text—turn out to be essential for understanding the meaning of memory in Proust's novel. But my discussion has already foreshadowed the sort of analysis I want to essay in what follows. If only in a figurative mode, the image obscurely visible in the window of the Grand-Hôtel, but everywhere else resisted in the novel, represents an identical dynamic by which Proust's text encounters the limits of its self-conception by momentarily and as if inadvertently violating them.

This pattern of momentary lapse or self-betrayal will seem familiar. The insistence, the strenuousness of Proust's doctrinal assertions, by which we come to suspect they represent expressive and ideological exigencies *beyond* their explicit contents, begins to look like the sort of distortion that around the same time Freud's analytic attention was learning to seize upon, the product of something like rationalization or repression. I want therefore to consider the hypothesis that in the overdrawn insistence of Proust's assertions—here, concerning the absolute autonomy of the aesthetic, elsewhere concerning the salvationist potentiality of "involuntary memory"—he presses not only against commonsense experience of such matters, but against something like an intuition that his own assertions may be deceived.

Of course this does not diminish the categorical, the positively apodictic tone of Proust's pronouncements. We may forget this tone in Proust, but it is characteristic of his style despite his aestheticizing strictures against the doctrinal and the theoretical. Consider this assertion from *Contre Sainte-Beuve*: "In art, there are no initiators, no precursors. Everything depends upon the individual, every individual begins the artistic or literary enterprise afresh, on his own ac-

28. The issue of connotation raised here challenges the analytic capacity of contemporary theories rooted in linguistic paradigms. For beyond linguistic competence, decoding a text requires competence in the realms of ideology and cultural knowledge that by their nature cannot be comprehended from within the linguistic paradigm itself. For an account of issues related to these paradigmatic tensions, see Vaheed Ramazani, *The Free Indirect Mode: Flaubert and the Poetics of Irony*, 26–29.

count" (220).[29] Even Baudelaire—to whose influential and ringing expressions of aesthetic intransigence I have repeatedly referred—never fantasized that individuality could attain such an extreme.[30] But it was an absolute and transcendent concept of individuality that Proust's insistence was calculated to safeguard and to promote.

Descombes has examined this Proustian fixation upon the "realization of the self" (see his *Proust*, 292–327). The attainment of individual distinction must be seen as another aspect of the antideterminist complex that Proust had inherited from the nineteenth century.[31] Descombes puts the stakes this way: "In the society Proust knew, the *institution of literature* permitted someone to claim and to obtain, under certain specified conditions, the status of autonomous individual" (295). The fundamental condition that had to be fulfilled was the attainment of "originality"—which we can understand as the art-critical code word denoting the hypostatized state of absolute transcendence Proust's aesthetic projects and valorizes. Original writers speak languages absolutely their own, as Proust asserted to his friend Madame Straus in November 1908, just as he was working on *Contre Sainte-Beuve* and the proto-*Recherche*: "[Writers] only begin to write well on the condition of originality, by creating their own language [*à condition d'être originaux, de faire eux-mêmes leur langue*]" (*Corr.*, 8:277).

Something *else* is being played out in the pristine—or brittle—absolutism of this state of aesthetic grace. What Proust projects with such tenacity is an individual wholeness and autonomy that he must have felt gravely threatened in his own experience or in the assumptions of his culture. Martha Nussbaum detects such an overdetermi-

---

29. Or this passage from "Journées de Lecture" (1904): "We can receive the truth from no one else, and we must create it ourselves" (*CSB* 177). Proust is more nuanced in his discussion of the role of the "précurseur" in *Sodome et Gomorrhe*. See *RTP* 3:211; *RTP54* 2:816.

30. In the *Salon de 1846* Baudelaire wrote that "individuality" had been exaggerated, to the detriment of collective originality, and sarcastically imagined that this had resulted from artists' dreams of finally possessing "that little *place of one's own* [*cette petite propriété*]" (*Oeuvres complètes*, ed. Le Dantec and Pichois, 949). I borrow my translation from Charles Baudelaire, *Art in Paris 1845–1862*, 116. But after 1848 Baudelaire abandoned this more nuanced view in favor of the doctrinal purities of the aesthetic formalism evidenced, for example, in the Gautier essay of 1859, which I discussed in Chapter 4.

31. I analyzed the historical and cultural dynamics of this preoccupation in *Discourse/ Counter-Discourse*, chap. 6, "The Paradoxes of Distinction."

nation of Proust's strategy. She seeks to frame his objective this wa,
"Isn't [the narrator's] whole enterprise just a new and more subtle
expression of the rage for control, and need for possession and certainty, the denial of incompleteness and neediness . . . ?"[32] These
needs are of course expressed in important diegetic and doctrinal
aspects of the *Recherche*. But whatever his motivation, the problem
Proust seeks to solve, the result he seeks so intensively to attain, is
the unification of the self, the resolution of its ambiguities and the
stresses dislocating it.

The psychological narrative in Proust's novel systematically refers
the etiology of this need back to childhood, as if the primitive experience of dependency and fragmentation—emblematized so memorably in the celebrated drama of the Combray good night kiss—had
projected itself through time to become a fate condemning us in
adulthood to the intolerable repetition of such archaic experiences. A
paradigm of determination by the past readable in Musset's *Confession* thus here is fully bodied forth.

If this hypothesis concerning the mystified determinations of
Proust's critique of determination is reasonable, what it says is that
his projection of individual existence and activity freed from the con-
tingencies of the quotidian, from the servitudes and constraints of
any mediations other than individual creative will and aesthetic
value, *fundamentally mystifies the operation of memory*. Proust's
doctrine construes as self-realization a constitutive bracketing, a *forgetting* of all the social experiences and ideological structures that
construct the self to begin with. But as I have been suggesting all
along, such a fundamental suspicion concerning the presence of the
past then seems comprehensible as a doctrine overdetermined by
the past itself—specifically, by phantasms emerging from the desper-
ate childhood needs that Proust represented more forcefully and
more poignantly than any other writer in the modern period. No
wonder, then, that as the crossing of such intense contradictions,
memory emerges as the central enigma in Proust's text. Then it seems
that no book in the period since the French Revolution narrates the
memory crisis with greater intensity or pertinence than Proust's.

In any case the system Proust has constructed to preserve what his

32. Martha C. Nussbaum, *Love's Knowledge: Essays on Philosophy and Literature*, 270.

novel and his doctrine understand as the integrity of the individual resists determination in the most determined ways. In one sense the threat it seeks to forestall seems completely indistinct or spectral—something like an archaic fear of drowning or self-dissolution. In another sense the constant anxiety at the dependence of the self of which the *Recherche* is the extended narrative bodies forth the menace in a brilliant and chilling representation. "Originality" might then seem an artfully designed compensatory formation whose objective was to re-suture an identity that Proust's three thousand pages ceaselessly reveal to be on the point of dissolution.

How can the stakes of originality have grown so weighty? Proust's fantasy concerning it was not unique. The *Recherche* may have given greater *extension* to such a notion than any other text. But it was propagated with comparable *intensity* among an entire portion of the aesthetic intelligentsia; it was part of a cultural tradition. Paul Valéry puts the stakes in terms that seem right for Proust as well as for Baudelaire to whom Valéry was specifically referring: "In the realm of creation . . . the necessity of distinguishing oneself is indivisible from one's very existence."[33] Individuality is thus elevated into a question of life and death. A striking passage from *La Prisonnière* gives a kind of backhand validation of this reading. The stakes that ride on "originality" are always at their highest when Proust describes his artists—Vinteuil, Bergotte, Elstir. Here, the narrator has been listening to Vinteuil's Septet. He finds himself astonished by the discovery of something that his novel has been strenuously, transparently claiming from the outset. His naïveté may strain our credulity, but his perception bears examination nonetheless: "[The impression] produced by these phrases of Vinteuil was so different from any other, that it was as if . . . *individuals existed*" (*RTP* 3:760; *RTP54* 3:255–56; emphasis mine). The logic of this insight seems clear. Through originality, individuals exist. We would seem constrained to conclude that without it, they don't.

Resonances of this existential apprehension—the threat to "individuality" from forces outside the self—emanate variously from the nineteenth-century tradition, from sources as diverse as the symbolists

33. Paul Valéry, "Situation de Baudelaire," in *Oeuvres*, 1:600.

and Nietzsche. The presence of the former in the ideological and aesthetic inheritance of the *Recherche* has been widely recognized since Edmund Wilson's *Axel's Castle* appeared in 1931.[34] But Nietzsche's relevance to the *Recherche* has perhaps not been adequately assessed. Proust was no partisan of Nietzsche, but he was well aware of him.[35]

Nietzsche's relevance to this discussion of "originality" arises not in any supposed "influence," but in the frame Nietzsche provided for the conceptual and ideological issues Proust was struggling with throughout the *Recherche*. Nietzsche produced the nineteenth century's most concerted polemic against the extrinsic determination of the individual: the second of his *Untimely Meditations*, widely known in English as "The Use and Abuse of History" (1874).[36] Proust may

34. See also Descombes, *Proust*, 255–56 and 299. Concerning Proust's convergence with symbolist themes, consider this quotation (in an English translation which is the only form of this text that has been conserved) from one of Mallarmé's essays on Manet: "The eye should forget all else it has seen, and learn anew from the lessons before it. It should *abstract itself from memory*, seeing only that which it looks upon, and that as for the first time" ("The Impressionists and Édouard Manet," 69; emphasis mine).

35. There are a number of Nietzschean references in Proust's first *Carnet* (see the epigraph to this chapter, and *Le Carnet de 1908*, 99, 100, 101). In the *Carnet*, Proust wrote the philosopher's name as "Nietche." He regularly spelled it wrong. In April 1909, at the request of his friend Robert Dreyfus, Proust promised to write a pastiche of Nietzsche (*Corr.* 9:75). There is no evidence that it was ever produced. The suggestion of one is itself piquant, however, since Proust had theorized pastiche as a mechanism for exorcising the influence—what, in a phrase which was to make its fortune, he called the "souvenirs involontaires" (letter to R. Dreyfus, 21 March 1908, *Corr.* 8:66)—of other writers' styles and ideas. It is provocative to think that Nietzsche might have penetrated Proust's consciousness to the point that a cure by pastiche (akin, one could say, to Freudian "abreaction") made sense to him. On the salubrious effect of pastiche, see Descombes, *Proust*, 132. In *A l'ombre des jeunes filles en fleurs*—in a revelation that itself explodes the notion that individuals are pre-scripted by "race" or "milieu," or predictable on the faith of them—we learn that the noble Robert de Saint-Loup is a committed Nietzschean (see *RTP* 2:92; *RTP54* 1:732). And at a different point the narrator ponderously joins an argument with Nietzsche's defense of friendship, which Proust was always at pains to condemn as yet another force threatening to erode the absolutism of authentic individuality (see *RTP* 2:688; *RTP54* 394). See *RTP* 2:1731 n. 1 for a detailed account of Proust's acquaintance with Nietzsche, in part through his friend Daniel Halévy, who wrote a biography of the philosopher that appeared in 1909.

36. R. J. Hollingdale gives the text a different title in his recent translation: "On the Uses and Disadvantages of History for Life." I cite this translation. Yet a third title appears in a new translation by Gary Brown: "History in the Service and Disservice of Life." I have found no evidence that Proust had read this work, although he did refer explicitly to the *fourth* Meditation ("Richard Wagner in Bayreuth," generally known in French as "Le Cas Wagner") in *La Prisonnière* (*RTP* 3:665; *RTP54* 3:159).

not have been familiar with this specific text or with the details of
Nietzsche's argument in it against the constraints that bind individuals and compress their existences into caricatures of their real potentiality, but the position is pervasive throughout Nietzsche's
works, and it resonates powerfully with preoccupations central to the
Recherche.

"The Use and Abuse of History" identifies the *past* as the origin of
constraint. Initially this might seem surprising. But Proust's intense
commitment to "originality" really claims nothing different. "Originality" arises in the ability to resist the human tendency toward uncritical homeostasis or involuntary iteration. The ability of the past to
reproduce itself automatically in the present and thereby to choke
originality was a persistent idea in the nineteenth century—evoked
nowhere more memorably than in Marx's chilling image from *The
Eighteenth Brumaire*: "The tradition of all the dead generations
weighs like a nightmare on the brain of the living."[37] Nietzsche draws
out the consequences of a parallel perception in his second *Meditation*.

Nietzsche's argument is simple. He conceptualizes how the investment of the present by the past—in the form of tradition, custom,
history, habit, style, and convention—colonizes the mind and restricts the creative potentiality of human beings. It does so in a vast
structure of routinized social and cultural practices that no one consciously elects and everyone inevitably experiences. The control exercised by these structures is uncannily spectral, and all the more
threatening for its invisibility. Authentic originality, decisive action,
thus require enforcing a rupture with the past. The burden of history
is a force with which human beings are required to contend and, if
they are to attain individuality, to break.[38] Nietzsche develops these
arguments with great analytic power. "All action," he writes, "requires forgetting" (62; translation modified). Creation in art, break-
through in science, calls for minds that can liberate themselves from
previous patterns. Realization of the individual and of the culture as
a whole depends on enforcing vigorous disjunction with the past.
"[Each one of us] must . . . rebel against a state of things in which he

37. Karl Marx, *The Eighteenth Brumaire of Louis Bonaparte*, 10.
38. See Hayden White, "The Burden of History," and David Lowenthal, *The Past Is a
Foreign Country*, 63–73.

only repeats what he has heard, learns what is already known, imitates what already exists" (123; translation modified).

It is striking how closely these arguments cohere with Proust's, particularly with his polemic against what he termed the "heavy veil of habit" (*RTP* 4:124; *RTP54* 3:544): "stupefying habit which during the entire course of our life conceals virtually the whole universe and, in the dead of night, without changing the label, substitutes for the most dangerous or the most intoxicating poisons something anodyne which procures no delight" (ibid.). Habit deadens everything. It normalizes and flattens experience. Habit is thus a mode, a Proustian name, for the dynamic that threatens the individuality of individuals and the originality of their perceptions and activity.

The terms of Proust's hypostasis of the individual—autonomous, disjunctive, irreducibly unique—reappear at the heart of this conception. Speaking of the authenticity of any perception of objects, Samuel Beckett makes this clear: "When the object is perceived as particular and unique and not merely the member of a family, when it appears independent of any general notion and *detached from the sanity of a cause*, isolated and inexplicable in the light of ignorance, then and then only may it be a source of enchantment" (*Proust*, 11; italics mine). Habit hobbles "enchantment" (see *RTP* 2:4–5; *RTP54* 1:643–44) by enforcing *relation*, and thereby subverting the ontological and temporal *difference* that in Proust's projection (or fantasy) constitutes the individual, the original, the unique.

Of course there are problems with such a notion, particularly when it is absolutized, as it tends to be in Proust. I've already referred to one manifestation of the paradox this vision entails: that the authentically unique, like the text in an unknown language, may equally well turn out to be authentically incomprehensible.[39] Proust seeks to recuperate this perplexity by projecting its erosion over time, but this naively hopeful gambit only displaces the enigma without beginning to suggest how contingency and relation could ever be constructed around an object that is constituted in its radical exemption from them.

Proust gets himself in this conceptual fix because he attempts to

39. On this disadvantage of originality, see Susan Stewart, *Crimes of Writing: Problems in the Containment of Representation*, 25.

purge from notions like "creation," "originality," the "individual"—
and in particular (as I will argue in the next chapter) from that absolute form of memory he terms "involuntary"—all trace of relation to
entities outside themselves that would open them to determination
or subject them to contingency. But such a vision leaves him in a
very awkward spot: conceptually afloat on a sea of indeterminate par-
ticulars in which everything stands pristine, *sui generis*—and irreducibly incomprehensible.

Theoretically, that poses a problem. In the face of it, we might be
tempted, along the lines of the tactic I described in Empson's dismissal of Proust's doctrinal conclusion in favor of his novel's much
more supple narrative texture, simply to overlook such incoherence.
But I consider it symptomatic, however internally contradictory it
may prove to be. Proust's conceptual system may seem flawed when
we attempt to rationalize it or to construct the world it would project. But its intransigence, its absolutism is its most salient and striking characteristic. It is particularly remarkable in a writer generally
associated with an almost excessive subtlety, nuance, and capacity for
modulation. When it comes to doctrines in the areas I have been
discussing, Proust turns into a conceptual terrorist. He wants utterly
to disable dialectics, exhaustively to eliminate relation as operators in
his conceptual scheme. This makes his world strangely incongruous.

For relation won't go away. Nietzsche was cannier than Proust in
this regard. His second *Mediation* brilliantly stigmatizes the "disadvantages" of history, the servitudes it imposes upon the present—
but Nietzsche never presumes that these can simply be erased in
some beneficent apocalypse. He prescribes a wary suspicion regarding the determinations of the past, but he stops short of projecting its
liquidation. In Proust this tension is manifestly different. Proust's
aesthetic seeks a way of theorizing the exclusion or transcendence of
determinations in every form. He wants each moment liberated from
all memory of what preceded—and presumably determined—it. But
for thousands of pages—presumably the reign of error preceding a
final flash of truth[40]—he rather narrates determination's extraordinary resilience and persistence. Through its own intensely counter-

40. See Proust's letters to Lucien Daudet, early September 1913, *Corr.* 13:259, and to
Jacques Rivière, 7 February 1914, *Corr.* 13:98–100.

discursive relation to Proust's doctrinal system, the
onstrates that the experience of the dialectic is irre
novel's own doctrine is wrong. Then, as I argued a
chapter, Proust's absolutism seems to collapse of
the failed epiphany at the book's conclusion.

This detour into Proust's aesthetic speculations may have seemed to
distance us from the ambiguities of memory in the *Recherche*. But
the confrontation of Proust with Nietzsche suggests that memory has
been at the heart of the issue all along. Nietzsche's reflections on the
contingency of any present help to explain how. The effort since the
nineteenth century to understand the determinations constraining
individuals in the absence of any overt military, political, or legal
compulsion has been a continuing theme in my argument. The gun
to the head is a coercion easy to understand, but the weight of tradition, the expectations of duty, the subtle dictates of style seem more
elusive. How do *they* constrain us? What is the agent of *their* power?
Twentieth-century theorists such as Antonio Gramsci and Louis Althusser have sought to formalize the difference between more overt
forms of determination on the one hand, and more atmospheric or
infrastructural ones on the other: Gramsci's opposition between
"rule" or "domination" [*dominio*] and "hegemony"; Althusser's between "repressive" and "ideological" apparatuses (see *Discourse/
Counter-Discourse*, 41–43).

   In connection with the enigma of these diffuse and puzzling forms
of control, what Nietzsche clarifies is that the infrastructural determinations of behavior, those that function through force of ideology
rather than force of arms, *are always mediated through memory*. And
memory is everywhere. What Proust termed the "immense edifice of
recollection [*l'édifice immense du souvenir*]" (*RTP* 1:46; *RTP54* 1:47)
then manifests itself as a malign complex bearing ceaselessly in upon
the present and the individual with the accumulated weight of the
past and of the collective.

   Memory is the most general form of determination. Memory is
how the past—and the anxieties and suffering that the overwhelming
weight of narration in the *Recherche* so powerfully represents within
it—sustains and projects itself into a present that never chose such
prolongation. Even "genius" can't make memory go away. This is

why, despite the celebratory and salvationist rhetoric that has surrounded the mnemonic realm since Proust produced his concluding apologia, memory remains the most fundamental and the most mystified problem in the *Recherche*. This resistance of the Proustian past to its effacement or transcendence, this tenacity of its determination, needs now to be rethought.

6

Hypermnesia—Memory in Proust
II. Displacements

The finding of an object is in fact a refinding of it.
  —Sigmund Freud, *Three Essays on the Theory of Sexuality* (1905), *SE* 7:222

. . . Les vrais paradis sont les paradis qu'on a perdus.
[The true paradises are the paradises we have lost.]
    —Marcel Proust, *A la recherche du temps perdu,*
    RTP 4:449; *RTP54* 3:870

Proust's mnemonic epiphanies begin less than fifty pages into the *Recherche*, early in "Combray." The narrator explains how he recovered the village of his childhood. Scholars have carefully probed the mechanism of this resurrection, but as happened with the cold fusion experiment, no one has been able to reproduce Proust's results. We need to consider why the experience of what Proust termed "involuntary memory" seems so peculiar, and what we can learn from its oddity.

Everyone talks about the *madeleine* as if it alone produced Combray. As Rebecca West once wrote, it must have been a very poetical cake.[1] But it may be that we have misidentified the agent that generated the miracle. Perhaps the secret of Combray's recovery was not

---

1. Rebecca West, *The Court and the Castle: Some Treatments of a Recurrent Theme,* 233.

the pastry at all, but rather the infusion Proust's narrator dipped it in.[2]

As a catalyst of mnemonic resurrection, *tilleul* (linden-blossom) appears to have had a modest but devoted following among the memory researchers in Proust's period. Combray was not the only childhood it restored. Here is the psychologist Frédéric Paulhan's evocation of an analogous revival, from his 1904 book *La Fonction de la mémoire et le souvenir affectif*: "We thus rediscover here and there, in our memory, distant recollections of impressions which seem to have nothing to do with the present, but which struck our mind at a favorable moment. . . . I thus recall the impression which the bland odor of falling linden blossoms [*fleurs de tilleul*] made upon me in the courtyard of the little school where as a young child I learned to read."[3]

Proust's linden-blossom resurrection is no doubt more memorable than Paulhan's. And two examples are insufficient to suggest that *tilleul* should be designated a controlled substance. My point in recollecting Paulhan is that Proust's mnemonic preoccupation—and his mnemonic technology—did not arise in a vacuum. Around the turn of the century, memory and memory phenomena were clearly on the cultural agenda. We will make more sense of the stakes the *Recherche* sets upon them if we examine the context in which these stakes were determined.

Frédéric Paulhan was only one among a number of French scientists of the period fascinated by the problems of memory.[4] The most

---

2. The *madeleine* has received more press. Proust described it charmingly and evocatively, but he also provided a carefully worked and intricately figurative description of the dried *tilleul* that his narrator was accustomed to shaking out of its pharmacy sack to prepare her infusion for Tante Léonie in Combray. In this bravura passage linden-blossoms also seem on their way to mythic status. See *RTP* 1:50; *RTP54* 1:51. Further on in "Combray," the narrator describes the linden trees that lined the Boulevard de la Gare and filled the summer air with a characteristic and powerful odor for which the infusion can be seen retroactively to serve as metonym (*RTP* 1:113; *RTP54* 1:114–15). *Tilleul* is the odor of Combray. Kevin Newmark discusses the *tilleul* imagery in "Ingesting the Mummy: Proust's Allegory of Memory," 166–68. Concerning references to and translations from Proust, see note 1 of Chapter 5. Translations from other writers in this chapter are my own, unless otherwise indicated.

3. Frédéric Paulhan, *La Fonction de la mémoire et le souvenir affectif*, 9.

4. In general, two groups of scientists were working on memory: psychologists and neurologists. Certain of the former did not possess medical degrees, but otherwise the research areas of the two specialties are hard to separate. Largely for purposes of clarity, I will concentrate upon the work of psychologists in the current chapter dealing with Proust,

important and celebrated of these researchers was Théodule Ribot, whose book on memory disorders, *Les Maladies de la mémoire* (1881), was regularly reprinted for five decades following its initial appearance. I will return to Ribot, but let me first examine some of Paulhan's concerns in his book on the functioning of memory. Here from the opening of his study is his description of memory's persistence:

> A considerable proportion of the psychic phenomenon often remains [after the initial stimulus or experience], and sometimes even more than would be desirable for mental functioning. In a more or less modified form it persists for a greater or lesser period, and above all it reappears, at the end of a certain amount of time, after it had disappeared. Our sensations, our feelings, our ideas, our images are not completely annihilated in the psychic whirlwind. They reconstitute themselves from time to time and we see them reappear in a form which resembles their initial one. They have even retained their freshness and sometimes their appearance of newness. Elements which seemed dissociated forever reconstitute themselves, those which seemed forever gone show themselves again. (*La Fonction de la mémoire*, 2)

And here is Paulhan's definition of "affective memory [*souvenir affectif*]":

> [This state] is one in which we witness the reminiscence, the spontaneous or willed reawakening, of affective facts as affective facts, complete with their affective character. (12)

Paulhan inherited his definition of "affective memory" from Ribot's pioneering work in chapter 11 of his *Psychologie des sentiments* (1896). And in acknowledging Ribot in 1904 he referred also to a

---

and turn to the neurologists and neuropathologists in my discussion of Freud in Chapter 7. It is interesting to note that, prior to the disciplinarization of psychology in France in the first half of the twentieth century, most of the nonmedical figures involved in this memory research were classified as "philosophers," and their work was published in journals such as the *Revue philosophique* (founded by Ribot) or collections such as the *Bibliothèque de Philosophie Contemporaine*. The *Journal de Psychologie*, the first French psychological journal, was founded in 1906 (Pierre Janet was its co-director). Elisabeth Czoniczer's research on a number of these figures has been essential to my own work. See her *Quelques antécédents de "A la recherche du temps perdu": Tendances qui peuvent avoir contribué à la cristallisation du roman proustien* (1957).

considerable tradition of research on the phenomenon; among other predecessors he names François Pillon and Marcel Mauxion (13, 24). The term "affective memory" was intended to include emotional and sensory phenomena, and to differentiate them from intellectual, volitional, or rational ones. By Proust's period it identified a commonplace distinction. As the narrator writes in "Combray," taste and odor were recognized as particularly effective triggers for such experiences, and could be relied upon long after other stimuli for carrying "the immense edifice of recollection" had faded: "l'odeur et la saveur restent encore longtemps . . . à porter . . . l'édifice immense du souvenir" (*RTP* 1:46; *RTP54* 1:47).

Several points seem worth emphasizing here. First, the notion of "affective memory" corresponds to a widely noted phenomenon. Reminiscences activated by emotional or sensory experiences have frequently been claimed to possess a particular capacity for vividness. In *The Invention of Memory*, Israel Rosenfield (citing Pierre Gloor's work on the limbic system and Wilder Penfield's on neurological localization of stored mental contents) acknowledges the existence of this capacity and attributes it to the archaic character of the limbic circuits that are activated by sensory stimuli.[5] There is an objective basis for crediting experiences like the intense reminiscence of Combray arising, as Proust claimed, from his narrator's cake and tea.

Second, Paulhan's account of the longevity of past mental contents contains a trace of suspicion that, however heady, such a capacity does *not* represent an unrelieved benefit for the individual who experiences it. One might have thought that exact and vivid reproduction of the past could only be a positive resource for subjects capable of such performance, but this view is undercut in the passage I quoted earlier. Regarding the surprising ability of material to persist seemingly verbatim in our memory, Paulhan added the following clause: ". . . sometimes even more than would be desirable for mental functioning." I want to flag the suggestion of a *pathology* associated with memory. I intend to develop it in what follows.

Third, Paulhan is interested in the relation between the mnemonic phenomenon he treats and aesthetic experience. He recalls that ex-

---

5. Israel Rosenfield, *The Invention of Memory: A New View of the Brain*, 222.

periences of affective memory play an important role in the work of Chateaubriand, and cites the *Mémoires d'outre-tombe* (69). As Proust's readers are well aware, Chateaubriand figures among the predecessors whose memory experiences the narrator of the *Recherche* cites as precedent for those he describes at the conclusion of the novel.[6]

In particular, Paulhan suggests that there may be a relationship between the success of an aesthetic work and the affective memory of its readers or viewers (119). Though Paulhan does not pursue his speculations on this point very far, he seems to be claiming that works which evoke affective recollection will tend to be remembered with the greatest immediacy, that intellection and rational analysis must be conceived as second-order phenomena in aesthetic experience. His idea implies that the evocation of archaic memory contents in the reader will produce the highest level of engagement with a text producing such reactions. Proust suggests an analogous notion concerning reader response in a passage very close to the end of the novel. He writes that he would only ask his readers to tell him "if I'd got it right [*si c'est bien cela*], if the words they read in themselves are really the ones I've written" (*RTP* 4:610; *RTP54* 3:1033). The tendency to depreciate analytical intelligence in the aesthetic realm clearly relates to the antipositivist polemic Proust conducted against Sainte-Beuve. It is a familiar and pervasive Proustian theme, which I will consider in greater detail.

These parallels between Paulhan and Proust are piquant, but what do they mean? What use can they be in understanding Proust's own writing? There has been considerable scholarship that has sought to ascertain where Proust got his ideas concerning memory, and to determine who influenced his notions on the subject.[7] This work is very

6. See *RTP* 4:306; *RTP54* 3:728. Proust makes the same point in his 1919 essay on Flaubert; see *CSB* 599.

7. Among the principal works contributing to this tradition are Czoniczer, *Quelques antécédents*; Elizabeth R. Jackson, *L' Évolution de la mémoire involontaire dans l'oeuvre de Marcel Proust*; and Joyce Megay, *Bergson et Proust: Essai de mise au point de la question de l'influence de Bergson sur Proust*. More recently, the question has occupied Antoine Compagnon in *Proust entre deux siècles*, and (from the philosophical side particularly) Anne Henry in *Marcel Proust: Théories pour une esthétique*. Perhaps the most extensive list of studies of "affective memory" in relation to Proust can be found in Harry

useful. It reveals the existence of a broad body of speculation about memory in the decades during which Proust was thinking about the memory problem. It enables us to map the intellectual context in which the *Recherche* evolved. But how does a work relate to its "context"? The memory problem lurks on the edge of this question.

The source-critical model according to which much Proust scholarship has conceived "influence" has been primitive. It has tended to see "ideas" as if they were property like real estate or stock certificates—objects that might be extracted from somebody's proprietorship and transferred to somebody else. The model imagines no mediations between source and receiver, no modulation of content in transmission. The fixity of the content transferred is matched by the passivity of the receiver and the overall transparency of the transaction. Such a conception looks like the literalist memory model I have termed "reproduction," in which a content laid down is simply retrieved intact and unaltered from storage.

Scholarship based on such a notion has posed its questions in pretty restricted ways. Typically, researchers have sought to determine whether Proust lifted his celebrated concept of "involuntary memory" from Bergson, or from specifically literary predecessors such as Chateaubriand, or from the experimental psychologists of his period. There is considerable evidence of Proust's acquaintance with Bergson's philosophy, and with the psychological and neurological speculations of his period. Proust himself was preeminently aware of the literary tradition. Nevertheless, it hardly suffices for an idea to have been present elsewhere for a novelist to snatch it up and stick it in a book. A complex process of selection and interpretation are involved in anyone's taking up any text. Proust can hardly have been a more passive victim in the reception of his period's speculation concerning memory than is the average reader in the face of the average text.

A notion of "influence" such as the one that has circulated in most Proust criticism cannot help us understand how a discursive context can *inflect* a text, how an intertextuality subtly changes language without leaving an overt mark of its presence. Scholars look for evi-

---

Redman, Jr., and Catherine Savage Brosman, "Further Nineteenth-Century Instances of Affective Memory," n. 2.

dence of the guilty contact between a writer and a "source." But "influence" is a slipperier operator than is suggested by the classic trio of means, motive, and opportunity. We can take it that Proust knew plenty about others' thoughts on memory. However, my model for assessing their effect upon the *Recherche* seeks to establish not the legal title to a given idea, but rather the subtle pressure that may have been asserted by discourses outside Proust's own on his representation of memory and hence upon our understanding of it.

Proust's own projection of the artist as a genius freed from external determination and exempt from the servitudes of the vernacular renders the question of influence—as of all determination by memory— opaque. But despite these Proustian implications I suppose that everyone within a culture speaks a language that is in large part common property. The existence of such transindividual discourses, and their capacity to "order" the conduct and the thought of individuals, has been one of the primary insights mobilized within the cultural criticism in our own period.[8]

My sampling of Frédéric Paulhan's psychological speculations about memory demonstrates a convergence with the familiar body of Proustian doctrine concerning the mnemonic realm. Our contemporary theory of "discourses" helps to understand such a convergence. The theory supposes a collective language, a set of common preoccupations, problems, and concerns, which inflect and influence the production of any specific locutor. In the dialectic between individual and cultural production of such discourses, determinations can surely flow in both directions. Writers *can* mold the language of a culture, but whereas in certain cases the effect of individual production may turn out to be great in modifying the collective discourse, the latter *inevitably* influences the former—and has always already done so whenever we begin to look. This model thus authorizes a reading of individual discourses that interprets them in relation to a collective discourse that may never be specifically articulated (still less explicitly referred to) within them. This collective discourse is not so much a "source" as it is a condition of possibility of individual ideas and texts.

8. See Richard Terdiman, *Discourse/Counter-Discourse: The Theory and Practice of Symbolic Resistance in Nineteenth-Century France*, 54–65.

To conceive how such pressure can be exercised from outside an individual discourse, we need a dialectical concept of the sign that emphasizes its theoretical incompleteness, its relationality, and hence the necessity of its inscription in an interpretive field that by itself it can hardly delimit or determine. If signs (like Proust's genius artists) are autonomous, then there is no place where "influence" upon their meaning might press upon or gain access to them. But if their meanings reach beyond their immediate content, then an intertextuality can act as what Charles Sanders Peirce called an "interpretant"—an element of the sign nowhere overt in its signifier, but essential for its functioning and for the interpretation of its signified (see *Discourse/Counter-Discourse*, 29–30). An openness to such inflection is inherent in any individual use of the collective medium of language.

In the attempt to understand the memory problem that occupies me here, the need for such a concept of individual discourses would seem clearer than anywhere else, for memory is the mechanism by which such transindividual mediations are exercised upon the individual production of language to begin with. *Context is the memory of language.* Words and concepts never stand alone and are never just synchronic. They carry the traces of their past, of the situations in which they have been made meaningful for their cultures, of the stresses under which they have come. Any specific signifier, any individual discourse, "remembers" the contents with which its culture has invested it. Its present always bears a past that the present is never free to ignore or to forget. This is the dialogic situation of all language, which Bakhtin sought to conceptualize through his notions of "heteroglossia" and "multiaccentuality" (see *Discourse/Counter-Discourse*, 35–41). Language is thus constituted by the adhesion of material it can neither speak nor forget. These spectral contents influence intention and expression; however, they do so not by baldly transferring the title of some item of linguistic or intellectual property to a new owner, but by changing the angle of the illumination by which a meaning becomes visible and can be interpreted.

This sort of hermeneutic revision bears a relation to the analytic rewriting of psychic contents that Freud was theorizing just around the time Proust's notions about memory were themselves developing. An intense preoccupation with memory obviously links the two figures.[9] In Chapters 7 and 8 I consider Freud's analysis of memory and the mnemonic system that underlies psychoanalysis. But anticipating that discussion, in a kind of analytic retroaction, I want to allow the Freudian perspective on memory to put some pressure on Proust's own treatment of the memory problem. I want to recover some of what I will claim are the repressed contents in Proust's own mnemonic triumph.[10]

Influence has an empirical component, answerable to certain facts. For example, Frédéric Paulhan's ideas about affective memory can't have come from Proust, who had published nothing on the subject when Paulhan's book appeared in 1904.[11] But as I just suggested, the reciprocal claim, that Proust more or less larcenously appropriated his mnemonic notions from one or another of his various predecessors, is equally misleading. He surely could have read Paulhan or any of the other psychologists whose research on memory strikingly parallels his conclusions—and he may well have done so, as I will suggest shortly. But *how* he may have read what he read remains to be established.

On the basis of the preceding considerations about "context," we can begin to interpret how the discourses concerning memory circulating in Proust's period brought pressure on his formulation and representation of memory in the *Recherche*. These in turn can begin to inflect—to "influence"—our own understanding of what Proust explicitly says about the issue. What Proust's speculations on mem-

9. There is a considerable literature examining relationships—factual, conceptual, representational—between Proust and Freud. For a recent bibliography, see Malcolm Bowie, *Freud, Proust and Lacan: Theory as Fiction*, 191 n. 1.

10. The modulations by which the mystified "influence" of signifiers and discourses arising somewhere else exercises itself upon any communicative act bear the strongest possible resemblance to the unconscious transformative mechanisms of the Freudian psyche that I consider in Chapter 8. It is worth speculating that the models involved in these two interpretive systems may be more than simply analogous or homologous, more than just mutually interpreting. They may be identical. As Freud conceived its action, the "influence" of the unconscious upon the formations of the psyche may theoretically be indistinguishable from the spectral contents circulating in the cultural and linguistic realm and linked through their dialogism to every conscious signifier. Like an invisible but powerful magnetic field, the presence of the distortions caused by such factors originating in personal or cultural history are recoverable only through some form of extrinsic analysis.

11. Anyway, as indicated earlier, Paulhan had sources enough in Ribot, Mauxion, and Pillon, whom he faithfully cites.

ory everywhere betray but never clearly express is the threat of a
mnemonic pathology constantly shadowing the triumph he celebrates
at the end of the *Recherche*. In what follows, I want to suggest how
the notion of such a pathology was attached to memory in Proust's
period, and how this conceptual cluster lying just outside the field of
Proust's own expression may have mediated the representations
within it.

To focus understanding of the context of discussion concerning
memory around the time of the *Recherche*, I turn to the most celebrated of the turn-of-the-century psychologists who dealt with the
problem, Théodule Ribot. The title of Ribot's most famous book, first
published in 1881, itself suggests the dialogic element that Proust's
Recherche repressed. *Les Maladies de la mémoire*—the diseases of
memory—maps a cultural preoccupation that Proust's representation
powerfully, if surreptitiously, reproduces.

Chapter 4 of *Les Maladies de la mémoire* deals with what Ribot
(following a tradition of medical usage) terms "hypermnesia": unexpected amplifications or recrudescences of memory, experiences in
which mnemonic contents that had seemed annihilated are "resusci-
tated" and "regain their intensity."[12] Two important issues arise in
connection with this idea. The first is the notion that *memory retains
everything*: that no experience, no content, is ever lost. The concept
has long had an intense attraction, and it fascinated a wide variety of
writers and theorists around the turn of the century. Proust referred
to it in his 1907 "Journées de lecture":[13] "Poets and philosophers have

---

12. Théodule Ribot, *Les Maladies de la mémoire*, 139. Freud refers repeatedly to this
tradition in connection with his discussion of the hypermnesia of dreams in *Interpretation
of Dreams*: "The fact that dreams are hypermnesic . . . has become one of the cor-
ner-stones of our teaching" (*SE* 5:589; see *SE* 4:11–17). Michael Roth surveys the literature on hypermnesia in the period in "Remembering Forgetting: *Maladies de la mémoire*
in Nineteenth-Century France." He provides a useful discussion of Ribot's analysis (57),
and an account of an 1897 medical dissertation, also titled *Les Maladies de la mémoire*, by
Albert Guillon (57–60).

13. Two different works by Proust are known by this title. The one cited here is Proust's
essay on the *Mémoires* of the comtesse de Boigne. Previously, the preface to his translation of John Ruskin's *Sesame and Lilies* (published in 1906), itself earlier called "Sur la
lecture," bore this title; see *CSB* 789, n. 1. On the permanence of memory, see note 36 to
Chapter 7. Proust had previously referred to the memory archive at the end of *Jean Santeuil*. The final, unfinished, sentence of the Pléiade edition of this unpublished material
from around 1898–99 reads as follows: "And the photograph of all that had taken its place
in the archives of his memory, archives so vast that for the greatest part he would never go

told us for a long time that . . . , no matter how great
destined for the immense oblivion which . . . devours an
even what seemed most certain to remain in the memo
beings. But suddenly the archaeologists and archivists c
on the contrary, that nothing is forgotten, nothing is destı
925). And the idea reappears in an important passage in *Albertine
disparue*. Proust compares the preservation of our past to the establishment of an endless archive: "Each day of our past has remained
deposited within us, as if in an immense library where, even of the
oldest books, there is a copy which doubtless no one will ever ask to
consult" (*RTP* 4:125; *RTP54* 3:544). The final clause of this sentence
is there to set up the novel's concluding revelation. We can ignore it.
But manifestly Proust's paradigm of "involuntary memory" suggests
the practical mobilization of the phenomenon—or the fantasy—that
the passage suggests: integral retention of the past, indeed effective
abolition of pastness altogether.[14]

But there is a second—and in Proust's case forgotten—aspect to
the question of hypermnesia. What Proust leaves aside in retrieving
this notion from the broader mnemonic discourse of his culture is the
aura of an uncanny pathology that is regularly attached to it. Ribot's
discussion in *Les Maladies de la mémoire* foregrounds this atmosphere clearly. Of course Ribot was not simply cataloging mnemonic
curiosities. His subject was the *diseases* of memory. So the question
of pathology was immediate for him. He was, however, somewhat
uncertain about how to assess it in connection with the memory "ex-
altations" of hypermnesia.

The medical paradigm that underlies Ribot's investigation construes "normality" as a state intermediate between two excesses: neither too much nor too little. Ribot thus casts hypermnesia as the
obligatory pendant to amnesia. There was of course no doubt for
him, as for a whole range of psychological and neurological re-

---

to see [the material in them], unless a chance event opened them up, as had the pianist's
wrong note that evening . . ." (898).

14. Freud's "unconscious" constitutes the most uncompromising and consequential version of such a theory of mnemonic permanence. I consider it in detail in Chapter 7. The
abolition of pastness is evident in the following reflection in *Le Temps retrouvé*: "The past
was made to encroach [*empiéter*] upon the present, and I was made to doubt whether I
was in the one or the other" (*RTP* 4:450; *RTP54* 3:871).

searchers in the period, that the various forms of amnesia are pathological. But is the contrary phenomenon—hypermnesia—morbid?
At first there is a flicker of hesitation in Ribot's position, but as he
continues he seems impelled by the logic of his own normalizing
model to associate experiences of hypermnesia with pathology: "At
the very least [hypermnesia] is an anomaly. If in addition we note
that it is always related to some organic disorder or to some unexpected and strange condition [*quelque situation bizarre et insolite*],
there can be no doubt that it comes within the frame of our subject
[that is, the diseases of memory]" (139). Ribot goes on to catalogue
the conditions that precipitate hypermnesia: "It frequently appears in
acute fevers. It is still more common in maniacal excitation, in ecstasy, in hypnosis; sometimes it appears in hysteria and in the early
stages of certain diseases of the brain" (140). Ribot then mentions
that experiences of heightened memory have frequently been reported in connection with fear of imminent death (141). Finally, he
speculates that hypermnesia may represent an anomalous appearance
of the phenomenon of pathological regression—the progressive loss
of memory that can afflict adults, so that eventually only the earliest
recollections are preserved, vivid by comparison with the mnemonic
emptiness that alone remains of the individual's recollection from
other periods of life (147).[15]

The pathologizing atmosphere of Ribot's discussion puts us at an
extraordinary distance from Proust's salvationist depiction of involuntary memory. Is it possible to make sense of this difference? If we
abstract the organic and neurological anomalies responsible, according to Ribot, for hypermnesic episodes, is there anything *intrinsic* to
this phenomenon that it would be reasonable to consider unhealthy?
As I have been arguing from the beginning, the answer to this question is unequivocally positive.

When it is not tempered by forgetting there is a deeply unsettling
side to memory. *Pure* memory: various myths are associated with
such a state. But (leaving Proust aside) perhaps the most celebrated
referent in the modern period is not mythological at all. In *The Mind
of a Mnemonist* (1968), the distinguished Soviet psychologist Alexander Luria described the case of "S.," a Russian whose memory

15. Today this affliction would no doubt be diagnosed as Alzheimer's disease.

capacity (as a somewhat astonished Luria discovered by careful experiment) "had no distinct limits" whatever.[16] "S." could remember
anything, and retain it indefinitely. We might have thought that such
a capacity—what is sometimes called "photographic" or "eidetic"
memory—would represent an extraordinary benefit. But Luria's
mnemonist suffered painfully from it. He was so overburdened with
irrepressible recollection that he sought to devise techniques for forgetting. For him, hypermnesia was deeply uncomfortable and chao-
tic (65).[17]

Without going to such extremes to make the point, analysis of
memory has regularly seen forgetting as a necessary complement to
recollection if mnemonic health is to be maintained. My discussions
of Musset's *Confession* and of Baudelaire's "Cygne" both led to such
a conclusion; my quotation from Paulhan earlier in the present chapter suggested it obliquely.[18] But the position was frequent in psychological speculation around the turn of the century. Remembering
without forgetting could be *dangerous*; hypermnesia could be an illness with dire consequences (see Roth, "Remembering Forgetting,"
63).

Such a conclusion of course diverges radically from the triumphant
assertions in *Le Temps retrouvé* concerning a sequence of mnemonic
experiences that look very much like hypermnesia. Proust might
seem simply to have rejected or ignored any suggestion that a pathology attached itself to the phenomenon upon which he counted for
epistemological and aesthetic salvation. But the *Recherche* bears its
traces nonetheless. For example, it coheres completely with the anguished and tortured representation of remembrance in *Albertine
disparue*. The catalepsy that follows Albertine's disappearance and
deepens after her death seems like nothing if not an ultimately ma-

16. Alexander R. Luria, *The Mind of a Mnemonist*, 11.
17. The paradox of such unlimited hypermnesia animated Jorge Luis Borges's caution-
ary story of Funes el Memorioso, who, unable to forget anything, was transformed into a
hallucinating insomniac afflicted by his experience of the simultaneity of everything (in
Ficciones). See Nicole Lapierre, "Dialectique de la mémoire et de l'oubli," 8. Oliver Sacks
discusses a comparable case in "The Landscape of His Dreams."
18. Compare the following sentence from Baudelaire's commentary on De Quincey,
evoking the pain experienced by a mind unable to purge the accumulated images laid
down in recollection: "Poetic memory, once a source of infinite pleasures, has become an
inexhaustible arsenal of torture instruments" ("Un Mangeur d'opium," in *Oeuvres complètes*, ed. Y.-G. Le Dantec and Claude Pichois, 429).

levolent memory effect, a prolonged hypermnesic crisis. Proust's depiction of anguish in the moment of loss has an elemental and primitive immediacy because (as I argued in Chapter 4) *in recollection,
loss is presence.*

The power of *Albertine disparue* arises in the unmediated intensity of the memory determining it. Only an excruciatingly protracted
and groping work of forgetting allows exhaustion of the anguish such
memory carries at its heart.[19] Hypermnesia thus carries a formidable
risk. If life is painful, its integral reproduction in hypermnesic recollection can hardly transform it into triumph. I want to argue that at
the heart of its representation the *Recherche* bears the knowledge of
this risk, despite Proust's concerted refusal to concede awareness of a
powerful tradition concerning it.

But in fact the odds are good that Proust was quite aware of this
tradition.[20] I want briefly to sketch the basis for this claim before
pursuing my interpretation of how Proust's representational system
incorporates the context of mnemonic speculation around the turn of
the century, while at the same time eerily veiling or resisting it.

During the first half of 1905 Proust spent considerable time reading the work of French specialists in nervous ailments.[21] He was preparing to enter Dr. Sollier's clinic in what was to be a futile attempt
to cure or moderate his asthma. Among the volumes he consulted
was Ribot's *Maladies de la volonté*. The book had been published by
Félix Alcan in 1883 in the Bibliothèque de Philosophie Contemporaine, the same collection in which *Les Maladies de la mémoire*
had appeared in 1881. Both volumes were constantly reprinted for

---

19. Proust himself makes a convergent observation in the course of presenting the narrator's anxiety after Albertine's disappearance. He speaks about "forgetting whose power I
was beginning to feel, and which is such a potent instrument of adaptation to reality" (*RTP*
4:137; *RTP54* 3:557). I analyze the course of the narrator's forgetting in my *Dialectics of
Isolation: Self and Society in the French Novel from the Realists to Proust,* chap. 9, "Narration in *La Fugitive.*" Proust judged that *Albertine disparue* ("the death of Albertine, the
forgetting [*l'oubli*]") was "the best thing I've ever written [*ce que j'ai écrit de mieux*]"
(letter to Gallimard [19 or 20 October 1921], in *Correspondance Proust-Gallimard, 1912–
1922,* 416).

20. Previous discussions of Proust's acquaintance with research in experimental psychology and neurology can be found in Jackson, *L' Évolution de la mémoire involontaire,* 12–
13 and 223–38, and Czoniczer, *Quelques antécédents,* passim. See also Élisabeth Roudinesco, *Jacques Lacan & Co.: A History of Psychoanalysis in France, 1925–1985,* 88–89.

21. George D. Painter, *Marcel Proust: A Biography,* 2:52–53.

decades afterward, and each was regularly advertised on the jacket of
the other. Proust refers to the Ribot volume ("his fine book [*son beau
livre*] on Diseases of the Will") in the preface to his translation of
John Ruskin's *Sesame and Lilies* ("Journées de lecture," *CSB* 179n).

Both Proust's father and brother were physicians. His father, Dr.
Adrian Proust, had been a student of Jean-Martin Charcot at the
Salpêtrière hospital, and had coauthored a work on neurasthenia in
1897 (Roudinesco, *Jacques Lacan, & Co.*, 88). Léon Daudet, with
whom Proust remained close despite Daudet's virulent anti-Semi-
tism, had also been a medical student and had known Charcot well
(they were neighbors on the Rue de Bellechasse).[22] Surrounded as he
was with medical discourse, it is difficult to imagine that Proust remained unaware of the pioneering work that in the period before the
turn of the century had made Paris the most advanced center of research in psychology and neurology in the world.

Sometime before the end of 1908 Proust had read and annotated
Henri Bergson's *Matière et mémoire* (originally published—also by
Alcan—in 1896).[23] Bergson, as a scholar and professional philosopher, was fully acquainted with contemporary memory research and
cited the literature repeatedly. In particular, he refers to Ribot's
Maladies de la mémoire in *Matière et mémoire*, chapter 2 (the same
chapter in which Bergson developed a distinction between two forms
of memory that has frequently been compared with Proust's own—a
convergence Proust denied with some irritation).[24]

Overall, we get the sense that the psychological, neurological, and
philosophical discourse about memory in his period swirled con-

22. Proust dedicated *Le Côté de Guermantes* to Daudet. Charcot is mentioned several
times in the *Recherche*: *RTP* 2:597; 3:274, 349, 439, 473; *RTP54* 2:301, 881, 959, 1051,
1087. On Proust's knowledge of Charcot, see Czoniczer, *Quelques antécédents*, 34–35,
and Jackson, *L' Évolution de la mémoire involontaire*, 12.

23. See Proust, *Le Carnet de 1908*, 113 and nn. 483–85; *RTP* 1:cxxx; and Painter, *Marcel Proust*, 2:52–53. Bergson is discussed in *Sodome et Gomorrhe*; I consider the passage
in note 36 to Chapter 7. On Proust's relations with Bergson, see the letter to Georges de
Lauris [end of April 1908], *Corr.* 8:106–7.

24. For Bergson's reference to Ribot, see *Matière et mémoire: Essai sur la relation du
corps à l'esprit*, 132. There are numerous other mentions of Ribot, Fouillée, and other
psychologists throughout Bergson's book. On Proust's relation with Bergson, see Proust's
1913 interview with Elie-Joseph Bois, in *Marcel Proust: Textes retrouvés*, 217, and
Proust's letter to René Blum, November 1913, *Corr.* 12: 295–96. See also Megay, *Bergson
et Proust*, and Georges Poulet's appendix on Bergson in *L'Espace proustien*.

stantly about Proust. There seems no proof that Proust had systematically sought to assimilate its multifarious strands as he was preparing to write the *Recherche*; but although there is no evidence sufficient to convict him of the sort of intellectual appropriation that
traditional scholarship has typically sought to demonstrate, it is clear
that he had sufficiently frequented the areas in which this work was
being carried on for us to conceive his representations of memory as
reactive to and overdetermined by it, rather than standing as a completely independent project. I therefore hypothesize that Proust covertly registers (if only through a meaningful omission) suggestions,
reiterated in the medical and philosophical literature, that consistently argued that memory bears a considerable danger.

I read involuntary memory in the *Recherche* against the grain of
Proust's own salvationist description. Let us accept that the theory of
involuntary memory in the novel quotes no one directly, and even
that the existence of explicit links between Proust's account of it and
the tradition of scientific description drawn from the research of his
contemporaries is generally uncertain (the discussion of Bergson's
theories at several places in Proust's corpus would be an exception).
It would thus be fruitless to seek precise parallels between Proust's
representation and more systematic or scientific descriptions of
memory phenomena drawn from the psychological research or philosophical speculation of his contemporaries.

But at the risk of increasing the provocation of my reading of memory in Proust, I want to suggest that *mémoire involontaire* in the
Recherche needs to be read, not "straight," but in the mode of a
Freudian reversal or negation. Despite Proust's efforts to mold our
understanding of it in salvationist directions, the phenomenon Proust
narrates as involuntary memory uncannily recalls the description in
Freud of the pathologies of traumatic injury and involuntary neurotic
reminiscence. Proust would strenuously have contested such a distortion of the valence he attached to involuntary recollection. I do
not ignore the resistance his account provides against such an interpretation, but I do propose to reinterpret it. Let me outline the
background for my perspective.

Except for the soteriological vision of the aesthetic whose fundamental symbol is the theory of involuntary memory, Proust's repre-

sentation of the world is almost unendurably somber. Family, friendship, love, travel, nature, even everyday reminiscence attributable to voluntary memory—all systematically fail to provide a reliable source of value, or even a credible reason for living on. Without the revelation of Memory and the salvation of Art, Proust might well stand as the most systematic and complete pessimist in the European literary tradition. For—excluding the utopianism of an aesthetic realm about which the least one could say is that its benefits would be difficult to democratize—Proust's pessimism bears not only upon the range of human activity to which individuals ordinarily appeal for the satisfactions of living, but upon the very medium of consciousness itself, upon the veracity and the reliability of the contents of our thoughts, our beliefs, and our perceptions.

Whatever their influence on each other may have been, Ribot, Paulhan, Bergson, and Proust each divided the mnemonic realm into two distinct forms of memory—typically, the memory organized by our intelligence on the one hand, and an autonomous affective or involuntary memory linked to sensory or emotional triggers on the other. There is an element common to these models that has not been sufficiently examined. All of them are founded upon a systematic distrust of the overt contents of mental representations. In Freud's interpretive paradigm such a vision is theorized and minutely operationalized, but it already functions powerfully in the suspicion which for Proust attaches to any recollected thought or emotion, any proffered interpretation—*to any memory save the epiphanic* upon which he rests responsibility for the redemption of the world.

This attitude of radical suspicion concerning consciousness must be analyzed.[25] It provides the affective and cognitive force behind a broad range of interpretive systems influential in the period I've been discussing. But what, fundamentally, does suspicion *suspect*?

In a complex of systems from the Proustian madeleine to the Freudian slip, interpretive privilege is granted to the *involuntary*: to what we never chose, to what we could not have manipulated to fit our conscious need, to what was not determined by any subjective

---

25. Carlo Ginzburg's "Clues: Morelli, Freud, and Sherlock Holmes" has influenced my discussion here considerably. I return to the notion of "suspicion" in Chapter 8.

instrumentality and can seemingly be exempted from any threat of falsification or distortion by it.

This is a fascinating epistemology. What accounts for it is an extraordinary distrust attaching to the *will*, to *intentionality*, to *consciousness*. Such an attitude determines a deeply divided model of the self and points to a deep paradox in Proust. In his reflection on originality and genius, Proust had sought to centralize everything in a sovereign subject, but involuntary memory fundamentally undercuts such a projection. "The best part of our memory is *outside of us*," he wrote in *A l'ombre des jeunes filles en fleurs* (*RTP* 2:4; *RTP54* 1:643; italics mine). It is true that the passage then continues: "Outside of us? Within us rather, but concealed from our own vision in a more or less prolonged forgetting." But either way, Proust conceives memory in a palpable and painful self-alienation. This inaccessibility of its own contents to consciousness is what authenticates as truth the range of involuntary and unpremeditated epiphanies or self-revelations for whose promulgation and promotion in this period we credit Proust and Freud.[26]

In the striking title essay of *Love's Knowledge*, which focuses on Proust's *Recherche*, Martha Nussbaum comes at this question of authentication of mental contents from an angle somewhat different from mine here. Her problem is the same: "The difficulty . . . becomes: how in the midst of this confusion . . . do we know what view of ourselves . . . to trust?"[27] Nussbaum emphasizes the self-validation of *suffering* (254). She examines the narrator's experience after Al-

26. The passage on memory from *Jeunes filles* to which I refer here recurs in more or less the same form in a manuscript addition to the typescript of *Albertine disparue* (*La Fugitive*). The editors of the new Pléiade edition relegate its second appearance to a note (see *RTP* 4:113 note *a*); Jean Milly, in the Garnier-Flammarion edition, prints it as part of the text (*La Fugitive*, 175 and n. 74). There is no way of telling whether, had he lived to complete *Albertine disparue*, Proust would have modified the passage in its second appearance to avoid simply repeating himself, or dropped it altogether. It forms part of the long section of the volume (250 pages in typescript, corresponding to well over 100 printed pages) that Nathalie Mauriac and Étienne Wolff argue Proust intended to cut entirely from the published version; see their edition of the newly discovered second typescript: Marcel Proust, *Albertine disparue*, 177–83. The issue is worth raising because the point in the *Recherche* at which Proust at least provisionally reattached this passage on the alienation of memory is marked by a despair perhaps as profound as any in the entire novel. Again the text suggests a connection between involuntary memory and *pain* that the salvationist construction of the mnemonic in most discourse about the novel simply suppresses.

27. Martha C. Nussbaum, *Love's Knowledge: Essays on Philosophy and Literature*, 261.

bertine leaves him, centering her analysis around Proust's own anguished realization at the beginning of *Albertine disparue*: "How much further suffering sees in psychology [*va plus loin en psychologie*] than does psychology itself" (*RTP* 4:3; *RTP54* 3:419). Nussbaum compares Proust's conclusion—that the lessons given to us by pain can be confidently relied upon—with the Stoic concept of *catalepsy*: "a condition of certainty and confidence from which nothing can dislodge us" (265). She asks why Proust might have held such a view about pain, and whether it might be epistemologically reliable.

Nussbaum privileges a different touchstone of truth than the one—involuntary memory—Proust attested himself, but her analysis converges with my own assessment of the logic of involuntary memory here. To begin with, following out Proust's suggestions, she provides a succinct account of the grounds for suspecting that the givens of consciousness cannot be relied on:

> To have an understanding of human psychology, it is necessary first to investigate oneself and to come to know the elements of one's own soul. But in order for this search to be successful, the searcher must get past certain powerful obstacles. First there is habit. . . . Second, there are more specific defenses that we erect against truths about our condition. . . . Finally, there is the obstacle erected by rationalization—an activity of self-explication engaged in at a superficial and intellectual level which, by giving us the confidence that we have accomplished a scientific analysis and arrived at exact truth, deters us from a deeper or fuller inquiry. . . . To remove these obstacles, we need, as Marcel [Proust's narrator] puts it, an instrument that is "subtle and powerful and appropriate for seizing truth." (254)

Conversely, having explored the unreliability of the data provided by consciousness, Nussbaum outlines the criteria that enable us to grant credibility to certain seemingly self-confirming experiences:

> What is it about the impressions of suffering [upon Albertine's departure] that makes them cataleptic? Why do they convince Marcel that truth is *here*, rather than in the deliverances of intellect? We are conscious, first of all, of their sheer *power*. . . . In addition to sheer force, there are also surprise and passivity. . . . For Proust

it is especially significant that surprise, vivid particularity, and extreme qualitative intensity are all characteristics that are systematically concealed by the workings of habit, the primary form of
self-deception and self-concealment. What has these features must
have escaped the workings of self-deception, must have come from
reality itself. (266–67)

My overly schematic summary of Nusbaum's argument cannot do
justice to the subtlety of her attempt to account for the potentiality of
truth in Proust's universe of almost overwhelming error. She surely
clarifies the basis for Proust's suspicion of subjectivity in the ordinary
mode, and for the need within the model he projects for some reliable criterion. And she agrees that whatever we are to credit must
somehow arise outside of our control.

But Nussbaum's effort to evaluate *pain* as Proust's candidate for
epistemological touchstone ultimately runs aground. Having established the basis for suffering's claim to be veridical, to have attained
the status of cataleptic knowledge, Nussbaum is finally obliged to
undercut that claim. The end of her essay echoes a long tradition of
modernist and postmodernist puzzlement over the aporias of language: "No form of discourse," she writes, "is cataleptic" (284). *Even
pain is aporetic.* Yet suffering in Proust, though it cannot provide a
reliable criterion for veracity, is nonetheless crucial for understanding the logic of the representation Proust offers of the dilemma of the
individual. Put simply, suffering is the mystified and repressed determinant of Proust's theory of involuntary memory, which he instituted to re-suture individuality.

However disappointing to our desire for certainty, the result
Nussbaum comes to is not surprising. Language, having turned un-
ruly, will not suddenly be cozened into docility despite our need.
But there is no question that in the modern period the intensity of
that need has grown urgently. Proust stands as earnest of its power.
No one has ever written of *desperation* as he does in the *Recherche*.
Yet this desperation at least can help us to measure the extraordinary
hypertrophy of the countervailing *hope* that Proust lodged in the
epiphanies of involuntary memory on which he sought to base reliance at the end of a three-thousand page demonstration of its utter
foundationlessness.

By its overdrawn urgency, by its fantastic totalizing exaggeration, Proustian involuntary memory transmits the intensity of a personal or cultural *need.* Those who would interpret its meaning can only conjecture about its source. But the problem must have been extreme to have called for such a solution.

It seems a long time since my discussion of Proust in *The Dialectics of Isolation* (1976) attempted to make sense of the profound pessimism that characterizes his representation of the world, as it does the worldview of a sequence of canonical novelists since the nineteenth century in France. In my approach to the question I was following a familiar tradition of ethical and political criticism of literary representation. In *Dialectics of Isolation* I worried about the cultural diagnosis that literary representations offer, and credited such representations as the projection of a potential or incipient critique.

Since the 1970s when *Dialectics of Isolation* appeared, criticism in this ethically and politically diagnostic mode has fallen out of style. *Language* preoccupies our readings. But as I attempt to make sense of the representation of memory in Proust, I want to recover the historicizing and politicizing impulse that animated my earlier effort. I am persuaded that it is impossible to understand the charge on "memory" in Proust without it. And I believe it is important to examine the convergence of this political concern with the semiotic and linguistic preoccupations of our criticism that have become familiar since the structuralist period, and in poststructuralism particularly.

In a very Hegelian way, my concern with politics in *Dialectics of Isolation* belonged to its age: to the dynamic of liberatory aspirations that had led to the revolts of 1968 and to the struggle against U.S. intervention in Southeast Asia from the mid-sixties onward. In a moment of even more intense and consequential political concern in Germany in the 1930s, Walter Benjamin wrote about Proust. His analysis is one of the rare critical treatments of the *Recherche* that has not been effectively absorbed by the novel's own intricate formalism and intense subjectivism. Though fragmentary, Benjamin's reflections remain pertinent to the problems raised by Proustian representation, and in particular by what increasingly seems his quite fantastic theory of *mémoire involontaire.*

In the twenties Benjamin translated Proust and wrote an essay on the *Recherche* to which I referred in Chapter 5 ("The Image of

Proust"). But on the question I am discussing here his acutest insights can be found embedded in one of his Baudelaire essays, "Some Motifs in Baudelaire" (1939).

Benjamin goes straight to the heart of the matter concerning Proust's theory of memory and its implications. He notes the *inadvertent, aleatory* character of the mnemonic miracle that Proust claims to depend on to make sense of the world. Benjamin terms the result of such epiphanies "forming an image": "According to Proust, it is a matter of chance whether an individual forms an image of himself, whether he can take hold of his experience."[28] But Benjamin contests Proust's naturalization of the individual's dependency on such adventitiousness. For Benjamin this chance is *determined*:

> It is by no means inevitable to be dependent on chance in this matter. Man's inner concerns do not have their issueless private character by nature. They do so only when he is increasingly unable to assimilate the data of the world around him by way of experience. . . . [Proust] coined the phrase *mémoire involontaire*. This concept bears the marks of the situation which gave rise to it; it is part of the inventory of the individual who is isolated in many ways. Where there is experience in the strict sense of the word, certain contents of the individual past combine with material of the collective past. The rituals with their ceremonies, their festivals (quite probably nowhere recalled in Proust's work), kept producing the amalgamation of these two elements of memory over and over again. They triggered recollection at certain times and remained handles for memory for a lifetime. In this way, voluntary and involuntary recollection lose their mutual exclusiveness. (112–13)

We can sense the influence here of an intensely politicized tradition of German critical sociology—in particular of the sort of social and institutional critique Tönnies sought to bring to bear in his notion of *Gesellschaft*.[29] Benjamin's implication is clear. For him it was

28. Walter Benjamin, *Charles Baudelaire: A Lyric Poet in the Era of High Capitalism*, 112. Proust strongly underlines this irrationality in connection with the madeleine incident in "Combray": "Il y a beaucoup de hasard en tout ceci" ["There is a large element of chance in these matters"] (*RTP* 1:43; *RTP54* 1:44).

29. This critique found parallel forms in Max Weber's *rationalization* and Lukács's *reifi-*

the shattering of experience that had become a commonplace of cultural diagnosis in the modernist period that determined the phantasmatic retotalization Proust projects in involuntary memory. It is difficult not to imagine that the fragmented and dispersed experience of subjectivity so consistently and powerfully represented in Proust's perspectivism (see Proust's interview with Élie-Joseph Bois, in *Marcel Proust: Textes retrouvés*, 217) is itself the perspective being compensated for in the magical epiphanies of the *Recherche*.

Such a diagnosis converges with the strain of more specifically linguistic preoccupation that in Chapter 4 I argued can be read in Baudelaire's encounter with the unreliability of language, and that became acute in his speculations concerning the consequences of this troubled perception of the medium of consciousness for consciousness's own constitution. The pathetic befuddlement of the swan/sign in "Le Cygne" I took as an emblem of the more consequential distortion inhering in all discourses, in all the modes of subjectivity and intersubjectivity, under the conditions of an increasing perfusion of mobile signs and messages. This confusion, I suggested, has expanded in proportion to the extension of the free-floating messages circulating in culture with no other warrant than the existence of a medium for propagating them. In Proust we can find the consequences and the institutionalization of the deep interpretive perplexity such a situation determines.[30]

The preconditions for the epistemological privilege Proust attrib-

_____

cation. I will return to the analysis of the fragmentation or dispersion of experience in the modernist period in Chapter 8.

30. There is a haunting connection between the Symbolist swan/sign pun that Baudelaire bequeathed to Mallarmé (cf. "Le vierge, le vivace et le bel aujourd'hui") and an experience at the heart of Proust's own encounter with the painful uncertainty of the semiotic. Proust's narrator had read Mallarmé's swan poem with Albertine. She came to love the text (*RTP* 4:39; cf. *RTP54* 3:455). At the height of the narrator's paralysis after her flight, in a futile attempt to persuade her to return, he writes her a letter in which he lists the gifts he was preparing to give her when she left. The substitution of words for objects, of signifiers for referents, that he seeks to perpetrate in this letter, his intended manipulation of discourses and of subjectivities, are excruciating and vertiginous. The narrator tells Albertine he had ordered her a Rolls-Royce and had chosen her yacht. He writes: "The yacht was almost ready; it was to be called, according to the desire you expressed in Balbec, the *Cygne*" (*RTP* 4:38; *RTP54* 3:455). But, like the lost and the shipwrecked in "Le Cygne," or the swan caught in the ice in Mallarmé's sonnet, Albertine never returns.

utes to the experiences of involuntary memory lie in such a perverse mobility of the meanings borne in language. Signs, Umberto Eco once wrote, are anything that can be used *in order to lie.*[31] The interpretive suspicion that Proust shares with Freud means that consciousness itself entails a propensity for deception. So the liberations of semioticity, the wantonness of language, profoundly subvert the reliability of the semiotic elements that consciousness offers in its representation of the world.

What then begins is a search for restabilization. The quest-structure of Proust's *Recherche* coheres with the logic of such an effort. Stabilization is what it seeks. Its preconditions arise in the historical experience of a disarticulated but powerfully expanded network of meanings, and in the consequent individual and commercial exploitation of messages (of whatever truthfulness) for producing "advantage." Signs become instrumentalized, whether nakedly—in commerce or in the narrator's letter to Albertine—or more covertly in a series of diverse tactics of consciousness—for example, in psychological "rationalization." In the conjuncture, this instrumentalization makes sense. For as the letter to Albertine most desperately suggests, in a limited economy there is always a possible advantage to be gained—whether this economy is one of time, of money, or of desire.

But the inherent lability of signs, ideas, messages, and meanings sets knowledge adrift. Promises function differently in such a world. They transform themselves into nothing more than clues on whose authentic meaning their recipient is constrained to speculate impotently. The semiotic aporias and uncertainties to which, in our own period, poststructuralism has sensitized us thus seem to migrate backward in time and turn up already fully formed and functional in Proust's *Recherche*. As de Man wrote in his essay on the difficulties of "reading" represented in Proust, "There seems to be no limit to what tropes can get away with."[32] "Reading" then increasingly appears impossible. Such unruliness at the heart of the medium on which we necessarily rely for the establishment of order entails far-

31. Umberto Eco, *A Theory of Semiotics,* 7.

32. Paul de Man, *Allegories of Reading: Figural Language in Rousseau, Nietzsche, Rilke, and Proust,* 62.

reaching consequences. In the face of the tropological caracoles and semiotic entrechats of which it appears to be constituted, conscious-ness then has somehow to mobilize *against itself* to recover the truths that its own process has distorted or concealed.

Whatever its significance in aesthetic or affective registers may be, "involuntary memory" is Proust's candidate to serve as the epis-temological discovery mechanism that might put a stop to such slip-pages, and distinguish the true from the counterfeit. Where every-thing floats in uncertainty, where everyone and everything lies, the unconjured recollections of the *Recherche* come to bear the mark of truth. Proust is unequivocal on this point:

> Whether it was a question of reminiscences like the noise of the fork or the taste of the madeleine . . . their most essential characteristic [*leur premier caractère*] was that I was not free to choose them, that they were given to me just as they were [*telles quelles*]. And I felt that this must be the mark of their authenticity [*Et je sentais que ce devait être la griffe de leur authenticité*]. I had not been searching for the two uneven paving stones of the courtyard where I had stumbled. But precisely the fortuitous and inevitable way in which I had met with this feeling proved the truth [*contrôlait la vérité*] of the past that it resuscitated. (*RTP* 4:457; *RTP54* 3:879)

What are the determinants, what are the consequences, of the in-tense mistrust of subjectivity and volition this passage evidences? Consider what Proust wrote early on about the unreliability of expe-rience, in *Jean Santeuil*, around 1898 or 1899. Speaking of the reality of life, which the novel's hero is unable to perceive or to enjoy in the moment of living it, Proust explains his disability in the following way: ". . . we cannot experience [reality] while we are living its mo-ments, *because we subordinate them to a self-interested purpose* [*car nous les rapportons à un but égoïste*], but . . . these sudden returns of disinterested memory . . . [make] us float between the present and the past in their common essence" (*JS* 537; italics mine; quota-tion modified for clarity).

Clearly by the time of *Jean Santeuil* Proust had already chosen a privileged form of memory as the means for transcending subjectivity's inherent limitation and constitutive unreliability. On this point his system will not vary. But what the passage from *Jean Santeuil* suggests perhaps more clearly than anywhere in the *Recherche* itself is the *mechanism* of the dilemma it is intended to resolve. We could describe it thus: the access of the conscious subject to reality is upset by subjectivity's own self-interested instrumentalism. This interference cannot be arrested by an act of will. It is an automatic process by which the intensities of immediate need, the pressures of intersubjective desire, the very exigencies of living, interfere with our ability to apprehend and to assess the reality of the world.

This is a depiction of subjectivity *in extremis*, of self-alienation brought to an exquisite pass. Its terms are these: although Proust's novel produces a projection of the self that, by all accounts, has never been exceeded in subtlety and range of analytic power; although no writer has ever gone so far in centering representation on the intricacies of consciousness, the ego on which Proust lavishes such unprecedented attention shows up in his analysis as constitutively mendacious. Proust projects the image of a self that has no clarity about its limits and no bounds to its potential for deception. Its blindnesses and its duplicities define it entirely. From beginning to end the narrative unremittingly repeats the discovery that the representations offered to us by consciousness—whether others' or our own—are counterfeits. The sovereign and all-absorbing subjectivity that it is the preeminent vocation of Proust's narrative to examine and to analyze turns out to be a fraud.

The world of the *Recherche* is a world of liars and of lies. Odette lies to Swann, Albertine lies to the narrator, Charlus lies to everybody—and all of them lie first and most profoundly to themselves. What Malcolm Bowie calls the "brilliant parade" of such deception in the novel continues endlessly (see *Freud, Proust, and Lacan*, 49). Ultimately, the *Recherche* represents that *life lies*.

For a narrator this presents an obvious difficulty. The liar's paradox is familiar. A story about liars becomes a problem when it is told by a liar—particularly by one who lies to himself. Proust needed to solve this difficulty by locating a site of subjectivity exempt from deception and self-deception. His narrative required a warrant. In response Proust produces one in the form of *mémoire involontaire*. His logic is compelling. All narratives instantiate recollection; all stories are practices of memory. So a guarantee *in and of memory* is the best we could possibly ask for. But the election of involuntary memory as the touchstone of truth in a world constituted by deceit and open to the most wanton interpretations has an unexpected consequence. The invention of involuntary memory paradoxically rehabilitates protocols of knowledge that privilege the accidental and the inadvertent. They seem to accredit nothing more powerfully than *fate*.

In the face of the sanction granted to an indeterminacy it absolutely can't control, subjectivity simply goes up in smoke. So at the end of the line in a process that seems to have as its object the affirmation of the ego, Proust finds himself radically subverting its most essential claims—in particular, the entire panoply of defenses he had erected around the notion of the individual's autonomy (genius, originality, individuality, and related values) that I examined in the preceding chapter.

Such paradoxes, by which we seem to achieve precisely the result that overturns the one we sought, have a familiar shape. They look like neuroses in psychoanalysis. It would be methodologically naive to homogenize the differences between Proust's representation of the individual and the corresponding analysis in Freud. But there is a sense in which their problematics converge remarkably. Such a convergence has three important elements: (1) an intense focus upon an entity variously named the individual, the psyche, the ego, or the self, which in turn generates a series of striking technical innovations for its analysis; (2) a powerful subversion in that analysis of the self-consciousness and self-identity attributable to that entity, which comes under increasingly radical interpretive suspicion; and (3) a resultant need to restabilize the very bases of analysis and interpretation, and the very identity of the self. Such restabilization must ultimately appeal to some transcendent agency to arrest the hermeneutic slippage that analysis itself has instituted. In what follows, I will seek to understand Proust's representation of and his response to the crux constituted by these successive moments of what is a fundamental crisis in the conception of the self.

. . . telle est la cruauté du souvenir. [. . . such is the
cruelty of memory.]
        —Marcel Proust, *Albertine disparue*, *RTP* 4:139;
        RTP54 3:558

Proust tells us that involuntary memory engenders joy.[33] I want
rather to explore the hypothesis that a profound experience of *unhappiness* systematically associates itself with these epiphanies, and
consequently that the celebration attending them calls for reinterpretation.

Proust shares a paradox with Freud. Both represent that the truest
of our memories are *the ones we cannot recall* (see note 37 to Chapter 7). Freud works out the logic of this irony in his theory of repression. Proust just lands us squarely in the middle of it. What is the
truth of these crucial, inaccessible memories? Freud's answer is
clear: for him the unconscious blocks our access not to random recollection, but to the memory of *trauma* in its various forms. With a
unique and mysterious power of discrimination, repression selects
out our calamities and our fiascos. Could it be that *mémoire involontaire* makes a parallel selection?

In Proust these moments of the past's uncanny projection into the
present unstring subjectivity. They subvert consciousness and confront us with the incomprehensible; they produce a feeling of inexplicable and irresistible surrender, of a fantastic penetration by the irrational. There is something terrifying about experiences of this power.
In framing his representation of them, Proust drew on the tradition
of the "sublime" that had become a pervasive figure for the overwhelming and the transcendent. Thus in a familiar Kantian or high-
romantic image he speaks of the "silent heights of memory" (*RTP*

33. "Combray": "Where can this powerful sense of joy [*joie*] have come from?" (*RTP*
1:44; *RTP54* 1:45). *Le Temps retrouvé*: ". . . my entire depression evaporated before the
same happiness [*félicité*] that at different periods of my life I had been given by the sight of
trees that I thought I recognized in a ride around Balbec . . . , by the savor of a madeleine
dipped in tea. . . . But why had the images of Combray and Venice . . . given me a joy
[*joie*] that seemed like certainty, and sufficient, with no other proof, to make me indifferent to death?" (*RTP* 4:445–46; *RTP54* 3:866–67). The word "joie" is repeated
twenty-nine times in *Le Temps retrouvé* alone; see Étienne Brunet, *Le Vocabulaire de
Proust*, s.v. "joie".

4:437; *RTP54* 3:858). And, in a passage whose conclusion I placed as an epigraph to this chapter, he evokes the pure air of paradise as analogue for the exalted atmosphere of these precious and privileged moments (*RTP* 4:449; *RTP54* 3:870).[34]

But as my epigraph suggests, these paradises of the sublime in Proust are constitutively and systematically *lost*. Even on Proust's own showing, there is something ominous inherent in this supposed joy. Of course this fact only strengthens the association of these experiences with the cultural complex of the "sublime." For the overwhelming is never unambiguous; it embodies a menacing, "uncanny" valence. Proust, and after him his critics, have tended to resist the implications of the ineffable's negative side. It needs to be reassessed. Let me sketch the *downside* of memory.

The ways in which a darker illumination associates itself with the experience of involuntary memory in the *Recherche* are diverse and dispersed. Consider, for example, Beckett's insight concerning the ambivalence of *Le Temps retrouvé*. Beckett observed that the victory that memory supposedly fashions over time in the first part of the Guermantes matinée is abruptly subverted in the "bal de têtes," the grotesque lineup of the decaying and moribund familiars with which the matinée concludes. This cortege of the ill and the dying figures a different, and much more sinister, form of recollection. In this subsequent "victory of Time," to which criticism has paid much less attention than to the mnemonic epiphanies with which the matinée begins, the vaunted negation of death chillingly mutates, as Beckett argues, into death's "affirmation."[35]

Or in a second register, consider the intense association throughout Proust's work between the memory of a parent and its profanation.[36] The episode in *Du côté de chez Swann* in which Mademoiselle Vinteuil and her lesbian lover spit upon the portrait of her dead father is notorious (*RTP* 1:157–63; *RTP54* 1:159–66), but its interpreta-

34. See Immanuel Kant, *Critique of Judgment*, sec. 29. In his notes on Stendhal, Proust comments on the importance of *height* and *exaltation* [*élévation*] in Stendhal's novels (*CSB* 654). For a general account of the tradition, see Thomas Weiskel, *The Romantic Sublime*.

35. Samuel Beckett, *Proust*, 51.

36. On the pervasiveness of this theme, see Compagnon, *Proust entre deux siècles*, 164–65.

tion is problematic. The invocation of sadism—Proust explicitly uses the term (157; 159)—explains little by itself, for it leaves unsettled the question of the *source* and the *meaning* of the charge that attends the act of profanation and gives it its erotic efficacity.

What is being desecrated—and thus, in however distorted a way, *commemorated*—in this act? By virtue of its scandalousness we easily recall the behavior of Mademoiselle Vinteuil and her friend observed by the narrator through the window at Montjouvain.[37] But the affect attending this action—motivating it—is more elusive. I want to focus on the scene's representation of a fundamental ambivalence in memory. The profanation vignette grapples with another aspect of what Proust represents as memory's dark side.

Nowhere is memory more burdened, nowhere more fraught, than in the commemoration owed by children to their parents. I considered the charge culture lays upon this configuration in my analysis of Musset's *Confession*. As I claimed in connection with that text, there can hardly be a more intense instantiation of the disquiet attending memory since the Revolution than the theme of intergenerational tension. The stories a culture tells about parents and children frame, as if in microcosm, the culture's conception of its inevitably problematic inheritance, of the present's perplexing relation to the past. Nietzsche's second *Meditation* may do no more than to raise this issue of the relations within the institution of the family to a higher level of generality, and provide it with a more explicitly political and ideological reading than do stories like Octave's in the *Confession* or Mademoiselle Vinteuil's in "Combray."

The memory stresses between children and their parents complicate the "profanation" at Montjouvain. In the Nietzschean violence of its repudiation of the past, its valence changes. Desecration then becomes comprehensible as a precondition for selfhood, as the enabling mechanism of independence and originality. Whatever assault such a conception may make upon traditional pieties—and indeed, precisely because it makes such an assault—this is a construction that an entire strain of modernist writers, of whom Georges Bataille might stand as emblem, would surely have recognized and approved. The profanation of Vinteuil's portrait, the implication of such an act of rejection of the parent and of the past in the present release of desire

37. This is yet another of the windows that section reality in modernist texts. I leave to Proust's biographers the analysis of how this perverse configuration plays out issues in his own life, particularly in his conflicted relationship with his parents.

and the production of pleasure, violently refocuses the normalized, reverential notion of a beneficent memory—much as Nietzsche sought to do.

The scene at Montjouvain insistently confronts the generations—and confronts the complication that the opposition between them inevitably poses. Proust's representation combines a dynamic of violent repudiation of the parent with another of virtual assimilation. The latter is a register of the scene to which critics have attended less carefully. In it the parent uncannily *absorbs* the child; the child unconsciously *mimes* the parent. Everything plays out the tensions of intergenerational memory in a pattern of ambivalence that works itself into the scene at Montjouvain.

The diegetic frame of the profanation scene invokes a second intergenerational pair: the narrator and *his* own father. As he tells us, the narrator falls asleep in the bushes behind Vinteuil's house exactly where he "used to wait for my father in the old days" (157; 159). The profanation scene takes place "in the room where [Mademoiselle Vinteuil's] father had received mine." In preparing the erotic ceremonial she enacts with her friend, Mademoiselle Vinteuil carefully puts the portrait of her father on the table where her father, in an identical ritual, disingenuously used to place the score he hoped the narrator's parents would ask him to play (158; 160). To express her simulated surprise at discovering what she has left on the table, the daughter then uses the very words her father habitually employed (160; 162). Beneath the playacted vulgarity of the gestures and intonations that Mademoiselle Vinteuil adopts in the scene of erotic arousal she has scripted with her friend, the narrator recognizes the manner of her father, which she involuntarily reproduces, unawareof how the memory of her own body rematerializes his absent presence (158–59; 160).[38] Her profanation, like the entire scene for all its actors, is irreducibly and integrally a practice of memory.

38. Proust explicitly associates such a body-memory with *involuntary* memory: "There seems to be an involuntary memory of the limbs . . ." (*RTP* 4:277; *RTP54* 3:699n). Despite his characterization of it as a "pale and sterile imitation of the other [variety of involuntary memory]," it is striking that he does *not* simply dismiss body-memory as a variety of habit. On body-memory, see Maurice Merleau-Ponty, *Phénoménologie de la perception*, 171 and 211 (citing a passage from *Du côté de chez Swann*); Pierre Bourdieu, *Outline of a Theory of Practice*, 94–95; and Elaine Scarry, *The Body in Pain: The Making and Unmaking of the World*, 109–11. Scarry's repeated litany ("What is remembered in the body is well remembered"; 110; cf. 109, 111–13) evokes the power of the somatic system of recollection. In *Discipline and Punish: The Birth of the Prison*, Michel Foucault offers a far-reaching analysis of the implication of the body in a variety of memory processes.

There is a final level of complication in the intricate mnemonics of
the scene at Montjouvain. Despite the apparently horrifying medium
she has chosen to express it, the narrator makes unmistakable the
parallelism between Vinteuil's musical genius and the form of his
daughter's perverse creativity. "Une sadique comme elle," the narrator writes; "est *l'artiste* du mal" ["A sadistic person like she was is the
artist of evil"] (162; 164; italics mine). "Artist" is a word Proust never
uses lightly. It resonates here as more than a metaphor: it becomes a
redefinition.

Two echoes of this scene later in the *Recherche* complicate and
strengthen the paradigm of perverse inheritance inscribed within it
for Proust. The first is the narrator's discovery of Albertine's acquaintance with Mademoiselle Vinteuil and her friend, which provokes
one of the most painful crises of their relationship (see *RTP* 3:499–
500; *RTP54* 2:1114–15):

> At these words, spoken as we were entering the Parville station, so
> far from Combray and Montjouvain, so long after the death of Vin-
> teuil, an image trembled in my heart, an image held in reserve for
> so many years that even if I had been able to guess in storing it up
> long before that it had a destructive [*nocif*] power, I would have
> thought that over the years it would have entirely dissipated; pre-
> served alive deep within me . . . for my torture, for my punish-
> ment, who knows? for having allowed my grandmother to die; per-
> haps suddenly surging from the depths of the night where it had
> seemed forever buried and striking like an Avenger in order to
> inaugurate for me a life at once terrible, deserved, and new.

Memory could hardly show up as more pathogenic than in this
scene.

The second is the fact that Mademoiselle Vinteuil's friend was responsible for transcribing the notes for the Septet, which Vinteuil
had only vaguely sketched before he died, which is taken, in the
credulous spirit typical of much Proust criticism, to represent an ex-
piation of the indecency at Montjouvain. But the more subterranean
paradigm of inheritance that I am examining here would suggest
that, rather than reversing the valence of the earlier scene, this indispensable work of artistic conservation only continues it (*RTP*
3:765–66; *RTP54* 3:261). Indeed, Proust makes clear that Mademoiselle Vinteuil's adoration of her father was the indispensable condi-

tion for the "sacrilege" by which she profaned his memory at Montjouvain. These are not separable dynamics, and they cannot be construed as progressing from a profanation to a reassuring confirmation of morality. On the contrary, Mademoiselle Vinteuil's blasphemous mnemonic ceremonial contradicts such a meliorist interpretation precisely through its demonstration of memory's obtuse persistence. There is a perverse and potentially violent moment in *any* memory, in *any* relation with the past.

Thus the vignette at Montjouvain suggests that art in the *Recherche* is never completely divorced from some version of the profanation of the past, which the scene of Mademoiselle Vinteuil and her friend only materializes more forcefully than any other in the novel. Such a subterranean link between profanation and creation might be offered to aestheticize even perversion, but in consonance with my exploration of Proustian memory's darker side, I offer a divergent interpretation. The scene at Montjouvain complicates the aesthetic, even at its most exalted (as in Vinteuil's music), with an aura of impropriety whose charge, whose perverse *cathexis*, is an irreducible effect of memory.

Consider a third register of this unexpected and unsettling association between memory and unhappiness, yet another strand of the ambivalence that seems inherent in the experiences of overwhelming power that earlier I associated with the romantic "sublime." If we credit the accounts Proust provides in the course of the *Recherche*, memory regularly releases a remarkable quantity and intensity of affect. As I recalled in opening this discussion of the valence of such memory, Proust systematically *speaks* of joy, but just as regularly, his description *evokes* a very different complex of emotion: pain, suffering, or anguish.

Perhaps the tears that evidence the affect elicited in these epiphanic moments are simply tears of joy? An examination of the cases in the *Recherche* will rather suggest that they are systematically the result of the recovery of experiences of profound unhappiness—typically, of experiences of painful and irreversible loss. For example, in a passage at the beginning of "Noms de pays: le pays" concerning the narrator's loss of Gilberte, of which I quoted a fragment earlier:

> The best part of our memory is outside of us, in a rainy breeze, in the musty odor of a bedroom or the smell of an early-season fire— wherever we rediscover of ourselves what our intelligence, having

no use for it, had rejected, the last reserve of the past, the best of all, the one which, when all our tears seem exhausted, *is able to make us cry again*. Outside of us? Within us rather, but concealed from our own vision in a more or less prolonged forgetting. It is thanks to that oblivion alone that we can from time to time rediscover the being that we were, can place ourselves in relation to things as that being was placed, can *suffer anew* [*souffrir à nouveau*]. (*RTP* 2:4; *RTP54* 1:643; italics mine)

The logic of the final sentence of this passage is startling. With no mediation, with no explanation, the narrator moves from the fact of the past's rediscovery to the evocation of *suffering* that attends it. For an experience elsewhere represented as the bearer of an ineffable joy, why should this association be so characteristic, so ready to hand, if it did not carry within it, however mystified, the *necessity* of such a content?

Examples like this one seem virtually to rise to the level of definitions. The reawakenings of involuntary memory regularly resuscitate *suffering*. Let us see how the narrator characterizes his experiences of the phenomenon in *Le Temps retrouvé*. He finds a comparison in Swann's history: "Remembering . . . the *sudden pain* that the little phrase of Vinteuil had caused in him by resurrecting those days themselves, such as he had once experienced them, I understood all too well that the feeling which the uneven paving stones, the stiffness of the napkin, the taste of the madeleine had reawakened in me had no relation to what I often tried to remember of Venice, or Balbec, or Combray, with the help of uniform memory" (*RTP* 448; *RTP54* 3: 869; italics mine). This reflection refers to the well-known passage in "Un Amour de Swann" in which Swann, persuaded that he has recovered from the loss of Odette—just as the narrator thought himself to have done with regard to their daughter at the beginning of "Noms de pays: le pays"—catastrophically discovers in hearing the Vinteuil Sonata how present and painful the past has remained within him: "But suddenly it was as if she had entered, and that apparition caused him such a *wrenching agony* [*et cette apparition lui fut une si déchirante souffrance*] that involuntarily he brought his hand to his heart" (*RTP* 1:339; *RTP54* 1:345; italics mine).

What follows is a bravura passage in which a cascade of associations triggered by Vinteuil's musical phrase resurrect the *pain* that is Swann's memory of Odette. Again, the epiphany turns out to be disastrous. The passage concludes as follows: "And Swann perceived, motionless in front of this resurrected happiness [of his memories of a time Odette loved him], a poor sufferer [*un malheureux*] for whom at first he felt pity because he did not recognize him immediately, to the point where he had to lower his eyes so that no one would see that they were full of tears. It was himself. . . . Then his pain became too great, he rubbed his hand across his forehead, dropped his monocle, polished the lens" (*RTP* 1:341; *RTP54* 1:347). The tears of involuntary memory are tears of pain.

Of course by selecting only cases in which the content was one of suffering I may have falsified my discussion of the phenomenon. But it does not seem that the experience of *mémoire involontaire* is indifferent to the emotion it resurrects. It *selects*. The problem is not exclusive to Proust, as my Freudian analogies suggest. Theoretically, the Freudian unconscious also contains an undifferentiated body of experiences. It archives everything. Yet for Freudianism, the fundamental postulate, the functionally crucial operator of repression selects from among all the traces registered in unconscious memory a critical number to which our access is strategically denied. I hypothesize a subterranean convergence between these two foundational memory systems—in particular between the explicitly *negative* moment in Freud's theory of memory (in repression, in neurosis) and Proust's seemingly contrary, insistently celebratory account.[39]

Let us examine two of the undisputed examples of involuntary memory in the *Recherche* to assess the emotional valence of the ma-

---

39. In a powerful examination in *Being and Nothingness: An Essay in Phenomenological Ontology,* Jean-Paul Sartre considered the mechanism in Freud that uncannily selects what will be made unconscious. The analysis led to a paradox: "The censor must choose and in order to choose must be aware of so doing. . . . [But] how can we conceive of knowledge which is ignorant of itself?" (52–53). In general terms, Freud anticipated this contradiction and sought to parry it through his doctrine that in the unconscious, ordinary laws (of logic, of temporality) do not operate. I will consider this paradigm in detail in Chapter 7, but at this point it is worth observing how deeply divided, even shattered, a model of the self is entailed by the operation of such a mysterious agent of discrimination. Precisely the same enigma arises in relation to the model I am developing here of Proust's involuntary memory and the mysterious process by which the objects of its resurrections are selected.

terial they resurrect. In *Le Temps retrouvé*, in quick succession, there are five cases in which the narrator's past projects itself vertiginously into his present. I will focus on the first and the last of these. Each involves some complication that needs to be factored into our understanding of what they function to retrieve, and what they tell us about Proustian memory.

Critics rarely discuss the initial epiphany from this concluding sequence, at least with regard to the substance of the resurrection it mediates. Why did Proust place it first in the series? And what does it call back? The facts are familiar. Entering the courtyard of the Hôtel de Guermantes, the narrator jumps aside to avoid being struck by a carriage passing through the *porte-cochère*. Off balance, he stumbles, and in regaining his equilibrium he finds himself standing on two slightly uneven paving stones in the courtyard. His body memory recollects a similar posture in the Baptistry of San Marco. The experience rematerializes Venice (*RTP* 4:445–46; *RTP54* 3:866–67).[40]

The Venice episode is by most accounts one of the least significant in the *Recherche*. Why open the series of concluding revelations with its retrieval? And what is the character of the experience associated with its resurrection? Venice is the object of a long obsession in the novel. The narrator's desire to visit the city is an insistent theme. Once, he comes very close to leaving for Italy, but the trip is aborted in a comic scene in which, in the throes of his anticipatory ecstasy on the point of departure, he discovers that his exaltation has in part a pathogenic cause, and his illness abruptly cancels the trip (*RTP* 1:386; *RTP54* 1:393). Later, throughout his love affair with Albertine and symbolizing his continuing fantasy of disengagement from her,

---

40. Proust planned a Venice episode early in the process of the novel's conception. In a fragment from *Le Carnet de 1908*, he had already determined the mechanism of the city's resurrection and associated it with the mystery of *mémoire involontaire*: "We believe the past is mediocre because we *think* it, but the past isn't that, it is a certain unevenness [*telle inégalité*] in the paving stones of the Baptistry of San Marco" (60). Later, in the catalog of place names recollected from the narrator's life only a few pages from the beginning of the *Recherche*, Venice appears along with the other principal sites in which the action of the novel will occur (*RTP* 1:9; *RTP54* 1:9). On the Venice episode, see Peter Collier, *Proust and Venice*; Christie McDonald, *The Proustian Fabric: Associations of Memory*, chap. 6; and Tony Tanner, *Venice Desired*, chap. 6. The version of the Venice episode in the newly discovered corrected second typescript of *Albertine disparue* (ed. Mauriac and Wolff), 127–59, is significantly different from the one on which previous editions have been based. See *RTP* 4:1028–38.

he is seized by desires to travel to Venice (*RTP* 3:674–75; *RTP54* 3:169). Finally, in the third and final stage of his recovery after her death, he actually goes there with his mother (*RTP* 4:202; *RTP54* 3:623).

What happens? The Venice episode juxtaposes a sequence—virtually a cascade—of vignettes in which the reality and the persistence of *loss* and of *pain* are powerfully foregrounded.[41] The emotional tonality of his stay Venice is determined—though *how* is something we will need to examine—by the flight and then the death of Albertine.

On the one hand, in this outflow of his bereavement there continue to be painful recrudescences. On the other hand, in a kind of proof *a contrario*, the narrator has an experience that he believes finally assures him that he has recovered from his anguish. He receives a telegram that appears to inform him—erroneously as it later turns out—that Albertine is still alive and wishes to renew their love affair. This incident leads to the realization that forgetting has at last sufficiently completed its process so that this startling news, which earlier would have released the most overwhelming affect, produces only a muted, almost a deadened reaction, accompanied by a long and intricate reflection on the process of change.

It thus might seem that the tonality of the Venice-complex—the cluster of associations with the city stored in the narrator's experience and evoked in their hypermnesic return in the Hôtel de Guermantes courtyard—is relatively sunny. Yet the recovery marked by the supposed telegram from Albertine is inevitably also the discovery of a destruction—of self, of time, of intense emotion—whose impli-

---

41. We even learn that while in Venice the narrator receives news that a series of unwise investments has reduced his fortune by four-fifths (*RTP* 4:219; *RTP54* 3:640). This would be distressing enough. But a persistent imagery in the volume establishes a close association—almost a symbolic interpenetration—of *money* and *memory*. Consider this reflection earlier in *Albertine disparue* concerning the narrator's intense desire to forestall the mnemonic entropy that inevitably will cause him, little by little, to forget Albertine: "The moments I had lived with . . . Albertine were so precious to me that I would have wanted to prevent every single one of them from being lost. And occasionally, *as one recovers the remnants of a squandered fortune*, I recaptured some of them that I had thought had vanished" (*RTP* 4:112; *RTP54* 3:531; italics mine). In Venice, with a logic that seems to collapse the seeming difference between capital and recollection, it turns out that the largest portion of *both* of these fortunes—the financial and the mnemonic—are simultaneously discovered to have disappeared forever.

cations, though less acutely painful, are just as somber as any other.
As he had observed at an earlier stage after Albertine had left him,
"my life seemed to me something . . . lacking the structure [*support*]
of an identical and permanent 'self'" (*RTP* 4:173; *RTP54* 3:594). The
involuntary resurrection of Venice in the courtyard of the Hôtel de
Guermantes is a reminder that this instability remains constitutive.
"Venice" is really the recovery of the ineluctable and painful *phenomenon of change* itself, of the implacable systematization of time
experienced as destruction. The Venice episode in *Albertine disparue* then foregrounds and instantiates what we could call the *loss
of loss*.

The text's language emphasizes this negativity in what might otherwise have appeared an atmosphere of relative optimism. Here is
how the narrator unexpectedly describes his cure: "Le monstre à
l'apparition duquel mon amour avait frissoné, l'oubli, avait bien,
comme je l'avais cru, fini par le dévorer" ["The monster at whose
apparition my love had trembled—forgetting—had indeed, as I had
suspected, ended up by devouring it"] (*RTP* 4:222; *RTP54* 3:643). It
would be hard to mistake the bestial imagery for an index of pleasure, reassurance, or enthusiasm. It pulls the narrator's recovery
back into the atmosphere of his illness; it marks a phantasmatic identification of the "cure" with the malady it only appears to supersede.
Venice thus symbolizes an exemplary experience of pain.[42]

One striking sign of the intensity and the *kind* of emotion in the
episode is the reappearance within it of a structure that in Proust
always signals the presence of acute stress and suffering. We encoun-

42. Compare the letter to Madame de Madrazo, [17 February 1916], in which Proust
summarized the Venice episode: "Now [in Venice] the Carpaccio in which I see the dress
[recalling the Fortuny gown he had given to Albertine] evokes Albertine and *makes Venice
painful*" (*Corr.* 15: 57; italics mine). In the sketches from Cahier 57 now published in the
new Pléiade edition, we find a curious project of association between Combray and Venice
that never found its way into the finished manuscript: "Important, when I speak of *François le champi* . . . join [*réunir*] Combray and Venice. . . . There were pages in *François le
champi* and in the book of (put in an art book) that I had read in Venice, between which I
saw Combray. . . . They had both become illustrated books . . . [in the case of *François le
champi*] thanks to the illustrations with which my memory had enriched it" (*RTP* 4:846–
47). I will return below to the valence of the George Sand novel in the symbolism of the
Recherche. It is worth recalling that the last thing the narrator does before he is struck
down by the news that Albertine has left him is to ring for Françoise to ask her to bring
him a guide to Venice (*RTP* 3:915; *RTP54* 3:414).

tered this topos in a passage I examined earlier in this chapter—the phantasmatic splitting of Swann into two alien and mutually observing fragments under the pressure of extreme emotional pain: "And Swann perceived, motionless in front of this resurrected happiness [of his memories of a time Odette loved him], a poor sufferer for whom at first he felt pity" (*RTP* 1:341; *RTP54* 1:347). The other before him, we recall, was Swann himself.

In connection with the material resurrected at the conclusion of the *Recherche*, such a personality fracture reappears twice, in a quite systematic distribution. The first of these appearances occurs in Venice, and it helps to take the measure of the emotional tonality that dominates what might otherwise seem a relatively happy portion of the text. To be sure the image arises obliquely. Here is the passage in question. It occurs after the narrator receives the telegram he believes to have been sent by Albertine:

> Then occurred in inverse direction what had happened concerning my grandmother: when I had learned *in fact* that my grandmother was dead I had at first felt no sadness. And I had only effectively suffered from her death when involuntary remembrances [*souvenirs involontaires*] had made her live for me. Now that Albertine was no longer alive in my thoughts, the news that she was living did not cause the joy I would have supposed. . . . And perceiving that I did not experience joy that she was alive, that I no longer loved her, I should have been more shaken than someone who, contemplating himself in a mirror after several months of travel or illness, perceives his hair has turned white and his face has been entirely changed, the face of . . . an old man. That unsettles us because it means: the man I was, the young blond man, no longer exists, I am someone else. (*RTP* 4:220–21; *RTP54* 3:641)

Obviously, this invocation of the personality's division or decomposition appears indirectly here—not the stark encounter with self-alienation that occurred in the case of Swann upon hearing the Vinteuil Sonata and rediscovering the pain of his love for Odette, but a more roundabout, hypothetical manifestation of the figure ("I *should have been* more shaken . . ."). Yet it is possible to be *too* rational about such emotion. The narrator in Venice experiences the same fracture that we saw Swann suffering—less acute, perhaps, but not less diagnostic. In Proust the topos of the split, of a painful self-dissolution, appears at the heart, and as the marker, of experiences of intense and painful emotion. We will see it again in the context of the final case of involuntary memory in the novel.

Let us return then to the original center of the entire complex Proust called involuntary memory—to Combray. Initially, we associate the resurrection of Combray with the madeleine incident. The narrator's famous cake and tea ceremonial and the consequent recovery of his childhood come nearly at the beginning of the *Recherche*, and hence nearly everything else in the novel is played out in their shadow. But not quite. There are two important inaccuracies in the view that attributes the recovery of Combray to the madeleine. The first is that Combray has already been the subject of a considerable portion of the text in the *baiser du soir* scene. The second is that *involuntary memory resurrects Combray twice*.

This latter fact is striking. Of all the experiences of *mémoire involontaire*, there is only one case of a mnemonic complex that is evoked by two separate epiphanies. Combray is revived by the madeleine incident, but it is reexperienced from a quite different—and, I will claim, considerably less mystified—vantage in the novel's final hypermnesic episode, triggered by the narrator's discovery in the Prince de Guermantes's library of a copy of George Sand's *François le champi*.[43]

The madeleine, as I suggested, is already Combray's *second* resurrection. It has been a commonplace that the Combray material in *Du côté de chez Swann* arises in a double demonstration of memory arranged by Proust to illustrate the structure of his theory: the bipolar system of *voluntary vs. involuntary* memory that he had devised to represent the arduousness of the past and its capacity for colonization of the present.

43. Proustologues will recognize that my claim that *only* Combray is evoked twice by experiences of hypermnesia is not quite accurate. In the sequence of five cases of the phenomenon at the end of the novel, both the third (triggered by the sensation of a starched napkin) and the fourth (produced by the noise of water in a pipe) call back Balbec. See *RTP* 4:447 and 452; *RTP54* 3:868–69 and 874. But these incidents have none of the differential structure that separates (in distance and in implication) the dual resurrections of Combray found in the novel's first and its final epiphanies. On the madeleine episode itself, see Jürg Bischoff, *La Genèse de l'épisode de la madeleine: Étude génétique d'un passage d' «A la recherche du temps perdue» de Marcel Proust*.

The first evocation of the village of his childhood (often identified in the critical corpus as "Combray I") is the celebrated bedtime melodrama, the "drame du coucher." The affective charge on this earlier and more fragmentary narration of the Combray material in the novel is intense. It rivals the most powerful moments of emotional pain anywhere in Proust, and it could hardly be confused with the deadened rehearsals of ordinary habit. But the narrator tells us that this partial, truncated recollection, symbolized by the narrow staircase leading up to his bedroom, was all he could recover of Combray until the day the cake and linden tea brought the village and his childhood experience there integrally back in what critics have dubbed "Combray II."

Beginning with Proust himself everyone thus says the same thing. There are two contrasting representations of Combray: the first, the two floors of Tante Léonie's house, linked by the narrow stairway the narrator is condemned to climb without the solace of his mother's goodnight kiss (*RTP* 1:43; *RTP54* 1:44); the second, the fully realized representation of the village in all its moods and hours. Ethically and esthetically, priority and privilege are clearly attributed to the second of these two narratives. The entire sequential structure focuses a fascination upon the hypermnesic mystery of the madeleine and its totalizing retrieval of time past.

My own perspective diverges from this orthodoxy. I want to disengage the representations Proust termed *mémoire involontaire* from Proust's own celebration of its salvationist implications. I think involuntary memory rather represents, with an extraordinary but displaced intensity, the pervasive and continuing perception at the heart of the memory crisis: that rather than being subject to our recapture, the past in fact malignantly captures us. A chilling sentence concerning Swann expresses the sense of disaster that elsewhere Proust's celebration of memory tends studiously to veil: "He marveled at the fearful re-creative power of his memory [*il admirait la terrible puissance recréatrice de sa mémoire*]" (*RTP* 1:362; *RTP54* 1:368). We *suffer* the past in these epiphanies. It is not then surprising that their content is itself an experience of suffering.

Proust's perspective—his glorification of the involuntary recapture of the past—resolutely contests mine here. Such reversals are by now familiar in the age of hermeneutic "suspicion" I mentioned in the preceding chapter and will return to in the next, but perhaps *this* reversal has not been suggested before. What evidence can be adduced for such a perverse reading of the letter of Proustian mnemonic theory? As a first point concerning the successive experiences of involuntary memory that turn Proust's novel toward its doctrinal conclusion, I think we can sense the operation of a screen, of some form of transformation or disguise of meaning, in the very vacuity of the representation of these recovered pasts. Proust claims they were overwhelming experiences essential to his epiphanic revelation of "art," but *they are not narrated*. With the exception of the Combray material to which I will shortly return, there is no representation anywhere in the *Recherche* of the experiences recaptured in *mémoire involontaire*.

Proust's power to characterize and depict is formidable and justly celebrated, but here it simply runs aground. To understand Proust's writing practices, to comprehend the relation between the narrative texture of the *Recherche* and the doctrinal assertions meant to frame and to explain it, we need to make sense of the *inadequacy* of his theory to his practice when it comes to representation of the material recovered in the experiences of hypermnesia. Why is it not more impressively foregrounded?[44] I think we need to read this mismatch not as a simple and empty mistake, but as meaningful and paradigmatically determined: as the evidence of a difficulty that intervenes between Proust's projection of value and a world that resists it.

But what *does* produce narration in the *Recherche*? If there is a productive memory throughout Proust's novel, it is the memory of *habit*—the routinized and insidiously coercive determinant of homeostasis and inertia whose role in defining Proust's own paradigm I considered in Chapter 5. However depreciated, *this* is the memory—involuntary in the negative, aversive sense—that produces nar-

44. Early in his career Proust seems to have conceived a novelistic texture composed *solely* of material generated out of experiences of *mémoire involontaire*, and presented as such. Such a texture is projected in a passage in *Jean Santeuil*: "I would write only when the past came back to life in an odor, a view" (401). Obviously such a model is very different from the one practiced in the *Recherche*. In *Le Temps retrouvé* the narrator seeks briefly to sanction the inclusion of material *not* produced by privileged memory: "I realized however that [the] truths which intelligence draws directly from reality are not entirely to be disdained, since they can frame . . . the impressions brought to us from outside of time . . . but which, more precious, are also too rare to permit a work of art to be composed with them alone" (*RTP* 4:477; *RTP54* 3:898). I considered this issue in *Dialectics of Isolation*, 171–73.

rative in the *Recherche*. In particular, the characteristic mode of diegesis that in my earlier study of Proust I termed "synthetic narration" (see *Dialectics of Isolation*, chap. 8) is quintessentially a depiction of the routine, the customary, even the chronic. "Le pépiement
matinal des oiseaux semblait insipide à Françoise"[45]—*that* is unmistakably Proustian narration. But it stands as far from the intense projections of epiphanic memory as we could imagine. Nothing in the
doctrinal superstructure of the *Recherche* valorizes this form of telling. Conversely, the experiences of involuntary memory recounted
in the book produce no systematic recapture or representation of the
past; rather, they produce a prolix argument for its privilege that
increasingly seems an abstraction and a rationalization, the result of
an ideological superstructure with a ponderous ax to grind.

My reading of involuntary memory is thus perverse. What of the
one experience in the novel in which an epiphanic moment *does* in
fact produce narration of the past restored in experience? What sense
can we make of the madeleine incident and of "Combray" which rises
magically out of it? The relationship between the narrator's representation of his childhood village and the theory of memory he seeks to
found in it requires a considerable reinterpretation.

As Proust's readers know, but as it is nonetheless easy for us to
forget, the recovery of the Combray material is divided over *three*
different sites in the *Recherche*. As we saw, "Combray I" and "Combray II" were carefully segregated to make Proust's doctrinal point.[46]
But Combray is then resurrected yet a third time in the novel's concluding epiphany. What appeared to have been recovered *without*
benefit of involuntary memory in "Combray I" (and hence was implicitly depreciated in the absence of its midwifery) is restored again
through its magic in *Le Temps retrouvé*. This diffused and reiterated

45. "The twittering of the birds at daybreak seemed insipid to Françoise" (*RTP* 2:309;
RTP54 2:9).
46. We might note in passing that originally these two versions of the childhood village
and the childhood trauma at the beginning of the novel were less hermetically compart-
mentalized than they became in the final text of *Swann*. The memorable exordium of
"Combray II"—"Combray, at a distance, from a ten-league radius, as we used to see it
from the train when we arrived there in the week before Easter, was no more than a
church symbolizing the village, representing it, speaking of it and for it to the surround-
ings" (*RTP* 1:47; *RTP54* 1:48)—was originally included in the sketch for material which
ended up in "Combray I"; see Bischoff, *La Genèse de l' Épisode de la madeleine*, 10–11
and 23.

resurrection muddies the neat theoretical distinction upon which
Proust had seemed to set such store in *Swann*.

Proust steadfastly claimed that he had composed the beginning
and the end of the *Recherche* simultaneously.[47] This insistence reflects a characteristic obsession. The problem with a capacity for
analysis as extraordinary as Proust's is that the Alpha and the Omega
of any reality can seem to spin off into radically different universes.
Disconnection and even dissolution always threaten. Under such
conditions, Proust's need to reassure himself that these far-flung elements actually belong to the same world, that they arose in the same
moment, that in some transcendent sense they have never really left
each other, is understandable.

With the publication of the sketches and drafts of the novel, we
can now identify with some precision just what Proust was referring
to. It turns out that the episode in "Combray I" in which the narrator's mother read *François le champi* to him through the night of the
drame du coucher was split in two. The second half of the text
moved from "Combray I" in *Swann* to the Prince de Guermantes's
library in *Le Temps retrouvé*—a dislocation that ended up spanning
some 2800 pages.[48]

So the structure of "Combray" upon which critics have so often
concentrated actually operates a repression or displacement of affect.
In "Combray I," the text powerfully evokes the narrator's childhood
anguish. But then it marginalizes or veils the pain of the bedtime
melodrama by privileging the more totalizing—and routinely ge-
nial—recovery of the village in the madeleine incident. This wreaths
the technology of *mémoire involontaire* with a misleading aura of be-
nignity—an impression that is in turn an essential precondition for
Proust's salvationist revelations of the meaning of involuntary memory in *Le Temps retrouvé*. Yet this displacement is forcefully undone
when the narrator comes upon the George Sand novel in the Prince's
library. And that is how, in the novel's concluding series of mnemonic epiphanies in *Le Temps retrouvé*, Combray is resurrected yet
another time around the story of the "baiser du soir," conveyed now
in an *involuntary* restoration of the most acute childhood anguish—
the last such experience in the book.

47. See the letter to Madame Straus, [approx.]16 August 1909, *Corr.* 9:163.
48. See Volker Roloff, "*François le Champi* et le texte retrouvé," and *RTP* 1:1120 n. 1,
identifying the text that Proust moved from the first volume to the last.

François le champi in fact represents anguish as powerfully and as unambiguously as any symbol in the *Recherche*. When critics mention Sand's book, they tend to limit their discussion to the few things the narrator says about it himself. Examinations of the thematic significance we might attribute to the novel itself are rare. Why did Proust choose it?[49] Two points are worth mentioning about *François le champi* in connection with the Proustian memory practices it is associated with in the first and final volumes of the *Recherche*.

First, in Berrichon dialect *champi* means "foundling" or "orphan." The thematic match with the narrator's anxiety in Combray, with what we might suppose were the childhood fears and phantasms that culminate in his bedtime drama at the end of "Combray I," is unmistakable.

Second, Sand's novel is founded on a plot that must have given the narrator's mother fits as she read the book to him on the night in Combray, even though we are told that for reasons of decency she skipped over the amorous portions of the story (*RTP* 1:41; *RTP54* 1:42). *François le champi* is the story of an incestuous love affair between a mother and her child. To be sure, the proprieties are technically preserved. Since François, the child, was a foundling, he bore no blood relation to the woman who raised him. But the detail seems immaterial; the psyche hardly concerns itself with such niceties. What is crucial is that *at the conclusion of Sand's novel the mother and the son get married*. Again the fit with what we can project as the narrator's phantasmatic desire in Combray is almost embarrassingly transparent.

Proust thus did not need to have read Freud to stage the Oedipus. The celebrated scene of the *baiser du soir* has hardly any latent content at all. Consider how, late into the night, the reading of Sand's story by the very object of his Oedipal longing must have resonated in the psyche of this child for whom, even decades later, the complex it determines would remain conspicuously unresolved. Consider how the apprehension of punishment by his angry father, and then his

49. He hesitated for some time before selecting this one from among the four "country" novels by Sand the narrator's grandmother had purchased as the gift for his *fête*. Previously Proust had thought to use *Indiana*—just as the narrator's grandmother had thought at first to purchase it for him. Even when he concluded that *Indiana* was inappropriate, we find *La Mare au diable* through several iterations of the passage in the drafts of "Combray." See *RTP* 1:41 n. 2 and 676 n. 1, and Ennid G. Marantz, "Les Romans champêtres de George Sand dans la *Recherche*: Intertextes, avant-textes et texte."

magical capitulation and retirement from the scene, must have po-
tentiated the narrator's desire and heightened his sensation of a network of quite violent affects. Consider the overwhelming intensity of
the guilt that is immediately and explicitly released in this experience: the self-subverting awareness, even while his mother spends
the night in his room, that the cost of his victory in the struggle for
her attention will inevitably have to be paid; that in this incident in
which for the first time he realizes that his parents had "raised him to
the dignity of a grown-up [*grande personne*]," and had "suddenly
brought him to a sort of puberty of unhappiness [*puberté du chagrin*]" (*RTP* 1:38; *RTP54* 1:38)—that at this moment of choice and of
transition, what should have produced joy in fact produced the
acutest unhappiness and remorse: "I should have been happy; I was
not. It seemed to me that my mother had made a first concession
that must have caused her pain, that it was a first abdication on her
part before the ideal she had conceived for me, and that, for the first
time, she, who was so brave, had had to declare herself beaten. It
seemed to me that if I had brought off a victory it was against
her . . . , and that that night began an era, that it would remain an
unhappy date on the calendar. If I had dared now, I would have said
to my mother, 'No, I don't want you to, you mustn't sleep here'"
(*RTP* 1:38; *RTP54* 1:38)

It would be easy to call attention to the (perhaps involuntary) double meanings detectable in this excerpt, as throughout the scene.
But it is not necessary to press the point. We need only observe to
what degree such ambiguities suffuse the entire passage with the
energy of an impossible erotics and the sadness of an unrealizable
desire. The narrated action of *François le champi* is what focuses the
fantasy of the narrator's desire—indeed the narrator himself tells us
(41; 42) that he fantasized through a considerable portion of his
mother's reading. Consequently, it is easy to understand how inti-
mately and how irretrievably the story of the Sand novel, and the
experience of his mother's reading it to him on that night in Combray, must intertwine with, and stand imaginatively for, the intense
and excruciating memory trace of the experience.

In an analytic setting such material would no doubt appear in disguise or displacement. The very force of the affect attaching to
it would tend to subject it to the intensest forms of repression. In

Proust it survives as if orphaned for decades in the depreciated voluntary recollection of "Combray I." But the repressed content finally reemerges and is finally accredited for what it is in the final epiphany of the *Recherche*.

The intensity of the recovery which then occurs is signaled, as if automatically, by the last appearance in the novel of the uncanny structure of "splitting"—associated in Freud with a variety of powerful distortions of the ego, and surfacing in Proust to dissolve or fracture Swann or the narrator himself at moments of extreme affective and mnemonic stress.[50] Here is the passage from *Le Temps retrouvé* at the moment of the narrator's hypermnesic encounter with *François le champi* in the Prince's library: "It was a deeply buried impression that I had just encountered. . . . At first I asked myself who was this stranger [*étranger*] who had arrived to do me harm. That stranger was me, it was the child I had been then, resurrected from within me by the book, which, knowing nothing of me but this child, had instantly summoned him up, wanting to be seen only by his eyes, to be loved only by his heart, to speak only to him" (*RTP* 4:462–63; *RTP54* 3:884).

If any doubt remained of the anguish that I have been claiming *systematically* subtends the experiences of hypermnesia in Proust and is its mystified determinant, it must evaporate at this last example. What returns at the novel's conclusion is the most archaic and most powerfully repressed of the painful contents the *Recherche* bears within it. The split of the self that this vertiginous restoration of the past produces is the unmistakable sign of the affect that it releases. Disaster might seem the contrary of epiphany. But in the *Recherche* it reveals itself as its double. In Proust, despite the density of salvationist rhetoric, memory remains acutely in crisis.[51]

At first glance it would seem that it should not be difficult to decide what is an epiphany in Proust. There are lists—Roger Shattuck's may

---

50. Freud's term is "Ichspaltung." See particularly "Splitting of the Ego in the Process of Defence" (1938), *SE* 23:275–78. Oliver Sacks speculates on the relation between memory and the phenomenon of such splitting or doubling of consciousness in "The Landscape of His Dreams," especially 59.

51. In "The Landscape of His Dreams," Oliver Sacks offers a striking speculation paralleling mine here concerning the origin of recollection in experiences of anxiety and discontinuity (60–61).

be the most complete and helpful.[52] However, the situation is more complicated than this taxonomic rationalism suggests. The reappearance of the crisis of "Combray I" at the culmination of the sequence of hypermnesic moments at the Guermantes matinée means that the seemingly simple opposition between voluntary and involuntary memory must be fundamentally reinterpreted.

The night of anguish in Combray is thus recovered in the final experience of *mémoire involontaire* narrated in the *Recherche*. But the truth of this resurrection still does not appear unambiguously at first. On the brink of its unmasking, mystification continues to distort the contents of authentic recollection. The repressed returns in stages—as if a series of lines of defense were successively being breached under the pressure of memory, but still intently contested.

When the narrator, waiting to enter the Princesse de Guermantes's salon at a break in the concert being held there, comes upon the volume of Sand's novel as he examines the books in the Prince's library, initially his impression is only of an incongruity: "I felt myself disagreeably struck by some impression excessively discordant with my current thoughts" (*RTP* 4:461; *RTP54* 3:883). The sight of the novel breaks the gravity of his mood, and (in a remarkably odd metaphor) he compares the experience to the shock felt by a child whose father's funeral is interrupted by the sound of a band suddenly striking up a "fanfare" (462; 883) outside the mortuary chamber—an interruption whose purpose turns out not to be to mock, as the son had feared, but rather to honor the deceased.

Then the narrator's mood changes to the impression of a rather agreeable memory triggered by the sight of the Sand novel: "This book that my mother had read aloud to me in Combray almost until morning had preserved in my mind all the charm of that night" (463; 884). This evocation of pleasure is truly surprising, given the gravity of the emotions with which the novel and the night had been linked in the opening volume. But the narrator's impression of "charm" turns out to be no more than another provisional screen.[53]

52. Roger Shattuck, *Proust's Binoculars: A Study of Memory, Time, and Recognition in "A la recherche du temps perdu,"* 70–74.

53. Compare the material in the sketches—for example *RTP* 1:1119: "My regrets were calmed, I let myself fall into the contentment [*douceur*] of that night with my mother near me. I knew that this would not happen again . . . , and even so I do not remember ever

What then intervenes is the long passage concerning the Sand novel and its resonances, which was simply lifted from the description of the "Combray" *drame du coucher* in one of Proust's early manuscript notebooks (Cahier 57), and inserted into the manuscript of the novel's conclusion at this point (see *RTP* 4:1261 n. 4). It is the narrator's final encounter with the involuntary recovery of his past. He returns to the figure of the indestructible memory archive that I have already considered—here, in the form of an imaginary library of the books to which in the course of life his feelings have become attached. Finally, the emotion that this series of tentative and provisional characterizations has functioned to hold at a distance becomes clear. The narrator observes that bibliophiles like the Prince organize their collections according to the associations their volumes accumulate with famous people. He contrasts his own fantasy of the library: "But it is rather in the history of my own life . . . that I would seek [beauty] . . . , as with this *François le champi*, contemplated for the first time in my little bedroom at Combray during what was likely the sweetest and saddest night of my life when I had, alas . . . , extracted from my parents a first abdication from which I could date the decline of my health and of my will, my constantly aggravated renunciation" (465; 886). Aestheticism is still trying to serve as mystification here. And the authentic negative emotion resurrected in *mémoire involontaire*—the "anguish about tomorrow" (464; 885)— will once again almost immediately be displaced and screened; the recovery of the most excruciating wound ever suffered by the narrator's childhood ego will, if we are to credit his hopeful construction, transform itself into the project of creation that germinates just before the novel ends.

But the anguish in this complex simply cannot be managed so neatly. *François le champi* surfaces one final time just four pages before the novel ends: "It was from that evening, when my mother had abdicated, along with the slow death of my grandmother, that I dated the decline of my will and of my health. Everything was decided in that moment . . ." (621; 1044). Given the unsettled state of

---

having experienced a feeling of calm and of happiness like the one I had during her reading." This serene atmosphere stands in profound tension with the narrator's perceptions of the irreducibly malign significance of the occasion, which I quoted earlier.

Proust's manuscript it would be unwise to make too much of the placement of this final evocation of anguish. Yet it is difficult not to sense in this reiterated memory of the novel's archetypal experience of *pain* a logic even more powerful than the metaphysics of *mémoire involontaire* that Proust elevated into such an insistent superstructure in the *Recherche*, and which so much in its narrative and affective structure nonetheless resists.

Proust's theory of memory is inevitably a mechanism for forgetting. To be sure, any theory determines what cannot be apprehended from within its closure. But the exclusions in this one may be more consequential, since they bear upon the very substance of experience, the very medium of knowledge.

Originality was essential to Proust's assumptions about art. In its idiosyncrasy, his celebration of hypermnesia seeks to sustain these, but it can only do so at the price of veiling or distorting—effectively repressing—a century-long tradition of anxiety about the difficulty of the past. Understanding memory in Proust means remembering what Proust's memory theory purposefully forgets. When we pull Proust back into the culture of memory that his claims to singularity necessarily bracket, powerful elements of convergence with the tradition of the memory crisis become clear. In concluding my analysis of his construction of the mnemonic, I want to reconsider the two sides of Proust's memory theory in this light.

The three-thousand page condemnation of "voluntary memory" in the *Recherche*, the coordinate attempt in his novel to see life *fresh*, then seems our culture's most powerful indictment of the past's malign persistence. Its perception is simple: that the negative corollary of experience is the loss of its immediacy, that *life* deadens *living*. Literature then lays down a quintessentially modernist claim: to be the alternative to existence. And of course the *Recherche* is nearly long enough to make this claim believable.

But we should observe that the entire construction operating in Proust is animated by a very simple binarism, by a familiar structure that organizes the repulsion of contraries. The parallel columns of its antinomies are familiar to any subject within the culture since romanticism:

life	death
fresh	frozen
immediate	insulated
multicolored	monochrome
aesthetic	quotidian
epiphany	history

. . . and so on.

There is an obvious paradox in such binarism. To condemn reduc-tionism it enforces a quite radical reduction. It substitutes precon-ceived structures for the immediacy of experience whose loss it seeks to forestall; it recollects the precise content of the past that it claims to depreciate. Proust's *theory* of memory thus practices the very form of memory it stigmatizes.

The notion that our experience bleeds over into the other spheres of our existence and contaminates them with contents from an irrele-vant past is at the heart of Proust's critique of experience itself. This degraded version of the past is the substance of what we remember through the deadening veil of habit. In Proust's doctrinal project, such banal forms of recollection simply reproduce banality. They jam the diverse into identities, the unique into the accustomed. They turn experience into something not experienced at all, but only dully rehearsed and mechanically reviewed.

So we might expect a systematic effort in the *Recherche* to eschew the habitual. But it is obvious that in his narrative practice Proust does not *really* condemn habit. As I suggested earlier in recalling my notion of "synthetic narration" in the *Recherche*, much of the di-egesis in Proust is rather a reproduction and celebration of the cus-tomary and the quotidian, the iterated and the familiar. The texture of recollection that emerges from the narrator's teacup could stand as a systematic paean to *Gemeinschaft* at its most chronically habitual. Recall the transcendent moment in "Combray" when (in a quintes-sential representation of dailiness evoked through synthetic narra-tion's verbs in the imperfect) Tante Léonie and Françoise debate the identity of an unfamiliar dog:

We knew [*connaissait*] everyone so well in Combray, both animals and people, that if my aunt had by chance seen a dog pass by "that she didn't know at all" she could not stop thinking about it nor devoting [*elle ne cessait d'y penser et de consacrer*] all of her inductive talents and her free moments to this incomprehensible fact.

"It's probably Mme Sazerat's dog," Françoise would say [*disait Françoise*] without much conviction, but in the hope of appeasement, so that my aunt would not "split her head."

"As if I didn't know Mme Sazerat's dog!" would answer [*répondait*] my aunt, whose critical intelligence did not give in so easily.

"Well then, it's probably the new dog that M. Galopin brought back from Lisieux."

"Oh, if that's it."

"They say he's a very friendly animal," Françoise would add [*ajoutait Françoise*]. (*RTP* 1:57–58; *RTP54* 1:58)

The opposition between the comforting village habitus of the "closed society" of Combray (*RTP* 1:109; *RTP54* 1:110) on the one hand, and the anonymity of modern life on the other is a theme in Proust as in much modernist writing. Balbec, for example, is thus cast as the antitype of Combray. In the dining room of the Grand-Hôtel, for the first time in his life, the narrator has the experience of being thrown into a universe completely indifferent to his existence.[54] This makes the Balbec dining room a particularly appropriate site for the window scene I analyzed in the preceding chapter. But Proust is far from systematic about this element of his demonstration. Even Paris, the metropolis, is represented with a comforting familiarity, and the habitual structures of synthetic narration occupy the Parisian scenes of the *Recherche* just as regularly as they do the others. The traditional contrastive geography of country vs. city does not quite seize the fundamental antinomy that Proustian memory theory projects onto the crisis of modern experience, and that animates his doctrinal energies.

But the reappearance—at the heart of his argument for its rejection—of precisely the reductive structure Proust's doctrine had sought to banish helps us to take the measure of the crisis that modernism's struggle with memory insistently registered and attempted to master. In his singular theory of involuntary memory Proust pro-

54. *RTP* 2:35; *RTP54* 1:674. Also see Vincent Descombes, *Proust: Philosophie du roman*, 182–83.

jected an antidote to this perplexity—indeed, sought to reason it out of existence.

Without doubt, the phenomenon of hypermnesia was a neurological fact recognized and extensively studied in Proust's period. I argued that this scientific context inevitably modulated Proust's construction of memory in his novel. In particular, it required suppressing the implication of a *pathology* attached to the totalizing retrieval of the past. And indeed this mnemonic pathology surely attached itself firmly to memory's *other* forms of appearance in the *Recherche*. My attempt to contextualize and historicize his representation of the memory crisis may help us to see the sort of distortion that Proust's demonstration obliged him to. For if the persistence of the past poses a problem for experience, how *a fortiori* could its absolute, totalizing reproduction not do so even more disastrously?

I began my discussion of involuntary memory by recalling how consistently Proust criticism has reproduced Proust's own understanding, his own valuation, of it. In the face of the contextual tensions and internal ambiguity of Proustian memory theory, we are now in a position to ask how we should understand involuntary memory ourselves. What should we *do* with involuntary memory? I am convinced that large numbers of Proust's readers have never truly believed that the phenomena Proust described was real enough to occupy the conceptual space he attributes to it, but rather that Proust's prestige and conviction alone induce us to credit this singular construction.

We need a way to modalize this material that can register the insistence of its assertion without forcing us to swallow it whole. The *mode of existence* of "involuntary memory" is a problem not often posed. Are we to believe in involuntary memory *literally*? Is it to be credited as the one element in Proustian representation that is self-interpreting and veridical? It purports to be a ground. Can we validate that claim?

I suggest that involuntary memory is rather a utopian projection. Involuntary memory, which promises the restoration of the past, is better understood as the intimation of an alterity potential in our present. Call it a "not-yet," since we lack other temporalities where it might conceptually be lodged. In any case it is surely evident that Proust's privileged form of memory does not only define a singular relation with time gone by. Involuntary memory is not just about the past. In a perfectly straightforward sense that registers the salvationist claim he makes for it, *mémoire involontaire* plots a relation to the future. We could understand it quite productively as science fiction. And it is culturally diagnostic as such.

Utopian representations inevitably project a time of otherness. But such alterity cannot be restricted to tomorrow. The time of its place is as uncertain as the paradoxical place of the "past" in memory. The modalization of thought that sustains and is expressed in the utopian project—something between belief and need—does not simply throw itself blindly forward into an unrealized future. It powerfully incorporates and recirculates contents and affects from the past and represents them in determinate transformation.

So we could say that involuntary memory transforms time, but not in precisely the manner that Proust claimed. For him, in the privileged moment of hypermnesia, time collapses in on itself. But in my projection here, involuntary memory rather locates a fold in temporality that opens it up from within to the possibilities of an existence that could rectify the deficiencies of the present, and that hence defines that present more rigorously than any direct characterization of it could manage to do.

This is why I have sought to subvert or to reinterpret the eudaemonism that Proust insistently attached to his privileged moments and could not abandon. I have wanted to search for the other side of involuntary memory's "joy": for the inevitable dystopian double of Proust's utopian postulation. Involuntary memory is a response to the anxieties of the memory crisis, but rather than resolving them it only calls them back more exactingly. The world it represents *should* be a different world, but as I have argued in analyzing what such memory really resurrects in the *Recherche*, this recollected world nonetheless perversely continues on its disastrous course.

Memory is the medium of these disasters. So with an urgent logic Proust calls upon memory itself to sublate them. And if we should conclude that the imperatives he sought to resolve in memory are so refractory as to force distortion of the very faculty upon which the salvationist potentiality was to have depended, even that deviation is comprehensible from within the canons of memory. The theory for *that* is Freud's. At just the moment Proust was seeking salvation in

hypermnesia, Freud was projecting memory as a consumn
perpetual trickster that transforms everything in accordan
needs of which we are not ourselves aware.

This notion of need seems increasingly urgent in Proust's theory
itself. The intensity of Proust's desire for the resolution involuntary
memory projects within the *Recherche* is really not different in character from the "terrible need for another person [*ce terrible besoin
d'un être*]" that he evokes from the depths of his anguish over Albertine and immediately connects with his apprenticeship to suffering in
Combray (*RTP* 3:130; *RTP54* 2:733). Here is the representation that
need projects: "If a sound, if an odor, once heard or smelled in the
past, is heard or smelled again, at once in the present and in the
past, real without being present, ideal without being abstract, immediately the permanent essence of things that is habitually hidden
finds itself liberated, and our true self . . . awakens, comes alive in
receiving the celestial nourishment that belongs to it. A minute freed
from the order of time has re-created within us to experience it a
being freed from the order of time. This being—we understand that
he is confident in his joy. (*RTP* 4:451; *RTP54* 3:872–73).

We can celebrate the extraordinary novel Proust wrote without at
the same time crediting the concerted mystification that inscribes
itself in the peculiar form of memory to which Proust attributed his
decision to write. Involuntary memory recovers anguish, misery, and
disappointment—but more than that, *involuntary memory is their
product*, they determine it. This is the painful side of recollection
that has haunted writers and thinkers throughout the period that I
have termed the "memory crisis." Recollection has been the site of a
continuing disaster. In the face of Proust's reversal of this valence, it
seems important to reestablish his relation to a century-long preoccupation with the malignancy of the mnemonic. Concerning modernity's most concerted obsessive of recollection, it would seem particularly ironic to misremember memory itself.

7

Mnemo-Analysis—Memory in Freud
I. Maieutics

> If anyone should feel inclined to over-estimate the state of
> our present knowledge of mental life, a reminder of the
> function of memory is all that would be needed to force
> him to be more modest. No psychological theory has yet
> succeeded in giving a connected account of the fundamen-
> tal phenomenon of remembering and forgetting.
>
> —Sigmund Freud, *The Psychopathology of Everyday
> Life* (1901), *SE* 6:134

Psychoanalysis is our culture's last Art of Memory. In this chapter
I explore how memory works in Freud. In particular, I examine
how psychoanalysis reacts to the problems arising in the presence of
the past that I have been calling the "memory crisis."

Freud always insisted that the therapy he theorized and the theory
he practiced sought to understand memory and help us to remember. "A psychological theory deserving of any consideration," he
wrote in 1895, early in his career, "must furnish an explanation of
'memory.'"[1] And almost two decades later, in one of the most important of his mature metapsychological essays, he defined the physician's objective in working with the patient as follows: "Remember-

---

1. Unless otherwise indicated, quotations from Freud are taken from *The Standard
Edition of the Complete Psychological Works*, ed. James Strachey et al., 24 vols. (London:
Hogarth Press, 1953–74), hereafter abbreviated *SE*. The passage cited is from Freud's
"Project for a Scientific Psychology" (1895), *SE* 1:299.

ing in the old manner—reproduction in the psychical field—is the aim to which he adheres."[2]

What happens when we consider psychoanalysis as an *Ars memorativa*, when we conceive of Freud's invention as a "mnemo-analysis"? What connections exist between the reconception of individuals, their culture, and their predicament in psychoanalysis and the problematic of memory that has concerned me in this book?

With Freud, preoccupation with memory proliferates and pervades psychological and cultural theory until the individual almost seems to have been reconceived as a cluster of mnemonic operations and transformations.[3] Desire, instinct, dream, association, neurosis, repression, repetition, the unconscious—all the central notions of psychoanalysis—then appear to have been rewritten as memory functions or dysfunctions. Moreover, they were theorized as such by Freud himself.

For psychoanalysis, memory is the heart of the matter. Memory constitutes us and undoes us simultaneously. In therapy, the exercise of memory is intended to heal the traumas whose capacity to disrupt our existence memory has itself perversely sustained.[4] In its diverse and seemingly incommensurable forms, memory thus comes to seem both the problem Freud sought to solve and the core of his solution.

2. Sigmund Freud, "Remembering, Repeating and Working-Through" (1914), *SE* 12:153. In what follows, I will have much to say about types of remembering *other* than the one Freud identified as the objective of treatment. Other versions of Freud's insistence on the relation between therapy and memory will be found in *SE* 7:253, 7:18, and 16:282. Freud regularly assumed the masculine gender for the therapist, as he did the feminine for hysteric patients. (It is true that the first female analysts—particularly, Melanie Klein and Anna Freud—did not begin active practice until the 1920s.) Contemporary usage diverges from his choice of pronouns.

3. In this chapter as elsewhere, I use "mnemonic" as an adjective equivalent to "memory-" or as an adjectival noun ("the mnemonic") designating "the memory realm." The editors of the *Standard Edition* chose the English "mnemic" to translate Freud's adjectival combining-form "Erinnerungs-" (or sometimes "Gedächtnis-"), as in *Erinnerungsspur, Erinnerungsrest, Erinnerungssymbol.* Hence "mnemic trace," "mnemic symbol," and so on. Like much of the terminology by which Freud's concepts have come to be known in English, "mnemic" is considerably less common than its German counterpart. I employ the *Standard Edition*'s "mnemic" only when quoting from their translation.

4. In *Language and Origins of Psychoanalysis*, John Forrester sorts out the positive and negative senses of "remembering" in Freud (132–33), but Forrester's discussion almost suggests that the ambivalence of "memory" might be resolvable by semantic clarification—as if two "kinds" of memory had somehow been confused. In Freud's view, however, the pathological and the therapeutic results of memory arise in *precisely* the same faculty. For psychoanalysis, memory's ambivalence is constitutive and irreducible.

In his attempt to unravel the complications of the mnemonic, he magnified its field, its centrality—and its ambivalence—more insistently and more powerfully than any other theorist in the modern period. He devoted intense and intricate attention to memory's covert and profoundly equivocal power, conceiving the understanding of individual and collective life as an increasingly complex recovery and reconception of what he might have called the "vicissitudes" of mnemonic material.[5] Thus (as I will argue in Chapter 8) the model of psychoanalytic *interpretation* bears an intimate—if sometimes forgotten—relation to Freud's paradigm of memory.

No modern theory of individual action or cultural process has made more of memory than Freud's. None has conceived the preservation of the past as more problematic in the present. But the very scope of the functions psychoanalysis ascribes to memory, the unprecedented theoretical imperatives that arise from Freud's totalizing vision of determination by the past, make solution of the memory problem arduous. Yet I think the stresses within Freud's theory are not simply complications internal to psychoanalysis. This is why an investigation of his memory theory has pertinence for an effort to elucidate the memory problem in modernity.

Freud assuredly did not set out to address the problem that has concerned me in this book—the sources and the significance of what I have termed modernity's "memory crisis," the anxiety about memory that came into focus in the nineteenth century, and whose representations pervade the period's self-conception and its social practices. Yet psychoanalysis developed an interpretive system that powerfully instantiates and illuminates this preoccupation. The virtuoso identification of memory's protean disguises in Freudian theory offers a persuasive confirmation that the generalized disquiet over memory that stressed cultural expression from the end of the French Revolution to Freud's own period was contending with something fundamental.

So I will claim that Freud's understanding of memory can help us read the memory crisis. Indeed, we might say that psychoanalysis exacerbates it to its point of greatest intensity and places it in its

5. Freud's term is *Schicksale*. See Sigmund Freud, "Instincts and their Vicissitudes" (1915), *SE* 14:111–40. Again, Freud's common word for the mutability of things was rendered in English by a considerably less common term.

most perspicuous light. Freud's account of the investment of the present by the past, his theorization of the material and psychological force of the constituted, reconceives the stresses that sought expression in a long series of nineteenth-century reflections concerning the perplexities of the mnemonic. By taking individual and collective memory as a site of crisis, by systematizing this preoccupation as a *science*, Freud's theory offers a prestigious cultural warrant for the reflection on the perplexities of memory that occupied his predecessors.

❧❧❧

> This brings us to the more general problem of preservation in the sphere of the mind. The subject has hardly been studied as yet.
> —Sigmund Freud, *Civilization and Its Discontents* (1930), *SE* 21:69

With Freud, the double bind of memory reaches a point of exquisite stress. In this concluding portion of my analysis of modernity's memory crisis, I examine the elements of Freud's theory of memory and the logic of the profound ambivalence within it. I seek to understand the unprecedented tension that Freud's conception of the psyche imposed on his account of our constitution by contents from the past.

In psychoanalysis—particularly in Freud's texts on psychoanalysis—the density and intensity of attention to the phenomena of memory, forgetting, false memories, and the like are evidence of the power of the past. Understanding this power might be said to have been the project of nineteenth-century reflection on the constitution of subjects. To recall and extend an analysis I began in my discussion of Musset's *Confession* in Chapter 3, we could say that for pre-Revolutionary society the overt compulsions of the law appeared to be the force constraining individuals—until the moment, in the late eighteenth century, when societies in Europe commenced a series of constitutional and political experiments that modified or suspended them. Then a slow process began in effect testing the theory that legal coercions were the source of individual constraints. The society of Estates was abolished; divine right was abrogated; economic "priv-

ileges" (restrictive licenses) were gradually revoked; property quali-
fications for political participation became more lenient; slavery and
serfdom were progressively abolished; women were slowly but increasingly admitted to full participation in civil and political society;
religious exclusions upon economic or political activity were loosened
or terminated. Yet it soon became evident that despite these forms of
juridical liberation the conduct of individuals and their possibilities
continued to be powerfully constrained. At that point, in the face of
these more diffuse and mysterious limitations, social theory began to
investigate how the social, cultural, and psychological past of individuals and groups seemed to preserve and impose itself even in the
absence of any overt compulsion. People appeared to imprison *themselves.* How did they come to do so, and why didn't they stop?

The problem was to understand the constitution of the present as
an unwitting, involuntary prolongation of the past. In such a structure, the bright independence of each moment of post-Revolutionary
time appeared to blur, to surrender its promise. Much more than the
present seemed present in the present. As the distinction between
then and *now* increasingly blurred, the persistence of the past, the
inertia of practice, the conservatism of habit, the subterranean obstinacy of belief increasingly became focused as a complex puzzle that
culture discovered at its heart and sought to comprehend in the service of its liberation.[6]

In that sense "memory" might be construed as the generic identi-
fier for the seemingly ineluctable *determinations* that give content
to, and create the conditions of possibility for, any present. Memory
names the mechanism by which our present is indentured to the
past, or, to turn the structure around, by which a past we never
chose dominates the present that seems the only place given us to
live.[7]

6. On this problem, see the introduction to my *Discourse/Counter-Discourse: The Theory and Practice of Symbolic Resistance in Nineteenth-Century France,* particularly 41–42. On the dialectical ambivalence of the past in Freudian theory, see Michael S. Roth, *Psycho-Analysis as History: Negation and Freedom in Freud.*

7. Psychoanalysis thus joins a number of other influential theoretical systems that seek to conceptualize the determination of the present by the power of the *constituted*: among others I would mention particularly Marx's notion of "reproduction" (and his related con-cepts of "forces" and "relations" of production, "constant capital," and "ideology"); Durk-heim's linked concepts of "social facts," "social forces," "material culture," and "collective

But the past is gone. It is always absent—this would seem its very definition. It may determine the present. The problem for cultural or psychological theory is to understand how in its absence and its impalpability it manages to do so. How does the constituted *constitute*? To employ a Freudian characterization, we might say that the constraints imposed by the past seem "uncanny," for their exercise is generally so invisible to us at the very moment we are under their control that we live in the illusion of an autonomy that the force of the constituted nonetheless continuously subverts.

The pre-Revolutionary compulsions of the law were easier to understand. Memory is a more obscure duress. The contents of the past that determines us in the present are not simply—bodily—*reproduced* in every succeeding moment of time. That is why the issue of memory becomes acute. To understand the significance of this, we need only fantasize the contrary case. Imagine that something like literal conservation of the past and its reproduction in the present were possible—not reproduction as Marx understood the term, but absolute replication in the mode of ontological totality. Such recurrence would of course contravene our most fundamental experience of the irreversibility of time: *the past would be here now.* By making what *has been* coincident and coterminous with what still *is*, this seemingly fantastical state of affairs would neatly abolish their difference.

The advantages of such a system would be striking—particularly for those of us who struggle to understand the history of culture. In a world of total "reproduction," comprehending the past would cease to be a problem. This would conveniently resolve the difficulty of theorizing and analyzing the forms through which an impalpable and irretrievable past still sustains a power in the present sufficient to swamp all our projections of free intentionality and individual autonomy.

Our intuitions of the world appear to require that we abandon this fantasy of the absolute abolition of time.[8] It is true (even in earth-

representations"; Gramsci's "hegemony"; Bourdieu's "habitus"; Althusser's "ideological apparatus"; Foucault's "discourse." On these diverse conceptualizations of the mechanisms through which the past's persistence is exercised, see my *Discourse/Counter-Discourse*, particularly 54–65.

8. But not completely by any means. For this paradigm of absolute temporal suppres-

quake country) that we generally wake up each morning with the buildings and the furniture of the night before still in their places. In this sense my fiction of a continuing coincidence between *then* and *now* might seem to bear some relation to experience. Yet this coincidence is never total and never assured; reproduction is never simply literal. We age, things change, we forget. The impossibility of absolute replication of the past restores the mystery, indeed the urgency, of the memory crisis about which the nineteenth century never ceased to worry. For if the reproduction of the past in the present is *not* the result of its ontological replication, how *does* the past contrive to determine us?

Resolving this question has been an urgent project of modernity. We might conceive the formation of the human sciences, in particular the disciplines we have come to know as history, political economy, sociology, and psychology, as the result of efforts by a series of seminal theorists to understand how our lives are in fact *determined.* Freud's psychoanalytic project to free individuals from the paradoxes of memory and the uncanny persistence of the past recirculates and resituates this long cultural interrogation concerning the *nature of determination.* The objective of Freud's work could then be articulated as follows: to discover how our past, despite being irretrievably absent, maintains the power of its presence, and, to the extent possible, to devise means for undoing this power.[9]

---

sion will recur with great force in Freud's fundamental notion of the timelessness of the unconscious. And it reproduces important features of Proust's doctrine of the integral resurrections of the past experienced in "involuntary memory."

9. As psychoanalytic theory developed, Freud was emphatic that *therapy* consisted of considerably more than the interpretation of unconscious material. As he puts it in *Beyond the Pleasure Principle* (1920), "At first . . . psycho-analysis was . . . an art of interpreting" (*SE* 18:18). But "this did not solve the therapeutic problem" (ibid.). Hence developing the theory in its therapeutic dimensions—while retaining the concern with interpretation—required addressing the specific resistances that had arisen and finding means to induce the patient to abandon them. I consider elements of that theory later. But since my purpose here is to understand the logic and the cultural stakes of psychoanalytic theory, I decline to discuss two related and deeply vexed questions: the practical efficacy of Freudian therapy and the dispute concerning its scientificity. These issues do not bear on my project in this chapter and the next. A summary listing of the vast and contentious literature on these twin controversies can be found in the bibliographical essay in Peter Gay's *Freud: A Life for Our Time,* 745. In addition to the items listed there, see B. R. Cosin et al., "Critical Empiricism Criticized: The Case of Freud"; Ludwig Wittgenstein, "Conversations on Freud; Excerpt from 1932–3 Lectures"; Jürgen Habermas, *Knowledge and Hu-*

In what follows I want to examine how the presence of the past is conceived in psychoanalysis. Most of the time, the formative determinations of the memory complex, being ubiquitous and constitutive of present reality, seem transparent. This induces us to ignore their evidence. But in those moments and at those sites where some disturbance of this transparency, some eddy in the seemingly unremarkable flow of past contents into the moving window of the present becomes perceptible, then suddenly the past no longer goes without saying.

These moments were the ones Freud's analytic attention detected and seized on, the moments when the presence and the power of the past detached themselves from the background of the unremarked and called out for an attention that few had granted them before Freud. When, in dreams, in parapraxes, in hysteria, and in the other transference neuroses, the present unexpectedly becomes *inexplicable* on its own terms, Freud discovered he could productively invoke, in order to understand it, the covert persistence of the past and the determinations of a memory whose extent and intensity no one before him had ever conceived as so ubiquitous or so sovereign.

∂∞∂

We must think of stronger means.
—Sigmund Freud, "The Psychotherapy of Hysteria"
(1895), *SE* 2:270

Where, then, is the past? And how can we gain access to it? Let us listen to Freud the artificer of memory. Early in his therapeutic work Freud decided that he should "start from the assumption that my patients knew everything that was of any pathogenic significance and

---

man Interests, particularly 214, 254–63; Sebastiano Timpanaro, *The Freudian Slip: Psychoanalysis and Textual Criticism,* particularly 47, 86–87, 216; Ilse Grubrich-Simitis, "Metapsychology and Metabiology," 102; and Carlo Ginzburg, "Clues: Morelli, Freud, and Sherlock Holmes," passim. A special mention should be made of the most notorious and negative critic of Freud's claims to scientificity, Adolf Grünbaum; see his *Foundations of Psychoanalysis: A Philosophical Critique.* I will consider the implications of claims for and against the scientific status of psychoanalysis in greater detail in the next chapter. Paul Robinson reassesses the anti-Freudian critiques of Frank Sulloway, Jeffrey Moussaieff Masson, and Adolf Grünbaum in *Freud and His Critics.*

that it was only a question of obliging them to communicate it"
(*Studies on Hysteria* [1895], *SE* 2:110). In "The Psychotherapy of
Hysteria" (part 4 of the *Studies*), Freud described a method he had
devised in order to get at the memories he believed lay at the origin
of his patients' symptoms, but which they had been unable to produce: "In these circumstances, I make use . . . of a small technical
device. I inform the patient that, a moment later, I shall apply pressure to his forehead, and I assure him that, all the time the pressure
lasts, he will see before him a recollection in the form of a picture or
will have it in his thoughts in the form of an idea occurring to him;
and I pledge him to communicate this picture or idea to me, whatever it may be" (*SE* 2:270).

In what follows, Freud expands on this pledge, on the patient's
commitment to avoid censorship of the memories the therapist's laying on of hands will have elicited—an early version of what he was
later to term the "fundamental rule" of psychoanalysis, the agreement by patients to say whatever they think and feel without selecting from the contents which come into their minds, even if they are
tempted to withhold or modify them.[10] This is the aspect of the passage from "The Psychotherapy of Hysteria" that has drawn the attention of commentators and critics. I want to consider it from a different angle. Let me recontextualize this early account of Freud's
therapeutic practice by examining an injunction from one of his mature papers on technique, "On Beginning the Treatment" (1913):
"Patients are occasionally met with who start the treatment by assuring us that they cannot think of anything to say, although the whole
field of their life-history and the story of their illness is open to them
to choose from. . . . Energetic and repeated assurances to the patient
that it is impossible for no ideas at all to occur to him at the beginning, and that what is in question is a resistance against the analyst,
soon oblige him to make the expected admissions or to uncover a
first piece of his complexes" (*SE* 12:137).

What these two passages, separated by nearly twenty years, make
evident is that the process for attaining individual recollection in-

10. The term "fundamental rule" first appeared in "The Dynamics of Transference"
(1912), *SE* 12:107, but the notion had been forming for a long time. See Jean Laplanche
and J.-B. Pontalis, *The Language of Psycho-Analysis*, s.v. "fundamental rule" and "free
association."

vokes a collective or dialogic instrumentality. *Anamnesis*—it might seem unexpectedly—*involves a system of two*. The pressure of my own hand alone can not achieve what the analyst's pressure manages.[11] But how can anyone else remember for me? Why should a recollection that everything suggests is personal require the assistance of a psychoanalytic interlocutor? What paradigm might make sense of a procedure by which the achievement and the expression of my memory passes through someone else?

The paradigm has come up before in this book. My discussion of Musset's *Confession* in Chapter 3 prefigured the structure of such mnemonic midwifery. By troping liturgical or juridical paradigms in his novel, Musset created a situation that transgressed the ordinary limitations of intersubjectivity. I claimed that in effect Musset placed Brigitte Pierson, his hero Octave's lover and confessor-interlocutor, "*within* Octave's process of memory." Brigitte's role in the tale resists containment within conventional narrative categories: she is neither simply a character nor simply a narratee. As a result of the anamnestic and confessional structure through which Musset represented the intersubjectivity at the center of his tale, the *content* of Octave's reminiscence—the repetition of the disabling emotional ties that the novel narrates—uncannily converged with, effectively *became its form*. In the *Confession* the relation narrated transformed itself into the narrative relation.

Musset's *Confession* thereby anticipated the Freudian paradigm of transference linking patient and analyst. The transference relation similarly blurs distinctions of content and form, observation and participation, objectivity and subjectivity. Freud claimed that this relation was an indispensable component of properly psychoanalytic therapy.[12] But other important psychoanalytic issues can be read in the mnemonic and therapeutic microcosm that Freud evokes in the two short passages I just quoted, in which Freud explains the techniques he used to elicit recollection from his patients.

The complex relationship that links remembrance and forgetting is

---

11. Freud's *self*-analysis presents obvious problems for such a conception. I consider the difficulty in note 14 to Chapter 8.

12. "[The treatment] only deserves the latter name ['psycho-analysis'] if the intensity of the transference has been utilized for the overcoming of resistances" (Freud, "On Beginning the Treatment" [1913], *SE* 12:143).

central to my argument concerning Freud's contribution to the framing of the memory crisis, but I can anticipate the psychoanalytic doctrine on the question I consider in greater detail below. It is that recollection and forgetting are not contraries, but rather differential modes of existence of the same process in the representation of the past. *Forgetting is a form of remembering.* The "resistance" that Freud identifies as the reason for the analytic patient's silence or apparent lapse of memory he reinterprets as a significant manifestation of the memory function itself.

It is not obvious how such internal resistance can be overcome. We might be tempted to say that the antidote to the patient's resistance is the analyst's coercion. With a laying on of hands or the imposition of a rule, the analyst commands performance. And it is true that, as the passages I cited suggest, Freud did not hesitate upon occasion to employ duress (he even spoke once of "blackmail")—most notoriously in the case of the "Wolf Man" whose analysis had become arrested on the threshold of Freud's concerted attack on the root neurosis from childhood that he believed underlay the Wolf Man's adult problems: "In this predicament I resorted to the heroic measure of fixing a time-limit for the analysis. At the beginning of a year's work I informed the patient that the coming year was to be the last one of his treatment, no matter what he achieved in the time still left to him."[13]

But the question of *why* coercion leads to the production of memories previously unavailable, and hence to the possibility of progress in the treatment, deserves further consideration. As I sought to suggest by recalling my discussion of Musset's *Confession*, the problem is that notions of "internal" and "external" turn baffling within the transferential paradigm. Clearly the patient's recollection, however "externally" coerced, could not have occurred if the "internal" memory contents in question had simply been obliterated. In that case no exercise of force could have recovered them. How then is forgetting

13. Sigmund Freud, "Analysis Terminable and Interminable" (1937), *SE* 23:217. Freud's self-characterization as blackmailer appears on the following page. The Wolf Man's case ("From the History of an Infantile Neurosis," *SE* 17) was composed in 1914 and published in 1918; the account of Freud's imposition of a time limit upon his patient is found on pages 10–11. The imposition of the "fundamental rule" at the outset of classical Freudian treatment—however salutary its effect may be—represents a clear case of parallel coercion.

reversible? Why does the analyst's opposition to the patient's silence, hence to the inaccessibility of remembrance, produce recollection? Why is a second consciousness necessary to undo the mnemonic paralysis of the first?

The answer would seem to be that the patient's continuing silence instantiates one of Freud's most striking insights, that forgetting is an instrumental behavior and involves a purposeful expenditure of energy. Forgetting is a determined activity—but one performed without the knowledge of its actor. The analyst's intervention can be efficacious because there is a *process* in which to intervene. If patients' forgetting were a simple absence, if their analytic silences were purely negative, there would be no place for the positivity of the other, the analyst, to gain access. Nothing could come of such a nothing.

For Freud on the contrary the patient's silence, and hence forgetting, must be conceived as a learned habit—as a *memory*—that makes certain recollection inaccessible. In the analytic silence the past is *already* expressing itself, a memory is being recalled. But the other, the therapist, has a different memory and a different past, and hence is not bound to the reproduction of this silence, to the recollected forgetting that has determined it. Anamnesis (whether in Freud or in Musset) is modeled as dialogic because undoing the remembered pattern of failure to remember, subverting the false stability of mnemonic blockage, requires the dynamism of an otherness. Transference can only make sense within a relation of difference.[14]

This is what enables rewriting the patient's silence as a communication. The analyst, not being the patient, hears the patient *differently*. Then the intersubjective difference through which patient and analyst are dialogically linked becomes the paradigm for a difference to be discovered and constructed in, and of, the self. Over the process of therapy, otherness becomes convertible into the possibility of self-transformation. In a classic instantiation of the dialectic's real productivity, the action of *difference* becomes the indispensable condition for a fuller realization of *identity*.[15]

14. Freud's most thoughtful reflections on the analytic situation as a system of *two* will be found in his "Constructions in Analysis" (1937), *SE* 23:257–69.

15. The analyst Leston Havens evokes this dialogism in *A Safe Place*: "The free passage of thoughts in the patient's speech and the therapist's mind occupies a space between the

To characterize the memory process enabled by the therapist's injunction to remember, I want to resurrect a splendid old word from the history of dialectic, the word I placed at the head of this chapter: *maieutics*. The term derives from the Greek *maia* (midwife). It originates in and refers back to the Socratic doctrine that teaching is based on eliciting recollection, on bringing forth that memory which the interlocutor has forgotten ever knowing. The relevance of such a paradigm to psychoanalysis is evident. From the Breuer period to the end of his career, Freud's procedures took as their instrumental condition and their teleology the continuous and concerted solicitation of remembrance.

꿍꿍

> There is in general no guarantee of the data produced by
> our memory.
> —Sigmund Freud, "Screen Memories" (1899), *SE* 3:315

Freud's own memory was excellent. "I am not in general inclined to forget things," he wrote in *The Psychopathology of Everyday Life* (1901). "For a short period of my youth some unusual feats of memory were not beyond me" (*SE* 6:135). In his biography of Freud, Peter Gay remarks on his subject's "unsurpassed memory for apt passages from poets and novelists" (*Freud*, 159; cf. 106). And in one of his classic papers on technique, Freud addressed a parallel issue: the seemingly formidable problem of keeping straight the names and details of numerous patients' stories. He referred to the incredulity that this feat of recollection stimulated among nonanalysts. But he represented himself as having no difficulty managing these memories— something he was able to do, he wrote, through use of the same "evenly-suspended attention" that he prescribed analysts maintain generally ("Recommendations to Physicians Practising Psycho-Analysis" [1912], *SE* 12:111).

Yet Freud's memory was subject to the same failures and confusions that all of us experience. For example, the phenomenon he

---

two; discoveries are not made by separate minds, but spring up in the common space"
(26). Freud termed this medium of the in-between a *Zwischenreich*. See Peter Brooks,
Reading for the Plot: Design and Intention in Narrative, 283.

termed "cryptomnesia"—what, adapting a charmingly understated British expression, we might translate as "forgetting with advantage." With his customary candor Freud recounted commissions of this lapse. For example he described how he had been brought by his friend Wilhelm Fliess to realize that he had completely blotted out recollection that Fliess had introduced him to the theory of "original bisexuality," a theory which he then played back to Fliess as if he had devised it himself.[16]

For most of us, lapses such as these function only as annoyances or embarrassments. But Freud—as is notorious—hypothesized that they could be made intelligible. The first significant result of his inquiry into quotidian experiences of memory loss and degradation was his essay "The Psychical Mechanism of Forgetfulness" (1898), which in a revised version became the opening chapter of *The Psychopathology of Everyday Life* (1901). Freud took many of the analyses of mnemonic lapses in this study from his own experience, including the classic case of his forgetting the name of the painter of the Orvieto Last Judgment frescoes.[17]

The result of his investigations strengthened Freud's conviction that such mental errors are always instrumental. He thus spoke of the "tendentious nature of our remembering and forgetting" (*SE* 3:296), and when he returned to the question the following year in "Screen Memories" (1899) he systematized his assertion: "Close investigation shows . . . that these falsifications of memory are tendentious—that is, that they serve the purposes of the repression and replacement of objectionable or disagreeable impressions" (*SE* 3:322). In *The Psychopathology of Everyday Life* he invoked the traditional juridical principle of "cui prodest?" (who benefits?) to summarize his doctrine that memory lapses always produce a gain to *some* psychic function, and that understanding them consequently requires identifying the beneficiary (see *SE* 6:144).

In the light of my discussion earlier concerning the puzzling and

16. See Freud, *Psychopathology of Everyday Life* (1901), *SE* 6:143–44, and Gay, *Freud*, 126–27 and 127 n. See also Freud, "Analysis Terminable and Interminable" (1937), *SE* 23:245.

17. It was Signorelli. See *SE* 3:290ff.; cf. 6:2ff. Timpanaro's analysis of Freud's own analysis of this lapse is a classic of anti-Freudian critique; see Timpanaro, *The Freudian Slip*, chap. 6.

stubborn *persistence* of memory, it is important to emphasize that Freud interpreted the experiences of "forgetting" he analyzed in these studies not as simple *trous de mémoire*, as mnemonic blanks, but as authentic experiences of remembrance. But the recollections recovered in them were inappropriate, at least to the conscious purpose for which they had been sought. In these lapses just as in any memory experience, the past has been projected into the present— but it is an unwanted past, indeed frequently an unacceptable one. In carrying into consciousness, in however disguised a form, the contents of a disagreeable mnemonic trace, memory lapses like those Freud analyzed in his work around the turn of the century involuntarily sustain what he called a *"motive of unpleasure"* (*The Psychopathology of Everyday Life, SE* 6:136; emphasis Freud's). And in the process they give a microcosmic but crucial glimpse of the general mechanism by which memory, seemingly a benign and neutral "archive" of our experience (*SE* 3:296), can turn pathological. Freud was explicit: "The example elucidated here [Freud's inability to recall the name of Signorelli] receives an immensely added interest when we learn that *it may serve as nothing more or less than a model for the pathological processes to which the psychical symptoms of the psychoneuroses . . . owe their origin.*"[18]

This hypothesis has of course proven extraordinarily productive. Through its varied manifestations, psychoanalysis (along with a series of diverse interpretive systems inspired by it) has been able to theorize entire areas of what had seemed meaninglessness as meaningful. Phenomena previously thought to be random or negative (for example, the seemingly entropic disappearance of a memory trace) have been reconceived as motivated and hence comprehensible.[19] This doctrine transforms forgetting from a flat and impenetrable absence

18. *SE* 3:295; emphasis mine. It is somewhat surprising that Freud seems not to have speculated that the intense frustration we experience when, unable to call up the "right" memory upon demand, we find only inappropriate sound-alikes, might actually carry in a disguised or displaced form the "unpleasure" of the repressed content that thus obliquely brushes against our consciousness. We might have imagined such an account on the model of Freud's analysis of the "uncanny," the affective power of which he interpreted as arising in the experience of an involuntary reminder of the repetition compulsion; see Freud, *Beyond the Pleasure Principle* (1920), *SE* 18:36.

19. Richard Wollheim, *Sigmund Freud*, xxxiii.

into a rich positivity—into remembrance. And it insists on the intimate "connection [*Zusammenhang*]" between the two, on their systematicity.[20]

Before Freud, forgetting had seemed an event about which no narrative could be offered, only an inarticulate and opaque conclusion. Freud insisted on the contrary that in the psyche there could be no results without causes, hence no denouements without stories. So if forgetting resulted, there was a story behind it. At the same time, he offered an explanation of why the pertinent story about our forgetting hadn't been known to everyone all along, why it had in effect been forgotten. To put his theory into movement, Freud projected a protagonist and a plot for the tale he was generating about forgetting. In effect he created a new narrative genre about the process of the mind.

The main character in this narrative had emerged as early as 1895 in the fourth part of the *Studies on Hysteria*, in Freud's discussion of the analytic technique he had developed in his work with hysterics: "The first and most powerful impression made upon one during such an analysis is certainly that the pathogenic psychical material which has ostensibly been forgotten, which is not at the ego's disposal and which plays no part in association and memory, nevertheless in some fashion lies ready to hand and in correct and proper order. . . . The pathogenic psychical material appears to be the *property* of an *intelligence* which is not necessarily inferior to that of the normal ego" (*SE* 2:287; emphasis mine). In Freud's image, the mysterious beneficiary of forgetting is thus provided with elements of a personality (intelligence) and even with a civil status (property holder). In the narrative of the psyche that Freud was composing, this entity functioned to withdraw from the ego's possession important facts about its perceptions, recollections, and behavior. But with this new character (the "unconscious") written into the story and the new plot motif ("repression"), which was its apparent goal, already functional, what I have been calling Freudian maieutics was crucially redefined, both in its necessity and its possibility. For although it now appeared

20. See Freud, *The Psychopathology of Everyday Life* (1901), *SE* 6:134. Paul-Laurent Assoun provides a suggestive treatment of the problem of forgetting in "Le sujet de l'oubli selon Freud."

absolutely indispensable to recover the memories the unconscious had withdrawn from the accessible archive of memory, this task of recovery simultaneously emerged as constitutively problematic.[21]

This resituation of the meaning and the function of memory requires asking once again, in the new tonality that it determines, the question I posed earlier. Now that we have projected an unconscious, *where is our past?* The paradox of Freudian construction of memory is that it defined for this constitutive instance of our psyche—of our self—both an irreducible presence and an infinite distance. The memory that Freud conceived in his complex and ambivalent projection in turn provides a perspective from which the urgency and the arduousness of the memory crisis of modernity must be reconsidered.

❧❧❧

> It is not easy to deal scientifically with feelings.
> —Sigmund Freud, *Civilization and its Discontents* (1930), *SE* 21:65

In my analysis of Baudelaire's Swan poem, I argued that in a world characterized by the mobility of signifiers that makes modern socio-economies possible, commodities are not alone in changing places. Language itself exhibits a fundamental lability. But once signs begin to flow and float, things become hard to restabilize. Even chronology turns insecure. Then the past can rematerialize like the classical Andromache in the heart of nineteenth-century Paris; the memories of the departed can seem more present than the present itself.

The paradox of Freudian "maieutics" lies on a continuum with this perplexity. The semiotic puzzle foregrounded in "Le Cygne"—the

---

21. On the history and prehistory of the unconscious, see particularly Henri Ellenberger, *The Discovery of the Unconscious: The History and Evolution of Dynamic Psychiatry*, and Lancelot Law Whyte, *The Unconscious before Freud.* In *The Interpretation of Dreams* (1900), Freud introduced the abbreviations *Ucs.*, *Cs.*, *Pcs.*, etc. to designate the topography of the psyche; see *SE* 5:540ff. He intended them to designate the *systemic* aspect of the psychic function to which they refer, in contrast to the adjectives "unconscious," "conscious," and so on, which he meant descriptively. See Sigmund Freud, "The Unconscious" (1915), *SE* 14:140 and n. 2. In Chapter 6 I referred to Sartre's critique of the agent of discrimination—the censor—responsible for determining the preservation of the patient's "pathogenic psychical material" in the unconscious; see note 39 to Chapter 6.

deceptive verisimilitude, the apparent *reality* of our memories of the nonexistent—had occupied Freud as early as the 1895 "Project for a Scientific Psychology." On the neurological level that was the focus of his attempt in the "Project" to construct a system of the psyche, Freud asked how we are able to tell the difference between a *presence* and an *absence*. We need, he wrote, "an external criterion in order to distinguish between perception [*Wahrnehmung*] and idea [*Vorstellung*]" or between "perception and memory" (*SE* 1:325; translation modified). [22]

At this relatively early stage of his career, Freud was committed to the positivism of the "neuropathology" in which he had been trained (*SE* 2:160). His system sought an explanation for the mechanism by which our neurons can distinguish between realities and representations. Both exist in the brain as what he termed *Vorstellungen* (depending upon context, the *Standard Edition* translates this term as "ideas," "representations," or "presentations")—a state of affairs that appeared to eclipse their seemingly obvious difference. If so, how can we tell a memory of the past from an experience in the present?

Freud might have been tempted to facilitate the solution of this conceptual difficulty by collapsing objective and subjective reality in some version of Idealism—equating *all* psychic representations, and thereby bleaching out the materiality of the real objects of our perception, which is where the epistemological problem arose to begin with. But at this stage of his work the paradigms of hard science won out over speculative philosophy. He therefore emphasized an uncompromising materialism in the face of his encounter with the mind-body problem. Not everything, he concluded, can be collapsed into the subjective paradigms of the psyche. Entities crucial for psychology exists external to the psyche itself. These entities are *things*.

The consequences of Freud's epistemological choice are considerable. "What we call things," he wrote, "are externalities that resist thought [*Was wir Dinge nennen, sind Reste, die sich der Beurteilung entziehen*]" (*SE* 1:334; translation mine). The concept of such re-

---

22. Since its publication in 1950, the 1895 "Project" has attracted considerable attention. Partial lists of the literature devoted to it can be found in Gay, *Freud*, 751, and David Farrell Krell, *Of Memory, Reminiscence, and Writing*, 323 nn. 1–2. Freud returned to this problem in *The Interpretation of Dreams* (1900), *SE* 5:565ff., and in "A Metapsychological Supplement to the Theory of Dreams" (1917), *SE* 14:231–32.

sistance is striking. It is particularly worth considering against the background of a period like our own characterized by the relative dominance of linguistic and semiotic paradigms, and—in the absence of extrasemiotic *hors-texte*—by the idea that the world somehow collapses into such paradigms. Freud's stance diverges. To put it in an image, for him we may juggle with our notions about the world, but the real objects that occupy it don't dance when we do so. Ideas, memory traces, word- and thing-presentations, the imagined objects of instinctual drives, fantasies, hallucinations—such psychic phenomena can imitate, stand for, refer to, represent, even deny the world external to the self and independent of its mental presentations. But methodologically Freud was not willing to confound them with it. He thus insisted upon confirming the irreducibility of the material objects the psyche's desires could evoke or react to, but not replace or control. This resistance of "things" will prove critical in unexpected regions of Freudian theory.

Freud's refusal to blot the problem out by collapsing reality into the neurological presentations available within the psyche only deepened the psychological puzzle. For in our experience—and particularly in the experience of the hysteric and neurasthenic patients Freud was working with throughout this period—the power of psychical presentations nonetheless seemed ceaselessly to displace the reality of the material world, just as some particularly energetic representations from the past appeared capable of interrupting and occupying the space of others seemingly more immediate, or more stimulated by immediate material reality. Neurotics *do* behave as if their memories were real. How could the difference between psychical and material reality be theorized in a way that granted each of these its requisite theoretical independence or autonomy, while still managing to leave conceptual room for the vertiginous interactions and substitutions by which their distinction seemed constantly subverted? And particularly, how could we understand—and how alter—the special power of certain intrapsychic traces to displace the products of immediate perception?[23]

23. Sigmund Freud, "Heredity and the Aetiology of the Neuroses" (1896): *"The memory will operate as though it were a contemporary event"* (SE 3:154; emphasis Freud's). This is the paper, originally written in French, in which the word "psychoanalysis" appeared for the first time. In a curious passage in *Totem and Taboo* (1913), Freud likened the power of

We could restate Freud's perplexity this way: *where does the reality of memory stop?* When does recollection end and experience begin? What lurks in these interrogations is the problem of memory's spectral *power*. We speak hopefully of the subject's memory, and psychoanalysis depends on it for the cure. But as Freud's therapeutic experiences began regularly and insistently to suggest, subjects' memories most often *subjected them.*

The pertinence of this reversal of agency had arisen dramatically in Freud and Breuer's early attempts to treat hysteria. Their diagnosis in the "Preliminary Communication" (1893) of the *Studies on Hysteria* concerning the etiology of this illness is justly celebrated: "*Hysterics suffer mainly from reminiscences*" (*SE* 2:7; emphasis theirs). Freud repeated this doctrine concerning the cause of hysteria regularly throughout his career, even as late as "Constructions in Analysis" (1937, *SE* 23:268), and most often with the same typographical emphasis it had first received in 1893. Moreover, he extended the earlier account of the etiology of hysteria to a much broader range of psychological illnesses. I want to examine particularly one of Freud's most evocative restatements of the notion, from his 1909 lectures at Clark University:

---

the absent to be present in memory to what he termed "spirit": "The 'spirit' of persons or things comes down to their capacity to be remembered and imagined after perception of them has ceased" (*SE* 13:94). Critical discussions of the indiscriminate fusing of the real and the imaginary tend to identify the phenomenon with the hallucinatory representations available in dreams. Freud surely emphasized the absence of "reality testing" in dream thoughts: "Real and imaginary events appear in dreams at first sight as of equal validity" (*Interpretation of Dreams* [1900], *SE* 4:288). However, it is important to underline that for Freud this blending of the veridical and the imaginary characterizes not just dreams or hallucinations, but *all* psychic representations: "*Psychical* reality is a particular form of existence not to be confused with *material* reality" (*SE* 5:620; emphasis Freud's). Freud needed to emphasize this precisely because in itself the psyche is unable *not* to confuse the presentations arising diversely in psychical and in material reality. Freud's most extended discussion of "reality testing" will be found in "A Metapsychological Supplement to the Theory of Dreams" (1917), *SE* 14:222–36. From the point of view of cultural theory, the absence of any secure distinction between "psychical" and "material" reality instantiates the impossibility of distinguishing, within the world bounded by their representations, between a semiotics of the "real" and a semiotics of the "imaginary"—an absence of distinction that constitutes semiotics to begin with. Umberto Eco makes this clear in *A Theory of Semiotics*: "Semiotics is concerned with everything that can be *taken* as a sign. A sign is everything which can be taken as significantly substituting for something else. This something else does not necessarily have to exist or to actually be somewhere at the moment in which a sign stands for it" (7).

I should like to formulate what we have learned so far as follows: *our hysterical patients suffer from reminiscences.* Their symptoms are residues and mnemic symbols of particular experiences. We may perhaps obtain a deeper understanding of this kind of symbolism if we compare them with other mnemic symbols in other fields. The monuments and memorials with which large cities are adorned are also mnemic symbols. If you take a walk through the streets of London, you will find, in front of one of the great railway termini, a richly carved Gothic column—Charing Cross. One of the old Plantagenet kings of the thirteenth century ordered the body of his beloved Queen Eleanor to be carried to Westminster; and at every stage at which the coffin rested he erected a Gothic cross. Charing Cross is the last of the monuments that commemorate the funeral cortège. At another point in the same town, you will find a towering, and more modern, column, which is simply known as "The Monument." It was designed as a memorial of the Great Fire, which broke out in that neighborhood in 1666 and destroyed a large part of the city. These monuments, then, resemble hysterical symptoms in being mnemic symbols; up to that point the comparison seems justifiable. But what should we think of a Londoner who paused to-day in deep melancholy before the memorial of Queen Eleanor's funeral instead of going about his business . . . ? Or again what should we think of a Londoner who shed tears before the Monument that commemorates the reduction of his beloved metropolis to ashes . . . ? Every single hysteric and neurotic behaves like these two unpractical Londoners. Not only do they remember painful experiences of the remote past, but they still cling to them emotionally; they cannot get free of the past and for its sake they neglect what is real and immediate. ("Five Lectures on Psycho-Analysis," *SE* 11:16–17; emphasis Freud's)

Freud materializes neurosis in a fantasy of London that conceives the city as an immense figuration of the memories of its inhabitants, as the concrete representation of their affective lives.[24] The parallel

24. On these urban memory constructions, see Marc Guillaume, "Mémoires de la ville," 139–40, and Michel de Certeau, "Les Revenants de la ville." This is of course not the only passage in which Freud takes the city as a metaphor for the psyche. Perhaps the most striking of such metaphors is the extended comparison of the psyche and Rome in *Civilization and Its Discontents* (1930): "Now let us, by a flight of imagination, suppose that Rome is not a human habitation but a psychical entity with a similarly long and copious past—an entity, that is to say, in which nothing that has once come into existence

with Baudelaire's vision of Paris in the Swan poem is irresistible. With Freud's urban fantasy before us, "Le Cygne" suddenly makes sense. How close to Freud's conception of the problem that memory poses for modernity is Baudelaire's evocation of memory's perverse persistence: "la forme d'une ville / Change plus vite, hélas! que le coeur d'un mortel" ["a city's form changes faster, alas, than a mortal's heart"]. Through a piquant example of what he would term *Nachträglichkeit*, the theory of neurosis that Freud articulated in his 1909 lecture retroactively elucidates and as we might say fills out the sense of Baudelaire's baffling transfer, exactly half a century earlier, of the mythical Andromache's mourning for Hector to a newly oblite-rated square in central Paris. But this in turn was a memory that replayed the affect of Andromache's loss fully two *dozen* centuries after both she and her husband had ceased in reality to exist.

Yet it is surely clear by now that both psychoanalyst and poet have transformed this last expression into a conceptual abyss. In the face of memories of this order and this power, what does "existence in reality" *mean*? In Freud's and Baudelaire's convergent and mutually legitimating visions, the seemingly secure materiality of the world of the here-and-now has been swamped and replaced by memory sym-bols whose longevity seems able to overmaster even the most per-durant constructions.

Nor does the power of these memories lie simply in their dura-bility. Against our will, unknown to our intention, they vertiginously upstage our present. Consider this passage from the "Dora" case: "When I set myself the task of bringing to light what human beings keep hidden within them, not by the compelling power of hypnosis, but by observing what they say and what they show, I thought the task was a harder one than it really is. He that has eyes to see and ears to hear may convince himself that no mortal can keep a secret. If his lips are silent, he chatters with his finger-tips; betrayal oozes out of him at every pore. And thus the task of making conscious the most

---

will have passed away and all the earlier phases of development continue to exist alongside the latest one" (SE 21:70). Such urban similes instantiate Freud's frequent practice of using archaeological analogies to illuminate his conception of the psyche; on such analo-gies, see "Constructions in Analysis" (1937), SE 23:259. The classical essay on Freud's archaeological themes is Suzanne Cassirer Bernfeld, "Freud and Archaeology." See also Donald Kuspit, "A Mighty Metaphor: The Analogy of Archaeology and Psychoanalysis."

hidden recesses of the mind is one which it is quite possible to ac-
complish." ("Fragment of an Analysis of a Case of Hysteria" [1905],
SE 7:77–78). The memory of what cannot be spoken imposes somatic
avowal; the mind writes it on the body. The idea here—that "truth
will out"—may be an old one, but Freud's originality was to specify,
however speculatively, the source and the mechanism of such involuntary rematerializations of the hidden. This source was the unconscious; the mechanism, the return of the repressed. In order to understand the extraordinary dilation of the memory function in
psychoanalysis, we need to examine how, for Freud, these psychic
agencies preserve and, at crucial moments, "betray" the past.

Conceptualizing this process and the consequences of this conservation and rematerialization of the past drove the mature theory of
psychoanalysis toward a reconception of the nature of psychological
"evidence" and of the paradigms for its interpretation. Freud had to
credit the seeming sovereignty of representations such as those
which involuntarily "ooze out" in neuroses or are acted out in hysteria—and to credit these behaviors not as unintelligible aberrations
but as products of the regular functioning of psychic processes:
*"What is suppressed continues to exist in normal people as well as
abnormal, and remains capable of psychical functioning"* (*The Interpretation of Dreams* [1900], *SE* 5:608; emphasis Freud's).

The adoption of such a stance was not obvious. To the naive ob-
server, the memories that irrupt we know not from where to over-
turn our present simply seem intolerable. Their rematerializations
violate the canons by which our world is supposedly ordered, and
call out for normalization. Indeed, the psychoanalytic patient has entered treatment precisely to eliminate them. But Freud learned to
forestall taking the perspective of the treatment's *end*—the suppression of pathological recurrence of these memory contents—in conceiving its material and its course. Epistemologically speaking, it was
as if achieving control over these archaic contents required abandoning our everyday realist bias and adopting *the point of view of memory itself*.

Producing Freud's mature theory of psychoanalysis thus involved
suppressing the tendency to devalue the data emerging in these moments when the past "inappropriately" recurs. We incline to such a
devaluation not only because of this inappropriateness, but for the

same reason that makes the influence of the past on the present an uncanny mystery to begin with: because the contents of the mind, like the impalpable contents of the past, seem nothing more than a fiction, an infinitely volatile will-o'-the-wisp. They maddeningly evade all attempts to exhibit their concrete referents or determine their specific locus. How can something that seems to exist nowhere be so energetic and so omnipresent?

In Freud's period the question of whether mental contents could be cognized as "real"—whether they had a verifiable material existence in the brain—was at the center of neurological and psychological research and was hotly debated. This debate occurred over the problem of what neurologists termed "localization." Attempts by nineteenth-century researchers to discover the neuronal site of mental processes and to map memory storage locations within brain tissue occupied many years and produced a voluminous literature.[25] The model according to which such contents were imagined to have been registered may have been primitive and mechanical, but it was credited by many in the period, and, with refinements, it has continued to attract adherents. On the other side of the argument, an alternative tradition has vigorously contested such views. It has sought to show that theories of localization badly misread the neurological evidence and lead to serious conceptual incoherences or limitations in psychology.

Beginning in the early "neuropathological" period of his work,

---

25. Such theories are homologous with and traceable to the traditional notion of memory as the product of a specific inscription in the brain. One of its earliest adherents was Plato. The Platonic analogy between memory and the impression of a seal in wax is one of the classical sources for theories of memory (see *Theaetetus* 191f., and Douglas J. Herrmann and Roger Chaffin, eds., *Memory in Historical Perspective: The Literature before Ebbinghouse*, 56–75). In the nineteenth century, researchers posited associations between specific mental functions and specific sites in brain anatomy based on work with patients who had suffered brain lesions. Broca, Wernicke, and, closer to our own period, Wilder Penfield are among the most influential of the theorists who have supported concepts of neuronal "localization" in some form. The question has been studied in detail by Robert M. Young, *Mind, Brain, and Adaptation in the Nineteenth Century: Cerebral Localization and Its Biological Context from Gall to Ferrier*. An excellent summary of the evolution of localization theories and the controversies concerning them can be found in Israel Rosenfield's *The Invention of Memory: A New View of the Brain*, part 1, though Rosenfield rehearses such theories in order to contest them. For the controversy concerning localization in more contemporary neurological research, see George Johnson, *In the Palaces of Memory: How We Build the World inside Our Heads*, 15–16.

Freud was a vehement antagonist of theories of neurological localization.[26] He remained an opponent of it to the end of his life. In his
essay "The Unconscious" (1915) he dismissed localization theory with
evident disdain: "Every attempt to . . . discover a localization of
mental processes, every endeavor to think of ideas as stored up in
nerve-cells . . . has miscarried completely" (*SE* 14:174). For Freud it
was critical to upset models that posited a simple correspondence
between brain anatomy and mental function. There could be no
equivalence linking "material" and "psychical" realities in such a way
that the latter could be conceived merely as the direct expression of
the former.

Those of us whose interests lie in the history and theory of culture
have a considerable stake in the debate over localization—as Freud's
vehement engagement with the issue as late as 1915, long after he
had abandoned his early "neuropathological" perspective, would suggest. Whatever the details of its mechanism, localization (particularly
of memory contents) envisages the laying down of a specific registration at some discrete site in the brain. Such a theory is prosaically
realist. It conceives "storage": a fixing of inscription, a recording of
data. The model—what Lowenthal calls "retrieving memories like
checked baggage"[27]—carries the implication that what went into the
brain can come out unchanged, that there exists an authoritative
master impression of any mental content against which any further
representation of the same content must be verified and measured.
Localization theory—like analogous theories of "original intent" or
"objective interpretation" in disciplines closer to the work of many of
us—is thus inherently and reductively literalist. The horizon of its
mechanism is an unproblematic, passive reproduction of the past:
memory as *proper* recording and *proper* recall. Localization envis-

26. His opposition is evident in the following injunction from *The Interpretation of
Dreams* (1900): "Ideas, thoughts and psychical structures in general must never be re-
garded as localized in organic elements of the nervous system . . ." (*SE* 5:611). David
Farrell Krell traces the roots of Freud's rejection of localization theory to his 1891 work on
aphasia and his 1893 article on paralysis; see *Of Memory, Reminiscence, and Writing*, 105.
Though Freud appears to be endorsing localization theory in a passage in *Beyond the
Pleasure Principle* (1920), *SE* 18:24, close examination of the passage demonstrates that his
adherence is only rhetorical, in order to make his own topographic theory of the psyche
(which he distantly analogizes to localization) comprehensible to the reader.

27. David Lowenthal, *The Past Is a Foreign Country*, 252.

ages a world of stable mental facts, the suppression of entropy, and the abolition of change. If localization theory were right, there would be no memory crisis.

It is easy to see why Freud resisted localization so strenuously. Against its literalism, psychoanalytic interpretation (as I will argue in the next chapter) supposes an unconstrainable *variability* and *mutability* of psychic representations. Any doctrine that tends to normalize such representations, or subject them to the superintendence of a criterion of simple fidelity to preexisting contents, would inevitably impoverish such a theory to the point of abolishing its field altogether.

For Freud the stakes in the tension between what we might term *literalist* and *interpretive* representations of the past thus were critical. And they arose at a crucial moment of inflection in the development of his paradigm—one that evokes a controversy still burning within Freudianism: the problem of "seduction theory." It is well known that early in his career, in one of his most startling hypotheses, Freud speculated that what he then termed "neurasthenia" (neurosis) resulted from an experience of childhood sexual molestation. In the course of therapy his patients had regularly produced recollections of such experiences. But in 1897 he began to be convinced that these accounts were likely to have arisen instead from what he termed "phantasies"—imaginary constructions, into whose formation the proportions of projection, invention, recollection, misrecollection, and retroflexive reconstruction were simply undecidable because *there was no master memory.* In the revision of the theory entailed by Freud's renunciation of belief in his patients' remembrance of early molestation, the entire field of the diagnostic data of psychoanalysis was sweepingly reinterpreted; the very notion of "data" was radically transformed. The consequences of such a move were profound.[28]

28. For an account of Freud's reasons for abandoning the seduction theory, see William McGrath, *Freud's Discovery of Psychoanalysis: The Politics of Hysteria,* chaps. 4–6. Given the vehemence of recent arguments around this issue, it is important to recall that Freud certainly never asserted that *all* accounts of molestation were delusive. Freud's renunciation of "seduction theory" is renarrated (and defended) by Peter Gay, *Freud,* 90–96 and 751. On the other side of the issue is Jeffrey Moussaieff Masson. In 1984, Masson published *The Assault on Truth: Freud's Suppression of the Seduction Theory,* in which he claimed that Freud's renunciation was determined by his feelings of isolation from the

In 1924, Freud republished "The Aetiology of Hysteria," which he had originally delivered in 1896 as a lecture to the Vienna Psychiatric and Neurological Society. The paper had been composed at a time when he still credited his patients' accounts of childhood molestation, and it summarized his "seduction theory" (his skepticism about the theory began to take hold the following year). On the article's republication in 1924, he added the following note to his wrenching description in the 1896 account of the pain that accompanied his psychoanalytic patient's recollection of infantile sexual abuse: "All this [the emotion patients experienced in rehearsing these memories] is true, but it must be remembered that at the time I wrote it I had not yet freed myself from my *overvaluation* of reality and my *low valuation* of phantasy" (*SE* 3:204 n. 1; emphasis Freud's).

In this remarkable addendum, Freud is reflecting on the implications of an epochal decision: to unlink the mnemonic *representations* elicited in treatment from any literal *reproduction* of specific past experiences. In essence, he is rehearsing the move that created the interpretive field in which mature psychoanalysis functions. What Freud means in this note by the "reality" he had previously "overvalued" is clearly what earlier we saw him conceiving as the objective or literalist realm of the "material" world; "phantasy," on the other hand, evokes the mobile representations of the "psychic" realm as the mature theory of psychoanalysis has conceived it. Such reconcep-

---

Vienna medical establishment—an isolation that Freud attributed to the shock his views on the etiology of neurasthenia produced in his colleagues—and was connected with the complex course of his affective relationship with Fliess. Convergent with Masson's conclusions, data and theory concerning the frequency and consequences of molestation of (particularly female) children developed by numerous researchers, many of whom associate their work with feminism, have tended to lead those who credit the responsibility of childhood molestation for the production of later pathologies to recode Freud's rejection of seduction theory (and its more contemporary analogues) as a more or less covert antifeminism. Some theorists on each side of the debate apparently believe it is possible to establish the factual truth or falsehood of Freud's own account of his abandonment of the theory. If so, from whatever side of the debate they may come, they concede (perhaps unwittingly) the fundamental methodological claim of seduction theory's supporters: that a unique authoritative and valid account of individual belief and behavior is attainable. The theoretical significance of Freud's abandonment of seduction theory subverts such a view, a point to which I will return. Among recent examinations of Freud's "seduction theory," see Katherine Cummings, *Telling Tales: The Hysteric's Seduction in Fiction and Theory*, and Gerald N. Izenberg, "Seduced and Abandoned: The Rise and Fall of Freud's Seduction Theory."

tion of the status of the issues and the evidence to which the analyst must attend—now no longer concerned with establishing the factual accuracy of the memories produced by his patients, but rather seeking the interpretation of the representations they offered, whatever the mechanism by which the psyche had generated them—is crucial to the reconception of psychoanalysis that underlies Freud's resituation of the memory problem.[29]

❧❧❧

This second system [the unconscious] . . . needs . . . to have the whole of the material of memory freely at its command.

    —Sigmund Freud, *Interpretation of Dreams* (1900),
     SE 5:599

Freud's opposition to models of neurological "localization" and his abandonment of "seduction theory" in favor of the more supple interpretive paradigms of mature psychoanalysis helped turn his conceptualization of psychic material from what I have been calling a model of "reproduction" (entailing the veridical replication and verbatim

29. In the case of Freud's assessment of what he came to call the "primal scene," the evolution of his thinking was more hesitant, and never reached the diagnosis of "phantasy" that intervened in his revision of "seduction theory." He debated the experiential status of childhood memories of witnessing parental intercourse over a long period (particularly with Jung and Adler) without ever resolving the issue completely. A succinct account of these hesitations can be found in Laplanche and Pontalis, *Language of Psycho-Analysis*, s.v. "primal scene." Ned Lukacher considers the problem in his wide-ranging discussion in *Primal Scenes: Literature, Philosophy, Psychoanalysis*, particularly in his introduction and in chap. 4. The term "primal scene" itself first appeared in print in 1918 in Freud's account of the "Wolf Man" case (Freud had used it in a letter to Fliess of 2 May 1897); see "From the History of an Infantile Neurosis," *SE* 17:38ff. Freud discussed the difficulty of determining the veracity of memories of such experiences at two principal points in the "Wolf Man" case, which he had been constrained to revise as his thinking on the question evolved; see *SE* 17:48ff. and 103 n. 1. Neil Hertz, in his *End of the Line: Essays on Psychoanalysis and the Sublime*, 119–20, rightly calls attention to Freud's "testy" tone in this latter note, in which Freud's assertion of his own originality in approaching the interpretation of such memories rings decidedly aggressive. Aggressive, perhaps, but nonetheless accurate in identifying the analytical stakes in the issue. Here is Freud in the note in question: "I admit that this [interpreting these childhood memories in the face of the problem of determining their veracity] is the most delicate question in the whole domain of psycho-analysis. I did not require the contributions of Adler or Jung to induce me to consider the matter with a critical eye, and to bear in mind the possibility that what

conservation of past contents) to one of "representation" (conceiving
rather the semiotic replacement of one content by another that is
understood to stand for it). When Freud opposed the literalism of
"localization" theory; when he came to credit the *meaningfulness* of
his patients' recollections of childhood seduction or of witnessing parental intercourse without thinking he must necessarily trust the
strict *veracity* of the memories thus evoked, he was projecting a conception of the contents of the psyche that approached these as interpretations rather than as facts. This is a theme in many accounts of
Freud. He is often taken as a principal mediator of a broad cultural
passage from the literalist positivism of the nineteenth-century hard
sciences and modes of knowledge modeled upon them, to the hermeneutic emancipation of our twentieth-century human sciences.

In my account of him to this point, Freud has thus increasingly
assumed the familiar aura of the contemporary hero of semiosis—
celebrant of the signifier's limitless mutability, and of our interpretive resourcefulness in the face of it. I've depicted a Freud who increasingly saw the contents of the psyche in terms of signs, and the
processes of the mind in terms of the substitutions and transformations that are the vocation of semiotic models of meaning. As Derrida
put it in a formula that can stand for many similar characterizations:
"The substitution of signifiers seems to be the essential activity of
psychoanalytic interpretation."[30]

But at this point a paradox intervenes. There are difficulties with
this construction of psychoanalysis, and they come into focus in the
problem of memory. For memory implicates the *directionality of
time*. Whatever else we may say about it, memory is somehow about
the *past*. The notion of the past thus invokes a temporal sectioning of
reality that any theory of reality needs to incorporate. Without time,
the memory problem simply becomes vacuous. Understanding memory requires being able to model time.

---

analysis puts forward as being forgotten experiences of childhood (and of an improbably
early childhood) may on the contrary be based upon phantasies created on occasions occurring late in life. . . . I was the first—a point to which none of my opponents have referred—to recognize both the part played by phantasies in symptom-formation and also
the 'retrospective phantasying' of late impressions into childhood and their sexualization
after the event." I will return to this "delicate question" in the course of considering the
issue of phantasy's relationship to memory in my final chapter.

30. Jacques Derrida, "Freud and the Scene of Writing," 210.

Semiotic paradigms based upon the Saussurian dyad of "signifier" and "signified" cannot manage this. For them time is simply not a dimension. A dyadic semiotics organized around Saussure's concepts has no difficulty in modeling change (A → B), but is incapable of representing its directionality. All transformations in such a semiotics are theoretically reversible (B → A); the system is perfectly indifferent to the direction of their movement. But because such a theory cannot represent the irreversibility of time, neither can it model timelessness. For a dyadic semiotics is blind to temporality; time is not a category in such systems. But as we will see, the concept of timelessness is crucial for understanding the Freudian unconscious. A Saussurian semiotics must thus inevitably experience trouble with psychoanalysis. This will generally be the case of theorists in the tradition of what in a familiar shorthand designation has come to be called "French Freud."[31]

Of all our psychic faculties, memory is the one that makes these limitations critical. For memory is irreducibly oriented: we have no memory of the future. Only our past is invoked in remembrance, and if we cannot represent the directionality of its determinations, there is no possibility of understanding how it has come to dominate our present. Under such conditions, the process of our development becomes theoretically opaque. Making sense of memory requires that directionality be central within any representation of its activity. The pertinence of such considerations becomes clear if we turn again to Freud's understanding of memory.

I argued earlier that when we come to the problems of psychology from the side of memory, it is memory's *persistence*, the seeming inertia of its traces, that calls out for explanation. Despite some ambiguities in the theory that I will examine shortly, the locus of memory in Freud's topography of the psyche reflects and attempts to understand this fixity. Freud conceived the unconscious (system *Ucs.*) as the timeless and immutable portion of the psyche. For psycho-

31. The term derives from the title of the influential issue of *Yale French Studies* (no. 48 [1972]), which introduced the work of a number of French psychoanalysts and theorists inspired by Saussurian structuralism—centrally, Jacques Lacan—to a wide public in the English-speaking world. Saussure was clearer about the limitations, or about the specifically limited applicability, of his model than some of those more recently inspired by it have proven. See Ferdinand de Saussure, *Course in General Linguistics*, 76, and Terdiman, *Discourse/Counter-Discourse*, 27–31.

analysis, I want to argue, this unconscious is memory's fundamental repository. My argument has several stages. The first is to recall that, as Freud repeatedly and emphatically insisted, *consciousness* has no capacity for the retention of anything. "Our memories—not excepting those which are the most deeply stamped on our minds—are in themselves unconscious" (*Interpretation of Dreams* [1900], SE 5:539; see also SE 5:540 n. 1). "Becoming conscious and leaving behind a memory-trace are processes incompatible with each other" (*Beyond the Pleasure Principle* [1920], SE 18:25).

Technically, Freud is asserting only that the repository of memory cannot be in consciousness—a position that goes back at least as far as the 1895 "Project for a Scientific Psychology" (part 1, section 3), and ultimately derives from Breuer. The reason for this limitation is initially neurological. As Freud explains in *Beyond the Pleasure Principle* (1920): "We find it hard to believe . . . that permanent traces of excitation . . . are . . . left in the system *Pcpt*.[perception]-*Cs*. If they remained conscious, they would very soon set limits to the system's aptitude for receiving fresh excitations" (SE 18:25).[32] Thus memories (or their traces) are "unconscious" in the sense that according to Freud's topography they must be registered by a part of the psyche other than system *Cs*. But this descriptive location still leaves a considerable ambiguity. For it does not select between the "preconscious" (system *Pcs*.) and the "unconscious" proper (system *Ucs*.) as the place of memory's inscription.

In an influential essay on the unconscious from within the tradition of Saussurian semiotics, Jean Laplanche and Serge Leclaire examined Freud's assertion that memories are unconscious. They understood him to mean only that the locus of memories is not in consciousness.[33] This position, although technically accurate, undermines the force of Freud's insistence on the unconscious locus of memory. It does not follow Freud far enough. Laplanche and Leclaire neglect the portion of memory that locates itself squarely in system *Ucs*.[34] But for psychoanalysis these memories in the uncon-

32. This is the problem Derrida examines in "Freud and the Scene of Writing"; see particularly 200–205.
33. Jean Laplanche and Serge Leclaire, "The Unconscious: A Psychoanalytic Study," 127 and n. 8.
34. Of course *some* memories must be inscribed in system *Ucs*. If *all* memory were in

scious (in the strong sense) have a singular privilege. For the unconscious is the source of the pathologies for which psychoanalysis seeks to be the therapy.

For this reason I want to interpret Freud's assertion about the locus of memory more radically than do Laplanche and Leclaire. Topographically, memory resides in the unconscious (whether *Pcs.* or *Ucs.*). But the memories to which psychoanalysis centrally attends, the memories that define its theoretical originality, are those which have been subjected to repression. These are inscribed in system *Ucs.* (though their derivatives, the "screen memories" and so on, are available to consciousness as part of the tactics by which repression protects itself). So *functionally*, what psychoanalysis means by memory—the traces of the past that will be determinant for the pathologies psychoanalytic therapy seeks to alleviate—is unconscious memory *strictly defined*, the memory of the mysterious, timeless system *Ucs.* It seems to me critical to foreground the consequences of this functional selectivity in any discussion of the problem of memory in Freud.

The repressed contents whose traces occupy system *Ucs.* then appear as the active pathologies that preoccupy psychoanalysis. The notion of this activity of the unconscious is omnipresent in Freud. One of its clearest statements is in the "Note on the Unconscious in Psycho-Analysis" (1912). There Freud recounts the etiology of symptoms in a hysteric patient, arising as an involuntary and unwitting response to the presence of unconscious contents, and then continues: "The same preponderance of active unconscious ideas is revealed by analysis as the essential fact in the psychology of all other forms of neurosis" (*SE* 12:262). This means that the memories crucial for our understanding of what is distinctive in Freud's *Ars memorativa* are those which become available *only* when they traverse the topographical boundary surrounding system *Ucs.* where their traces are located. For Freud, these memories lodge in the realm of the timeless. Their persistence in consciousness and in behavior is theorized as a result of their permanence in the psyche.

---

the preconscious, if all the determinations of our past were potentially available to consciousness upon demand, we could simply abandon the hypothesis of the unconscious altogether, and with it the entire theory of psychoanalysis.

Unconscious memory thus reproduces the uncanny, counterintuitive fantasy of the literal conservation of the past and its absolute replication in the present, hence of the effective annihilation of time, that in a seemingly absurd *reductio* I conjured up earlier in this chapter. This unexpected reappearance of an apparently unthinkable paradox at the heart of Freudian theory complicates our understanding of psychoanalysis and of the logic of Freud's paradigm considerably.

As I noted, the argument is regularly made that Freud's conception of psychic contents progressively turns from a model based on the literalism of "data" to one deploying the more supple, labile practices of "interpretation." At the heart of this inflection lies a rethinking of how the past is conserved and processed, of how memory arises, affects us, and can be comprehended. For this past is the evidence to which psychoanalysis must attend, and the diverse forms of its recollection are all the analyst has to go on. But with my recentralization of the unchanging memory registrations of system *Ucs.*, a tension within the model begins to be perceptible. In effect, the immutable inscriptions of the unconscious unsettle the paradigm of interpretive mobility usually thought of as defining psychoanalysis.

What positivism thought of as a "fact" depended on the absolute identity of its content over time, thus on what we might imagine as a kind of automatic internal memory function assuring unchanging "reproduction." In the positivist's view, no matter when or how we look at it, the "fact" remains the same. It never forgets its facticity. This notion supposes the secure stability of meaning that permits meaning to seem unproblematic—which is just how positivism saw it. But when this intrinsic capacity to sustain self-identity, this signifying homeostasis, is interrupted or called into question, as most accounts argue results from Freud's reconception of psychic contents, then the positivist guarantee of the identity—the "facticity"—of such contents evaporates. What intervenes, in the face of their constant potentiality for transformation, is the necessity of bringing to bear the continual reassessment of the "data" continuously produced from the past that we call "interpretation."

Many have taken this to justify rethinking Freud in terms of the semiotic model I have referred to. But the problem of memory complicates this inflection in a puzzling way. The bearing of this destabilization is to make the mobile transfers that characterize semiotic systems fit much less comfortably within the logic of Freudianism than might have first appeared to be the case. For in the face of a semiotic paradigm cognizing the psychic world, Freud's timeless and unchanging unconscious poses a critical conceptual difficulty. Can *this* unconscious cohere with the movement toward the mobile interpretations characteristic of semiotic systems? The question arises because Freud's concept of the unconscious, although it specifically avoids the *anatomical* literalism of "localization theory," in an important respect still functions precisely in the manner the "localization" theorists conceived. The unconscious, as Freud tells us, lays down authoritative and unchanging master registrations of our past. It records and preserves such contents absolutely identical to themselves—moreover it preserves them with such tenacious fidelity, with such unerring stability, that in its registrations the force of our history lives on undiminished, its substance unaltered. This leads to a surprising result. At the heart of a paradigm of luxuriant interpretation, the unconscious turns out to be a realm of *facts*.[35]

Freud's unconscious thus unexpectedly revives something that functions very much like the positivist model of the past—a paradigm of data unerringly and permanently recorded—that he had been at such comprehensible pains to contest when it dominated neuropathology.[36] Moreover, this notion of the timelessness of the

35. At these extremes of the ineffable, we can hardly expect precise definition. With this caution, I will mention that a relation exists between the frozen representations of the past preserved in the Freudian unconscious and the depreciated Platonic field of "writing" (and allied concept of the "monument" [*hupomnesis*]), which Derrida examines in "Plato's Pharmacy"; see *Dissemination*, particularly 132–34.

36. This notion of permanence was assuredly not credited by Freud alone. An assumption that *early* memories, at least, produced permanent, unchanging impressions in the brain had been widespread in medicine and neuropathology (even among researchers suspicious of physicalist explanations) since the early nineteenth century. See Michael S. Roth, "Dying of the Past: Medical Studies of Nostalgia in Nineteenth-Century France," 9–10 and n. 10. More generally, as Roth points out elsewhere, "one of the presuppositions shared by most late-nineteenth-century writers on memory was that, despite the fact that we have limited recall of the past, nothing is permanently lost to our memories" (Michael S. Roth, "Remembering Forgetting: *Maladies de la mémoire* in Nineteenth-Century France," 65). For example, the important French psychologist Théodule Ribot took this position on the permanency of memory in his influential *Maladies de la mémoire* (1881), 148. The notion was also current in certain strains of philosophy. In the curious section of *Sodome et Gomorrhe* in which Proust's narrator reflects on sleep, drugs, and memory, Proust (or at least the "Norwegian philosopher" who appears seemingly for this purpose at

unconscious seems itself to have been absolutely stable over time.
Here are some of Freud's statements of it from the different periods
of his work.[37]

From *The Interpretation of Dreams* (1900):

> It is a prominent feature of unconscious processes that they are
> indestructible. In the unconscious nothing can be brought to an
> end, nothing is past or forgotten. . . . A humiliation that was expe-
> rienced thirty years ago acts exactly like a fresh one throughout the
> thirty years. (*SE* 5:577–78)

From *The Psychopathology of Everyday Life* (note added in 1907):

> It is generally thought that it is time which makes memory uncer-
> tain and indistinct. It is highly probable that there is no question at
> all of there being any direct function of time in forgetting. . . . In
> the case of *repressed* memory traces it can be demonstrated that
> they undergo no alteration even in the course of the longest period
> of time. The unconscious is quite timeless. The most important as
> well as the strangest characteristic of psychical fixation is that all
> impressions are preserved, not only in the same form in which
> they were first received, but also in all the forms which they have
> adopted in their further developments. This is a state of affairs
> which cannot be illustrated by comparison with another sphere.

Mme Verdurin's soirée) attributes belief in mnemonic permanency to Bergson; see *RTP*
3:374 and 321 n. 6. In response to this statement of Bergsonian doctrine—perhaps to
distance himself from increasingly frequent assimilations of his own theories of memory to
Bergson's—Proust goes on in the same passage to express skepticism about a permanent
memory that is preserved while remaining at the same time *unknown* to its "holder": "But
what is a memory which one doesn't recall?" Proust's question would, of course, immediately cast doubt on the concept of the unconscious in Freud. But (as I suggested in
Chapters 5 and 6) the later course of Proust's own novel demonstrates that memories
unknown or hidden for long periods of our lives are crucial to Proust's understanding no
less than to Freud's. In *Albertine disparue* Proust approvingly compares the preservation
of our past to the establishment of an endless archive: "Each past day has remained deposited within us, as in an immense library where, even of the oldest books, there is a copy
which doubtless no one will ever ask to see" (*RTP* 4:125).

37. With Freud's conceptual restructuration of the psyche in his second "topographic"
theory after 1920, the system *Ucs.* disappeared and the characteristic of timelessness was
inherited by the "id." Cf. *New Introductory Lectures on Psycho-Analysis* (1933), *SE* 22:74,
in which Freud speaks of the id's exemption from time and change in terms precisely
paralleling his earlier descriptions of system *Ucs.* I bracket this terminological change here
since it is irrelevant for the purposes of my argument concerning memory.

Theoretically every earlier state of the mnemic content could thus be restored to memory again. (*SE* 6:274 n. 2)[38]

From "Notes upon a Case of Obsessional Neurosis" [The "Rat Man"] (1909):

I then made some short observations upon . . . the fact that everything conscious was subject to a process of wearing away, while what was unconscious was relatively unchangeable; and I illustrated my remarks by pointing to the antiques standing about in my room. They were, in fact, I said, only objects found in a tomb, and their burial had been their preservation. (*SE* 10:176–77)

From "The Unconscious" (1915):

The processes of the system *Ucs.* are *timeless*; i.e. they are not ordered temporally, are not altered by the passage of time; they have no reference to time at all. (*SE* 14:187)

From *Civilization and Its Discontents* (1930):

Since we overcame the error of supposing that the forgetting we are familiar with signified a destruction of the memory-trace—that is, its annihilation—we have been inclined to take the opposite view, that in mental life nothing which has once been formed can perish [*im Seelenleben nichts, was einmal gebildet wurde, untergehen kann*]—that everything is somehow preserved and that in suitable circumstances (when, for instance, regression goes back far enough) it can once more be brought to light. (*SE* 21:69)[39]

38. Freud seems never to have completely resolved the technical question of whether the registrations preserved in the unconscious also include records of the subsequent stages of the transformations of unconscious material as it passes into other systems of the psyche. In "The Unconscious" (1915) he writes: "Are we to suppose that this transposition [from *Ucs.* to *Cs.*] involves a fresh record—as it were, a second registration—of the idea in question . . . ?" (*SE* 14:174). He returns to this question repeatedly in the paper, without ever settling it (it is in particular not resolved in his assertion [*SE* 14:201] that conscious presentation differs from unconscious in its inclusion of a word-presentation). See also *SE* 14:175, 180, 192. Laplanche and Leclaire examine these hesitations in "The Unconscious: A Psychoanalytic Study," parts 2 and 4.

39. Several pages later Freud considers the possibility that he may be exaggerating this permanence. "Perhaps," he writes, "we ought to content ourselves with asserting that what

Finally, from "Constructions in Analysis" (1937):

> All of the essentials are preserved [in the psyche]; even things that
> seem completely forgotten are present somehow and somewhere,
> and have merely been buried and made inaccessible to the sub-
> ject. Indeed, it may, as we know, be doubted whether any psychi-
> cal structures can really be the victim of total destruction. (*SE*
> 23:260)

This projection of psychic *fixity* must discomfit semiotic theories of
the mind. We need to consider its consequences more closely.

❧❀❧

> The repressed is foreign territory to the ego—internal for-
> eign territory.
> —Sigmund Freud, *New Introductory Lectures* (1933),
>   *SE* 22:57

Because of the immutability of its contents the unconscious as
Freud projected it is *not* easily or entirely conceivable as a semiotic
system. The unconscious isn't structured precisely like a language. In
certain key aspects, it rather functions as something like the opposite
of one. For in the timeless unconscious as Freud hypothesizes it, *no*
content stands for any other. Instead, each stands uniquely and im-
mutably for itself.[40] This produces a puzzling result. In the unconscious, because there can be no change, *in a sense there can be no
signs*.

This claim might seem absurd. Surely I cannot be proposing that
the content of our unconscious, if it is not semiotic, is instead "referential"—that our minds are tenanted by the material world we have
experienced. Mallarmé playfully warned us in "Crise de vers" that

---

is past in mental life *may* be preserved and is not *necessarily* destroyed"; however upon
reflection he concludes as follows: "It is possible, but we know nothing about it. We can
only hold fast to the fact that it is rather the rule than the exception for the past to be
preserved in mental life" (*SE* 21:71–72).

    40. Laplanche and Leclaire seek to understand this puzzling situation from within the
paradigm of a dyadic semiotics in "The Unconscious: A Psychoanalytic Study," 162–63.
Their construction is not persuasive, since it is limited by the paradigmatic characteristics
of Saussurianism that I discussed earlier.

this was impossible. We cannot expect the "real" world to be present in our representations, he pointed out, because it could never fit.[41] On the other hand, signs seem an appropriate size for Freud's system *Ucs*. How then can I suggest that anything other than semiotic representations could be lodged there?

This puzzlement ignores an insight from within semiotics itself. For although the notion of the "sign" seems wonderfully impalpable and capable of heady volatility, one of its parts remains obtusely rooted in the world of matter. "Signifiers" require a real substrate, they are constituted by a concrete "sign-vehicle" (Eco's term, *Theory of Semiotics*, 14, summarizing Saussure; cf. *Course in General Linguistics*, 66). Signifieds may belong to the ideal realm, but signifiers are freighted with their materiality. If there is a sense to seeing signs in the unconscious at all, this materiality must be emphasized. At the least, the presence of such materiality in the semiotic signifier provides a basis, a kind of theoretical analogue, for the stability, the intractable resistance to change Freud conceptualized as essential to the unconscious. We need to recall the massive, inert, and unchanging presence of the London monuments Freud likened in 1909 to these strange unconscious registrations of the past in order to begin to grasp their peculiarity.

It may be that our familiar Saussurian concept of the dyadic sign (Saussure, *Course in General Linguistics*, 67) conceives the unification of its parts too unreflectively. Freud's unconscious may invite us to understand the "conceptual" separation of signifier and signified as real and corporeal. Perhaps we need to view the unconscious as populated exclusively with signifiers understood in a sense that emphasizes the *fixation*, the *materiality* that attaches to their notion. It is difficult to find a language for discussing such a situation because nothing in conscious experience corresponds to its oddity. Thinking of signifiers fixedly subsisting without signifieds is like trying to imagine a naked quark. Perhaps the best that can be done is to offer some glancing and approximate analogies to suggest how this situation might be conceived.

Two approaches may be helpful for understanding the sense in which the contents of the unconscious seem to resist or exceed the

41. Stéphane Mallarmé, *Oeuvres complètes*, 366.

familiar categories of the semiotic. The first arises from Freud's supposition that the unconscious registers the totality of our perception and our experience, and maintains these in an immutable one-to-one ordering with the original experiences they record.[42] In seeking a term of comparison for this mnemonic mechanism, we might consider another of the classical accounts of memory, Augustine's evocation of the "fields and spacious palaces" of memory in which the whole treasure of our perception and experience has been laid up.[43] In this memory palace, Augustine continues, "things come up readily, in unbroken order, as they are called for." Augustine's image colorfully recapitulates the reproductive vocation of the antique *artes memorativa*, whose object was to ensure the faithful and unchanging rehearsal of contents previously recorded. But in these compendia of the past convergent—we might almost say coterminous—with the past's own reality, something in the concept of the sign is transgressed. For signs never equate absolutely to their referents, never simply totalize them. Rather, signs live in their *difference* from what they represent. However divergent they may be on other grounds, the Augustinian memory palace and the Freudian unconscious together project one-to-one reproduction of the referential in the mechanism that conserves it. They evoke something approaching the total adequation of signifier to signified, their identity. But such an identity would suppress semioticity to begin with. If we had the referents themselves, we wouldn't need their stand-ins.

This leads to a second perspective from which the tension between the Freudian unconscious and the categories of semiosis may be suggested. In my discussion of Baudelaire's Swan poem, I argued that the cause for the astonishment and the unease underlying this text arose in Baudelaire's discovery of (or confrontation with) what one might term the disorienting "compliance of the linguistic material": the ease with which language, without the slightest rupture, accom-

---

42. Recall the passage from "The Psychotherapy of Hysteria" (1895) that I cited earlier: "The first and most powerful impression made upon one during . . . analysis is certainly that the pathogenic psychical material which has ostensibly been forgotten . . . , nevertheless in some fashion lies ready to hand and in correct and proper order" (*SE* 2:287).

43. Augustine, *Confessions*, 10.8; see Frances A. Yates, *The Art of Memory*, 46–49, and Jacques Le Goff, *Histoire et mémoire*, 134 and 169.

modates the transformation of the meaning-system in which it is embedded. Language will stand indifferently for whatever you like. This
unfixity defines the sign: it can be anything and substitute for anything. But the description I offered a few lines earlier for this wanton
lability of the semiotic—"compliance of the linguistic material"—is
in fact Freud's own characterization for the contents of consciousness
(*Psychopathology of Everyday Life* [1901], *SE* 6:222). And it invites
confrontation with his directly contrasting evocation of the thought-
resistant materiality of *things* (*SE* 1:334) that I examined earlier.
Language is compliant; things are resistant. The contents of the
Freudian unconscious resist change as if they were in this sense
"things."[44]

Whatever occupies the unconscious as Freud conceived it is not
entirely conciliable with the paradigms of semiosis. Perhaps, re-
sponding to its contradictions with the resources of an oxymoron, we
could term unconscious contents "nonsemiotic representations." But
the important point for understanding the memory problem as psychoanalysis sought to frame it in what is surely the most sophisticated
and far-reaching of the models available to us for conceiving how the
past invests our present is this: the contents of the unconscious cannot have the character of a sign since they do not have its mobility. It
is not that the traces which occupy the unimaginable space of
Freud's system *Ucs.* can replace nothing else. It is rather that *nothing can replace them.* They cannot be signified; they are a memory
that never forgets and thus is never altered. The past they carry is
not past at all. And this is what makes the issue of the *cure* so arduous for psychoanalysis.

44. In order that my point not be mistaken here, I should distinguish my claim from the
more familiar idea that *words* are absent from the unconscious. Cf. "The Unconscious"
(1915): "The conscious presentation [*Vorstellung*] comprises the presentation of the thing
plus the presentation of the word belonging to it, while the unconscious presentation is the
presentation of the thing alone" (*SE* 14:20). If the contents of the unconscious are conceived in terms of the inert and unchanging materiality I am seeking to image here, other
attributes regularly insisted upon by Freud may become less puzzling. Their impervious-
ness to doubt, contradiction, or negation, for example, is hard to explain if their nature is
semiotic, but requires no explanation if their nature is material. *Things* can't experience
uncertainty or negate each other. The fixity of their substance prohibits their entering into
"logical" or "conceptual" relations at all.

✿✿✿

It is . . . legitimate to assume that the neuroses must
. . . bear witness to the history of the mental development
of mankind.
                    —Sigmund Freud, "Overview of the Transference
                    Neuroses" (1915), 11

At this point in my consideration of the uncanny permanence of the
unconscious, the paradigmatic *necessity*, or at least the compelling
internal logic, of Freud's psychic Lamarckianism—his belief that the
individual's memory preserves an inherited recollection of the entire
species—comes into theoretical focus. The notion that a phylogenetic memory parallels the ontogenetic one conserved in our psyche
has been a scandal for many who otherwise admire Freud. Peter Gay
calls it "one of Freud's most eccentric and least defensible intellectual commitments" (*Freud*, 290n).

The issue has been widely and contentiously discussed. It has recently rebounded into prominence with Ilse Grubrich-Simitis's unexpected rediscovery, in 1983, of Freud's unpublished twelfth metapsychological essay, written in 1915. Freud had planned a book on
the theory of psychoanalysis (*Preliminaries to a Metapsychology*),
which was to have included twelve papers. The essay in question was
to have been the last. But he abandoned the project and eventually
published only five of the papers. It is known that the other seven
were more or less completed from late 1914 to summer 1915. Freud
presumably destroyed them; however in July 1915 he had sent a
draft of the twelfth essay to Sándor Ferenczi, among whose papers
Grubrich-Simitis found it. To date it is the only one of the seven
unpublished papers known to have survived in any form.[45]

Freud titled the draft of his twelfth paper "Overview of the Transference Neuroses," although this title is misleading.[46] The second section of the paper, which Freud referred to as his "phylogenetic fantasy," provides a highly speculative account of relations between the

45. Freud, "Overview of the Transference Neuroses" (1915). The five published essays
are "A Metapsychological Supplement to the Theory of Dreams," "Mourning and Melancholia," "Instincts and their Vicissitudes," "Repression," and "The Unconscious."
46. See the foreword, by Axel Hoffer and Peter T. Hoffer, to Sigmund Freud, *A Phylogenetic Fantasy: Overview of the Transference Neuroses*, ix–xi.

development of the individual (ontogeny), the development of the species (phylogeny), and the pattern of onset of the two categories of neuroses—the narcissistic and the transference neuroses. In Freud's speculation, neuroses arise not only from the memories of our own past *but of the past of our entire culture.* "This series [of transference neuroses] seems to repeat phylogenetically an historical origin. What are now neuroses were once phases of the human condition" (letter to Ferenczi, 12 July 1915, in *A Phylogenetic Fantasy*, 79; see also 18, n. 40). "One can justifiably claim that the inherited dispositions are residues of the acquisitions of our ancestors" (*A Phylogenetic Fantasy*, 10). The paper thus carried further Freud's celebrated (and, for some, notorious) speculations in *Totem and Taboo* (1912–13) concerning the inheritance and unconscious activity in the individual psyche of memories of a prehistoric "primal crime," the murder of their father by a group of rebellious sons, thus putting an end to the patriarchal horde. Freud's theorization along this Lamarckian line then continued in *Moses and Monotheism* (1934–38).[47]

My own argument has no stake in the veracity of Freud's construction of our psychocultural past. What interests me here is that he made such a claim to begin with, that he insisted on forcing even beyond his thesis of its timeless stability in the *individual* unconscious the notion that *all* human experience, *all* psychic material is conserved. His seemingly perverse Lamarckianism is homologous with such structures and reproduces them in an analogue of such mnemonic conservation, now on the level of cultural existence. As he put it in *Moses and Monotheism*: "If we assume the survival of these memory-traces in the archaic heritage, we have bridged the gulf between individual and group psychology" (*SE* 23:100).

Freud's Lamarckianism shocked (and still shocks) biologists and anthropologists—and Freud himself was well aware that the empiri-

47. A summary of the argument and its context will be found in Gay, *Freud*, 324–35 (Gay discusses the "phylogenetic fantasy" on 368). Grubrich-Simitis's essay, "Metapsychology and Metabiology" in her edition of the twelfth paper provides a careful examination of many aspects of the issues raised by Freud's insistence on a Lamarckian position concerning the psyche. The question was previously examined by F. J. Sulloway, *Freud, Biologist of the Mind: Beyond the Psychoanalytic Legend.* See also Norman O. Brown, *Life Against Death: The Psychoanalytic Meaning of History*; Herbert Marcuse, *Eros and Civilization: A Philosophical Inquiry into Freud*; and Marie Moscovici, "Un Meurtre construit par les produits de son oubli."

cal evidence he had drawn from those disciplines for his metapsychological speculations had become less credible year by year: "My
position . . . is made more difficult by the present attitude of biological science, which refuses to hear of the inheritance of acquired
characters by succeeding generations" (*Moses and Monotheism, SE*
23:100). For us the puzzle must be to explain why in the face of such
increasing disconfirmation he persisted in his phylogenetic theses.
The logic of my answer—itself inevitably speculative—is rooted in
my attention to Freudianism as a theory of memory.[48] Freud's extension of the mechanism by which the past is preserved and can be
projected into the present *completes the form* of total memory conservation in the unconscious. With Freud's Lamarkianism, the
psyche's registration of the dynamic toward recuperation of the past
seems to consummate itself. Now *everything* in human existence—
not only the things I have repressed and no longer recall from my
own past, but even things I never experienced from a past beyond
myself—becomes the object of permanent memory inscription
within my unconscious. For consideration of what I have termed
Freudian "maieutics," the consequences of this reiterated insistence
upon the scope and the fixity of the unconscious are considerable.

꧁꧂

> It almost looks as if analysis were the third of those "im-
> possible" professions in which one can be sure beforehand
> of achieving unsatisfying results.
> —Sigmund Freud, "Analysis Terminable and
> Interminable" (1937), *SE* 23:248

Freud's mnemonics of the unconscious thus totalizes experience *radically*. Without doubt, the unconscious he conceived projects a conception of memory unparalleled in any modern theory of the individual or of culture. Freud's vision of the reproduction of the past in the
unconscious is so absolute that it might only be comparable to certain
mystical and eschatological representations of an integral recuperation of the world.

---

48. Grubrich-Simitis's reflections on the logic of Freud's position look rather to his desire to assert the transcultural claims of psychoanalysis. See Freud, *A Phylogenetic Fantasy*, 99.

The unconscious conserves everything. The problem is on its *border*. Let us revert to the question that worried Freud in "The Unconscious" (1915). Freud asked what happens when an unconscious representation—for example, one of the memories forever fixed there—becomes conscious (see *SE* 14:174). Does the same material simply undergo a change of state, or is there a separate second inscription (*Niederschrift*), a new registration of it elsewhere in the psyche? Freud, I observed, was not able to decide precisely how to resolve this conceptual puzzle; however, my aggressive reconceptualization of the nature of unconscious representations and their relation to semiosis obliges a more decisive response. There must be an entirely new version of the unconscious content registered somewhere in consciousness. The reason for this is simple. I argued that the eternal memory traces preserved in system *Ucs.* act more like things than like signs. By denying that the contents of system *Ucs.* can unproblematically be conceived in semiotic terms, the fundamental problem becomes their *translation into signs* somewhere on its border.[49] But clearly the *remainder* of the psyche manipulates its contents very much as if they were signs. The question is, how outside of the fundamental, unchanging registrations of the unconscious do they acquire semiotic status to begin with?

Denying the character of signs to the content of the unconscious emphasizes the impression of irreducible "foreignness" that Freud regularly attributed to it. To press the image, the unconscious does not simply speak a different dialect from the other agencies in the psyche—for in that case, we could learn the foreign tongue and make it our own with relative ease (on the notion of the dialects of the unconscious, see "The Claims of Psycho-Analysis to Scientific Interest" [1913], *SE* 13:177). But the seemingly irreducible *length* of analysis that Freud examined in "Analysis Terminable and Interminable" (1937) seems to suggest that this cannot be. Rather, in some mysterious sense whose ineffability I was struggling to frame earlier, the unconscious must somehow not use language at all. That, as I observed, is true in the weak sense emphasized by Freud that no

49. It may be unnecessary to recall that, like Freud's, my adoption of this topographic imagery is intended only figuratively. But, as he argued (*Interpretation of Dreams*, *SE* 5:611), such figuration appears "expedient and justifiable" if we are to achieve any theoretical grasp on our constant experience that representations in the psyche do not circulate freely and cannot freely be called upon by consciousness.

words exist there, but it seems it must be true in a stronger sense as well.

Thus conceived, this unconscious, which Freud called the "true psychical reality," (*Interpretation of Dreams* [1900], *SE* 5:613) upsets the conception of the remainder of the psyche of which it is the truth. The split in the psyche is a split between the semiotic and its other. It is at this border between them that the problem of Freudian theory becomes acute. The question of such a border is the question of psychotherapy itself. Early on, Freud evoked it suggestively thus: "The account given by the patient sounds as if it were complete and self-contained. It is at first as though we were standing before a wall which shuts out every prospect and prevents us from having any idea whether there is anything behind it, and if so, what" ("Psychotherapy of Hysteria" [1895], *SE* 2:293). This is only an early member of a long series of images through whose figures Freud sought to describe what the mind was like behind this wall, to understand the unimaginable parallel world of the unconscious, and to discover how this "internal foreign territory" of which he spoke in 1933 in the *New Introductory Lectures* (*SE* 22:57) could be negotiated.

The paradox of the psychoanalytic cure should now be apparent. The power of unconscious memories arises in the fact that we are not free *not* to live them. The unconscious memory traces at the source of a neurotic symptom clearly produce "output" to the rest of the psyche—but perhaps they produce only this, and, in the state in which they were laid down, are inaccessible to input, moderation, modulation, or diminution. To cure neurosis must mean to act upon the archaic registrations lying at its source, registrations which the unconscious has integrally conserved. The problem, however, is to imagine how this could happen. For if the unconscious is timeless and immutable, if memories are inexorably fixed, it would seem difficult to conceive how *any* activity taking place outside of it could interrupt them. How can the changeless be changed?

I think this puzzlement must be at the origin of the growing pessimism Freud expressed toward the end of his career concerning the therapeutic ambitions of psychoanalysis. His theory in some sense constrained this reserve. It is particularly visible in "Analysis Terminable and Interminable" (1937). The editors of the *Standard Edition* take particular note of the relative gloom expressed in the essay concerning the possibility of the cure (see *SE* 23:211). What is striking in the analysis

offered in "Analysis Terminable and Interminable" is a seeming convergence between the sources of Freud's reserve concerning the possibility of cure and my depiction of an unconscious whose difference from
the other portions of the psyche is so radical that its very contents exist
in what we might almost think of as an alternate ontological mode.

Analysis can really only cure by some form of *displacement* or *substitution*. The formula in which Freud made this point is celebrated
(if its detail is notoriously opaque): "Where id was, there ego shall be
[*Wo Es war, soll Ich werden*]" (*New Introductory Lectures* [1933],
SE 22:80). But in my examination of whether the contents of the
unconscious (or the "id") could be the object of replacement, could
be *substituted for* and thus fulfill the quintessential function of signs,
I claimed that precisely this was impossible if the timeless character
Freud attributed to unconscious contents was not to be fatally com-
promised.

Lest it be thought that my argument depends too heavily on
Freud's sybilline formulation of the cure, which I have just quoted,
let us look at some other accounts. I've chosen two—one from the
beginning, the other from the end of Freud's career. In "The Psychotherapy of Hysteria" (1895), Freud described the mechanism by
which the patient exhausts the damaging memory image at the origin
of hysteria: "*The patient is, as it were, getting rid of it by turning it
into words*" (*SE* 2:280; emphasis Freud's). This procedure of "abreaction" in the period of Freud's "cathartic" treatment of hysteria is well
known, as are the reasons he later offered for his abandonment of the
techniques by which it was managed. These were essentially that the
"abreacted" memory trace *nonetheless persisted*: one hysteric symptom might disappear, but another would supersede it. In essence,
Freud discovered that the *symptom* in hysteria could be substituted
for, but the *cause*—the unconscious memory trace—remained intact. This discovery is easily conciliable with my reading of the nonsemiotic nature of such traces.

At the other end of his life, in the atmosphere of therapeutic
pessimism to which I've already referred, Freud tried, against the
background of a much more highly modulated theoretical paradigm,
to understand to what extent the "talking cure" could cure.[50] As the

50. The phrase "talking cure" was Anna O.'s and appears in Freud's account of her case;
see *Studies on Hysteria* (1893–95), SE 2:30.

editors of the *Standard Edition* note (*SE* 23:212), to Freud in his last years the limit of such therapeutic capacity seemed to depend upon the refractory nature of the psychic contents determining neurotic behaviors. Freud calls this factor "the strength of the instincts," and defines the cure as "permanently disposing of an instinctual demand" (*SE* 23:224).

Abstracting the manifold intricacies of psychoanalytic theory, two points in "Analysis Terminable and Interminable" relating to my argument seem clear. First, the locus of effectiveness of the instincts, which are there identified as the source of neurosis and the opponent of the treatment, lies in the unconscious (more exactly, instincts are elements of the "primary process"; see *SE* 23:225). Second, the origin of instincts and their mode of existence is not primarily psychological, but organic—biological and physiological (see *SE* 23:212).

These observations would seem to isolate the source of neurosis from any access to the talking cure. In its struggle to overcome pathology, psychoanalysis in effect attempts to oppose the force of *matter* with *words*, to set signs against materiality. It is not surprising that in the face of such a mismatch, in "Analysis Terminable and Interminable" Freud restricted the ambitions of the cure substantially. In particular, with regard to the source of symptoms (the "instinctual demand"), he made it clear that there was little prospect of the treatment's eliminating it. "This," he wrote, "is in general impossible" (*SE* 23:225). Rather, he continued, "we mean something else, something which may be roughly described as a 'taming' [*Bändigung*] of the instinct. That is to say, the instinct is brought completely into the harmony of the ego."

Although the therapeutic operation thus proposed is more subtle, it nonetheless constitutes a version of the same *substitutive* move that I pointed to previously. The old paradigm of abreaction still lurks on the edge of the model for explaining the cure that at this late stage in his career Freud had come to. For in effect the "harmony" into which instinctual demands are to be brought—unless we are to imagine it as an inconceivable conciliation of realities comprised of distinct philosophical substances and occupying completely diverse ontological states—suppresses the constitutive *difference* posited by Freud himself between the *material* nature of the content inducing neurosis (the instinct) and the *psychical* nature of the agency into harmony with which treatment is supposed to induce its entry (the ego).

The problem may be irreducible within the structure of the psyche as Freud conceived it. The cure projects something that psychoanalysis strongly suggests may be impossible: *replacement or extinction of an unconscious trace.* The theoretical energy Freud devoted, from one end of his career to the other, to establishing the timelessness and the stability of the memories in the unconscious rebounded at the moment of the cure to subvert coherent accounts of its very possibility.[51]

In this way, the eidetic memory that Freud attributed to the unconscious and by which it achieves total preservation of the past mutates into something more like memory's nightmare. For as we saw at the outset of my discussion of the relation between memory and the unconscious strictly defined (system *Ucs.*), what is repressed in the unconscious, what is denied entry into consciousness and cut off from development, nonetheless remains banefully active in our lives. In the unconscious such memories withdraw from the possibility of their erosion; once laid down there, they become exempt from exhaustion. The unconscious is thus the unerring repository of our past; but its particular and disheartening privilege is to conserve the contents most harmful to us (or at least to our conscious selves) in a place where their toxicity will suffer no diminution.

The recollected contents of Freud's Art of Memory, the consequences of his maieutic enterprise, thus turn out unexpectedly dire. It is surely possible to reconnect with the deepest memories conserved within us; their manifestations in consciousness are extraordinarily diverse, but always lead back to an unchanging source. Such

51. The problem is not whether psychoanalytic cure is possible. I take no position in *that* debate; rather, I seek to illuminate here whether Freud's theoretical model makes sense of the reality it seeks to render comprehensible. To the extent that it cannot, the task of criticism becomes to see to what degree that failure can be rendered interesting— not simply an opaque negativity, but a puzzle productive of further discourse and understanding. Attempts within psychoanalysis to understand how the fixity of the unconscious can be reconciled with the possibility of the cure replay the memory problem that has concerned me all along. Memory must have more stability than the randomness of signifiers in general; yet just as certainly stability threatens the possibility of any present to realize the unprecedented, to produce itself as something more than an indentured prolongation of the past. The long debate between dialectical and epistemic models of history arises in questions such as these.

multiform manifestations become the substance on which psychoanalysis exercises its practice, and on the basis of them the evidence
Freud could offer for the existence of the unconscious (however indirect) is surprisingly persuasive.

Such a structure embraces the extremes of Freud's construction of
memory. These extremes span a range unprecedented in modernity.
The conflict between memory as the *absolute reproduction of unchanging contents* and memory as the *mobile representation of contents transformed* stresses and might really be said to construct
Freudian analytic theory. On the one hand, his insistence on the
absence of loss in the mnemonic world of the unconscious can be
interpreted as a paroxysm of the reproductive model of memory. The
totalizing retention and recovery of the past has never been conceived more radically. On the other hand, his techniques for interpreting relations linking the constantly changing manifestations of
psychic content as constituting a form of continuous and uninter-
rupted recollection (to which my discussion now turns) provides us
with the most sophisticated theory of mnemonic representation yet
devised. But as my pessimistic analysis suggests, the extremes to
which Freud felt it necessary to go in order to embrace the protean
diversity and power of memory's presence in our lives may have led
him to a structure so internally stressed that it may be capable of no
resolution at all. If so, psychoanalysis preserves the memory crisis as
tenaciously as any trace in the timeless and immutable unconscious
that it conceives as the repository of memory to begin with.

8

Mnemo-Analysis—Memory in Freud
II. Hermeneutics

> Actually, we can never give anything up; we only ex-
> change one thing for another.
>
> —Sigmund Freud, "Creative Writers and
> Day-Dreaming" (1908), *SE* 9:145

The past is always problematic, but in periods of change its difficulties deepen. Freud reflected powerfully on the process and
the substance of such change (see, for example, "Thoughts for the
Times on War and Death" [1915], *SE* 14:273–302). An entire age was
trying to understand and to manage the upheavals, the perturbations
of individual and collective life, that had dominated Europe since the
twin revolutions of the nineteenth century. We know these convul-
sions as modernity. In their shadow, psychoanalysis reflected and
reflected on the stresses of the present's relation to its history. We
could then construe Freud's "mnemo-analysis" as modernity's most
powerful and most influential theory of the difficulties that arise in
the complications of the present and the intractability of time. With
it, Freud takes the measure of modernity's memory crisis.

In Freud, memory lives in a contradiction framed by psychoanalytic topography. Freud's unconscious lodges an integral and unchanging *reproduction* of the past (though not the past our conscious self
has lived), whereas consciousness circulates a mobile and unground-
able *representation* of these contents to which direct access is theoretically impossible. These two memories cohabit within us but co-

here nowhere; these two pasts constitute us but conflict ceaselessly.
Freud thus conceives memory through two divergent, perhaps irreconcilable models for understanding the past's presence and its effec-
tivity. In Freud, the theory of memory has been stretched to exquisite extremes.

In "The Unconscious" (1915), Freud sought to understand how a
relation between the two memory systems he had projected might
be modeled (see particularly *SE* 14:188–89). I considered his uncertainties in the preceding chapter. Of course the arduousness of theorizing how a junction between systems *Ucs.* and *Cs.* (or between the
non- or pre-semiotic contents of the unconscious on the one hand
and the sign-organized material of consciousness on the other) could
be negotiated does not prevent such passages from being the experience of every minute of our lives. A modesty before the limitations of
our models constrains us to recognize that existence does not depend
upon our ability to theorize it in order to occur.

But for Freud's *theory* the difficulty remains. Could the orthogonal
memory worlds of the unconscious and of consciousness produce a
comprehensible model for understanding the presence of the past?
Our conception of the individual subject depends on the answer to
this question. As I argued in my discussion of Baudelaire in Chapter 4,
all manner of reflection on our condition has sought to ground identity in our memory. What else could be its guarantor; what else
seems constant as we change? Such views have been familiar over a
long portion of the history of the West. Yet modernity put this foundational idea into crisis. Suddenly memory does not ground us—it
rather registers our drift.[1] What I have been calling the "memory
crisis" arises in this change. Freud did not initiate this broad reconception of the stability of memory, but psychoanalysis carried it further than it had ever been brought before.

Let me state the magnitude of the problem clearly. For Freud,
whatever the eerie fixity of the registrations preserved in uncon-

1. Theodor Adorno discusses this point as follows: "The unstable character of traditional philosophy's solid identity can be learned from its guarantor, the individual human
consciousness. To Kant, this is the generally predesigned unit underlying every identity.
In fact, if an older person looking back has started early on a more or less conscious
existence, he will distinctly remember his own distant past. It creates a unity. . . . Yet the
'I' which he remembers in this unreality . . .—this I turns simultaneously into another,
into a stranger to be detachedly observed" (*Negative Dialectics*, 154).

scious memory, in *consciousness* recollection exhibits a positively wanton disloyalty to the truth. There seems no seduction before which its representations will not yield. Consider this note Freud added in 1910 to *The Psychopathology of Everyday Life*: "None of us has been able to portray the phenomenon [of the influence of affective factors on memory] and its psychological basis so exhaustively and at the same time so impressively as Nietzsche did in one of his aphorisms (*Jenseits von Gut und Böse*, IV, 68): 'I did this,' says my Memory. 'I cannot have done this,' says my Pride and remains inexorable. In the end—Memory yields" (*SE* 6:146 n. 2).[2] "There is," Freud dryly wrote in *The Interpretation of Dreams*, "no guarantee of the correctness of our memory" [1900], *SE* 5:515).

Thus if we turn our attention from the unconscious to consciousness, the problem of characterizing the absolute, uncannily inert and stable record of the past that Freud theorized was inscribed in system *Ucs.* mutates into the problem of understanding a vertiginous representational mobility in the memories of which awareness is permitted to us. Under such conditions, I am tempted to twist a well-known aphorism. In psychoanalysis, I want to say, it is *consciousness* that is structured like a language. For the reckless lability of psychic representations resembles nothing more closely than language's potentiality for slippage and dissemination. In the face of such seemingly perverse mobility, which it became Freud's theoretical and therapeutic objective to interpret, we might be reminded of the aphorism—generally attributed to Talleyrand—according to which language has been given to human beings so that they can disguise their thoughts. Or of Eco's doctrine—mentioned earlier in connection with my discussion of Proust—that semiotics is the discipline that studies anything that can be used in order to lie.[3] For as Freud framed it, consciousness shifts its ground like the most unprincipled of charlatans.

In its protean volatility the memory function exercised in consciousness proliferates and diffuses extravagantly. With Freud the theory of memory thus reaches a critical pass. The psychic life we

2. Freud's attention was drawn to this passage from Nietzsche's *Beyond Good and Evil* by his patient the Rat Man; see *SE* 10:184. See also Friedrich Nietzsche, *Beyond Good and Evil: Prelude to a Philosophy of the Future*, trans. Walter Kaufmann, 80.

3. Umberto Eco, *A Theory of Semiotics*, 7.

experience or can observe directly is a perpetual movement of transformations and substitutions—ordered, determined perhaps (as we
will consider), but potentially interminable. As Freud put it in "The
Dynamics of Transference" (1912), "Unconscious impulses do not
want to be remembered in the way the treatment desires them to
be, but endeavor to reproduce themselves in accordance with the
timelessness of the unconscious and its capacity for hallucination" (*SE*
12:108). But once even *hallucination* has been admitted as a mode of
meaning, then psychoanalysis has committed itself to resolving heroic problems in interpretation.

The untrammeled play of exchanges and transformations of meaning that psychoanalysis projects as the business of conscious memory
subverts the coherence through time and the reality check that
memory was long supposed to provide. In psychoanalysis, recollection rather appears as a hypocritical counterfeiter. Freud thus
threatens to dissolve the stable definitional element that made memory a special and restricted form of representation, and to merge it
with the unlimited plasticity—we might almost say the indifferent
mendaciousness—of representation in general. In psychoanalysis,
the art of memory becomes an art tending toward memory's dissolution.

This extravagant mobility of psychic contents preoccupied Freud.
It both defined his paradigm of interpretation and caused him concern because of its vertiginousness. Consider this passage (highly excerpted here) from "Screen Memories" (1899):

> There are numerous possible types of case in which one psychical
> content is substituted for another. . . . The essential elements of an
> experience are represented in memory by the inessential elements
> of the same experience. . . . The process which we see here at
> work—conflict, repression, substitution involving a compromise—
> returns in all psychoneurotic symptoms and gives us the key to
> understanding their formation. . . . The assertion that a psychical
> intensity [cf. *SE* 3:67] can be displaced from one presenta-
> tion . . . on to another . . . is as bewildering to us as certain
> features of Greek mythology. (*SE* 3:307–9)

But his increasingly intricate conception of the bewildering exchanges within the psyche did not cause Freud to recant. He rather

intensified his rewriting of the paradigms of the mnemonic. In consciousness, Freud reconceived memory as transformation. Henceforth, in a vision that has had great influence since Freud's own period, *remembering means changing.*

Within Freud's construction of the psyche the tension between the paradigms of *reproduction* and *representation* (as I have called them) may be theoretically unresolvable. But the topographic localization that structures the psyche segregates each of these paradigms in its own realm. Reproduction is conserved in the one portion of the psyche (system *Ucs.*) for which our evidence is always indirect and distorted. "How are we to arrive at a knowledge of the unconscious? It is of course only as something conscious that we know it, after it has undergone transformation or translation into something conscious" ("The Unconscious" [1915], *SE* 14:166). But as this passage suggests, in the remainder of the psyche—in that capacious and internally differentiated area that is called consciousness—an altogether different paradigm functioned. In consciousness, memory is constrained only by the vertiginous (as Freud had said, the "bewildering") exchanges that characterize representation.

For Freud, the psyche is thus a mechanism for establishing and experiencing relation. But as Henry James once observed, "relations stop nowhere."[4] Thus in the psyche, everything *moves.* "Not only is it [repression] . . . *individual* in its operation, but it is also exceedingly *mobile*" ("Repression" [1915], *SE* 14:151; emphasis Freud's). Psychoanalytic understanding is characterized by an unlimited readiness to tropological exchanges and transformations. We might recall the sentence of Derrida's that I quoted in the preceding chapter: "The substitution of signifiers seems to be the essential activity of psychoanalytic interpretation."[5] For the model of the mind that psychoanalysis projects, the normal mode of existence for psychic contents is thus not homeostatic but transferential—transferential not in the special sense Freud attaches to the notion of "transference" in the cure (though the transference relationship instantiates precisely the same process of displacement of psychic material), but in a specifically rhetorical or figural way. In psychic material, *things keep*

4. Henry James, preface to *Roderick Hudson*, in *The Art of the Novel: Critical Prefaces*, 5.
5. Jacques Derrida, "Freud and the Scene of Writing," 210.

changing into other things. A readiness to perceive this constitutive lability and plasticity, to consider it as the zero-degree reality in the psyche, is fundamental to Freudian hermeneutics.

Reinterpretations of Freud along Saussurian lines have preoccupied important strands of critical theory over the past thirty years or so.[6] We have become familiar with the notion that the Freudian model of meaning-transfer, of metonymic relays and metaphoric indices, of a seemingly uncontainable displacement of significations, bears a persuasive similarity to the structures of semiosis as they became conceptualized and propagated at the very period Freud's own theory was being systematized (Saussure's lectures took place between 1906 and 1911). It almost seems that semiotics was dreaming up psychoanalysis at the same time as Freud himself.

But one qualification should be emphasized. The account of the mode of existence and displacement of psychic material in terms of tropology is not itself metaphorical. We could say that the latent content of a dream relates to the recollected manifest content as tenor to vehicle, in the familiar mode of metaphor.[7] But we could hardly say that the relationship between the parts of a metaphor is *itself* tropological. A metaphor isn't metaphorical metaphorically: it *really is.* This is pertinent because the transition to a psychoanalytic mode of thinking means accepting that the psychic objects of analytic discourse truly *do* transfer their meanings. And they do this not as a figuration, but in a *literality analogous to figuration.* Transfers are how they work—not in the mode of "as if," but veritably. Thus to call the relations between different manifestations of psychic material tropological is itself a metaphor—and not a particularly helpful one, for it disguises the fact that the multifarious transfers, which nonpsychic existence accustoms us to think of as metaphorical, *in the psyche are the real, literal mode of existence.*

Consider the following passage from Freud's account of the Wolf Man case. It occurs in the course of Freud's uneasy analysis of the

6. On these, see particularly Élisabeth Roudinesco's *Jacques Lacan & Co.: A History of Psychoanalysis in France, 1925–1985.*

7. Cf. Freud, "On Dreams" (1901): "The transformation of the latent dream-thoughts into the manifest dream-content . . . is the first instance known to us of psychical material being changed over from one mode of expression to another" (*SE* 5:642).

Wolf Man's recollection of witnessing parental intercourse—a theoretical crux I considered in my discussion of Freudian "maieutics" in the preceding chapter. For Freud the question arose, are such scenes *memories* or *fantasies?* Freud writes: "I am not of the opinion . . . that such scenes must necessarily be phantasies because they do not reappear in the shape of recollections. It seems to me absolutely equivalent to a recollection, if the memories are replaced (as in the present case) by dreams the analysis of which invariably leads back to the same scene and which reproduce every portion of its content in an inexhaustible variety of new shapes. *Indeed, dreaming is another kind of remembering"* ("From the History of an Infantile Neurosis" [1918], *SE* 17:51; emphasis mine). In Freud's analysis a psychic content has been transferred. It appears not as a memory per se, but as a dream. The situation, however, is analytically the same ("It seems to me absolutely equivalent to a recollection . . ."). This produces an arresting result. It could be said that the paradox of Freud's Art of Memory is that *it abolishes memory as a specific faculty.* Memory establishes connections, and connections are what is at issue in psychoanalysis. But at a certain level all connections look the same. The passages, shifts, and slippages of representation to which I've already referred, the seemingly wanton transfers of meaning that constitute the mode of existence of psychic material, make of memory no more than a special case of the psychic transfers whose distinction increasingly seems to lack a difference. In Freud's mnemo-analysis the search for memory has led us perplexingly to the point of memory's disappearance.

In Chapter 1, I noted how natural the objectivity of the past seems to us despite the evident problematization of its notion in numerous strains of contemporary theory. We have learned to believe that the "past," however consecrated it may appear, however necessary its lineaments may seem to our conception of the world, is subject to the same contingency as any cultural fact. Freud is one of the prosecutors of this reconception. With Freud the past and the faculties by which we conceive and register it mutate before our eyes. The minimalist model for memory I offered at the beginning of this book went as follows: a content of some sort is registered, with whatever reproductive fidelity the registering system can manage. A represen-

tation appears, presumably related to the content previously registered. Such conservation and reappearance in a representation defines a memory effect. However, such a structure will only seem a
model for memory if the temporal displacement between the two
moments upon which the model focuses is itself foregrounded. Otherwise, the model is simply a paradigm for the transfer of meaning:
for representation. But as I argued in the preceding chapter, semiotics (at least in its dyadic versions) has no ability to model time. Consequently, from the side of such a semiotics, memory appears as an
entirely indifferent form of transfer. In the generality of representations, its specificity dissolves. Then the past with all the weighty
prestige of its determinations is reduced to seeming no more than a
commonplace site for interpretation. At that point, *memory itself
seems forgotten.*

❧❀❧

> Like the physical, the psychical is not necessarily in reality
> what it appears to us to be.
> —Sigmund Freud, "The Unconscious" (1915), *SE* 14:171

What follows might appear an unwitting swerve in the course of my
argument—from the character and practices of *memory* in the
Freudian account of the psyche toward an account of the nature of
Freudian *interpretation*. It might seem that I have negligently
traded mnemonics for hermeneutics. At the outset of this apparent
digression I want to make the claim that it is no such thing. The
problems of memory and of interpretation in Freud are indissociable;
on the theoretical level they cannot legitimately be distinguished.
This convergence is a critical element of one of our century's most
influential mnemonic theories and practices. Asserting it reconceives
what for many has been the most characteristic reflex of modernism:
the irreducible necessity of interpretation, for whose pervasiveness
the name of Freud has itself become emblematic far beyond the
therapeutic realm of psychoanalysis. It thereby radicalizes the claim
that has echoed in my argument all along: that in the modern period
memory has most powerfully and influentially been construed in the

mode of *representation*, with all the burden of nontransparency and contingency that this term supposes and emphasizes.

How do these two registers—the mnemonic and the hermeneutic—unfold and intertwine in Freud's theory? Freudian interpretation is fundamentally *genealogical*. It supposes the reality, and the potential verifiability, of a flow of temporal transformations of psychic contents. However arduous in practice, Freud thus conceives interpretation as a *realist* act. It then becomes simple to say how the problem of memory relates to the problem of interpretation. *We need hermeneutics when memory fails*: when the transparency of our access to the meanings transmitted to us from the past is troubled or interrupted. I have called these perturbations a memory crisis. But how do such troubles manifest themselves? At first we might imagine that the crisis of memory simply implies a diminishing trustworthiness or clarity of recollection, a decline in faithful reproduction. And indeed, everyone knows the frustration that arises in the loss of mnemonic definition, in the experience of "I can't quite recall."

But as I've argued from the beginning, the memory crisis has more daunting forms than this disturbance of the accuracy of our recollection. In particular, memories malfunction when they cast their net too widely, when they recall *too well or too much*. Then their meanings become problematic by virtue of their very multiplicity and their diffusion. In such cases interpretation is how we choose between the profusion of possible contents that present themselves for credence even as they mutually subvert the competing claims each makes to faithfulness and undermine the reliability of the faculty that has perversely produced them, helter-skelter, in our consciousness.

In my discussion of Baudelaire's Swan poem I observed that memory can remember *anything*—there is no objective limit to the references it may retrieve, no restriction to its potential associations. This problem recurs powerfully in Freud, and it has a considerable urgency for this concluding portion of my book. The *reconstructive-interpretive* paradigm of psychoanalysis is entirely homologous with the *associative-productive* paradigm of the mnemonic such as it emerges in "Le Cygne." But this homology is limited by a crucial constraint: the constraint of history. For Freud, real lives are freighted by limitations that confine the volatility of semiotic transfers—or at least by constraints on interpretation of their meaning. The weight of an already constituted materiality and the obstinacy of time's unidirectionality thus bear heavily upon Freudian hermeneutics. Viewed from the side of memory's limitless associations, *any* association can link *any* content with *any* other. But that door swings only one way. Once an association is constituted, once a mnemonic trace replacing one content by another is laid down in the unconscious, then the unconstrainable freedom of mnemonic productivity mutates into the servitude of a hermeneutic that must detect and reconstruct the history of *just these* mnemonic linkages. At any point, *any* linkage is still theoretically possible; but punctually only *one* such linkage will actually have occurred and been retained in the psychic contents of which, and out of which, the analyst must make sense. The determined productivity of time thus converts mnemonics into hermeneutics.

To put this less abstractly, psychoanalysis must construct the meaning of an entity, the psyche, whose meaning is not given on its surface, but as Freud made clear in "Constructions in Analysis," it can only claim to do so as a *re*-construction. It performs the interpretive equivalent of "reverse engineering": given a product, it seeks to understand how the product came to be, how it was made. It walks back up the chain of relations that in their accumulated effects produced the psyche it strives to understand. Freud conceived this process as fundamentally *realist*. His model is considerably more complex than Ranke's celebrated paradigm for historians, but however complex, at bottom Freud's interpretive practice still seeks to understand "how it—the transformation of the psyche's contents—*really happened.*" This is why memory and interpretation in Freud ultimately name the same phenomenon and cannot be dissociated. Under such circumstances, the apparent recession of the memory problem in my discussion is the paradoxical (but ultimately comprehensible) effect of the problem itself. The memory crisis was never a complication to be *solved*. It was always a disquiet about origins, and arose in a sudden opacity of the relation between *then* and *now*. With the perturbation of the past, even memory necessarily recedes. The memory crisis thus could be understood as an instantiation of itself. The difficulty it emblematizes is the arduousness of recovering even its own genesis, of reproducing even the memory of how the bizarre sense of disconnection, the eerie temporal flatness of modernity arose to begin with.

At a certain point, the memory crisis yields to its period's anxious interrogation—not by delivering its secret, but by dissolving back into the culture out of which it, and its urgency, had precipitated in the first place. To put this differently, a cultural problem like the memory crisis can take on such a centrality that in the end it loses its very definition and diffuses to become one of the conditions of existence of the culture for which it had arisen as a crisis. It returns to transparency not by having been resolved but by having been routinized along with the recollected experience of time upon which it inevitably depends. Then the notion of "origin," and the entire model of determinant temporality it presumes, appear to become irrelevant. The culture's question about where its uncertainties came from dissolves like the Cheshire cat.

The effort to resolve this cultural disquiet by seeking to recover its development runs into a blank wall. The nature of the problem makes this result inevitable. For the memory crisis can't be solved by an act of memory. In the face of its obduracy it changes into a familiar puzzlement, the question of what cultural (and individual) disquiet *means*. Maieutics thus mutates into hermeneutics. This means that our fascination with interpretation carries the displacement of modernity's century-long puzzlement about memory.

So the concerted attention that Freud devotes to the problem of memory by no means contradicts the virtual dissolution of the faculty that had been the object of such concern for psychoanalytic theory and interpretive practice. The problem for a good portion of the nineteenth century had been to understand how the constituted *was constituted*, to comprehend the uncanny presence of the past in a time when the recession of that past, the disappearance of felt or securely remembered connection with it, increasingly left individuals experiencing the present as a kind of depthless enigma. But at the end of the road of that interrogation of memory, through a kind of catastrophization or Hegelian reversal that produces the experience and the paradigm of modernity as such, the past simply appeared to dissipate altogether. Freud's double, contradicted paradigm of mem-

ory instantiates both moments of this evolution in his dualistic model
of the psyche. It commemorates the frozen hypostatization of the
past as a localizable, recoverable body of experience, and simultaneously its increasing dissolution in the practices of an endless
world of exchanges of meaning.

But even transformed, forced beyond its own name in that second
moment of the Freudian problematic, memory can nonetheless be
reinscribed as central, for the fundamental axiom of the hermeneutic
deployed in psychoanalysis is that *some content is always preserved*—retained, transferred, recollected—across even the most
vertiginous mutations undergone by representations within the
psyche. These transfers inevitably center in memory, instantiate its
processes, and convey its materials. As for the specifically interpretive activity of psychoanalysis, of course it has no other content than
memories to work with. "We have to do our therapeutic work on [the
present state of the patient's illness], which consists in large measure
in tracing it back to the past" ("Remembering, Repeating, and Working-Through" [1914], *SE* 12:152). This hermeneutic exercise can be
seen as a fundamental process of anamnesis.

Each transformation of psychic contents augments the problem of
elucidating the new *form* in which the content appears, of specifying
the determinations of the representation assumed. But the fundamental crux to which they all point is detection of the originary content that has been carried forward from the most primitive registrations conserved in the psyche. Yet if these originary memories (the
changeless contents of system *Ucs.*) are the ground of interpretation,
in practice they can provide only the most distant warrant for our
understanding. In the meantime, psychoanalytic hermeneutics must
contend with a signifying volatility just as heady and (to repeat
Freud's characterization) potentially just as "bewildering" as the
mythological metamorphoses to which he compared the transformations of psychic contents.

So not only does *remembering* mean changing in Freud: *meaning*
means changing too. The fundamental interpretive rule of psychoanalysis thus is: *everything is transformed, everything requires interpretation.* No psychic content gives itself to us unmediated; none
carries transparent significance. In his brilliant and acerbic critique
of Freud, Sebastiano Timpanaro brandishes Gilles Deleuze against

Freud on this point, apparently in the belief that the Deleuzian witticism he cites can help him to stigmatize the unprincipled and indefensible slipperiness he attributes to the Freudian doctrine that patients do not know the meaning of what they say. Timpanaro writes: "The 'interpretive mechanism' of psychoanalysis, rightly observes Gilles Deleuze, can be summarized as follows: whatever you say, it means something else."[8] But Deleuze doesn't undermine Freud in the way Timpanaro seems to think. Timpanaro considers the Freudian analyses of lapses and parapraxes sophistical and believes that the methods of philology can unpack them more rationally than psychoanalysis does. But in a sense these are intraparty quarrels. The "method of the tedious philologist" was Ferenczi's description of psychoanalysis itself.[9] And Freud's own comparisons of his method of interpretation to the operations characteristic of textual science are well known (see, for example, his analysis of defenses in terms of the censorship of books in "Analysis Terminable and Interminable" [1937], *SE* 23:236). There is more linking philology and psychoanalysis than Timpanaro is willing to believe.

Fundamentally, philologists and psychoanalysts hold parallel attitudes toward the sanctity of texts and meanings, even if the mechanisms each employs for their correction or more perfect comprehension diverge considerably. Both willingly subvert the authority of the text; both rely on the reinterpretation of a seemingly original utterance; both produce parallel demonstrations of its false immediacy, of its distortion or derivation. Both see the locus of meaning lying behind or beyond the text, rather than on its surface. And both realize that there is an irreducible element of conjecture in the interpretations they offer. Past these convergences, the argument between philology and psychoanalysis might almost seem a matter of detail.[10]

8. Sebastiano Timpanaro, *The Freudian Slip: Psychoanalysis and Textual Criticism*, 46.

9. John Forrester, *Language and the Origins of Psychoanalysis*, 198.

10. Carlo Ginzburg strikingly parallels the reliance of philology and the various branches of medicine on conjectural reasoning in "Clues: Morelli, Freud, and Sherlock Holmes," 92. Jürgen Habermas clarifies the similarities and differences between psychoanalytic and philological paradigms in *Knowledge and Human Interests*, 214–17. See also Timpanaro, *Freudian Slip*, particularly 19, 41, 86–87.

Psychoanalysis is justly suspicious.
—Sigmund Freud, *Interpretation of Dreams* (1900),
    SE 5:517

In the *Introductory Lectures on Psycho-Analysis* (1916–17), Freud
speculated about the damage done by scientific doctrine to the self-
regard of human narcissism:

> In the course of centuries the *naïve* self-love of men has had to
> submit to two major blows at the hands of science. The first was
> when they learnt that our earth was not the centre of the universe
> but only a tiny fragment of a cosmic system of scarcely imaginable
> vastness. This is associated in our minds with the name of Coper-
> nicus. . . . The second blow fell when biological research de-
> stroyed man's supposedly privileged place in creation and proved
> his descent from the animal kingdom and his ineradicable animal
> nature. This revaluation has been accomplished in our own days by
> Darwin, Wallace and their predecessors, though not without the
> most violent contemporary opposition. But human megalomania
> will have suffered its third and most wounding blow from the psy-
> chological research of the present time which seeks to prove to the
> ego that it is not even master in its own house, but must content
> itself with scanty information of what is going on unconsciously in
> its mind. (*SE* 16:284–85; emphasis Freud's)[11]

Freud attributed a portion of the notorious resistance to psychoanalysis in the period of its development to the narcissistic injury it
caused to individuals' self-conception. We hate to be told we don't
know what we're doing. And (as the Deleuze quotation that Timpanaro sought to use against Freud makes pugnaciously clear) psychoanalysis tells us precisely that.

   Yet in the modern period such disauthentification of our intentionality, such devaluation of our self-knowledge feels uncannily familiar. In particular, it hardly seems necessary today to reargue the
doctrine that texts, messages, utterances, representations—*meanings*—mean beyond and beneath what they appear to say, or what

---

11. Freud expanded his argument concerning these narcissistic injuries at the hands of
science in "A Difficulty in the Path of Psycho-Analysis" (1917), *SE* 17:139–41.

their locutors *intended* them to say. All of modernism supposes such multileveled, decentered, and often internally conflicted production of meaning. This skepticism about our capacity completely to possess our consciousness has become a consecrated habit during precisely the period in which memory itself has turned troublesome.

In the preceding chapter I speculated on the diffuse discovery that—despite the promises of the Enlightenment—the social and political revolutions of the late-eighteenth and nineteenth centuries had failed to produce an unequivocal liberation of human beings and of their societies. This unwelcome realization, I argued, led to the development of disciplines (what we have come to know as the "human sciences") that sought to understand the more mysterious, more covert constraints on our freedom. Each of these emergent disciplines speculated upon hidden *internal* barriers to our emancipation. Thus in effect each projected the same second-guessing of subjectivity or dethroning of consciousness that Freud referred to here.

In a well-known analysis, Paul Ricoeur termed this attitude "suspicion." Here is the passage in which Ricoeur's idea appeared:

A general theory of interpretation would . . . have to account not only for the opposition between two interpretations of interpretation, the one as recollection of meaning, the other as reduction of the illusions and lies of consciousness; but also for the division and scattering of each of these two great "schools" of interpretation into "theories" that differ from one another and are even foreign to one another. This is no doubt truer of the school of suspicion than of the school of reminiscence. Three masters, seemingly mutually exclusive, dominate the school of suspicion: Marx, Nietzsche, and Freud. It is easier to show their common opposition to a phenomenology of the sacred, understood as a propaedeutic to the "revelation" of meaning, than their interrelationship within a single method of demystification. It is relatively easy to note that these three figures all contest the primacy of the object in our representation of the sacred. . . . It is also easy to recognize that this contesting is an exercise of suspicion in three different ways: "truth as lying" would be the negative heading under which one might place these three exercises of suspicion. But we are still far from having assimilated the positive meaning of the enterprises of these three thinkers. . . . Beginning with them, understanding is hermeneutics: henceforward, to seek meaning is no longer to spell out the consciousness of meaning, but to *decipher its expressions*. . . . For Marx, Nietzsche, and Freud, the fundamental category of consciousness is the relation hidden-shown or, if you prefer, simulated-manifested. . . . What all three attempted, in different ways, was to make their "conscious" methods of deciphering coincide with the "unconscious" *work* of ciphering which they attributed to the will to power, to social being, to the unconscious psychism. . . . All three, however, far from being detractors of "consciousness," aim at extending it.[12]

But like any other element of culture the meaning of "suspicion" is neither obvious nor simple. To interpret Ricoeur's term we should begin with some speculation on its history. Although my evidence is circumstantial, I want to propose a skeleton tradition for the notion of suspicion itself. I would begin in just the period with which I began this book. In a celebrated (if somewhat telegraphic) passage in his *Souvenirs d'égotisme* (1832), Stendhal foregrounded the term "suspicion": "Poetic genius is dead, but the genius of *suspicion* has come into the world. I am deeply persuaded that the only antidote which might make the reader forgive the repetitions of the 'I' which the author will employ is complete sincerity."[13] In this passage, and more generally in the *Souvenirs* from which it is drawn, Stendhal was seeking to frame a new and anxious notion of subjectivity—one that bears a striking parallel to the conflicted sense of self that at the outset of this book I argued Musset was defining in his nearly contemporary *Confession* (1836). The first-person fiction of autobiographic anamnesis, the consequent ironic decentering of the remembered "I" that Stendhal and Musset have in common, are striking constants linking the two books. In unmasking a mystified discontinuity of consciousness, both works instantiate the inflection in our understanding of subjectivity that has been at the center of my analysis. What both Stendhal and Musset expose is just the narcissistic injury to the sovereignty of consciousness that Freud was theorizing much more systematically in his *Introductory Lectures* in 1917.

12. Paul Ricoeur, *Freud and Philosophy: An Essay on Interpretation*, 32–34; emphasis Ricoeur's.
13. Stendhal, *Souvenirs d'égotisme*, 7; emphasis Stendhal's.

In 1956, Nathalie Sarraute published an influential volume of essays on the novel, *L'Ere du soupçon*. It focused upon this uncertainty of subjectivity and its consequences for representation in the fictions of modern culture. Sarraute borrowed the key word in her title from Stendhal. A notion of "suspicion" bearing upon our conceptualization of subjectivity was thus in play at just the moment that Ricoeur was writing his book on Freud, which appeared in 1965. Rather than proposing this genealogy of Ricoeur's "school of suspicion" in the mode of traditional source-criticism, I want simply to suggest that it provides historical and conceptual depth—a kind of familiarization or Freudian "facilitation" [*Bahnung*]—lying behind and sustaining Ricoeur's analysis of the incompleteness of subjectivity that makes a hermeneutics indispensable.

If we unpack what seems concentrated in Ricoeur's notion of suspicion, four strands emerge as particularly important:

- Suspicion assumes *transformation* as the normal process through which meaning is transmitted.
- Suspicion presumes *intelligibility*, and seeks to produce understanding out of the enigmas of distorted meanings.
- Meaning *disseminates*; it has no obligatory end point.
- The production of meaning is *dialogic*: its generation requires an interlocutor.[14]

In what follows, I want to examine the consequences of these principles.

---

14. The hermeneutic bootstrapping operation that was Freud's solo self-analysis presents an obvious problem for such a conception—as it did for Freud himself. In a letter to Fliess (14 November 1897) he expressed the difficulty unequivocally: "My self-analysis remains interrupted. I have realized why I can analyze myself only with the help of knowledge obtained objectively (like an outsider). True self-analysis is impossible; otherwise there would be no [neurotic] illness" (*The Complete Letters of Sigmund Freud to Wilhelm Fliess*, 281; the text also appears in *SE* 1:271). A similar pessimism can be found in a text from much later in Freud's career, "The Subtleties of a Faulty Action" (1935), *SE* 22:233–35, see especially 234. He took a more positive view in "On the History of the Psycho-Analytic Movement" (1914), *SE* 14:7–66, see especially 20. Whatever Freud's view may have been, the implications of self-analysis for the location of interpretive authority present particular conceptual difficulties.

> I think . . . that the Roman emperor was in the wrong
> when he had one of his subjects executed because he had
> dreamt of murdering the emperor. He should have begun
> by trying to find out what the dream meant; most probably
> its meaning was not what it appeared to be.
>   —Sigmund Freud, *Interpretation of Dreams* (1900),
>   *SE* 5:620

Freud supposes that there is no knowledge outside of interpretation, but for him there is surely knowledge in it. Everything in the Freudian scheme, the entire hermeneutic energy that psychoanalysis deploys, has as its object the fixation and revelation of meaning, the substitution of adequate interpretation for the inadequacies of immediacy. Psychoanalysis thus makes unequivocal and uncompromising truth claims—even if, as figures from Ricoeur and Jürgen Habermas to Adolf Grünbaum and an entire tradition seeking to debunk the scientificity of Freudianism suggest, the meaning and validity of such truth claims is problematic.

It is axiomatic that the truths such a hermeneutic produces cannot be fully articulated from within the subjectivity whose truths they are. To produce them, interpretation suspends and supersedes the authority of this subject's own self-understanding. Interpretive suspicion *rewrites*. But here a problem arises. Once the rewriting of the object of interpretation begins; once transfer, transposition, what Freud termed *Umsetzung* (*New Introductory Lectures on Psycho-Analysis* [1933], *SE* 22:100–101) are accepted as legitimate for understanding its *real* meaning, then it becomes difficult to see how to *limit* such revisions. The hermeneutics of suspicion maintains that things do not mean what they say. But then the difficulty becomes knowing how they might not mean anything at all.

Freud resolutely refuses uncontrollable and endless rewriting. He wants to find the real meaning concealed within the psyche and stop there. His insistence on this point establishes him as a partisan of determinable intelligibility in a world about to slip into the aporias of radical dissemination. But the disjunction between Freud's belief in determinate meaning on the one hand and familiar poststructuralist theories of unlimitable semiotic transfer on the other is not as great as it might first appear. The paradigms of significatory free play beckon at the limit of Freud's hermeneutic protocols. The very procedures by which interpretive demystification (whether Freudian, Marxian, or Nietzschean) proceeds simultaneously establish the preconditions for these postmodernist attitudes. To recall a neologism I offered earlier, the members of Ricoeur's school of suspicion "disauthenticate" the authority of the object they interpret. But once its self-understanding is destabilized in the interpretive act, restabilization requires a very strong argument. If an object of analysis (of whatever sort) does not adequately control and possess its meaning, can its analyst securely inherit the privilege of determining the meaning that has been withdrawn from it?

Marx and Freud together theorize the displacement of authority from a previously sovereign object to the analyst whose role is to elucidate it. Marx expresses the necessity for such displacement this way: "All science would be superfluous if the form of appearance [*Erscheinungsform*] and the essence of things directly coincided."[15] In the absence of such coincidence, the meanings hidden must be brought to light through the agency of analysis. The authority of the traditional sites of subjectivity (individual consciousness, memory, experience, and so on) is thus disinherited. Postmodernism refuses the comfortable relocation of this authority. Once interpretive privilege is called into question, it remains in question. Nietzsche had already adumbrated this further reorientation. Postmodernism insists on taking it all the way. It stigmatizes the foundation of *any* analytic or discursive authority.

A crucial tension in Freud thus arises in the necessity of allowing for *some* interpretive movement without legitimating *all* such movement—which by making its product absolutely indifferent would amount to disestablishing interpretation altogether. How to become the theorist of a mediated meaningfulness, of an intricate and possibly unreproducible hermeneutic, *without* involuntarily finding oneself the apologist for meaning's radical disintegration? *Determinate meaningfulness* (on the one hand) and *variability of representation* (on the other) are the interpretive and epistemological imperatives that conflict in any hermeneutics of suspicion, and in Freud's in par-

15. Karl Marx, *Capital: A Critique of Political Economy, Volume 3*, 956; translation modified. On this point, see Gerald A. Cohen, *Karl Marx's Theory of History*, Appendix 1. Cf. Nietzsche: "It is not true that the essence of things 'appears' in the empirical world" ("On Truth and Lies in a Nonmoral Sense," 86).

ticular. Freud wants to credit both the *lability* of representations in
the psyche and, simultaneously, despite it, their *intelligibility*. His
hermeneutics thus stands uneasily on the border between a vision of
the unpredictable *contingency* of representations and a conviction of
their *determination*.

Consider a characteristic Freudian assertion analyzing the contents
of human fantasies: "Feces—money—gift—baby—penis are treated
. . . as though they meant the same thing, and they are represented
too by the same symbols" (*New Introductory Lectures* [1933], *SE*
22:101). At first glance the relations between these symbols may
seem absurd. But that is not the problem. As I argued earlier, establishing and maintaining relations—even the most singular or unexpected—is the characteristic business of the psyche. Nothing in the
form of Freud's reasoning should therefore be surprising. My claim
then is not that the connection between specific psychic contents
that Freud asserts in this brief passage is unthinkable. It is only that
once you establish such connections, the question arises of how you
know where to *stop*.[16] In particular, once the exchange of signifiers in
the psyche is enabled up to and including the point of what in a
passage I quoted earlier Freud called "hallucination," how can we
tell what signifiers are *not* exchanged? The transfer and transformation of contents is an intensely powerful dynamic. The question is,
how can an interpretation contain it?

This problem underlies reflection throughout Freud's career. He
acknowledged it in a forthright and crucial passage in *The Interpretation of Dreams* (1900): "The dream-thoughts to which we are led by
interpretation cannot, from the nature of things, have any definite
endings; they are bound to branch out in every direction into the
intricate network of our world of thought" (*SE* 5:525). In one of his
last essays, the difficulty that this boundlessness poses appears in the
form of a deceptively simple question. Freud asked how we can
know when an analysis is finished. From the point of view of the

16. Wittgenstein posed precisely this question in his attack on Freudianism: "This procedure of free association and so on is queer, because Freud never shows how we know
where to stop—where is the right solution. Sometimes he says that the right solution, or
the right analysis, is the one which satisfies the patient. Sometimes he says that the doctor
knows what the right solution or analysis of the dream is whereas the patient doesn't: the
doctor can say that the patient is wrong" ("Conversations on Freud; Excerpt from 1932–3
Lectures," 1). Yet it must be acknowledged (as I will seek to show in what follows) that
Freud was more reflective about these problems than Wittgenstein allows.

theory and practice of psychoanalytic interpretation, the puzzlement implicit in the title of this celebrated paper—"Analysis Terminable and Interminable" (1937, *SE* 23:216–53)—identifies a problem that may be incapable of solution within the hermeneutic system Freud devised. Indeed, *no* hermeneutics of suspicion may be able to resolve it.

❧

> All this is not entirely arbitrary.
> —Sigmund Freud, letter to Wilhelm Fliess, 22
> December 1897, in *The Complete Letters*, 288

Freud's analyses produce the impression of an extraordinary hermeneutic ingenuity, of a dazzling interpretive brio. His cases make brilliant narratives (in the *Studies on Hysteria* [1893–95] he commented himself on their unexpected—and unwelcome—resemblance to fictions; *SE* 2:160). For example, "From the History of an Infantile Neurosis" ["The Wolf Man"] leads the investigation through a vertiginous unfolding of memory screens, detours, and disguises, through intricate and unpredictable transformations of psychic contents to arrive, eventually, at the Wolf Man's recollection of a primal scene—an event that, as I observed earlier, Freud speculates may not have happened at all.

The problem is to know *how we know* that one particular psychic content is related to another. We could believe that relation was the essential modality of the psyche without having any way to be sure *which* relations obtained in any given situation. Richard Wollheim puts the difficulty clearly: "Observation of an idea . . . depends upon our capacity to recognize or reidentify that idea: and it is precisely this capacity that seems put in doubt if the idea undergoes the transformations or takes on the characteristics peculiar to the contents of the system *Ucs.*"[17] Meaning has to be preserved through even the giddiest transformations within the psyche. But when is it possible to say that a particular content retains or "remembers" another one to which our access is blocked, or whose appearance leads to no obvious assumption of its connection with the content before us?

Freud termed the disparate manifestations of such preserved con-

17. Richard Wollheim, *Sigmund Freud*, 194–95.

tents "substitute formations": "We find that derivatives of the *Ucs.* become conscious as substitute formations and symptoms—generally, it is true, after having undergone great distortions" ("The Unconscious" [1915], *SE* 14:193).[18] This notion of substitution is central in the Freudian understanding of interpretation. In Freud, things constantly stand for other things. Sentences like this one from "Mourning and Melancholia" (1917) are characteristic of the process by which, according to Freud, the analyst arrives at the meanings the unconscious does not want to reveal: "The narcissistic identification with the object then becomes a substitute for the erotic cathexis" (*SE* 14:249). *This* for *that. Quid* pro *quo.*

Within the model established by such assumptions, the connections between the various manifestations of "substitute formations" and the contents for which they substitute are normally hidden. That is why the hermeneutics of suspicion arises to begin with, and why analysis is necessary: such relations, such connections are *never* transparent or self-interpreting. Yet simultaneously, Freud believes that interpretation of these transfers is a realistic aim. Psychoanalytic theory supposes that the transfers through which connections between seemingly diverse psychic contents are established *really occur*, and occur for a determinable reason. That is why I argued earlier that to understand the psyche's transfers purely in tropological terms, solely in the mode of "as if," misleads us. It hardly makes sense to speak of them as "distortions" (as we saw Freud doing a moment ago in "The Unconscious") unless one accepts the theoretical postulate that such transfers are more than just a "manner of speaking": that they are real psychic events and embody real determinations.

So for Freud transfers *really happen*. But they leave no direct record of their occurrence. Or at least none can be exhibited or discovered anywhere in the psyche. These transfers of meaning are our history, but for consciousness *there is no history of them*. Everything is preserved in the psyche *except* direct registration of the transfers by which psychic contents (ideas, presentations, affects) substitute for other contents. This is an important point, because it locates precisely where recollection runs aground, where the memory crisis

18. On "substitute formations," see also Freud's "Repression" (1915), *SE* 14:154, and his "Overview of the Transference Neuroses"(1915), 7.

manifests itself within Freudian thinking about the processes of the mind. Everything that psychoanalysis can cognize necessarily arises from a process of memory. Only through the zero-degree recollection that is the narrative of their existence can patient and symptom "present" themselves to analytic attention. *But memory fails absolutely to register how psychic contents are transformed.* This failure is what justifies interpretive "suspicion" and requires the intervention of the analyst. This is what necessitates the restoration of memory that from the beginning to the end of his career Freud conceived therapy to be.

Freud had no doubt that the process and the content of the substitutions that psychoanalysis seeks to retrace can be made intelligible. The memory of psychic transfers can be recovered. This is what it means to say that for psychoanalysis the psyche is a realm of meaningfulness. But such a claim of intelligibility is immediately equivalent to a claim about memory. For the process of the mind by which contents are retained while being transferred and transformed is the very mechanism that, read from the other direction, *constitutes* intelligibility.

Everything that happens in the narrative that is our psyche is thus purposive, hence comprehensible. Here are some of Freud's thoughts on this point from the formative period of his career:

> Experience has taught me to require that every psychical product shall be fully elucidated. ("On the Psychical Mechanism of Forgetting" [1898], *SE* 3:294)

> The dream-thoughts are entirely rational. (*Interpretation of Dreams* [1900], *SE* 5:506)

> [Previous writers on dreams] have underestimated the extent to which psychical events are determined. There is nothing arbitrary about them. (Ibid., 514)

> I believe in external (real) chance, it is true, but not in internal (psychical) accidental events. (*Psychopathology of Everyday Life* [1901], *SE* 6:257)

These are strong claims. What kind of conception of the psyche could make sense of them?

Psychic contents have a history and, in principle at least, this history can be produced. These claims are predicated on a conception of determination that supposes the operation of strict causality within the psyche. To understand a mental representation within psychoanalysis thus implies the possibility of mapping the representations (conscious and unconscious) carrying transformations of its content. It supposes that the specific genesis and form of each substitution can be explained by reference to determinations that are not simply offered *sui generis*, but have some sort of objective existence and functioning within the psyche. To put it more briefly, Freud says that within our psyches contents circulate, many of which are disguised or distorted derivatives of others to which access is denied us. He claims that through psychoanalysis these substitutes can be identified for what they are, and brought back into their proper relation with the real contents that are represented within them only through such distortion. In effect, analysis will enable us to remember what was purged from our memory.

Of course the possibility of sustaining these claims has been vociferously contested. The holders of such antipsychoanalytic positions dispute the epistemological postulates of Freud's interpretive model. In a classic argument, Karl Popper maintained that Freudianism was not a scientific theory because it could not be tested—in particular, Popper said, its hypotheses could not be falsified. He consequently viewed the theory's accounts of psychic events as scientifically vacuous. Adolf Grünbaum, though no less hostile to Freud than Popper, has contradicted Popper's claim that psychoanalytic propositions are untestable. Grünbaum rather argued that they can indeed be tested, and that when they are they can be shown to be inadequate or mistaken. Ludwig Wittgenstein attempted an independent attack that maintained that whereas Freud thought he was giving *causal* arguments for the presence of particular representations in the psyche he was only giving *aesthetic* ones: putting two factors together in a kind of delusive repetition of the "post hoc ergo propter hoc" fallacy. Sebastiano Timpanaro subscribed to Popper's doctrine of falsifiability and believed that Freudian explanations were necessarily underdetermined, leaving room for such a superabundance of explanatory hypotheses that none of them could be regarded as demonstrable.[19]

19. The general thrust of the "nonfalsifiability" argument can be seen in this extract

On the other side of the argument, let us consider two approaches that seek grounds for crediting Freud's claim to elucidate the real relations obtaining between psychic contents, despite the divergence of his paradigm and practices from what is often assumed to be the situation in the "hard" (or deductive) sciences.[20] Both arguments seek to enlarge the category of the scientific by noting that certain disciplines are widely believed to attain it without exhibiting a complete parallelism with experimental physics. Jürgen Habermas aligns psychoanalysis with history. He elucidates a category he calls "narrative explanation": "We show how a subject is involved in a history" (*Knowledge and Human Interests*, 262). Such an account is not predictive but retrospective; it cannot establish in advance which of many possible outcomes will eventuate, but it *is* capable after the fact of explaining both the conditions of possibility of what happened and, to some degree, its meaning.[21] In effect, it parallels the implicit (and often explicit) promise of psychoanalysis to *restore memory*: to recover the connections that obtained in an individual's history, but whose traces were lost through unconscious repression.

A second (though convergent) approach is taken by Carlo Ginz-

---

from Popper: "It is a typical soothsayer's trick to predict things so vaguely that the predictions can hardly fail: that they become irrefutable" (*Conjectures and Refutations: The Growth of Scientific Knowledge*, 37). See also Adolf Grünbaum, *The Foundations of Psychoanalysis: A Philosophical Critique*; Wittgenstein, "Conversations on Freud"; and Timpanaro, *The Freudian Slip*. Ricoeur summarizes the classical criteria in philosophy of science for the scientificity of a theory in *Freud and Philosophy*, 345–46.

20. Concerning the scientific claims of psychoanalysis itself, Richard Wollheim argues that for Freud, with his early training in the positivist atmosphere of nineteenth-century neuropathology, the thesis of psychic determinism was equivalent to a commitment to science, which Freud understood according to the deductive paradigms that were credited with scientificity in his period. Wollheim believes that although the details of Freud's analytical protocols evolved considerably following his early neurological work, the model of science implicit in the 1895 "Project for a Scientific Psychology" continued to define the standard of reasoning to which his work aspired; see *Sigmund Freud*, 59, 72. Habermas, though sympathetic to the claims of psychoanalysis to interpretive truth, believes that Freud's conflation of psychology and natural (or experimental) science was simply a mistake; see *Knowledge and Human Interests*, 253.

21. This notion has clear Hegelian roots. It seems generally convergent with the view Freud takes in "Constructions in Analysis" (1937), his final reflection on the complex of questions at issue here; see *SE* 23:257–69. Habermas identifies the distinction between such contingent, historical accounts on the one hand and the deductive claims of experimental or "hard" sciences on the other as one between "interpretations" and "theories"; see *Knowledge and Human Interests*, 261. Ricoeur also understands the disciplinary methodology of psychoanalysis as resembling that of history; see *Freud and Philosophy*, 374.

burg (see "Clues: Morelli, Freud, and Sherlock Holmes"). The term
of comparison to which Ginzburg appeals in seeking a basis for the
claims of psychoanalysis to scientific status is the group of disciplines
that constitute what Ginzburg calls the "conjectural" sciences. These
disciplines (history, archaeology, geology, physical astronomy, pale-
ontology, and particularly medicine) cannot meet the criteria of deductive reasoning derived from "Galilean" science, and do not claim
to do so. Results in these disciplines always carry "an element of
chance" (92). The sort of certainty we believe may be possible in
physics is unattainable for them. The causes of this limitation or divergence are basically two. To explain them Ginzburg takes medicine as an exemplary case. First, he points out, a disease presents
itself differently in each patient; second, our knowledge about it is
always to some degree indirect, since the secrets of the living body
are generally out of reach. In the "conjectural" sciences, experiments
cannot be controlled or repeated. Causes cannot be replicated; hence
there is no alternative but to infer them from their effects (103). But
for Ginzburg such inference is reliable. After all, we take the medicine the physician prescribes.

I have not summarized these diverse positions to decide whether
or not psychoanalysis is a science. That debate will continue. Rather,
I want to point out how closely its terms repeat cardinal elements in
the century-long disquiet about memory that has been my concern in
this book. In particular, the dispute about the truth claims of psychoanalysis recalls the contrasting memory models of *reproduction* and
representation that have arisen repeatedly in my discussion—the
first endowed with just the same digital certainty, the same capacity
to rematerialize reality, that locks out randomness in the structure of
formal deduction in physics; the second functioning to establish a
series of irreducibly unpredictable connections in the mode of unlimited semiosis or transfer of significations that nonetheless remains a
perfectly coherent model of meaning—contingent, but never random. Elements of both of these divergent paradigms coalesce and
intertwine in Freud's theory of the preservation of our past and simultaneously stress it to the point of internal contradiction. This intrinsic heterogeneity within the psychoanalytic paradigm may help to
explain the intensity and the irresolution that have characterized the
debate over the scientificity of Freudianism. For within the structure
of Freud's model these perhaps irreconcilable elements nonetheless

cohere, each on its own separate side, with crucial doctrines of the competing models of scientificity that have been marshaled for and against the claims of psychoanalysis. The memory crisis parallels this debate and to a degree may even be said to foreshadow it. Reading psychoanalysis within the frame of the memory crisis casts reciprocal illumination upon each of the terms and helps us to frame their cultural significance.

What is still and always at stake is the warrant for understanding our present and our past. The progression from a purely deductive conception of the basis of psychoanalysis to the more speculative and interpretive models offered by its defenders still leaves unresolved the question of when such a warrant expires. For example, Ginzburg's argument for a possible basis for psychoanalytic truth claims nonetheless construes them as more speculative than even Habermas did. With Ginzburg, we take yet another step away from the sort of positivist account of truth concerning the psyche that Freud seems to have been attracted to over the greatest portion of his career. The question is, how far can one conjecture and speculate concerning the character of the relations posited between psychic contents before any reasonable claim to have "understood" or "interpreted" these contents collapses under the weight of underdetermination and uncertainty?

✿❀❁

> One and only one of these logical relations is very highly favoured by the mechanism of dream-formation; namely, the relation of similarity, consonance or approximation— the relation of "just as."
>
> —Sigmund Freud, *Interpretation of Dreams* (1900), *SE* 4:319–20

> Reversal, or turning a thing into its opposite, is one of the means of representation most favoured by the dream-work.
>
> —Sigmund Freud, *Interpretation of Dreams* (1900), *SE* 4:327

In Freud the postulate of intelligibility is sustained at the cost of significantly lowering the threshold for licit explanation. In effect,

intelligibility is attained by allowing for absurd connection. There is
nothing intrinsically shocking in such a move. If we are to understand the activity of the psyche, such an extension of our concept of
rationality seems indispensable. As in Freud's early work on parapraxes, a scientific psychology is obliged to make sense even out of
phenomena, behaviors, and relations that make no apparent sense.
For as I have repeatedly observed, *anything* in the psyche can substitute for *anything else at any time*. There is no a priori constraint
whatever on psychic associations and transfers. Yet each such connection must in principle be comprehensible. This consequence was
sufficiently disquieting that Freud was led repeatedly to address it.
For example, concerning the fantastical relations obtaining between
the elements of dreams, with a suitably restrained amusement he
wrote: "No connection was too loose, no joke too bad, to serve as
a bridge from one thought to another" (*Interpretation of Dreams*
[1900], *SE* 5:530).

But the effect of this bewildering lability is not simply humorous.
If we remind ourselves of the *anxiety* attending mnemonic and semiotic slippage that I first considered in connection with Baudelaire's
Swan poem, the affect accompanying the experience of such slippage
from sign to sign, from psychic content to psychic content, from
meaning to meaning, can manifest itself as disquiet or even as dread.
In this book I have spoken repeatedly of the distress engendered by
the memory crisis, by modernity's experience of an uncertain and
tense relation to the past. As this "crisis" is manifestly a metaphor,
the anxiety I claim attends it may have also seemed metaphorical.
But whatever its status before psychoanalysis, with Freud this anxiety becomes literalized. And psychotherapy takes relieving it as a
critical social and individual goal. In Freud's understanding, psychoanalysis arises in response to the disorienting disjunction of consciousness from its past, hence from the affective locus of much upon
which we call to stabilize the present. In seeking to account for the
problems and pathologies that stress our lives, we look for explanation to our own histories. We attempt to recover the origins and the
determinants that indenture our present. But our investigation
leaves us afloat in the aporias of memory, in the limitless and seemingly haphazard associations sustained within our psyche, none of
which unproblematically elucidates *how* the past remains so banefully active within us. We have too many associations to have mean-

ing. Memory overloads us as it simultaneously under-explains us. The disquiet that arises in such a situation might remind us of Pascal's image of human beings adrift in anguish in a boundless and dizzying cosmos.[22]

Psychoanalysis combats the anguish of memory's lability by offering the security of interpretation. Interpretation settles the seeming limitlessness of association. The uncontrollable exchange of *everything* finds its antidote in the projection of some *specific* thing, which calms the vertigo and reestablishes the present as a site of stability. But what founds such restabilization itself? The chain of logic underlying the Freudian interpretive enterprise rests (as I have argued) on two principles whose function is to insure intelligibility and interpretive boundedness: that chance is not to be credited in psychic life, and that the unconscious memory is eternal. The first of these principles warrants the interpretive chain offered by the analyst; the second provides the ground legitimizing such chains. The past is thus recaptured for the present. And (at least in its most optimistic construction within psychoanalysis) it is managed in such a way that its impenetrability for this present is resolved.

To produce these effects, psychoanalytic interpretation, having taken a realist view of the psyche's processes of distortion and substitution, projects its interpretive procedures as their epistemological analogue. In this sense we might say that Freud conceives *analysis* in the image of *repression*. The work of interpretation is like the dreamwork; its procedures are imagined to be of precisely the same order—specifically, just as purposive and just as materially realist—as those it seeks to undo. It maneuvers in the same space as the transfers and substitutions that have necessitated its intervention to begin with, and plays them backward.

Thus if the representations of psychic contents exhibit what Freud termed "condensation," (see *Interpretation of Dreams* [1900], *SE* 4:279), analytic interpretation will unpack them; if conscious contents have lost experiential ties with their real determinants through "displacement" in a chain of associations, analysis will retrace the metonymic connections to their authentic source (see *SE* 5:339). In all cases interpretation seeks to exchange psychic substitutes for their originals. In this way the conversion into the somatic that early on

22. Blaise Pascal, Pensée 197, in *Pensées*, 1:139-43.

Breuer and Freud defined as the *symptom* (*Studies in Hysteria* [1893–95], *SE* 2:206) is linked back in therapy to a traumatic excitation that could not be otherwise managed by the patient. Such a notion of the reestablishment of original connection is a constant in the development of psychoanalysis. In "Constructions in Analysis" (1937) Freud returns to it: "We know that [the patient's] present symptoms . . . are the consequences of repressions . . . : thus that they are a substitute for these things that he has forgotten" (*SE* 23:258).

Conceptually, the simplest substitute formations bear the most patent connection to the contents they replace. This is what Freud called the relation of "just as" (*Interpretation of Dreams* [1900], *SE* 4:320). The most transparent case is neurotic repetition, where the relation is straightforwardly mimetic. In the psyche (as Freud had theorized in his early neuropathological work) certain patterns become "facilitated" (*SE* 2:206–9). Recurrences are programmed by such preestablished patterns. For example: "[The dream-work] merely follows the paths which it finds already laid down in the unconscious" (*Interpretation of Dreams* [1900], *SE* 5:346). Or: "[Defenses] become fixated in [the patient's] ego. They become regular modes of reaction of his character, which are repeated throughout his life whenever a situation occurs that is similar to the original one" ("Analysis Terminable and Interminable" [1937], *SE* 23:237). Beyond noting the similarity that constitutes it, understanding the pattern means tracing it to the repressed experience it involuntarily imitates, and in which it was first established.

Such patterns become diagnostic by virtue of their very persistence. This is what makes transference a powerful analytic resource:

> Each individual . . . has acquired a specific method of his own in his conduct of his erotic life—that is, in the preconditions to falling in love which he lays down, in the instincts he satisfies and the aims he sets himself in the course of it. This produces what might be described as a stereotype plate . . . which is constantly repeated—constantly reprinted afresh—in the course of the person's life. . . . The libidinal cathexis of someone who is partly unsatisfied [will] be directed as well to the figure of the doctor. . . . This cathexis will have recourse to prototypes, will attach itself to one of the stereotype plates. ("Dynamics of Transference" [1912], *SE* 12:99–100)

Patients reenact their most characteristic life patterns in relation to the analyst. But patterns repeat and proliferate generally. Thus the structures characteristic of what Freud termed "erotic life" become paradigmatic for other behaviors: "A man's attitude in sexual things has the force of a model to which the rest of his reactions tend to conform" ("Notes upon a Case of Obsessional Neurosis" [The "Rat Man]" [1909]; *SE* 10:241). Such generalizations of initially restricted or local behaviors instantiate an interpretive insight that Carlo Ginzburg believed was itself characteristic of Freud's period: that an individual's identity "can be recognized in his every characteristic, even the most imperceptible and slightest" ("Clues: Morelli, Freud, and Sherlock Holmes" 107). Here metonymy is taking on the force of a sovereign determination.

Conceptually, these paradigmatic behaviors are substitute formations because their connection with the determining experience they reenact has been repressed. They stand in for conscious memory, and hence become subject to interpretation. As Freud put it, "[the patient] is obliged to *repeat* the repressed material as a contemporary experience instead of, as the physician would prefer to see, *remembering* it as something belonging to the past" (*Beyond the Pleasure Principle* [1920], *SE* 18:18; emphasis Freud's. See also "Remembering, Repeating, and Working-Through" [1914], *SE* 12:151).

Freud found himself attending to a variety of repeating phenomena through which, as in a kind of involuntary memory very distant from Proust's, the past was inappropriately projected into the present: the distorted recollection of early material in dreams and symptoms; the recurrence of behavior patterns that he termed "acting out"; the imitation of more general paradigms in the transferential relation to the analyst. "[The patient] repeats all his symptoms in the course of the treatment" ("Remembering, Repeating, and Working-Through" [1914], *SE* 12:150). Repression may make it difficult to recover the memory traces at the root of such recurrent and apparently aberrant behaviors, but their resemblance to the behaviors that reenact them makes establishing their responsibility a relatively straightforward interpretive act.

But those are the simple substitutions. In other cases, connections can be much less evident. They can attain an abstraction or an intricacy that appears positively eerie. The metalepses that the psyche generates (or at least that Freud attributes to its functioning) can be truly vertiginous. The Wolf Man case exemplifies the sort of tangled interpretive rewritings of clinical evidence that psychoanalysis generates in a search for the truths it can never attain through direct observation of the data of the unconscious.

Opponents of psychoanalysis fault Freud on two fundamental grounds. Some accept the notion that neuroses arise in repression, but argue that Freud's interpretations in a specific instance were intrinsically underdetermined: that the pattern of facts adduced could equally support a different construction (or many different constructions) of the neurotically causal repression. Many critical accounts of Freud's handling of the Dora case take this tack. Opponents in this group point to the notion that Freud's own concept of "overdetermination" itself argues that no unilinear or unambiguous connection from fact to interpretation, from cause to result, can exist in the world of the psyche.[23] Other opponents of psychoanalysis simply deny that repression operates in the ways Freud hypothesized—examples would be Wittgenstein or Grünbaum.[24]

My concern here is to comprehend Freud's "mnemo-analytic" model for understanding our past, not to attempt to adjudicate claims concerning the validity of psychoanalysis. Even if Wittgenstein or Grünbaum are right, we would still have to account for the extraordinary influence of Freud's interpretive system on comprehension in the most diverse areas of the human sciences; for, foundational arguments against Freud aside, claims of *underdetermination* and *misinterpretation* made against him need to be considered in the context of an attempt to understand the basis of his hermeneutics. They point to areas of play within psychoanalysis that suggest just how profound a rethinking of the empirical is entailed in Freudian interpretation.

I want to address this problem by examining Freud's concept of "negation [*Verneinung*]." Negation (or "denial," as it is sometimes called) institutes a seemingly simple form of interpretive rewriting.

23. See particularly a number of the essays in Charles Bernheimer and Claire Kahane, eds., *In Dora's Case: Freud—hysteria—feminism*. This is also the general position of Timpanaro, who believes that Freud's interpretations are arbitrary; see *Freudian Slip*, 88, 179.

24. See Wittgenstein, "Conversations on Freud," particularly 7, and Grünbaum, *Foundations of Psychoanalysis*, particularly chap. 8.

In the spirit of its own arithmetical designation, we can say that it adds a minus sign to a content in the psyche. Freud gives negation a particularly interesting status. In his essay on the concept, he writes: "A negative judgement is the intellectual substitute for repression; its 'no' is the hall-mark of repression, a certificate of origin—like, let us say, 'Made in Germany'" ("Negation" [1925], *SE* 19:236). Negation, in this sense, is as close as consciousness can get to repression without losing consciousness itself. We could say that negation seizes the disappearance of its referent "in the act"; it catches it at the very moment of its slippage into the epistemological limbo of system *Ucs*.

Here we leave the world of Freud's analogical and mimetic "just as" and enter a realm of more radical, even heroic, interpretive transformations. Negation may be arithmetically simple—but *hermeneutically* it is a much trickier operation. The analyst rewrites the "no" of negation as a "yes." There can be no more flagrant example of the arrogation of psychoanalytic authority against the patient. If we can simply invert what we hear from consciousness, need our hermeneutic dominion *ever* end? Freud was acutely aware of the scandal such untrammeled analytical sovereignty appeared to pose to the canons of rationality. He took up the problem quite strategically at the opening of "Constructions in Analysis" (1937), his final paper on psychoanalytic technique. Speaking of a scientist who had generally been fair-minded about psychoanalysis, Freud continued as follows:

> On one occasion, nevertheless, he gave expression to an opinion on analytic technique which was at once derogatory and unjust. He said that in giving interpretations to a patient we treat him upon the famous principle of "Heads I win, tails you lose." That is to say, if the patient agrees with us, then the interpretation is right; but if he contradicts us, that is only a sign of his resistance, which again shows that we are right. In this way we are always in the right against the poor helpless wretch whom we are analysing, no matter how he may respond to what we put forward. (*SE* 23:257)

Freud's humorous adoption of this paradigmatic objection (cast toward the end of the passage in an ironic *style indirect libre* that might have done credit to Flaubert) leads of course to a defense of the procedures of psychoanalysis. Freud is at pains to show that interpretation is never simply free to deny the patient's denial. As the

mark of science is rule-bound, disciplined constraint, so Freud seeks
to demonstrate that the analyst's procedures are principled. Freud
consequently addresses the problem of the limits of interpretation.

I will return to the theory and practice of these constraints, but
first I want to consider the consequences of the rewriting that
Freud's concept of negation instantiates. It is evident that the model
of *Verneinung* applies to situations beyond the explicit denial on the
part of an analytic patient of a fact or an interpretation offered by the
analyst. Negation is the paradigmatic instantiation of the founding
principle of any hermeneutics of suspicion, that things do not mean
what they say. In particular, this structure brings us back to Freud's
understanding of memory, to his doctrine that forgetting is a *form of
recollection*. The inversion of meanings shared by these interpretive
structures (*no* means *yes*; *forgetting* is *remembering*) permits re-
situating the question of the mutation of signifiers within the field
of psychoanalysis. These mutations contain the propensity for the
convergence, indeed the fusion, of contraries. Such reversals are intrinsic to what Timpanaro termed the "mode of reasoning" within
Freudianism (*Freudian Slip*, 11). They produce a paradox that psychoanalysis focuses more acutely than any of the other interpretive
systems with which Ricoeur associated it, a limiting case for the modulations of meaning.

When a signifier can come to signify its contrary, when the rule of
noncontradiction is itself rewritten such that *p* and *not-p* may show
up as synonymous, the instability of meaning reaches a critical point.
Having once established the decoupling of appearance from signification, the effort to limit this instability or lability then becomes the
essence of Freudian interpretation. Positivism claims that facts interpret themselves. Positing the essence/appearance disjunction
abruptly annuls this axiom. But then the necessity arises of theorizing restabilization of what otherwise risks becoming significatory disorder. What is necessary is a kind of meta-modulation theory: a
methodology that preserves the "play" in the system that permits
what virtually no one questions—that things often bear non-apparent
meanings—while at the same time forestalling the abyss of absolute
slippage or pure relativism in which nothing can reliably be *said* to
mean anything. A meaning-system must be finite. At this point,

Freud's projection of analysis as possibly "interminable" locates the most troubling implication of his own insights.

彩❖彩

> [You will argue that] in consequence of the reversals of every kind of which dreams are so fond, it is open to the interpreter to carry out a reversal like this in connection with any passage in the dream he chooses.
> —Sigmund Freud, *Introductory Lectures on Psycho-Analysis* (1916), *SE* 15:228

The paradigm of negation only repeats the general form of the connections psychoanalytic interpretation always establishes: one thing—one presentation, affect, or idea—replaces another. "Owing to the repression of its proper representative [the affective or emotional impulse] has been forced to become connected with another idea, and is now regarded by consciousness as the manifestation of that idea" ("The Unconscious" [1915], *SE* 14:177–78). But for consciousness the original association has been lost, and the substitute that has replaced it will demonstrate no necessary link whatever with the content it now represents. The consequences of this interruption of cognizable relation are considerable.

As the links it traces become less mimetic, less rooted in recoverable experience, less motivated by the naturalized connections of Freud's "just as," the interpretive rationality of the Freudian system tends increasingly to mutate from substantive to formal.[25] The transformed presentations of psychic contents produced (say) in "transference" assuredly alter the appearance of such contents. Yet at the same time the mimetic relation between admittedly diverse terms— like Freud's "just as"—that "transference" determines appears rela-

25. Max Weber made the tendency toward increasing abstraction and formalization in interpersonal and conceptual relations—and the corresponding diminution of their ethical or experiential content—a powerful tool for understanding the process of modernization. See *Economy and Society: An Outline of Interpretive Sociology*, 1:85–86, and *From Max Weber: Essays in Sociology*, 298–99. For an account of Weber's more general relation to culture and modernity, see Lawrence A. Scaff, *Fleeing the Iron Cage: Culture, Politics, and Modernity in the Thought of Max Weber*.

tively natural to us. We search for a way to characterize the apparent
accessibility to our understanding of such connections; we speak of the
"organic" or "felt" relationships between the terms that lie at the heart
of metaphor. But not all the forms of substitutions and exchanges that
psychoanalysis defines appear so naturally accessible to understanding.

As we move from "transference" to "negation," the felt relations of
metaphor seem to mutate into the more abstract successions of
metonymy. To be sure, both of these figures of relation between
diverse terms "make sense." But the model of sense-making each
instantiates nonetheless separates them considerably along the vector
that runs from affect to intellection. And as they approach the latter,
more formal pole of the typology of possible relations psychoanalysis
seeks to cognize, I think we could agree that the increase in abstraction becomes a source of the anxiety that accompanies the necessity
of interpretation to begin with.

Such a result is not surprising. It does no more than to register the
affect that necessarily accompanies any hermeneutics of suspicion.
Psychoanalysis theorizes a fundamental interruption in the supposedly "natural" relationship between our conscious emotions and
memories on the one hand and their ostensible referents on the
other. This separation opens the space for interpretation and simultaneously makes it indispensable, but such a reconception of the
reliability of memory and the authenticity of feeling necessarily resonates in feelings themselves. *"Suspicion" has emotional consequences.* The more we conceive conscious psychic manifestations as
decoupled from retrievable affective roots, the more their contents
are autonomized or reattributed, the more we will then experience
such abstraction as disorienting or even as malevolent.[26]

In the modern period there has been a powerful tradition of seeing

26. As was true when I employed the term "malevolence" in the course of considering
Proust's analysis of memory, my use of this term here is intended to recall my discussion
in Chapter 4 above of the unexpected emotional resonances produced by an analogous
decoupling that Foucault claimed emerged in nineteenth-century characterizations of the
sign. I argued that such a decoupling was essential to Baudelaire's "Le Cygne," and accounted for much of the poem's affective charge. Around the same time as Foucault's
essay, in a passage that I already cited as an epigraph to Chapter 4, Jacques Lacan discussed the emotional consequences of such semiotic mutations strikingly: "The slightest
alteration in the relation between man and signifier . . . changes the whole course of
history by modifying the moorings that anchor his being" ("The Agency of the Letter in the
Unconscious, or Reason since Freud," in *Écrits: A Selection*, 174).

abstraction in such terms. We could trace it (for an early and influential example) to the Hegel of the *Phenomenology of Spirit* (1807), in particular to Hegel's discovery that by virtue of its exclusion from the productive activity of those it nominally commands, even the seeming sovereignty of Lordship is unexpectedly subverted.[27] Abstraction in this pejorative sense arises when the experience of individual or social process has been fragmented, thus when the recoverable *memory* of some subject's activity has been shattered or suppressed. The issues that have concerned me in this book are foregrounded in such conceptions. Modernity's self-consciousness has produced a concerted critique of the increasing splintering of experience. Much of social theory in the modern period has been a reaction to it. Whether in Tönnies's notion of *Gesellschaft*, in Weber's *rationalization*, in Lukács's *reification*, or (though no doubt this is a more controversial claim) in Freud's *repression*, such perceptions have animated analyses of the denaturalization of traditional social forms, of human relations, of processes of production, of cultural expressions, and of subjectivity itself.[28] This broad critique has been focused in the image of an uncanny disruption in the experiences of time and particularly of recollection. In the fragmented memory of modernity, identity seemed no longer to have any secure foundation. Time's disarticulation and memory's dysfunction have been variously attributed to the increasingly urban, industrial, and instrumental reality of post-Revolutionary existence, or to the psyche's stressful accommodation to culture's demands. But whatever the causes, these effects have provided modernity's registers of the fragmentation of experience and the abstraction of felt connection with its contents.

What I have been calling the memory crisis is experience's intu-

27. G.W.F. Hegel, *Phenomenology of Spirit*, sec. 190–96.
28. Fredric Jameson has provided suggestive discussions of this issue throughout his work, often focusing on the notion of reification and allied concepts. See particularly *The Political Unconscious: Narrative as a Socially Symbolic Act*, 62–63, in which there is a brief but striking analysis of Freud in relation to this problem, and *Late Marxism: Adorno, or, the Persistence of the Dialectic*, 16, in which Jameson examines neurosis and repetition in the light of Adorno's critique of "identity" theories. See also Ferdinand Tönnies, *Community and Society*, and Georg Lukács, "Reification and the Consciousness of the Proletariat," in *History and Class Consciousness*. On Weber's relation to this problem, see note 25 to this chapter. On several other thinkers in whom a parallel problematic is active, see David Frisby, *Fragments of Modernity: Theories of Modernity in the Work of Simmel, Kracauer, and Benjamin*.

ition of this complex. This intuition projects a world whose meanings have been radically displaced or emptied out: a world in the image of the three thousand six hundred disarticulated seconds that accumulate every hour in Baudelaire's "L'Horloge." These radically impersonal beats materialize time's mockery of our desire for meaning as— to return to the Freudian mode—they unrelentingly tick off our progress toward Thanatos. This portrayal of abstraction and lost connection bears arresting resemblances to tendencies in Freud's account of the psyche and its truths. The experientially emptied links that are all that repression leaves behind in consciousness seem to instantiate the same dissociation that modernism's critics have stigmatized more generally. We think of relations as providing cognitive grasp on the phenomena they relate, but the modern period has subverted such a logic and produced a paradoxical paradigm of linkage whose function is to *disconnect*. For Freud, relationless relations of this character are the heart of the experience of consciousness. Such structures defeat affective memory and comprehensible meaning, and replace these with something like Baudelaire's dead logic of ordinality, a series of replicating metonyms whose significance, whatever it might be, is always elsewhere.

⋆⋆⋆

"A far-fetched, forced explanation," it will be said.
　　—Sigmund Freud, "The Psychical Mechanism of
　　　Forgetfulness" (1898), SE 3:293 n. 1

The recession of meaning thus constitutes the hermeneutics of psychoanalysis, not as a danger toward which the system tends, but as a fundamental presence. In Freud's psyche, I claimed earlier, *meaning means changing*. Having devised an unprecedented hermeneutic complex by which such vertiginous transformations are theorized as having been produced, psychoanalysis requires another complex to restabilize them. For by virtue of its progressive bleaching out of the experiential connections that characterize metaphor, the logic of pure metonymy that Freud had formalized in the psychic mechanism of "displacement" risks becoming a kind of meta-trope for psychoanalysis itself. The diffusion and disappearance of any authoritative

subject who could be said to have *chosen* the transfers of meaning
that characterize signification in the Freudian psyche threatens to
leave us only with a totally abstract structure of contiguity. In effect,
from this perspective, psychoanalysis puts logic on the threshold
of the Lyotardian "link."[29] The discourse of consciousness is thus
conceived as cohering in terms only of the most attenuated forms of
connection. On this reading, in which the subterranean contiguities
of modernist and postmodernist models surface once more, history
risks transformation into a narrative of increasingly radical parataxis: recollection, perhaps, but (as we might say) recollection loboto-
mized.

The analytic process is intended to palliate these limitations. Although the relations between psychic contents and their substitute
formations may appear abstract or incomprehensible to the patient,
the analyst sees meaningful connections. The transformations with
which analysis works may not be predictable, but they are made retrospectively intelligible by the quasi-historiographical process of interpretation theorized by Ricoeur or by Habermas. And they are pat-
terned according to the taxonomy of psychical transformations that
has become synonymous with Freudianism.

The taxonomy of these "transfers" of meaning is well known. The
concepts of the Freudian technical vocabulary are paradigms for the
modes of transfiguration of the psyche's contents. Here are the principal operators into which Freud classified such transformations:

> *condensation, displacement,* and *secondary revision* (man-
>   ifested in dreams and in other psychic representations)
> *rationalization*
> *compromise formation*
> *conversion*
> *repetition* (involuntary "acting out")
> *transference*

29. The "link" (*enchaînement*) envisions the maximum possible suppression of any logic
of determination and leaves only sequentiality: *this*, then *that*. It aims at freeing discourses
from the domination of pre-scripting. On the "link," see Jean-François Lyotard, *The Differend: Phrases in Dispute*. See also Richard Terdiman, "On the Dialectics of Postdialectical Thinking," 113.

repression (and the displaced reversals known as the *return of the repressed*)

projection

introjection

reaction formation

screen memories, deferred action [Nachträglichkeit], and *retroaction* (distortions of recollection)

reversal

negation

sublimation

These are the named and charted processes that in its developed form psychoanalysis cognizes in its attempt to follow the transmutations of the psychic contents we are unable to observe directly. At various points in his work, Freud offers skeleton checklists that catalog the varieties of systematic distortion to which the representations of consciousness may have been subjected, and plot the modes of their analytic decoding and retranslation. For example:

> In interpreting any dream-element it is in general doubtful
>   (a) whether it is to be taken in a positive or negative sense
>   (as an antithetic relation)
>   (b) whether it is to be interpreted historically (as a recollection),
>   (c) whether it is to interpreted symbolically, or
>   (d) whether its interpretation is to depend on its wording.
>   (*Interpretation of Dreams* [1900], *SE* 5:341)

Such repertoires of the orders of distortion and transformation might almost remind us of the protocols for manipulating the subject in a classical fugue (a genre whose rules allow its theme to be sounded straight, or upside-down, or backward, or both at once). Freud's list of possible variations offers interpretation the solace of a pattern; however the existence of such patterns, as I have been arguing, is far from conclusively reassuring. Indeed, the passage from *The Interpretation of Dreams* in which Freud lays out what Peter Gay termed his dream-work tool kit continues with a logic that is more discouraging than heartening: "Yet, in spite of all this ambiguity, it is fair to say that the productions of the dream-work . . . present no greater difficulties to their translators than do the ancient hieroglyphic scripts to those who seek to read them."[30] But Champollion (who deciphered hieroglyphics in 1822) was able to count on the stability of the source language whose translation he sought. Only its connections with the target language were difficult to establish; and he had the Rosetta stone to guide him. In his interpretive practice Freud was obliged to assume not only the protean arduousness of the connections to be elucidated, but a positively hallucinatory instability in the source itself. On Freud's own showing, Champollion had the easier job.[31]

Yet the arduousness of interpretation does not imply its impossibility. However difficult, the retranslation of psychic substitutions seems reasonable in principle. If they happened, they should be able to be uncovered. But how can the analyst know that the *right* substitution has been detected? No doubt we must assume an irreducible quotient of interpretive finesse that it would be impossible to reduce to purely mechanical operations. Freud did not decline this less rationalizable component of hermeneutic acumen—what he terms "skill . . . , experience and . . . understanding" (*Introductory Lectures* [1916], *SE* 15:229).[32] But however credible they may be in the hands of expert practitioners, such claims of *métier* cannot found an interpretive science by themselves. Freud put the object of the exercise clearly in "Constructions in Analysis" (1937): "What we are in search of is a picture of the patient's forgotten years that shall be alike trustworthy and in all essential respects complete" (*SE* 23:258). But in deciding the trustworthiness or exhaustiveness of any inter-

30. Freud, *Interpretation of Dreams* (1900), *SE* 5:341. Peter Gay's phrase is from *Freud: A Life for Our Time*, 113.

31. In "Constructions in Analysis" (1937) Freud pursued an analogous comparison between psychoanalysis and archaeology, concluding that the psychoanalyst "works under more favorable conditions than the archaeologist" because of the availability of a live and responsive patient (*SE* 23:259). This conclusion is far from self-evident.

32. Whence the sort of nontransmissible claim of authority in Freud's assurance to the young man whose inability to recall a complete quotation from Virgil's Dido Freud had narrated in a celebrated analysis in *The Psychopathology of Everyday Life*. To this man's testimony that he could discern no connection between his slip and a thought that had crossed his mind when he considered it, Freud breezily replied, "You can leave the connection to me" (*SE* 6:11). Timpanaro was particularly irritated by this seemingly cavalier assumption of authority ("Once again, the 'connexion,' the famous connexion which could 'be left' to Freud"). See *The Freudian Slip*, 55, 139.

pretation there must be principles upon which reliance can be placed. Freud theorized several that the analyst might count on to select among the potentially unlimited interpretations of a given psychic content.

The problem was to find a foundation that could limit the slippage of significations, to locate a point where meaning stabilizes instead of simply repeating its protean referral to yet another substitute signifier in the chain of interpretive rewritings. If it is not to risk incoherence, every hermeneutics of suspicion must appeal to such a foundation. For Marx, in the extended sense he and his interpreters gave to the term, this pertinent ground is the "economy." For Freud, in a similarly expanded definition which he struggled to establish against the prurient reductionism of psychoanalysis's early opponents, it is "sexuality."[33]

The appeal to such foundations always seeks to reground the lability of thought and the endless variability of interpretation that characterize diverse forms of Idealism—and constitute their paradigmatic limitation—in some material base that can norm their meanings and limit their otherwise endless mutability. The privilege of materiality is paradoxical. It lies in the prosaic *lack* of imagination by which matter seems phlegmatically to go on being itself, whatever our thoughts about it. Of course nothing is quite that simple, and this independence from the conceptual which we attribute to materiality in a first attempt to frame its defining difference turns knottier in all manner of theoretical attempts to understand how we might make sense of it. But the dull stability of a world somehow distant from thinking and insulated from its extravagant flights is the desideratum at the heart of the attempt, in any hermeneutics of suspicion, to discover the material *limit* of what can be suspected of disguise.

33. "In psycho-analysis the concept of what is sexual comprises far more [than the need for coitus or analogous acts producing orgasm and emission of the sexual substances]; it goes lower and also higher than its popular sense. This extension is justified genetically; we reckon as belonging to 'sexual life' all the activities of the tender feelings which have primitive sexual impulses as their source, even when those impulses have become inhibited in regard to their original sexual aim or have exchanged this aim for another which is no longer sexual. For this reason we prefer to speak of *psychosexuality*, thus laying stress on the point that the mental factor in sexual life should not be overlooked or underestimated. We use the word 'sexuality' in the same comprehensive sense as that in which the German language uses the word *lieben*" ("'Wild' Psycho-Analysis" [1910], *SE* 11:222–23).

In the effort to locate such a limit, Freud concentrated upon three touchstones that might cloture the slippage of analytic understanding.

The first was the projection of an ultimate ground on which all interpretations must be based and by which they could be validated. The logic of such a ground is easy to understand. Stuart Hampshire put the objective of psychoanalysis in these terms: "If the hypothesis of total memory is correct, the earliest memories of the earliest instinctual needs, and of primitive frustrations of instinctual need, must be the terminus of explanation."[34] If up to that terminus everything risks slippage, the terminus could stop it. In this spirit Freud proposed that "we follow a pathogenic complex from its representation in the conscious . . . to its root in the unconscious" ("Dynamics of Transference" [1912], *SE* 12:103). Presumably, the interpretive effort could be arrested there. But the daunting problem of the boundary between systems *Ucs.* and *Cs.*, which I discussed in Chapter 7, makes this procedure problematic. It is clear what salutary ground it would offer for analysis. If we could know the contents of the unconscious, they would offer a wonderfully cogent warrant for any interpretation. But offering them as such a warrant begs Freud's question quite precisely, for the contents of the unconscious are the problem psychoanalytic interpretation must solve to begin with. They can hardly interpret themselves.

In "The Aetiology of Hysteria" (1896) the dilemma of signifying slippage and the consequent problem of the ground were already unmistakable. Freud wrote: "We must . . . ask ourselves: where shall we get to if we follow the chains of associated memories which the analysis has uncovered? How far do they extend? Do they come anywhere to a natural end?" (*SE* 3:197). His answer was unequivocal: "Whatever case and whatever symptom we take as our point of departure, *in the end we infallibly come to the field of sexual experience*" (199; emphasis Freud's). Sexuality, as he put it in this early essay, was the "*caput Nili*," the source of the neuropathological Nile (203). It became the source of the psychoanalytic one as well.

The interpretive privilege of sexuality for Freud is perceptible in this hydrological metaphor, and in alternative geological analogies through which he regularly expressed it. It would indeed be reassur-

34. Stuart Hampshire, "Disposition and Memory," 90.

ing to discover a material *source* or *base* to bound the otherwise
labile space of analysis. Toward the end of his career, Freud increasingly leaned toward an explicit hypothesis that such a foundation was
organic or material: that "sexuality" (inevitably a complex and mobile
phenomenon in the more volatile realm of psychology) was ultimately an expression of "biology" (whose objective, physical substrate restored some of the stability of the empirical to the otherwise
vertiginous permutations of psychic contents).

Thus in "Analysis Terminable and Interminable" (1937), speaking
of two "themes" that psychoanalysis had identified as irreducible
characteristics of males and females respectively, Freud wrote the
following: "We often have the impression that with the wish for a
penis [the female "theme"] and the masculine protest [the male
"theme"] we have penetrated through all the psychological strata and
have reached bedrock, and that thus our activities are at an end. This
is probably true, since, for the psychical field, the biological field
does in fact play the part of the underlying bedrock" (*SE* 23:252).[35]

In this way, at the end of his career, and at the end of an essay that
itself takes the *possibility of ends* as its fundamental preoccupation,
Freud (at least tentatively) locates the point at which psychoanalytic
activity attains a conclusion. That conclusion is that *conclusion is outside psychoanalysis*. For whatever biology may be, it is not cognizable through the protocols that attend to the profoundly diverse
realities that compose Freud's psychic topography. To rely on the
facts of materiality to arrest the slippages of psychoanalytic interpretation inevitably takes you beyond psychoanalysis itself.

Of course from within psychoanalysis Freud is explicit in indicat-
ing where you should look for an interpretive stopping point. He had
begun by projecting psychoanalysis as the rehabilitation of memory—as producing the "trustworthy" picture of the patient's "forgotten years" about which he spoke in "Constructions in Analysis" (*SE*
23:258). In Chapter 7 I considered certain limitations of dyadic semiotics, in particular the inability of structuralist theories to model the
directionality of time. But Freudian psychoanalysis is not similarly

35. It is well known that Freud's identification of the fundamental gender themes has
been powerfully and cogently contested by more recent theorists. The issue here, however, is not the content, but the biological *locus* he attributed to psychoanalysis's interpretive "bedrock." Recently, Joseph Sandler has edited an important collection of studies of
Freud's celebrated essay: *On Freud's "Analysis Terminable and Interminable."*

restricted. Not only can psychoanalysis model time's direction, but it explicitly privileges the archaic, "the earliest memories of the earliest instinctual needs" of which Stuart Hampshire speaks in the passage I quoted. If we could establish these contents, analysis could terminate quite neatly.

But these memories are unconscious, and however imperishable they may be, they are also systematically inaccessible.[36] Indeed, this is why the attempt to attain the traces that ground all other contents in the psyche institutes the hermeneutic paradigm of transfer, exchange, and rewriting that has concerned me in this chapter. But *that* paradigm cannot cognize time, only directionless (and as Freud himself clearly saw, limitless) connection. And unfortunately nothing in this *second* theoretical field can tell you whether a psychic content is veridical or hallucinated, whether it is earlier or later, whether it is fundamental or derivative. So Freud's reasoning in "Analysis Terminable and Interminable" means that memory can have no security within psychoanalysis, nor can the past ever offer a reliable warrant for interpretation. Biology may well impose a limit to the signification of psychic contents, a "bedrock" for understanding. But if so, it does this from *outside*, and through determinations theoretically disjunct from the logic of interpretation Freud otherwise prescribed for analytic meaning.

The second principle Freud essayed to ground the potentially limitless rewriting of psychic contents that emerged as a consequence of his interpretive system was the hypothesis of a general lexicon of psychic symbolism that could potentially make interpretation a version of "translation" and provide an objective control on it.[37] The interpretive issue to be resolved was the seemingly unconstrainable

36. In particular, they are the theoretical victims of what Freud termed "infantile amnesia," which affects the first years of life, and which he theorized arose as a result of the repression of infantile sexuality. See *Three Essays on the Theory of Sexuality* (1905), *SE* 7:174–76. In a classic reconsideration of the problem in 1947, Ernest Schachtel proposed an interpretation of childhood amnesia that depends upon the inability of human beings to register memories prior to the formation of conventional patterns (schemata), which are absent in early development. He was concerned with an anomaly in Freud's account, that failed to suggest why *all* recollection of early childhood (and not just the memory of infantile sexuality) should be obliterated in consciousness. See "On Memory and Childhood Amnesia."

37. In the *Introductory Lectures* (1916) Freud explicitly terms such symbols "stable translations" (*SE* 15:151).

variability of psychic associations, the structure of a seemingly free circulation of meanings that will allow anything to represent anything else. But if there were *invariant* elements in the representations in dreams and more generally in the psyche, these would establish an objective limit to the displacements that threatened the system's overall ability to produce stable meaning.

Freud's attitude concerning such a hypothesis was complicated by his painful dispute with Jung, for whom such universal symbolism (associated with Jungian concepts of "archetypes" and "collective unconscious") became a key doctrine (see Forrester, *Language and the Origins of Psychoanalysis*, 194). Given the notorious sense of betrayal Freud experienced at Jung's defection, it may seem surprising how much convergence exists between their theoretical positions, at least in the restricted area of universal psychic symbolism and its consequences for interpretation. But the notion that there are invariants in such symbolism grew progressively in Freud's conceptualization. In *On the History of the Psycho-Analytic Movement* (1914) he acknowledged Wilhelm Stekel's influence on this point, though never Jung's (see *SE* 14:19; see also *Interpretation of Dreams*, *SE* 5:350 [passage from 1925]). A dispute exists about whether such a doctrine was present in Freud's theory from the first, or whether it only arose in the later course of his development.[38] But it is clear that the most significant statements of it in Freud's work are from the period of his maturity. In particular, the important section in *The Interpretation of Dreams* devoted to "representation by symbols" only took on its fully developed form in 1914 (see *SE* 5:351–404; see also the *Introductory Lectures* [1916], *SE* 15:151–65).

In Chapter 7, in relation to the overall question of memory's permanence in his notion of the psyche, I attempted to construct the logic of Freud's Lamarckianism. Despite the discomfort it has caused to many of his most fervent supporters, the scandal of Freud's commitment to the doctrine that acquired characteristics can be inherited resurfaces here in connection with his hypothesis of universal symbolism. Consider this passage from the *Introductory Lectures* (1916): "It seems to me . . . that symbolic connections, which the

38. Jean Laplanche and J.-B. Pontalis, *The Language of Psycho-Analysis*, s.v. "symbolism."

individual has never acquired by learning, may justly claim to be
regarded as a phylogenetic heritage" (*SE* 15:199). This is no casual
claim. As Grubrich-Simitis put it, "the basic biogenetic-Lamarckian
concepts, including the idea of the inheritability of archaic layers of
the world of symbols, runs like a warp through the fabric of [Freud's]
total work."[39] Freud's Lamarckianism has predictably been downplayed or ignored by theorists more attracted to the heady play of
unlimited semiosis that they attribute to the interpretive paradigms
of psychoanalysis. But however perverse it may seem, Freud's
Lamarckianism won't go away.

The meaning of this tendency in his thinking must now be clear:
Lamarckianism provides a *ground*. It clotures the unpredictability of
individual associations and provides a lexicon against which they can
be read. To revert to Freud's analogy of the decipherment of hieroglyphics, universal symbols provide the Rosetta stone that can open
up the seeming arbitrariness of the rest of the psychic text. Whatever
the clinical evidence that may have induced Freud to credit the hypothesis of universal symbolism, it is important to see how clearly
such a doctrine answers the theoretical need in the system of psychoanalysis to find a "bedrock" that might stabilize the interpretive process and allow for its principled termination.

But even admitting that benefit to interpretation, it is important to
note the degree to which the reality that affords it—the preservation
of an ageless inheritance of fixed meanings set against the seemingly
infinite mobility of psychic associations that Freud had otherwise
theorized—splits the theoretical field of psychoanalysis in a manner
that must appear theoretically arbitrary. From the perspective of interpretation, the archaic constancy to which interpretation can appeal to stabilize itself is at the same time totally opaque: a fact that
may be true and that if so will surely help to establish truth, *but that
in itself makes no sense*. There is an irony that the very element to
which one might appeal to cloture the randomness of psychic associations itself appears so random. Like the reference to biology that I
examined in the preceding section, there is something irreducibly
reductionistic in this solution to the problem of psychoanalytic interpretation.

39. Ilse Grubich-Simitis, "Metapsychology and Metabiology," 97.

The third and final hermeneutic touchstone Freud entertained in
the effort to discover how meaning might be determined within his
system is somewhat different. It is the hypothesis that interpretation
can be verified by the patient's reaction to it. For the purposes of my
discussion this is the least useful of the three principles Freud entertained, since its logic is restricted to the analytic situation and cannot
be generalized beyond it. However, some comment may nonetheless
be worthwhile.

Freud's pronouncements on this matter can be found throughout
his work, and they vary little. But as has already become clear, his
attention to the problem of interpretive randomness intrinsic to his
theory is most acute in the two 1937 essays to which I have referred
repeatedly in the course of discussing this issue. Here is what he says
in "Constructions in Analysis": "At the very start, the question arises
of what guarantees we have while we are working on these constructions that we are not making mistakes and risking the success of the
treatment by putting forward some construction that is incorrect" (*SE*
23:261). Indeed, that is the essential question. Freud's answer has
several parts.

Freud first explains on the basis of "analytic experience" how one
can know that a proposed construction is *incorrect*: "The patient remains as though he were untouched by what has been said and reacts
to it with neither a 'Yes' nor a 'No.' . . . If nothing further develops
we may conclude that we have made a mistake" (261).

Second, Freud addresses the problem (to which he has recurred
repeatedly throughout his work) of assessing the danger that, given
the intrinsic uncertainty of our grasp on psychic truths, a suggestion
by the analyst may in effect *substitute* for such truth and block access
to it. "The danger of our leading a patient astray by suggestion, by
persuading him to accept things which we ourselves believe but
which he ought not to, has certainly been enormously exaggerated. . . . I can assert without boasting that an abuse of 'suggestion'
has never occurred in my practice" (262)[40]

Third, Freud seeks to provide an answer to the objection that,
granted the hermeneutic sovereignty that psychoanalysis seems to

---

40. This assertion occurred as early as "The Psychotherapy of Hysteria" (1895); see *SE*
2:295.

authorize, analysts are free to turn either assent or denial on the part of their patients into verification of whatever interpretive hypotheses they desire—on the argument that "yes" means yes, but "no" means yes too. I deferred consideration of Freud's response to this widespread criticism when the issue arose earlier in this chapter. But in connection with my discussion of the possibility of stabilizing interpretation in psychoanalysis, it is important to consider it now. Essentially, Freud's answer is this: in psychoanalysis neither *yes* nor *no* necessarily means *any* specific thing. "We do not accept the 'No' of a person under analysis at its face value; but neither do we allow his 'Yes' to pass" (262). These signifiers, like all the others within the interpretive field of psychoanalysis, have no particular privilege and fall into the familiar Freudian pattern of hermeneutic indeterminacy. Freud's interpretive consistency would thus appear seamless.

But then something unsettling happens. To his assertion that patients' conscious reactions are no less equivocal than any other signifier in the world of the psyche, Freud adds the unexpected claim that, nonetheless, certain *indirect* signs produced by patients and accompanying their explicit responses to the analyst's proposed construction provide a completely reliable basis for assessing the accuracy of the analyst's suggestion. Freud puts it this way: "It appears . . . that the direct utterances of the patient after he has been offered a construction afford very little evidence upon the question whether we have been right or wrong. *It is of all the greater interest that there are indirect forms of confirmation which are in every respect trustworthy*" (263; emphasis mine). To those not practicing psychoanalysis, the clinical details of these confirmatory procedures may be of little interest.[41] But that they exist at all is surprising. For in a realm of daunting indeterminacy, they suddenly offer the promise of interpretive "bedrock." And indeed, Freud's language throughout the entire discussion of this issue in "Constructions in Analysis" demonstrates a particularly decided assurance: "such an abuse of 'suggestion' has never occurred in my practice"; "there is no

41. In brief, Freud claims that a correct interpretation will stimulate the production of new memories and connections on the part of the patient (261; cf. "Remarks on the Theory and Practice of Dream-Interpretation" [1923], *SE* 19:115). Or the patient will offer an indirect concession of the truth of the analyst's suggestion: "I didn't ever think" (263; cf. "Negation" [1925], *SE* 19:239).

justification for accusing us"; "forms of confirmation which are in every respect trustworthy."

The most troubling interpretive problem within Freudian theory is to know how we know when we have found the correct explanation for anything in the psyche. This is the issue that constantly underlies the two 1937 essays I have been considering here, "Constructions in Analysis" and "Analysis Terminable and Interminable." It may seem a facile move to analyze the analyst, but the apodictic tone of Freud's remarks, their untroubled and unhesitating resolution of the most profoundly worrisome difficulty within psychoanalytic theory, leaves the impression that this interpretive complication has been surreptitiously skirted or displaced.

As in the cases of Freud's reduction of psychic complexes to biology, or his projection of a lexicon of unambiguous symbolism that might be used to decode the labile substitutions and exchanges in the individual psyche, again we have a situation in which the logic of psychic associations, where any content can be related to any other, is suspended and a mode of univocal signification deftly substituted for it. Limitlessness is abruptly limited. In a world of ambiguity, it is convenient to have protocols of verification. But precisely by their secure resolution of the uncertainties of psychoanalysis, these mechanisms violate its assumptions so thoroughly that they seem the product of a *deus ex machina*, an external accident, rather than a response to any potentiality theorized from within the psychoanalytic system itself.

✿❀✿

> Is there such a thing as a natural end to an analysis—is there any possibility at all of bringing an analysis to such an end?
>
> —Sigmund Freud, "Analysis Terminable and Interminable" (1937), *SE* 23:219

Psychoanalysis is stressed between postulates of absolute intelligibility and absolute mobility of meaning. Stated thus, the problem seems to take the form of a logical antinomy. But of course the processes of the psyche are not primarily determined by abstract con-

cepts. They are real, material activities. Consequently, these theoretical imperatives look different in analytic practice. To begin with,
Freud is forthright in declaring that the theoretical ideal of complete
understanding cannot universally be achieved. The question arose in
The Interpretation of Dreams (1900), and his response was unequivocal: "It is in fact never possible to be sure that a dream has been
completely interpreted" (*SE* 4:279). And it recurred in the *Three Essays on the Theory of Sexuality* (1905): "It is not always possible to
trace the course of . . . connections with certainty" (*SE* 7:155). In
"'Wild' Psycho-Analysis" (1910) he says this: "One may sometimes
make a wrong surmise, and one is never in a position to discover the
whole truth" (*SE* 11:226). And finally, in "Constructions in Analysis"
(1937), he acknowledges that "every . . . construction is an incomplete one" (*SE* 23:263).

In analytic practice the theoretical contradiction setting the intelligibility of the psyche's processes against their uncertainty takes a
temporal form. The arduousness of interpretation, we might say,
translates into the *length* of the effort required to achieve it. As
Freud had acknowledged as early as "The Psychotherapy of Hysteria"
(1895), psychoanalysis is "laborious and time-consuming" (*SE* 2:265).
Or as he put it in *The Interpretation of Dreams* (1900), the analyst
"must bear in mind Claude Bernard's advice to experimenters in a
physiological laboratory: 'travailler comme une bête'—he must work,
that is, with as much persistence as an animal" (*SE* 5:523). Though
the theoretical contradiction between intelligibility and mobility can
not be sublated or erased, in interpretive practice it plays out as the
prolongation of the treatment, which cannot stop until the multiform
resistances of the unconscious succumb and release and reveal what
the psyche has repressed.

Analysis takes time. The implications of this prolongation in time
are more complex than they might seem at first.[42] As I have argued,
making time a factor in semiotic models presents problems. Viewed
narrowly, the tropological relations, the exchanges of meaning, the
bewildering transfers of "intensities" of which Freud had spoken in
"Screen Memories" and which characterize the fundamental activity

42. Ricoeur has considered the issue I raise here (and particularly the reasons psychoanalysis involves *work*) from a somewhat different angle. See *Freud and Philosophy*,
406–7.

of the psyche, appear instantaneous. They do not seem to involve temporality at all. But this is only one side of the psyche's process as Freud conceived it. In the traditional opposition between idealism and materialism that has repeatedly emerged as an issue in the development of his conception of the psyche, time locates itself on the side of the material, just as it did in my discussion of the registrations of system *Ucs.* in the preceding chapter. Time projects not a world of instantaneous (and presumably instantaneously reversible) exchanges, but a world of energies, entropies, and resistances, of work done and inscriptions laid down, of material, inherently directional change.

The problem of memory might appear to have faded from this portion of my discussion, but it resurfaces strategically here. For *memory inscribes the factor of time* that is absent in the labile and instantaneous exchanges of semiosis. Memory is how the mind *knows* time and registers change. In a tantalizing note in "On Narcissism" (1914) Freud speculated that the two faculties—remembering the past and perceiving time—developed together in the psyche. He considered the faculty of self-observation as their common source: "I should like to add to this . . . that the developing and strengthening of this observing agency might contain within it the subsequent genesis of (subjective) memory and the time-factor" (*SE* 14:96 n. 1).

This was only a tentative hypothesis, and Freud seems not to have pursued it further.[43] But it raises a consequential point. For what lies at the heart of the commonality he suspected may link the origins of *memory* and *time* as they function in the psyche is that both involve the establishment or registration of change in the material world. This characteristic had been present in his thinking about the psyche since his early neurological speculations in the "Project for a Scientific Psychology" (1895). There he wrote that "a main characteristic of nervous tissue is memory: that is, quite generally, a capacity for being *permanently altered* by single occurrences" (*SE* 1:299; emphasis mine).

In this sense, memory differs from perception and intellection. These latter processes seem inherently labile. To use the language Freud employed in "The 'Mystic Writing Pad,'" they form "no per-

---

43. He offered several speculations on the origin of the concept of time that related it to a vaguely sketched discontinuity in the functioning of system *Pcpt.-Cs.*; see *Beyond the Pleasure Principle* (1920), *SE* 18:28, and "The 'Mystic Writing Pad'" (1925), *SE* 19:231.

manent traces" (*SE* 19:230). Time is not a factor for them, for as they can form in an instant so they can disappear—literally—without a trace. But laying down a memory means (however microscopically) that *the world has been changed.* Memory's process inherently inscribes itself in time. Consequently, it becomes the analogue—and perhaps even the source—of the prolongation of the process of psychoanalysis itself. *Memory is why psychoanalysis takes time.*

For unconscious resistance is also a memory and possesses the material inertia of any memory system. Its inscriptions have irreversibly changed the psyche. They were brought about, as Freud put it in *The Interpretation of Dreams,* by "laborious work" (*SE* 5:578). Undoing them, canceling the determined forgetting they ensure, likewise means doing work in time. So interpretation is hard because (as we might say) it must lift the material weight of memory. Therapy is long because memory takes time.

No transformations occur within the psyche without there being an expenditure of energy. Any interpretation of Freudian interpretation that fails to take account of this materiality, that sees the flows and exchanges of signification as a gratuitous *combinatoire,* as the unconstrained play of infinitely compliant signifiers, fundamentally misleads us. On the level of practice, as I have suggested, it is impossible to say in advance why a particular content cannot mutate with what seems like absolute lability into any other through the seemingly limitless processes of displacement, condensation, and so on that carry out the relational business of the psyche. But in every case the reduction in unpleasure or gain in pleasure because of which the transmutations takes place reconnects the process of the psyche with process itself: with the materiality of time.

❧❀❧

> In the further course of the dream the figure of Irma acquired still other meanings.
> —Sigmund Freud, *Interpretation of Dreams* (1900),
>   SE 4:292

With the uncompromising and irreducible materiality of these processes in mind, what can we say in response to the critical question that lives at the heart of Freud's 1937 essay? Is analysis—is recollection, is interpretation—terminable?

In a note to "Analysis Terminable and Interminable," the editors of the *Standard Edition* cite a letter Freud wrote to Fliess (16 April 1900) that implies a reserved response to this question. The letter suggests that the work of analysis moves toward termination, but without ever attaining its end: "The asymptotic termination of the treatment is substantially a matter of indifference to me; it is for outsiders rather that it is a disappointment" (*SE* 23:215). And in the body of the essay itself, as I observed in the preceding chapter, Freud is gloomy about the possibilities of completing the cure and concluding the treatment. He even suggests that the analysis of the analyst must *itself* be regarded as always incomplete: "This would mean . . . that not only the therapeutic analysis of patients but his own analysis would change from a terminable to an interminable task" (*SE* 23:249).

On a practical level this conclusion is of course unrealistic. And Freud immediately reverts to practicality in suggesting that "whatever one's theoretical attitude to the question may be" (249), therapy *does* help patients. Once they have been helped they can stop their treatment. But the theoretical question thus put to the side remains haunting. Understanding the past, gaining control over the harm it causes, means achieving an interpretation of its contents that can bring their irrationality to reason. This isn't the same thing as comprehending *everything* in our psyche and exhaustively mapping its determinations. The latter task is authentically endless. As Stuart Hampshire wrote concerning the structure of understanding implied by Freud's model of the psyche: "If we accept the hypothesis of total memory of past satisfactions and frustrations, it certainly follows that we could only approach complete explanation of inclination and behaviour in any individual case through an interminable analysis" ("Disposition and Memory," 89). But short of that, a more general understanding may be possible. Despite the labyrinthine perplexity of a limitless but inaccessible memory, on the level of practice we achieve this every day. Therapy terminates; the patient learns to manage the ongoing anxiety of a past not fully rationalized or rationalizable. Such a modus vivendi may be enough, and may be all we can hope for within the swirling enigmas of the mnemonic.

But these questions measure the problem that has focused discussion from the outset of this book. Our memories are both a constant resource and an ongoing difficulty, an indispensable support and an unresolvable conundrum. Everyday life induces us to foreground the practical perspective. Yet on a theoretical level the deeper disquiet about memory persists in the very structure of the theory that enabled such a coming-to-terms on the level of practicality. At its origin psychoanalysis set out to reclaim recollection from the past's perversity and pathology—as I might put it in the perspective of this book, from the systemic disquiet that haunted a hundred years of the memory crisis. And in a sense that measures how consequential Freud's theory has been in reframing our understanding of the history alive within us, this effort to understand the past has largely *succeeded*. For modernity following Freud the range and role of memory has dilated extraordinarily, and it has been radically unlocked. Everywhere we look for meaning, memory's determinations focus our concern.

Yet for all this apparent centering of meaning in memory, memory's contradiction perversely subsists. Indeed, it has only grown more anxious as psychoanalysis has forced our understanding of the presence of the past further and deeper than ever before. In psychoanalysis, in a magnified image of the intractability of the memory problem, memory, while everywhere, is lost forever in an unconscious we can neither access nor change. And understanding, whose ambiguous but intimate links to the contents of the past conserved in memory I have sought to suggest, has become the most persistent puzzle of modernity. We could put it this way. In Freud, memory has entirely filled the psyche. Yet it has entirely disappeared within us. Psychoanalysis then seems a catastrophization of the mnemonic anxieties this book has sought to trace, a paroxysm of the memory crisis.

Conclusion:
Reading Memory

J'ai plus de souvenirs que si j'avais mille ans.
[I have more memories than a thousand-year-old.]
    —Charles Baudelaire, "Spleen,"
      in *Oeuvres complètes*, 69

Chaque jour ancien est resté déposé en nous.
[Each day of our past has remained archived within us.]
    —Marcel Proust, *A la recherche du temps perdu*,
      RTP 4:125; *RTP54* 3:544

The paradox of memory that emerges more clearly in Freud than anywhere before him rematerializes the problems that have occupied me in this book. Does the past ever go away? Can we ever gain control over it? Can we ever resolve its enigma? Psychoanalysis focuses these concerns with particular urgency, but they are not Freud's preoccupations alone. We could call them modernity's questions. And they lead to some consequences I want to consider in concluding my argument.

This book has been a reflection on the persistence of the past into the present, on the investment of contemporaneity by history. Such temporalities normally seem discrete, but they conjugate in memory. As I put it in Chapter 1, in memory time doubles back on itself. Its enigma arises in this convolution. There are, however, other modes of such folding in the neat successions of chronology. As memory pulls the past into the present, so desire and intention draw the fu-

ture toward us, or stretch contemporaneity beyond itself. By mo-
bilizing the dynamism potential in presentness, they shrink the field
of the not-yet, they begin to reverse its uncertainty.

The enterprise of theory displaces temporalities in the same way.
A theory programs *now* what may happen *then*. This anticipation of
what may be from the perspective of what is defines the sort of productivity one might hope for from any inquiry that tries to make
sense of how we understand our world. For inevitably the effort to
make sense aims at *changing* things. We seek to make them different
as a result of our work upon them. So in my attempt, in concluding
this book, to strike the balance of what may have been illuminated in
it, I want at the same time to project a *different* time. In particular, I
hope my analysis of the memory crisis might suggest some modification in our activity as interpreters. For the image I have given of
memory upsets some orthodoxies concerning how we understand the
past. The memory crisis particularly destabilizes a distinction that in
cultural theory has virtually become an article of faith. If this is so, we
might inflect a bit of our future as analysts of texts and of culture under
the influence of what we can recover in thinking about memory.

We say there are no facts, only interpretations.[1] What happens if
we bring this doctrine into contact with the problems of memory that
have concerned me in this book? Nietzsche's antipositivism then acts
to depreciate what I have been calling *memory as reproduction* in
favor of an unconstrained vision of *memory as representation*. Such a
position privileges the relationship to knowledge and to the past in
the mode that hermeneutics has defined, and conversely marginalizes or problematizes the empirical registers of our own or our culture's history. Psychoanalysis has frequently been understood along
these lines, just as Freud has been conceived as what I called a "hero
of semiosis."

Yet in my projection of it, psychoanalysis doesn't quite accommodate such a construction. Because of its centralization of memory,
psychoanalysis makes it harder to distinguish between the past's re-

1. The source of this familiar idea is Friedrich Nietzsche, *The Will to Power*, sec. 481.
Its circulation today owes most to the rediscovery of Nietzsche by French poststructuralism. See, in particular, Michel Foucault, "Nietzsche, Freud, Marx" and "Nietzsche, Genealogy, History." On Nietzsche's "perspectivism" and his critique of notions of "fact," see
Alexander Nehamas, *Nietzsche: Life as Literature*, chap. 2.

covery and the understanding we might have of it. Freud thus complicates our thinking about two questions that twentieth-century theory has increasingly (and I would argue reductively) disconnected: *How do we remember?* And *how do we interpret?* As modernity has inflected into postmodernism, these problems have increasingly seemed to refer to incommensurable epistemologies. But foregrounding the role of memory in culture and in our individual lives upsets the disjunction between them. However unexpected it might seem, this reconvergence can be understood on a straightforward basis. For as we have repeatedly noticed in the course of my argument, memory cannot distinguish between the register of facts and that of interpretations. It is unable to conceive their difference.

Both Proust and Freud make this clear with epochal force. Proust surely represents that our truth arises in our recollection of the past. But it is not only that in the experience of hypermnesia the recovered world has an immediacy, a reality as credible as the one we had been occupying when we tasted the *madeleine*. For Proust the convergence of significance and recollection is even more fundamental: it is that the meaning of our experience materializes in memory. Indeed, where else could it come from? Yet the strange structure of involuntary recollection upon which Proust insisted makes ordinary understanding of this situation suddenly problematic. For the notion that meaning is located in memory leaves open the question of *which* memory it lodges in or emerges from. Yet this question is crucial to understanding the relation between mnemonics and hermeneutics that I considered in detail in Chapter 8.

As I have argued throughout this book, memory is far from a unified or transparent register of our past. The pasts we carry but do not entirely cognize regularly rise to colonize our present. But once we admit the ways—whether subtle and subterranean, or entirely overt—by which this eerie domination of *now* by *then* can happen, then memory turns labyrinthine. At that point any notion of a self-identical and accessible subjectivity as the straightforward agent of interpretations of our lives—past *and* present—spins off into perplexities that disable the paradigms that might have seemed to credit the dominion of the hermeneutic. In particular, how might we integrate the repeated and insistent rematerializations of pain and unhappiness that I argued Proust purposefully and systematically screened with his doctrine of salvation by memory? Such experiences place the Nietzschean privilege granted to interpretation under the most consequential stress. For even as they *evade* conscious interpretation, they remain massively present and determinant nonetheless. Given their seemingly sovereign influence over our present and our consciousness, we might almost be tempted, despite Nietzsche's injunction from *The Will to Power*, to think of them as *facts*.

Freud was more systematically reflective concerning such matters. For him the impossibility of distinguishing memories from facts, or recollection from perception, had become an axiom as early as his 1895 "Project for a Scientific Psychology." I quoted the relevant passage (*SE* 1:325) in Chapter 7, and observed that Freud regularly assumed its doctrine and developed its significance in a series of later texts. But the consequences of this cognitive uncertainty are not simply abstract or theoretical, for psychoanalysis embodies and seeks to recontain a contradiction of extraordinary intensity between the mobile—even wanton—representations of psychic contents that circulate in consciousness on the one hand, and the massive *facticity* of the unconscious mnemonic registrations that on the other Freud posited as their source and cause. Notions of "free" interpretation must give way in the face of the timeless and monumental reproduction of the past that psychoanalysis lodges in the memory of system *Ucs.* These complications discomfit the Nietzschean dismissal of an order of the *constituted* that might resist the free rewriting of our meanings and *determine* interpretation. This is particularly an issue for the tradition of Nietzschean postmodernism, with its powerful commitment to evade subjection to any pre-scripting, any entailment, any master discourse.[2]

In our own period Nietzsche's doctrine has been taken as justification for an increasingly limitless hermeneutics. But something is missing in such a construction. However protean, volatile, or inaccessible our memories may be, they have a massive determining power that models of unlimited hermeneusis misrecognize. In this sense the Nietzschean position can be insidiously reductive, for it collapses precisely the tension that sustained the memory crisis and gave it its cultural force throughout the period I have been discussing in this

2. See Richard Terdiman, "On the Dialectics of Postdialectical Thinking."

book. By absorbing memory entirely into subjectivity, the complication of a problem that absorbed Europe for more than a hundred
years is simply made to evaporate. But it is difficult to believe that a
disquiet of that intensity could be so neatly resolved.

So I would argue that the Nietzschean dogma concerning facts and
interpretations has itself been interpreted with insufficient discrimination. The salutary effort in Nietzsche's "perspectivism" to supersede the naïveté of positivism's flat-footed belief in facticity in effect
induced a symmetrical distortion, in which it has almost come to see
that interpretation is entirely arbitrary, constrained by nothing at all.
But even if the memory model that I have been calling *reproduction*
now seems untenably simplistic, the effort to understand how memory has been understood in the modern period has made clear how
misleading it would be to construe the alternative model—what I
have termed *representation*—as insulated from any pressure exerted
by the weight of the constituted and the contents of the past.

I want therefore to raise again the problem of the mnemonic and
its relation to the hermeneutic, and seek to restore the power of its
paradox. To be sure, this must be done with delicacy. "Recollection"
at first might seem to throw us back to the supposedly docile world
of data that nineteenth-century positivism projected, to the realm of
"how it really was" that Ranke conceived as the historian's field of
knowledge. And it is true that at one time much humanistic research
sought simply to recover the "facts"—to resurrect lost elements of
knowledge that (at least for those alive in the period when they had
been functional) once posed no mystery at all. Scholars made their
careers by reversing entropy; they sought to solve the mysteries that
the passage of time had produced by rediscovering information once
patent and unproblematical. Such research presumed stable archives
that awaited the moment when they would be called upon to deliver
up their secrets. Information was *there*; it only needed discovery.
These conceptions seem distant now. But if we transfer the archive
inward, the paradigm is not so far from the Freudian and Proustian
projections of how we understand ourselves.

As I have tried to show, such archives of the contents of the past
were a particular obsession in the period of the memory crisis. A
variety of neurological, cultural, and psychological theories held that

events once recorded were preserved forever.[3] Proust's involuntary memory and Freud's system *Ucs.* look like the diegetic and psycho-analytic analogues of such stable and unerring repositories of the past. Proust of course made the analogy central to his work. As for Freud, such a parallel between the *unconscious* and the *archive* is far from an imposition of extrapsychoanalytic interpretation. Beginning with his discussion in "The Psychical Mechanism of Forgetfulness" in 1898 (see *SE* 3:296), Freud made constant reference to such archival repositories—in history and culture on the one hand, in the psyche on the other—in the course of his efforts to explain psychoanalysis and to elucidate how it could bring our lost meanings back to light. I alluded to two cases of which Freud made much: the arduousness of relearning Egyptian hieroglyphics (see *SE* 5:341) and the difficulty of recovering the significance of London's Charing Cross (see *SE* 11:16–17). Both of these projects sought to restore elements of the past that time had converted from commonplaces to arcana. Freud and Proust thus converge in rooting understanding in the recovery of vanished memories.

Today the positivist model of data once known, then lost, then found again seems archaic. We live in a time when the human sciences have focused their inquiry on the intricacy of interpretation rather than on the resurrection of facts. Contemporary paradigms of cultural theory have little sympathy for what they conceive as the naive empiricism of interrogations of "history" in the effort to recover for the present what the past knew perfectly well. But Freud's projection of the psyche as a memory machine upsets the heady lability of hermeneutics and the now-consecrated depreciation of fact in favor of interpretation. In psychoanalysis (as I argued) much of the work of interpretation is understood as a resurrection of the past of our psychic processes—their contents, their origins in experience, and their successive transformations.

Such a paradigm thus hardly suggests that our understanding can be freed from the dominion of the constituted and the servitude to

3. See Chapter 6. See also Chapter 7, particularly note 36. Compare Baudelaire's image of memory in one of his "Spleen" poems as a "chest of drawers overstuffed with accounts [*bilans*]" (Charles Baudelaire, *Oeuvres complètes*, ed. Y.-G. Le Dantec and Claude Pichois, 69).

facts. It makes the past irreducibly determinant in our comprehension of the present. And thereby it complicates the segregation of *fact* and *interpretation* that contemporary paradigms have tended to presume—indeed to celebrate. In our contemporary understanding of psychoanalysis, the intricate *inter*-determinations of memory and meaning have often been shadowed by Freud's more heroic hermeneutic feats. But in its essence psychoanalysis is still a mnemo-analysis. And memory still incorporates a powerful intuition that the past is not just our own invention. *The past still answers us and still constrains our own response to it.* We need a model that can frame the weight by which such a mnemonic register bears down upon our understanding as it does upon our lives.

We can understand the importance of the dynamics in Freud's paradigm that downplayed the sovereignty of the empirical. Freud needed to clear a space for interpretation. Recall his 1924 addendum to "The Aetiology of Hysteria," cited in Chapter 7, in which he wrote about how important it had been for him and for the evolution of his science to free himself from what he called "my *overvaluation* of reality" (*SE* 3:204 n. 1; emphasis Freud's). Yet as I tried to show in the course of discussing this passage, such a move only displaced the importance of the empirical realm from consciousness to the uncanny but immutable registrations of the unconscious. There is no doubt that this displacement—however crucial to the model of mature psychoanalysis—reintroduced a tension in Freud's paradigm. However troublesome we might find it, this tension cannot be resolved by simply ignoring one of its terms. Psychoanalysis is constitutively ambivalent about how it construes the mnemonic realm and how it comprehends the past. But at the least it complicates the depreciation of the empirical that has become a contemporary orthodoxy. Today the space for interpretation has stretched to the horizon. What is necessary now is to see how it might be bounded.

So we need to consider again the seemingly disparate categories of *fact* and *interpretation*, of *reproduction* and *representation*. The essential tension between them in Freud's framing of the psyche suggests rebalancing the paradigms of interpretation. Then recovery of the data so dismissively associated with positivism—and seemingly so outworn in our interpretive practice—would be rehabilitated. My notion is admittedly heterodox, but if it has any value, it arises be-

cause we have tended to forget how deeply implicated in our interpretations are the contributions to them rooted—in however equivocal and complex a manner—in our memories. This complex intertwining of mnemonics and hermeneutics might help us to resituate
our thinking about what we do when we read a text, or participate in
culture, or seek to understand our present so profoundly invested by
the past.

Marx's reconception of the commodity early in the memory crisis
is a prototype of the reframing of memory's role in interpretation that
psychoanalysis later forced to new levels of centrality and pervasiveness. As reifications are forgettings (see Chapter 1), *so inevitably interpretations are recollections.* At the foundation of Western attempts to make systematic sense of things, Plato had argued that
hermeneutics is always a maieutics. Findings are always *re*-findings,
as Freud maintained in a passage I cited as epigraph to Chapter 6
(see *SE* 7:222). Marx's model is convergent on this point at least. In
his reconceptualization of the commodity, understanding must recover the frozen and forgotten history of the object to reconceive it
as a process. The commodity then becomes comprehensible as a
story about its production, and about the production of a society in
which its own production became the object of a strategic suppression. Reification deprives objects of their history; it cancels our memory of their past. To be sure, in its manifestation as what Bourdieu
termed "genesis amnesia," such mechanisms of arrest enable creation
of the stable entities necessary for middle-class intellectual or economic practice. But by implying the necessity of reversing the process of such memory loss in our efforts at understanding, "genesis
amnesia" also marks the space in which the destabilization of such
reified entities can begin, and in which the recovery of forgotten
activity and practice can gain a purchase upon the real. In the course
of such an interpretation it becomes clear how much the hermeneutic always owes to the mnemonic.

Such a dialectical model of understanding stands awkwardly between the apparent clarities of positivist facticity on the one hand
and unlimited semiosis on the other. Both of these latter paradigms—however intricate they may prove in practice—posit a simple principle at their hearts. But restoring the tension *between* such
polar simplifications lets us see to what degree these models were

themselves obliged to institute a repression of elements not conso-
nant with their univocity. These are the elements—always in danger
of getting forgotten—that a theory of meaning attentive to the meaning of the memory crisis might help us to restore. Interpretation is
thus neither so bound as the positivists believed, nor so free as the
celebrants of the untrammeled play of signifiers have claimed. But
these twin, symmetrical reductions of the interpretive problem situate its difficulty. The *complications* of memory turn out to be what
both of these paradigms are unable to apprehend. Such intricacy is
what my investigation of the memory crisis has tried to recall.

What we need now is a model of cultural and textual understanding that could conceive how the contents of our memory and our past
retain—and how they could assert—the capacity to ground or norm
interpretations, so that the relativism of the latter might be brought
into contact with a principled and nuanced complex of constraints.
What would be the character of such interpretations normed by
memory, but responsive to its representational and transformative
nature? In order to begin to see what such a model might look like,
let us return to Freud. Freud believed that two kinds of knowledge
underlie an interpretation within psychoanalysis. The first was structural, based on certain dynamics in ontogenetic development (the
"stages" and so on), and on the topography of the psyche—elements
he posited were the same in all humans. These structures, we might
say, are "hard-wired" into us. In determining our psyche they become effective *in the form of memory*. That, in essence, was what
(following his surprising Lamarckianism) I argued concerning Freud's
belief in phylogenesis. Here is one form, then, in which the psyche's
memory system necessarily constrains interpretation.

The second area of knowledge is the analyst's experience with the
patient. This experience essentially seeks to map the analysand's own
memory. The process by which it does so parallels and may be said
to adapt fundamentally literary protocols of reading—in thematics
and stylistics particularly. By organizing the remembered patterns
active within an individual psyche, it seeks (out of the psyche's limitless flux) to foreground the elements that are already forceful—often
banefully so—in the patient's psyche.

There is no question that, given sufficient acquaintance and hermeneutic skill, powerful and coherent interpretations of this recol-

lected and reenacted material are possible. But how much authentication of such interpretation would it be reasonable for us to expect? In particular, what chance exists that the analyst's interpretation will turn out to be the *right* one? Here the *representational* side of memory's dialectic intervenes to suggest modesty in our expectations. The experience of generations of readers suggests strong reasons for skepticism concerning claims for the univocal truth of any interpretation. The notion of articulating a single correct reading is subverted by the multiplicity of intelligent and persuasive—but distinctly divergent—interpretations offered by readers of texts. The conditions of psychotherapy of course proscribe a parallel situation. For although two readers can be said to read the same text of *Hamlet* or *The Interpretation of Dreams*—each interpretation destabilizing its rivals and being destabilized by them—the psychoanalytic situation makes such control procedures impossible.[4]

My point is not to attack interpretation within psychoanalysis, but rather to urge us to view the hermeneutic system that Freudianism proposes with less insistence on some unattainable decision concerning truth claims and more on an assessment of the tensions existing within and indeed motivating the system of interpretation itself. The aim would be to achieve a more adequate and a more critical understanding of what is really at stake in psychoanalysis as a paradigm for making sense of individuals, and, simultaneously, to enable a more powerful reintegration of the analytic project in cultural dynamics operating beyond the quasi-medical or therapeutic setting in which analysis situates itself.

Two principles, standing in a relation of dialectical tension, form the basis on which such a reinterpretation of psychoanalytic interpretation must be founded. The first emphasizes the weight of past

---

4. We should also note how divergent are the views within psychoanalysis itself even concerning the *structural* paradigms that frame understanding of the patient's individual case—since these also represent "readings" of the situation of which interpretation must make sense. If we consider the notion of developmental "stages" and psychic processes, we immediately encounter differences between the original structures Freud proposed and his own and subsequent revisions. None of these paradigms has achieved hegemony, and the divergent schools of analysis struggle over them still. For example, consider the differences between Melanie Klein's, Jacques Lacan's, and Otto Kernberg's diverse understandings of what Freud originally termed *Spaltung* ("splitting"). On Freud's concept, see Jean Laplanche and J.-B. Pontalis, *The Language of Psycho-Analysis*, s.v. "splitting of the ego."

Conclusion

contents laid down in personal and even in collective or species history, and recoverable in the extraordinarily diverse forms of memory that modernity has powerfully brought to light and laid bare. The second points to a constitutive *underdetermination* inherent in the functioning of texts. Texts—or memories—cannot constrain us to any *specific* interpretation. Perceptions of this underdetermination in the relation between text and interpreter have emerged with particular pertinence and acuteness in the modern period. There is too much going on in texts or in the psyche for any interpretation to exhaust them and their potentiality for generating meaning. There is too much loaded on words, images, symbols, and recollections for their significance to be entirely *re*-producible within the compass of an analysis. The interpretation whose length exceeds that of the object it nominally responds to has thus become familiar—my own analysis of Baudelaire's "Le Cygne" in Chapter 4 is such a case. To be sure, getting analysis right is less consequential when one reads *Hamlet* than when one seeks to help someone overcome the suffering of neurotic repetition. For despite the virulence of some battles for interpretive dominance, the literary world has room for everyone's reading. But the human realities of the analytic setting, in which there is real suffering to be alleviated, make such an openness to alternatives more troubling. Yet the fact that we might wish for greater certainty in that setting does not automatically produce the mechanism for achieving it.

The truth is that "truth" is a derivative objective of interpretation. Our encounters with any form of constituted representation—texts or memories—are intrinsically *underdetermined*. Any attempt exhaustively to exhibit their determinations fails, not because of any lack of critical stamina or acumen, but because the horizon of such exhaustiveness is an impossible form of *possession* of the impalpable. This is straight Freudian doctrine. In "Negation" (1925) Freud derived the function of "judgment" from the instinctual impulses of the oral stage: "'I should like to eat this,' or 'I should like to take this into myself and to keep that out'" (*SE* 19:237). But we cannot ever *possess* texts, memories, language, or symbols in that way. What we can know and articulate in any communicative situation—whether literary or psychological—cannot be fenced off or absolutely bounded, owing to characteristics inherent to language, subjectivity, and epistemology.

The notion that one can only legitimate an interpretation by a claim of its veridical character has two equally deleterious results. First, it forestalls the free-floating attention to the material presented for understanding that captures the conditions under which interpretation must actually be conducted. Such a sense of the material's manifold *possibility* is closed off when an essentially interminable process is put under an injunction to conclude. Second, it constrains the repression of those dissonant elements that pull in the direction of the *interminable* side of the temporal binary that Freud considered in his celebrated essay. The notion of a univocal interpretation represents a kind of parti pris, a bias whose unscientific character constitutes an example of the impulse to *shut down* interpretive possibilities. But a sense of the range of such possibilities constitutes the interpretive situation itself.

More and less adequate interpretations surely exist. Everyday experience demonstrates this persuasively. But the move from "adequate" to "correct" is a different matter. It may have little consequence for the practice of psychoanalysis, since a person can only have one analysis at a time. Its conduct is therefore subject to no experimental control, and the procedures that might authenticate it (as I argued in Chapter 8) are ambiguous at best. But the postulate of "correctness" has profound significance for cultural history and understanding. One may be able to cure or alleviate suffering with an *adequate* interpretation, but such a cure does not end the tension inherent in any claim that an interpretation is founded in truth, that from the materials available to the analyst one can integrally and unerringly reconstruct the psychic transfers whose own manifold uncontainability on a different register Freud so brilliantly illuminated. Overdetermination itself denies the theoretical possibility of an exhaustive "rightness."[5] In the functioning of communicative systems there can be no warrant that understanding has exhausted its object—has (in Freud's terms) completely "swallowed" and possessed or fully digested it. In the signifying world in which interpretation is necessary to begin with, something always escapes recuperation. Sig-

---

5. "The same dream may perhaps have another interpretation as well, an 'overinterpretation' which has escaped [a beginner in the business of interpreting dreams]. . . . My readers will always be inclined to accuse me of introducing an unnecessary amount of ingenuity into my interpretations; but actual experience would teach them better" (Sigmund Freud, *Interpretation of Dreams* [1900], SE 5:523).

nifiers do not cease to be significant at any given point, nor fully deliver up their meanings at some final moment of reckoning. "In the further course of the dream the figure of Irma acquired still other meanings" (*Interpretation of Dreams* [1900], *SE* 4:292). There is no end to this movement.

The problem is not getting the right reading, but getting reading right. The point is not to *possess* the past, but to *understand the force of its claim upon the present* without thereby supposing that such a claim is sovereign, or that contemporaneity is simply swamped or displaced by memory. This more open attitude toward interpretation resembles a complex of impulses we can detect throughout Freud's career and at diverse places in his theoretical development—from his commitment to resisting the literalism of "localization" theories, to his growing indifference to the veridical status of certain recollections emerging in treatment, to his skepticism about the possibility of ever reaching the end of the associative chains whose existence and pertinence he had theorized more powerfully than anyone else. If his commitment to what he conceived as science at times induced him to speak as if the objective of psychoanalysis was to produce an unimpeachable and univocal account of psychic reality, the multifariousness and uncontainable diversity of that reality elsewhere led him to stretch the bounds of interpretation (as in his regular speculations about "yet one more" layer of meaning in a dream) to the point where the very notion of a bound seemed itself to have been superseded. Interpretation can best be understood in the equipoise and in the tension of these polar, contradictory dynamics. It has increasingly seemed that memory works in just that way.

The figures I have been considering in this book, and Freud perhaps most consistently among them, have refigured the way the past subsists within us. Memory increasingly seems not a faculty but a trajectory.[6] The closer we look at how memory has been conceived

---

6. In this, Freud agrees with much recent research holding that there is no specific memory locus in the brain—neither a place where a specific registration is stored nor a specific region where storage occurs (see Israel Rosenfield, *The Invention of Memory: A New View of the Brain*). The retention of sensory, affective, and cognitive material diffuses through our neural tissue—as if we had to conceive of memory not as a "department" of neurological function, but as coextensive with functioning itself. A model that might be

since the nineteenth century, the clearer becomes the need t balance it in the delicate dialectic—between reproduction and representation, between fact and interpretation, between recollection and understanding—that we still need to devise and to refine.

In the modern period the weights attributed to the notions of "identity" and "change" have mutated radically. Historical experience and the reflexes of such experience in thought have made continuity seem extraordinary, and the extraordinary more or less constant. A Heraclitan willingness to normalize *change*, to conceive stasis—identity, reproduction, univocal preservation or replication—as exceptional or unattainable, has increasingly claimed cogency. Not surprisingly, such significatory mobility has not been integrated into cultural assumptions without strain or conflict. Consider the nostalgia for grounded, ascertainable, and *total* recuperation of the past that, however ambiguous its covert determinations, becomes acute in Proust, or the desire for recovery of the archaic memory traces at the origin of symptoms and neurotic patterns that underlies Freud's concept of the psyche.

But as the dynamics within modernity have been internalized, these impulses to retain or rehabilitate the fantasy of mnemonic *reproduction* have given way to an almost provocatively cool insouciance concerning the possibility of *any* authoritative registration, conservation, or transmission of the traces of our history, of the contents of the past. The medium in which memory functions has increasingly become conceived as an unceasing transformative flow of time, indifferent to direction and dubious about cause. Such a postmodern mutation of the object of my investigation, such a diffusion of the problem of memory into the general process of culture, make this book itself terminable. I began by claiming that even memory has a history. I argued that in the early nineteenth century something significant divided people's experience of and speculations

---

seen as reaching toward a comparable formulation—the concept of "organic memory"—was conceived in 1867 by Henry Maudsley, and became influential after its reformulation in 1870 by Ewald Hering. They conceived that every cell registers the memory of the experiences undergone by all the cells from which it is descended. Versions of this model reappear in other nineteenth-century paradigms. Clearly it converges with Freud's Lamarckianism. On "organic memory," see Stephen Kern, *Culture of Time and Space, 1880–1918*, 40–41.

about it from what their ancestors had experienced only a short time
before—or at least from what post-Revolutionary Europeans *thought*
they had experienced. That perceived division instituted my problem in *Present Past* and posited its far boundary. Now at this reciprocal *present* point in the analysis, we may be essaying the *nearer* border of such a mnemonic periodization, the perimeter that divides
today's practice and understanding of memory from a now "classical"
modernism. Thus, in contemporary terms, as the dull facticity of the
past modulates into complication, as the enigma of the past's retention expands to become indistinguishable from the experience of the
representations by which and within which we live, the time line
appears to turn definitively circular and eventually to diffuse altogether. Then memory and its problem seem almost to disappear.

In an intriguing metalepsis Carlos Fuentes calls this epochal contemporary rearticulation of the mnemonic realm "remembering the
future, inventing the past."[7] Such projection of the future is a consecrated cultural desire. Fuentes's provocation can be brought into relation with a memorable passage from Freud, the final paragraph of
The Interpretation of Dreams: "And the value of dreams for giving us
knowledge of the future? There is of course no question of that. It
would be truer to say instead that they give us knowledge of the
past. For dreams are derived from the past in every sense. Nevertheless the ancient belief that dreams foretell the future is not
wholly devoid of truth. By picturing our wishes as fulfilled, dreams
are after all leading us into the future. But this future, which the
dreamer pictures as the present, has been moulded by his indestructible wish into a perfect likeness of the past" (*SE* 5:621). There might
at first seem little room in this quotation for the optimism of
Fuentes's formula. In this concluding paragraph of his most celebrated book, Freud seems to project the future as captive to a present banefully colonized by the past. The force that might ventilate
that airless closure is not named in the passage, but it is the subject
that underlies the entire book the passage concludes, and indeed all
of Freud's work: the *change* that human beings can bring to experi-

7. Carlos Fuentes, "La Mémoire du futur," 95. Piquantly, perhaps involuntarily,
Fuentes's paradox itself recalls another that I discussed in Chapter 2 (see note 36): Lewis
Namier's conundrum, which holds that historians "imagine the past and remember the
future." See David Lowenthal, *The Past Is a Foreign Country*, 234.

ence, by which they can intervene in the reproduction of what has been in order to reconceive what might be. That is how the past is to be reinvented and the future remembered.

As the inner horizon of memory, the oldest content of life is Thanatos, the lifelessness from which life emerged, so the outer horizon is an intense struggle between repetition and innovation, between past and future. *Too much memory, or too little.* As I have sought to suggest in this book beginning with its title, the time line by which we imagine our experience has been sectioned is neither so unequivocal nor so unidirectional as we might have thought. The enigma of *present past* identifies a problem that has not ceased to disquiet our present, but it also projects the space and the need for a future—exquisitely contingent, deeply problematic, but irrepressibly potential.

Works Cited

Adorno, Theodor W. *Negative Dialectics* (1966). Trans. E. B. Ashton. New York: Seabury, 1973.

Assoun, Paul-Laurent. "Le Sujet de l'oubli selon Freud." *Communications* 49 (1989): 137–47.

Baczko, Bronislaw. "Le Calendrier républicain: Décréter l'éternité." In *Les Lieux de mémoire, I: La République*, ed. Pierre Nora, 37–83.

Bakhtin, M. M. *The Dialogic Imagination: Four Essays*. Trans. Caryl Emerson and Michael Holquist. Austin: University of Texas Press, 1981.

——[V. N. Vološinov, pseud.]. *Freudianism: A Marxist Critique*. Trans. and ed. I. R. Titunik and Neal H. Bruss. New York: Academic Press, 1976.

——[V. N. Vološinov, pseud.]. *Marxism and the Philosophy of Language*. Trans. Ladislav Matejka and I. R. Titunik. New York: Seminar Press, 1973.

Balzac, Honoré de. *La Cousine Bette* (1838). In Balzac, *La Comédie humaine*, ed. Pierre Citron, vol. 5. Paris: Gallimard-Pléiade, 1966.

Barbéris, Pierre. *Balzac et le mal du siècle*. 2 vols. Paris: Gallimard-Bibliothèque des Idées, 1970.

Barthes, Roland. *Critique et vérité*. Paris: Seuil, 1966.

——. "Myth Today." In *A Barthes Reader*, ed. Susan Sontag, 93–149. New York: Farrar, Strauss & Giroux, 1981.

Bate, Walter Jackson. *The Burden of the Past and the English Poet*. Cambridge: Harvard University Press, 1970.

Baudelaire, Charles. *Art in Paris 1845–1862*. Trans. Jonathan Mayne. Ithaca: Cornell University Press, 1965.

——. *Correspondance*. 2 vols. Ed. Claude Pichois and Jean Ziegler. Paris: Gallimard-Pléiade, 1973.

——. *Oeuvres complètes*. Ed. Y.-G. Le Dantec and Claude Pichois. Paris: Gallimard-Pléiade, 1961.

——. *Oeuvres complètes*. Ed. Claude Pichois. 2 vols. Paris: Gallimard-Pléiade, 1976.

Beaujour, Michel. "*Memoria* à la Renaissance." *Corps écrit*, no. 11 (1984): 103–10.

Beckett, Samuel. *Proust*. New York: Grove Press, 1931.

Bell, Clive. *Proust*. New York: Harcourt, Brace, 1929.

Benjamin, Walter. *Charles Baudelaire: A Lyric Poet in the Era of High Capitalism*. Trans. Harry Zohn. London: NLB, 1973.

——. *Gesammelte Schriften.* Ed. Rolf Tiedemann, Hermann Schweppenhäuser, Theodor W. Adorno, and Gershom Scholem. 7 vols. Frankfurt am Main: Suhrkamp, 1972.

——. *Illuminations.* Ed. Hannah Arendt. Trans. Harry Zohn. New York: Schocken, 1969.

——. "The Image of Proust" (1929). In Benjamin, *Illuminations,* 201–15.

——. *Reflections: Essays, Aphorisms, Autobiographical Writings.* Trans. Edmund Jephcott. New York: Harcourt Brace Jovanovich, 1978.

——. "Some Motifs in Baudelaire" (1939). In Benjamin, *Charles Baudelaire: A Lyric Poet in the Era of High Capitalism,* 107–54.

——. "The Work of Art in the Age of Mechanical Reproduction." In Benjamin, *Illuminations,* 217–251.

Berger, John. *Pig Earth.* New York: Pantheon, 1979.

Bergson, Henri. *Matière et mémoire: Essai sur la relation du corps à l'esprit* (1896). Paris: Presses Universitaires de France, 1939.

Bernfeld, Susan Cassirer. "Freud and Archaeology." *American Imago* 8, no. 2 (1951): 107–28.

Bernheimer, Charles, and Claire Kahane, eds. *In Dora's Case: Freud—hysteria—feminism.* New York: Columbia University Press, 1985.

Bersani, Leo. *Marcel Proust: The Fictions of Life and of Art.* New York: Oxford University Press, 1965.

Bischoff, Jürg. *La Genèse de l'épisode de la madeleine: Étude génétique d'un passage d'«A la recherche du temps perdu» de Marcel Proust.* Bern: Peter Lang, 1988.

Blanchot, Maurice. "Le Paradoxe d'Aytré." *Les Temps modernes* 9 (June 1946): 1576–93.

Borges, Jorge Luis. "Funes, the Memorious" (1942). Trans. Anthony Kerrigan. In Borges, *Ficciones,* 107–15. New York: Grove Press, 1962.

Bourdieu, Pierre. *Outline of a Theory of Practice* (1972). Trans. Richard Nice. Cambridge: Cambridge University Press, 1977.

Bourdieu, Pierre, and Jean-Claude Passeron. *Reproduction in Education, Society, and Culture.* Trans. Richard Nice. London: Sage, 1977.

Bowie, Malcolm. *Freud, Proust, and Lacan: Theory as Fiction.* Cambridge: Cambridge University Press, 1987.

Boyarin, Jonathan. "Un Lieu de l'oubli: Le Lower East Side des juifs." *Communications* 49 (1989): 185–94.

Braudel, Fernand. *The Structures of Everyday Life: The Limits of the Possible.* New York: Harper & Row, 1982.

——. *The Wheels of Commerce.* New York: Harper & Row, 1982.

Brewer's Dictionary of Phrase and Fable. New York: Harper, n.d.

Brombert, Victor. "'Le Cygne' de Baudelaire: Douleur, Souvenir, Travail." *Études Baudelairiennes* 3 (1973): 254–61.

Brooks, Peter. *Reading for the Plot: Design and Intention in Narrative.* New York: Vintage, 1984.

Brown, Norman O. *Life Against Death: The Psychoanalytical Meaning of History.* New York: Vintage, 1959.

Brunet, Étienne. *Le Vocabulaire de Proust.* Geneva: Slatkine; Paris: Champion, 1983.

Buck-Morss, Susan. *The Dialectics of Seeing: Walter Benjamin and the Arcades Project.* Cambridge: MIT Press, 1989.

Burton, Richard D. *Baudelaire in 1859: A Study in the Sources of Poetic Creativity.* Cambridge: Cambridge University Press, 1988.

——. *The Context of Baudelaire's "Le Cygne."* Durham, U.K.: Durham Modern Language Series, 1980.

Cameron, Rondo. *France and the Economic Development of Europe, 1800–1914.* 2d ed. Chicago: Rand McNally, 1961.

Casey, Edward S. *Remembering: A Phenomenological Study.* Bloomington: Indiana University Press, 1987.

Certeau, Michel de. *See* de Certeau, Michel.

Chambers, Ross. "Are Baudelaire's 'Tableaux Parisiens' about Paris?" In *On Referring in Literature,* ed. Anna Whiteside and Michael Issacharoff, 95–110. Bloomington: Indiana University Press, 1987.

——. "Du temps des 'Chats' au temps du 'Cygne.'" *Oeuvres et critiques* 9, no. 2 (1984): 11–26.

——. *Mélancolie et opposition: Les Débuts du modernisme en France.* Paris: J. Corti, 1987.

Chantal, René de. *Marcel Proust, Critique littéraire.* 2 vols. Montréal: Presses de l'Université de Montréal, 1967.

Chateaubriand, Francois-René de. *Mémoires d'outre-tombe* (1841). Ed. Maurice Levaillant. 4 vols. Paris: Flammarion, 1982.

——. *René.* In Chateaubriand, *Atala, René,* ed. Fernand Letessier. Paris: Classiques Garnier, 1958.

Chevalier, Louis. *Laboring Classes and Dangerous Classes in Paris during the First Half of the Nineteenth Century.* Trans. Frank Jellinek. New York: H.Fertig, 1973.

Choay, Françoise. *The Modern City: Planning in the Nineteenth Century.* Trans. Marguerite Hugo and George R. Collins. New York: George Braziller, 1969.

Citron, Pierre. *La Poésie de Paris dans la littérature française de Rousseau à Baudelaire.* 2 vols. Paris: Éditions de Minuit, 1961.

Clark, T. J. *The Painting of Modern Life: Paris in the Art of Manet and His Followers.* New York: Knopf, 1985.

Cohen, Gerald A. *Karl Marx's Theory of History: A Defence.* Princeton: Princeton University Press, 1978.

Colet, Louise. *Lui, A View of Him.* Trans. Marilyn Gaddis Rose. Athens: University of Georgia Press, 1986.

Collier, Peter. *Proust and Venice.* Cambridge: Cambridge University Press, 1989.

Compagnon, Antoine. *Proust entre deux siècles.* Paris: Seuil, 1989.

Corbin, Alain. "L'Arithmétique des jours aux XIXe siècle." *Traverses* 35 (1985): 91–97.

——. *The Foul and the Fragrant: Odor and the French Social Imagination.* Cambridge: Harvard University Press, 1986.

Cosin, B. R., C. F. Freeman, and N. H. Freeman. "Critical Empiricism Criticized: The Case of Freud." In *Philosophical Essays on Freud*, ed. Richard Wollheim and James Hopkins, 21–59.

Cummings, Katherine. *Telling Tales: The Hysteric's Seduction in Fiction and Theory.* Stanford: Stanford University Press, 1991.

Czoniczer, Élisabeth. *Quelques antécédents de "A la recherche du temps perdu": Tendances qui peuvent avoir contribué à la cristallisation du roman proustien.* Geneva: Droz, 1957.

Davis, Natalie Zemon. *The Return of Martin Guerre.* Cambridge: Harvard University Press, 1983.

de Certeau, Michel. "Le Corps et les musiques de l'esprit." *Le Monde*, 19–20 January 1986, 12.

——. *L'Invention du quotidien: Arts de faire.* 2 vols. Paris: Union générale d'éditions-10/18, 1980. Volume 1 translated by Steven F. Rendall under the title *The Practice of Everyday Life*. Berkeley and Los Angeles: University of California Press, 1984.

——. "Les Revenants de la ville." *Traverses* 40 (1987): 74–85.

——. *The Writing of History.* Trans. Tom Conley. New York: Columbia University Press, 1988.

de Lattre, Alain. *La Doctrine de la réalité chez Proust.* 3 vols. Paris: Corti, 1978–85.

Deleuze, Gilles. *Marcel Proust et les signes.* Paris: Presses Universitaires de France, 1964. Trans. Richard Howard, under the title *Proust and Signs*. New York: George Braziller, 1972.

de Man, Paul. *Allegories of Reading: Figural Language in Rousseau, Nietzsche, Rilke, and Proust.* New Haven: Yale University Press, 1979.

——. "Literary History and Literary Modernity." In de Man, *Blindness and Insight*, 2d ed., 142–65. Minneapolis: University of Minnesota Press, 1983.

Derrida, Jacques. "La Différance." In Derrida, *Marges de la philosophie*, 1–29. Paris: Minuit, 1972.

——. *Dissemination* (1972). Trans. Barbara Johnson. Chicago: University of Chicago Press, 1981.

——. "Freud and the Scene of Writing." In Derrida, *Writing and Difference*, trans. Alan Bass, 196–231. Chicago: University of Chicago Press, 1978.

——. "Plato's Pharmacy" (1968). In Derrida, *Dissemination*, 61–171.

——. "The Principle of Reason: The University in the Eyes of Its Pupils." *Diacritics* 13 (Fall 1983): 3–20.

Descombes, Vincent. *Proust: Philosophie du roman.* Paris: Minuit, 1987.

Diderot, Denis. *Le Rêve de d'Alembert.* In Diderot, *Oeuvres philosophiques*, ed. P. Vernière, 257–385. Paris: Classiques Garnier, 1961.

Dimendberg, Edward. "Film Noir and Urban Space." Ph.D. diss., University of California, Santa Cruz, 1992.

Doubrovsky, Serge. *Writing and Fantasy in Proust: La Place de la Madeleine.*

Trans. Carol Mastrangelo Bové and Paul Bové. Lincoln: University of Nebraska Press, 1986.

Droz, Jacques. *Europe between Revolutions, 1815–1848.* Trans. Robert Baldick. New York: Harper & Row, 1967.

Duchet, Claude. "Preface." In Alfred de Musset, *La Confession d'un enfant du siècle,* ed. Maurice Allem, i-xxvii.

Eco, Umberto. "Un Art d'oublier est-il concevable?" *Traverses* 40 (1987): 124–35.

———. *A Theory of Semiotics.* Bloomington: University of Indiana Press, 1976.

Ellenberger, Henri F. *The Discovery of the Unconscious: The History and Evolution of Dynamic Psychiatry.* New York: Basic Books, 1970.

Empson, William. *Seven Types of Ambiguity* (1930). 2d ed. Harmondsworth, U.K.: Penguin, 1965.

Engels, Friedrich. "The Housing Question." In Karl Marx and Friedrich Engels, *Selected Works,* 557–635. Moscow: Progress, 1962.

Enzensberger, Hans Magnus. *The Consciousness Industry.* Ed. Michael Roloff. New York: Seabury, 1974.

Faulkner, William. *Light in August* (1932). New York: Modern Library, 1968.

Ferguson, Margaret W. "Saint Augustine's Region of Unlikeness: The Crossing of Exile and Language." *Georgia Review* 29, no. 4 (1975): 842–64.

Flaubert, Gustave. *Correspondance.* Ed. Jean Bruneau. 3 vols. Paris: Gallimard-Pléiade, 1973–91.

———. *L'Éducation sentimentale* (1869). Ed. E. Maynial. Paris: Classiques Garnier, 1964.

———. *Madame Bovary* (1857). Ed. C. Gothot-Mersch. Paris: Classiques Garnier, 1971.

Forrester, John. *Language and the Origins of Psychoanalysis.* New York: Columbia University Press, 1980.

Foucault, Michel. *Discipline and Punish: The Birth of the Prison.* Trans. Alan Sheridan. New York: Vintage, 1979.

———. "Film and Popular Memory" (1974). Trans. Martin Jordin. In *Foucault Live (Interviews 1966–84),* ed. Sylvère Lotringer, 89–106. New York: Semiotext(e), 1989.

———. *Histoire de la sexualité, I: La volonté de savoir.* Paris: Gallimard, 1976. Trans. Robert Hurley, under the title *History of Sexuality: An Introduction.* Vol. 1. New York: Vintage, 1990.

———. "Nietzsche, Freud, Marx" (1964). *Cahiers de Royaumont,* 6 (1967): 183–200.

———. "Nietzsche, Genealogy, History" (1971). In Foucault, *Language, Counter-Memory, Practice: Selected Essays and Interviews,* ed. Donald Bouchard, 139–64. Ithaca: Cornell University Press, 1977.

———. *L'Ordre du discours.* Paris: Gallimard, 1971. Trans. Rupert Swyer [sic] under the title "The Discourse on Language," in Foucault, *The Archaeology of Knowledge,* 215–37. New York: Pantheon, 1972.

———. *The Order of Things: An Archeology of the Human Sciences.* New York: Random House, 1970.

Fournel, Victor. *Paris nouveau et Paris futur*. Paris: Lecoffre, 1865.

Fournier, Édouard. *Paris démoli: Mosaïque de ruines*. Paris: Jules Dagneau, 1853.

Freccero, John. "The Fig Tree and the Laurel: Petrarch's Poetics." *Diacritics* 5, no. 1 (1975): 35–37.

Freud, Sigmund. *Civilization and Its Discontents* (1930). New York: W. W. Norton, 1961.

——. *The Complete Letters of Sigmund Freud to Wilhelm Fliess, 1887–1904*. Trans. Jeffrey Moussaieff Masson. Cambridge: Harvard University Press, 1985.

——. "Overview of the Transference Neuroses" (1915). In Freud, *A Phylogenetic Fantasy: Overview of the Transference Neuroses*, 5–20.

——. *A Phylogenetic Fantasy: Overview of the Transference Neuroses*. Ed. Ilse Grubrich-Simitis. Trans. Axel Hoffer and Peter T. Hoffer. Cambridge: Harvard University Press, 1987.

——. *The Standard Edition of the Complete Psychological Works*. Trans. and ed. James Strachey, Anna Freud, Alix Strachey, and Alan Tyson. 24 vols. London: Hogarth, 1953–74. [*SE*]

[*Specific works cited from* The Standard Edition:]

"The Aetiology of Hysteria" (1896). *SE* 3:189–221.

"Analysis Terminable and Interminable" (1937). *SE* 23:209–53.

Beyond the Pleasure Principle (1920). *SE* 18:3–66.

"The Claims of Psycho-Analysis to Scientific Interest" (1913). *SE* 13:165–91.

"Constructions in Analysis" (1937). *SE* 23:255–69.

"Creative Writers and Day-Dreaming" (1908). *SE* 9:141–53.

"A Difficulty in the Path of Psycho-Analysis" (1917). *SE* 17:137–44.

"The Dynamics of Transference" (1912). *SE* 12:97–108.

"Fragment of an Analysis of a Case of Hysteria" ["Dora"] (1905). *SE* 7:7–122.

"Freud's Psycho-Analytic Procedure" (1904). *SE* 7:249–54.

"From the History of an Infantile Neurosis" [The "Wolf Man"] (1918). *SE* 17:3–124.

"Heredity and the Aetiology of the Neuroses" (1896). *SE* 3:141–58.

"Instincts and Their Vicissitudes" (1915). *SE* 14:111–40.

The Interpretation of Dreams (1900). *SE* 4–5.

Introductory Lectures on Psycho-Analysis (1916–17). *SE* 15–16.

"A Metapsychological Supplement to the Theory of Dreams" (1917). *SE* 14:222–35.

Moses and Monotheism (1934–38). *SE* 23:3–137.

"Mourning and Melancholia" (1917). *SE* 14:239–58.

"Negation" (1925). *SE* 19:236–42.

New Introductory Lectures on Psycho-Analysis (1933). *SE* 22:3–183.

"A Note on the Unconscious in Psycho-Analysis" (1912). *SE* 12:260–66.

"Notes upon a Case of Obsessional Neurosis" [The "Rat Man"] (1909). *SE* 10:155–249.

"A Note upon the 'Mystic Writing-Pad'" (1925). *SE* 19:227–34.

"On Beginning the Treatment (Further Recommendations on the Technique of Psycho-Analysis I)" (1913). *SE* 12:121–44.
"On Dreams" (1901). *SE* 5:633–86.
"On Narcissism: An Introduction" (1914). *SE* 14:69–102.
"On the History of the Psycho-Analytic Movement" (1914). *SE* 14:7–66.
Outline of Psycho-Analysis (1938). *SE* 23:141–207.
"Project for a Scientific Psychology" (1895). *SE* 1:295–387.
"The Psychical Mechanism of Forgetfulness" (1898). *SE* 3:287–97.
The Psychopathology of Everyday Life (1901). *SE* 6.
"The Psychotherapy of Hysteria." In *Studies on Hysteria* (1893–95), *SE* 2:253–305.
"The Question of Lay Analysis." *SE* 20:183–258.
"Recommendations to Physicians Practising Psycho-Analysis" (1912). *SE* 12:109–20.
"Remarks on the Theory and Practice of Dream-Interpretation" (1923). *SE* 19:108–21.
"Remembering, Repeating and Working-Through" (1914). *SE* 12:145–56.
"Repression" (1915). *SE* 14:143–58.
"Screen Memories" (1899). *SE* 3:301–22.
"Some Additional Notes on Dream-Interpretation as a Whole" (1925). *SE* 19:127–38.
[With Josef Breuer.] *Studies on Hysteria* (1893–95). *SE* 2.
"The Subtleties of a Faulty Action" (1935). *SE* 22:233–35.
"Thoughts for the Times on War and Death" (1915). *SE* 14:273–302.
Three Essays on the Theory of Sexuality (1905). *SE* 7:125–247.
Totem and Taboo (1913). *SE* 13:xiii–163.
"The Unconscious" (1915). *SE* 14:161–204.
"'Wild' Psycho-Analysis" (1910). *SE* 11:219–27.
Fried, Michael. "Painting Memories: On the Containment of the Past in Baudelaire and Manet." *Critical Inquiry* 10, no. 3 (1984): 510–42.
Frisby, David. *Fragments of Modernity: Theories of Modernity in the Work of Simmel, Kracauer, and Benjamin.* Cambridge: MIT Press, 1986.
Fuentes, Carlos. "La Mémoire du futur," trans. Céline Zins. *L'Écrit du Temps* 10 (Autumn 1985): 93–105.
Gaillard, Françoise. "A Little Story about the *bras de fer*; or, How History Is Made." In *Flaubert and Postmodernism*, ed. Naomi Schor and Henry F. Majewski, 84–99.
Gaillard, Jeanne. *Paris, La Ville 1852–1870.* Paris: H. Champion, 1977.
Gale, John E. "De Quincey, Baudelaire and 'Le Cygne.'" *Nineteenth-Century French Studies* 5, nos. 3–4 (1977): 296–307.
Gastinel, Pierre. *Le Romantisme d'Alfred de Musset.* Paris: Hachette, 1933.
Gauthier, Alain, and Henri-Pierre Jeudy. "Trou de mémoire, image virale." *Communications* 49 (1989): 137–47.
Gautier, Théophile. *Poésies complètes.* Ed. René Jasinski. 3 vols. Paris: Nizet, 1970.

Gay, Peter. *Freud: A Life for Our Time.* New York: Anchor Books, 1988.

Gearhart, Suzanne. "Philosophy *Before* Literature: Deconstruction, Historicity, and the Work of Paul de Man." *Diacritics* 13 (Winter 1983): 63–81.

Gershman, Herbert S., and Kernan B. Whitworth, Jr., eds. *Anthology of Critical Prefaces to the Nineteenth-Century French Novel.* Columbia: University of Missouri Press, 1962.

Giedion, Sigfried. *Space, Time, and Architecture: The Growth of a New Tradition.* 5th ed. Cambridge: Harvard University Press, 1982.

Ginzburg, Carlo. "Clues: Morelli, Freud, and Sherlock Holmes." In *The Sign of Three: Dupin, Holmes, Peirce*, ed. Umberto Eco and Thomas A. Sebeok, 81–118. Bloomington: Indiana University Press, 1983.

——. "Clues: Roots of an Evidential Paradigm," trans. John and Anne C. Tedeschi. In Ginzburg, *Clues, Myths, and the Historical Method*, 96–125. Baltimore: Johns Hopkins University Press, 1989.

Goncourt, Edmond de, and Jules de Goncourt. *Journal: Mémoires de la vie littéraire.* Ed. Robert Ricatte. 22 vols. Monaco: Imprimerie Nationale, 1956–58.

——. *Pages from the Goncourt Journal.* Trans. Robert Baldick. Harmondsworth, U.K.: Penguin, 1984.

Goodkin, Richard E. *Around Proust.* Princeton: Princeton University Press, 1991.

Goody, Jack. *The Domestication of the Savage Mind.* Cambridge: Cambridge University Press, 1977.

Gould, Carol C. *Marx's Social Ontology: Individuality and Community in Marx's Theory of Social Reality.* Cambridge: MIT Press, 1978.

Goux, Jean-Joseph. *Économie et symbolique.* Paris: Seuil, 1972.

——. *Les Monnayeurs du langage.* Paris: Galilée, 1984.

Greimas, Algirdas-Julien. "Structure et histoire" (1966). In Greimas, *Du sens*, 103–15. Paris: Seuil, 1970.

Grubrich-Simitis, Ilse. "Metapsychology and Metabiology." In Freud, *A Phylogenetic Fantasy: Overview of the Transference Neuroses*, 73–107.

Grünbaum, Adolf. *The Foundations of Psychoanalysis: A Philosophical Critique.* Berkeley and Los Angeles: University of California Press, 1984.

Guillaume, Marc. "Mémoires de la ville." *Traverses* 36 (1986): 134–40.

Habermas, Jürgen. *Knowledge and Human Interests* (1968). Trans. Jeremy J. Shapiro. Boston: Beacon, 1971.

Hahn, Aloïs. "Contribution à la sociologie de la confession et autres formes institutionalisées d'aveu: Autothématisation et processus de civilisation." *Actes de la Recherche en Sciences Sociales* 62/63 (June 1986): 54–68.

Halbwachs, Maurice. *La Mémoire collective.* Paris: Presses Universitaires de France, 1950. Trans. Francis J. Ditter and Vida Yazdi Ditter, under the title *The Collective Memory.* New York: Harper & Row, 1980.

Hampshire, Stuart. "Disposition and Memory." In *Philosophical Essays on Freud*, ed. Richard Wollheim and James Hopkins, 75–91.

Hartog, François. "L'Évidence de l'histoire." Typescript. Translated into Italian under the title "L'Evidenza della storia." *Nuove Effemeridi* 3 (1989): 67–72.

Harvey, David. *The Condition of Postmodernity: An Enquiry into the Origins of Cultural Change*. Oxford: Basil Blackwell, 1989.

——. *Consciousness and the Urban Experience: Studies in the History and Theory of Capitalist Urbanization*. Baltimore: Johns Hopkins University Press, 1985.

Havens, Leston. *A Safe Place*. New York: Ballantine, 1989.

Hawkes, Terence. *Structuralism and Semiotics*. Berkeley and Los Angeles: University of California Press, 1977.

Hegel, G.W.F. *Phenomenology of Spirit*. Trans. A. V. Miller. New York: Oxford, 1977.

Heidegger, Martin. "The Question Concerning Technology." In Heidegger, *The Question Concerning Technology and Other Essays*, trans. William Lovitt, 3–35. New York: Harper & Row, 1977.

Henry, Anne. *Marcel Proust: Théories pour une esthétique*. Paris: Klincksieck, 1981.

Herbermann, Charles G., et al. *The Catholic Encyclopedia*. 15 vols. New York: Appleton, 1907–12.

Herrmann, Douglas J., and Roger Chaffin, eds. *Memory in Historical Perspective: The Literature before Ebbinghaus*. Berlin: Springer-Verlag, 1988.

Hertz, Neil. *The End of the Line: Essays on Psychoanalysis and the Sublime*. New York: Columbia University Press, 1985.

Hirschman, Albert O. *The Passions and the Interests: Political Arguments for Capitalism before Its Triumph*. Princeton: Princeton University Press, 1977.

Hobsbawm, E. J. "Introduction: Inventing Traditions." In *The Invention of Tradition*, ed. E. J. Hobsbawm and Terence Ranger, 1–14.

——. "Mass-Producing Traditions: Europe, 1870–1914." In *The Invention of Tradition*, ed. E. J. Hobsbawm and Terence Ranger, 263–307.

Hobsbawm, E. J., and Terence Ranger, eds. *The Invention of Tradition*. Cambridge: Cambridge University Press, 1983.

Hollier, Denis, ed. *Harvard History of French Literature*. Cambridge: Harvard University Press, 1989.

Horkheimer, Max, and Theodor W. Adorno, *Dialectic of Enlightenment*. Trans. John Cumming. New York: Seabury, 1972.

Hugo, Victor. *Les Misérables*. Ed. Maurice Allem. Paris: Gallimard–Pléiade, 1951.

Hutton, Patrick H. "The Art of Memory Reconceived: From Rhetoric to Psychoanalysis." *Journal of the History of Ideas* 48 (July–September 1987): 371–92.

Izenberg, Gerald N. "Seduced and Abandoned: The Rise and Fall of Freud's Seduction Theory." In *The Cambridge Companion to Freud*, ed. Jerome Neu, 25–43. Cambridge: Cambridge University Press, 1991.

Jackson, Elizabeth R. *L'Évolution de la mémoire involontaire dans l'oeuvre de Marcel Proust*. Paris: Nizet, 1966.

James, Henry. *The Art of the Novel: Critical Prefaces*. New York: Charles Scribner's Sons, 1934.

Jameson, Fredric R. *Late Marxism: Adorno, or, The Persistence of the Dialectic*. London: Verso, 1990.

———. *Marxism and Form: Twentieth-Century Dialectical Theories of Literature.* Princeton: Princeton University Press, 1971.

———. *The Political Unconscious: Narrative as a Socially Symbolic Act.* Ithaca: Cornell University Press, 1981.

———. "Postmodernism and Consumer Society." In *The Anti-Aesthetic: Essays on Postmodern Culture,* ed. Hal Foster, 111–25. Port Townsend, Wash.: Bay Press, 1983.

Janis, Eugenia Parry. "Demolition Picturesque: Photographs of Paris in 1852 and 1853 by Henri Le Secq." In *Perspectives on Photography: Essays in Honor of Beaumont Newhall,* ed. Peter Walch and Thomas Barrow, 33–66. Albuquerque: University of New Mexico Press, 1986.

Jay, Martin. *Marxism and Totality: The Adventures of a Concept from Lukács to Habermas.* Berkeley and Los Angeles: University of California Press, 1984.

Johnson, Barbara. *The Critical Difference: Essays in the Contemporary Rhetoric of Reading.* Baltimore: Johns Hopkins University Press, 1980.

Johnson, George. *In the Palaces of Memory: How We Build the World inside Our Heads.* New York: Knopf, 1991.

Joinet, Louis. "L'Amnistie: Le Droit à la mémoire entre pardon et oubli." *Communications* 49 (1989): 213–24.

Joyce, James. *Ulysses.* Ed. Hans Walter Gabler. New York: Random House, 1986.

Kann, Robert A. *The Problem of Restoration.* Berkeley and Los Angeles: University of California Press, 1968.

Kant, Immanuel. *Critique of Judgement.* Trans. J. H. Bernard. London: Collier-Macmillan, 1951.

Keller, Luzius. *L'Épisode de la madeleine dans les cahiers de brouillon de Marcel Proust.* Paris: Jean-Michel Place, 1978.

Kemp, Anthony. *The Estrangement of the Past: A Study in the Origins of Modern Historical Consciousness.* New York: Oxford University Press, 1991.

Kern, Stephen. *The Culture of Time and Space, 1880–1918.* Cambridge: Harvard University Press, 1983.

Kittler, Friedrich A. *Discourse Networks 1800/1900.* Trans. Michael Metteer and Chris Cullens. Stanford: Stanford University Press, 1990.

Krell, David Farrell. *Of Memory, Reminiscence, and Writing: On the Verge.* Bloomington: Indiana University Press, 1990.

Kristeva, Julia, "Mémoire." *L'Infini* 1 (Winter 1983): 39–54.

Kuspit, Donald. "A Mighty Metaphor: The Analogy of Archaeology and Psychoanalysis." In *Sigmund Freud and Art: His Personal Collection of Antiquities,* ed. Lynn Gamwell and Richard Wells, 133–51. Binghamton: State University of New York, 1989.

Lacan, Jacques. *Écrits: A Selection.* Trans. Alan Sheridan. New York: W. W. Norton, 1977.

Laclau, Ernesto, and Chantal Mouffe. *Hegemony and Socialist Strategy: Towards a Radical Democratic Politics.* London: Verso, 1985.

Lapierre, Nicole. "Dialectique de la mémoire et de l'oubli." *Communications* 49 (1989): 5–10.

Leplanche, Jean, and Serge Leclaire. "The Unconscious: A Psychoanalytic Study." *Yale French Studies* 48, no. 2 (1972): 118–85.

Laplanche, Jean, and J.-B. Pontalis. *The Language of Psycho-Analysis.* Trans. Donald Nicholson-Smith. New York: W. W. Norton, 1974.

Leakey, F. W. "The Originality of Baudelaire's 'Le Cygne': Genesis as Structure and Theme." In *Order and Adventure in Post-Romantic French Poetry: Essays Presented to C. A. Hackett,* ed. E. M. Beaumont, J. M. Cocking, and J. Cruickshank, 38–55. Oxford: Blackwell, 1973.

Le Goff, Jacques. *Histoire et mémoire.* Paris: Gallimard-Folio, 1988.

Lévi-Strauss, Claude. "Mythe et oubli" (1975). In Lévi-Strauss, *Le Regard éloigné,* 253–61. Paris: Plon, 1983.

Lewis, Bernard. "Masada et Cyrus le Grand." *Communications* 49 (1989): 161–84.

Locke, John. *Essay Concerning Human Understanding.* Ed. Campbell Fraser. Oxford: Oxford University Press, 1894.

Loftus, Elizabeth F. *Eyewitness Testimony.* Cambridge: Harvard University Press, 1979.

Lombardo, Patrizia. "Hippolyte Taine between Art and Science." *Yale French Studies* 77 (1990): 117–33.

Loraux, Nicole. "De l'amnistie et de son contraire." In *Usages de l'oubli,* ed. Yosef H. Yerushalmi et al., 23–47. Paris: Seuil, 1988.

Lotman, Yuri M., and B. A. Uspensky. "On the Semiotic Mechanism of Culture" (1971). *New Literary History* 9 (Winter 1978): 211–32.

Lowenthal, David. *The Past Is a Foreign Country.* Cambridge: Cambridge University Press, 1985.

Lukacher, Ned. *Primal Scenes: Literature, Philosophy, Psychoanalysis.* Ithaca: Cornell University Press, 1986.

Lukács, Georg. *The Historical Novel.* Trans. Hannah Mitchell and Stanley Mitchell. Lincoln: University of Nebraska Press, 1983.

——. *History and Class Consciousness: Studies in Marxist Dialectics.* Trans. Rodney Livingstone. Cambridge: MIT Press, 1971.

Luria, Alexander R. *The Mind of a Mnemonist.* Trans. Lynn Solotaroff. New York: Basic Books, 1968.

Lyotard, Jean-François. *La Condition postmoderne: Rapport sur le savoir.* Paris: Minuit, 1979. Trans. Geoff Bennington and Brian Massumi, under the title *The Postmodern Condition: A Report on Knowledge.* Minneapolis: University of Minnesota Press, 1984.

——. *Le Différend.* Paris: Minuit, 1983. Trans. George Van Den Abbeele, under the title *The Differend: Phrases in Dispute.* Minneapolis: University of Minnesota Press, 1988.

McDonald, Christie. *The Proustian Fabric: Associations of Memory.* Lincoln: University of Nebraska Press, 1991.

Macfarlane, Keith H. "'Le Cygne' de Baudelaire: 'falsi Simoentis ad undam.'" *L'Information littéraire* 27, no. 3 (1975): 139–44.

McGrath, William. *Freud's Discovery of Psychoanalysis: The Politics of Hysteria*. Ithaca: Cornell University Press, 1986.

MacInnes, John W. *The Comical as Textual Practice in "Les Fleurs du mal."* Gainesville: University of Florida Press, 1988.

Mallarmé, Stéphane. "The Impressionists and Édouard Manet" (1876). In *Documents Stéphane Mallarmé*, ed. Carl Paul Barbier, 1:57–91. Paris: Nizet, 1968.

——. *Oeuvres complètes*. Ed. Henri Mondor and G. Jean-Aubry. Paris: Gallimard-Pléiade, 1945.

Marantz, Ennid G. "Les Romans champêtres de George Sand dans la *Recherche*: Intertextes, avant-textes et texte." *Bulletin d'informations proustiennes* 13 (1982): 25–36.

Marcuse, Herbert. *Eros and Civilization: A Philosophical Inquiry into Freud*. New York: Vintage, 1955.

Marx, Karl. *Capital: A Critique of Political Economy. Volume 1.* Trans. Ben Fowkes. New York: Vintage, 1976.

——. *Capital: A Critique of Political Economy. Volume 2.* Trans. David Fernbach. New York: Vintage, 1978.

——. *Capital: A Critique of Political Economy. Volume 3.* Trans. David Fernbach. New York: Vintage, 1981.

——. *The Eighteenth Brumaire of Louis Bonaparte*. Moscow: Progress, 1954.

——. *Grundrisse: Foundations of the Critique of Political Economy*. Trans. Martin Nicolaus. New York: Vintage, 1973.

——. *The Letters of Karl Marx*. Ed. Saul K. Padover. Englewood Cliffs, N.J.: Prentice-Hall, 1979.

Marx, Karl, and Friedrich Engels. *The Communist Manifesto* (1848). Trans. Samuel Moore. Ed. A.J.P. Taylor. Harmondsworth, U.K.: Penguin, 1967.

——. *The German Ideology*. Ed. C. J. Arthur. New York: International Publishers, 1970.

Masson, Jeffrey Moussaieff. *The Assault on Truth: Freud's Suppression of Seduction Theory*. New York: Farrar, Straus, & Giroux, 1984.

Megay, Joyce. *Bergson et Proust: Essai de mise au point de la question de l'influence de Bergson sur Proust*. Paris: Vrin, 1976.

Megill, Allan. *Prophets of Extremity: Nietzsche, Heidegger, Foucault, Derrida*. Berkeley and Los Angeles: University of California Press, 1985.

Meikle, Scott. "Dialectical Contradiction and Necessity." In *Issues in Marxist Philosophy*, vol. 1, *Dialectics and Method*, ed. John Mepham and David-Hillel Rubin, 5–35. Atlantic Highlands, N. J.: Humanities Press, 1979.

Merleau-Ponty, Maurice. *Phénoménologie de la perception*. Paris: Gallimard, 1945.

Moscovici, Marie. "Un Meurtre construit par les produits de son oubli." *L'Écrit du temps* 10 (Autumn 1985): 127–44.

Musset, Alfred de. *La Confession d'un enfant du siècle* (1836). Ed. Gerard Barrier. Paris: Gallimard-Folio, 1973.

——. *La Confession d'un enfant du siècle* (1840). Ed. Maurice Allem. Paris: Classiques Garnier, 1968.

Nehamas, Alexander. *Nietzsche: Life as Literature.* Cambridge: Harvard University Press, 1985.

Neisser, Ulric, ed. *Memory Observed: Remembering in Natural Contexts.* San Francisco: W. H. Freeman, 1982.

Nelson, Lowry, Jr. "Baudelaire and Virgil: A Reading of 'Le Cygne.'" *Comparative Literature* 13, no. 4 (1961): 332–45.

Newmark, Kevin. "Ingesting the Mummy: Proust's Allegory of Memory." *Yale French Studies* 79 (1991): 150–77.

Nietzsche, Friedrich. *Beyond Good and Evil: Prelude to a Philosophy of the Future.* Trans. Walter Kaufmann. New York: Vintage, 1989.

———. "History in the Service and Disservice of Life" (1874). Trans. Gary Brown. In *Unmodern Observations,* ed. William Arrowsmith, 87–145. New Haven: Yale University Press, 1990.

———. "On the Uses and Disadvantages of History for Life" (1874). In *Untimely Meditations,* trans. R. J. Hollingdale, 59–123. Cambridge: Cambridge University Press, 1983.

———. "On Truth and Lies in a Nonmoral Sense." Ed. and trans. Daniel Breazeale. In *Philosophy and Truth: Selections from Nietzsche's Notebooks of the Early 1870s,* 79–97. Atlantic Highlands, N.J.: Humanities Press, 1979.

———. *The Will to Power.* Trans. Walter Kaufmann and R. J. Hollingdale. New York: Random House, 1967.

Nora, Pierre. "Entre mémoire et histoire: La problématique des lieux." In *Les Lieux de mémoire, I,* ed. Pierre Nora, xvii–xlii. Trans. Marc Roudebush, under the title "Between Memory and History." *Representations* 26 (Spring 1989): 7–25.

———, ed. *Les Lieux de mémoire, I: La République.* Paris: Gallimard-Bibliothèque des Histoires, 1984.

———, ed. *Les Lieux de mémoire, II: La Nation.* 3 vols. Paris: Gallimard-Bibliothèque des Histoires, 1986.

Nussbaum, Martha C. *Love's Knowledge: Essays on Philosophy and Literature.* New York: Oxford University Press, 1990.

O'Neill, John. "Critique and Remembrance." In O'Neill, *On Critical Theory,* 1–11. New York: Seabury, 1976.

Painter, George D. *Marcel Proust: A Biography.* 2 vols. London: Chatto & Windus, 1959, 1965. 2d ed. in 1 vol. New York: Random House, 1989.

Pascal, Blaise. *Pensées.* Ed. Zacharie Tourneur and Didier Anzieu. 2 vols. Paris: A. Colin, 1960.

Paulhan, Frédéric. *La Fonction de la mémoire et le souvenir affectif.* Paris: Alcan, 1904.

Perrot, Michelle, ed. *From the Fires of Revolution to the Great War.* Vol. 4 of *A History of Private Life.* Trans. Arthur Goldhammer. Cambridge: Harvard University Press, 1990.

Pinkney, David H. *Napoleon III and the Rebuilding of Paris.* Princeton: Princeton University Press, 1958.

Plato. "Lesser Hippias." In *The Dialogues of Plato*, 2:715–29. Trans. Benjamin Jowett. New York: Random House, 1937.
———. "Theaetetus." In *The Dialogues of Plato*, 2:143–217. Trans. Benjamin Jowett. New York: Random House, 1937.
Popper, Karl R. *Conjectures and Refutations: The Growth of Scientific Knowledge*. London: Routledge & Kegan Paul, 1963.
Poulet, Georges. *L'Espace proustien*. Paris: Gallimard, 1963.
Prince, Gerald. *A Dictionary of Narratology*. Lincoln: University of Nebraska Press, 1987.
Proust, Marcel. *A la recherche du temps perdu*. Ed. Pierre Clarac and André Ferré. 3 vols. Paris: Gallimard-Pléiade, 1954. [*RTP54*]
———. *A la recherche du temps perdu*. Ed. Jean-Yves Tadié. 4 vols. Paris: Gallimard-Pléiade, 1987–89. [*RTP*]
———. *Albertine disparue*. Ed. Nathalie Mauriac and Etienne Wolff. Paris: Grasset, 1987.
———. *Le Carnet de 1908*. Ed. Philip Kolb. Cahiers Marcel Proust, n.s. 8. Paris: Gallimard, 1976.
———. *"Contre Sainte-Beuve," précédé de "Pastiches et mélanges," et suivi de "Essais et articles."* Ed. Pierre Clarac and Yves Sandre. Paris: Gallimard-Pléiade, 1971. [*CSB*]
———. *Correspondance*. Ed. Philip Kolb. 19 vols. to date. Paris: Plon, 1970–. [*Corr.*]
———. *Correspondance Proust-Gallimard, 1912–1922*. Ed. Pascal Fouché. Paris: Gallimard, 1989.
———. *La Fugitive*. Ed. Jean Milly. 2d ed. Paris: Garnier-Flammarion, 1986.
———. *"Jean Santeuil," précédé de "Les Plaisirs et les jours."* Ed. Pierre Clarac and Yves Sandre. Paris: Gallimard-Pléiade, 1971. [*JS*]
———. *Marcel Proust: Textes retrouvés*. Ed. Philip Kolb and Larkin B. Price. Urbana: University of Illinois Press, 1968.
———. *Remembrance of Things Past*. Trans. C. K. Scott-Moncrieff and Terence Kilmartin. 2 vols. New York: Random House, 1981.
Quémar, Claudine. "Autour de trois 'avant-textes' de l' 'Ouverture' de la *Recherche*: Nouvelles approches des problèmes du *Contre Sainte-Beuve*." *Bulletin d'informations proustiennes* 3 (1976): 7–29.
Rabinbach, Anson. *The Human Motor: Energy, Fatigue, and the Origins of Modernity*. Berkeley and Los Angeles: University of California Press, 1992.
Rabinow, Paul. *French Modern: Norms and Forms of the Social Environment*. Cambridge: MIT Press, 1989.
Raczymow, Henri. *Le Cygne de Proust*. Paris: Gallimard, 1989.
Ramazani, Vaheed K. *The Free Indirect Mode: Flaubert and the Poetics of Irony*. Charlottesville: University Press of Virginia, 1988.
Redman, Harry, Jr., and Catherine Savage Brosman. "Further Nineteenth-Century Instances of Affective Memory." *Essays in French Literature* 22 (November 1985): 12–20.
Reid, Martine. "La Confession selon Musset." *Littérature* 67 (October 1987): 53–72.

Ribot, Théodule. *Les Maladies de la mémoire* (1881). Paris: Alcan, 1924. Trans. William H. Smith, under the title *Diseases of Memory*. New York: Appleton, 1882. Reprinted Washington, D.C.: University Publications of America, 1977.

Rice, Shelley. "Parisian Views." *VIEWS: Supplement* (1986): 7–13.

———. "Souvenirs." *Art in America* 76 (September 1988): 156–71.

Richards, Thomas. *The Commodity Culture of Victorian England: Advertising and Spectacle, 1851–1914*. Stanford: Stanford University Press, 1990.

Ricoeur, Paul. *Freud and Philosophy: An Essay on Interpretation*. Trans. Denis Savage. New Haven: Yale University Press, 1970.

———. *Time and Narrative*. Trans. Kathleen Blamey and David Pellauer. 3 vols. Chicago: University of Chicago Press, 1984–88.

Riffaterre, Michael. "Flaubert's Presuppositions." In *Flaubert and Postmodernism*, ed. Naomi Schor and Henry F. Majewski, 177–91.

Robinson, Paul. *Freud and His Critics*. Berkeley and Los Angeles: University of California Press, 1993.

Roloff, Volker. "*François le Champi* et le texte retrouvé." In *Études proustiennes 3* (Cahiers Marcel Proust, n.s., 9). Paris: Gallimard, 1979.

Rosenfield, Israel. *The Invention of Memory: A New View of the Brain*. New York: Basic Books, 1989.

Rossi-Landi, Ferruccio. *Linguistics and Economics*. The Hague: Mouton, 1975.

Roth, Michael S. "Dying of the Past: Medical Studies of Nostalgia in Nineteenth-Century France." *History and Memory* 3, no. 1 (1991): 7–29.

———. *Psycho-Analysis as History: Negation and Freedom in Freud*. Ithaca: Cornell University Press, 1987.

———. "Remembering Forgetting: *Maladies de la mémoire* in Nineteenth-Century France." *Representations* 26 (Spring 1989): 49–68.

Roudinesco, Élisabeth. *Jacques Lacan & Co.: A History of Psychoanalysis in France, 1925–1985*. Trans. Jeffrey Mehlman. Chicago: University of Chicago Press, 1990.

Rousseau, Jean-Jacques. *Confessions*. Ed. Jacques Voisine. Paris: Classiques Garnier, 1964.

Ryan, Michael. "The Marxism-Deconstruction Debate in Literary Theory." *New Orleans Review* 11 (Spring 1984): 29–35.

Sacks, Oliver. "The Landscape of His Dreams (A Neurologist's Notebook)." *New Yorker*, 27 July 1992, 56–66.

Sainte-Beuve, Charles-Augustin. *Nouveaux Lundis*. 13 vols. Paris: Michel Lévy, 1863–70.

Salaman, Esther. "A Collection of Moments" (1970). In *Memory Observed: Remembering in Natural Contexts*, ed. Ulric Neisser, 49–63.

Sandler, Joseph, ed. *On Freud's "Analysis Terminable and Interminable."* New Haven: Yale University Press, 1991.

Sartre, Jean-Paul. *Being and Nothingness: An Essay in Phenomenological Ontology*. Trans. Hazel Barnes. New York: Philosophical Library, 1956.

Saussure, Ferdinand de. *Cours de linguistique générale*. Ed. Charles Bally and Albert Sechehaye. Paris: Payot, 1964. Trans. Roy Harris, under the title

Course in General Linguistics. Ed. Charles Bally and Albert Sechehaye. 3d ed. London: Duckworth, 1983.

Scaff, Lawrence A. *Fleeing the Iron Cage: Culture, Politics, and Modernity in the Thought of Max Weber.* Berkeley and Los Angeles: University of California Press, 1989.

Scarry, Elaine. *The Body in Pain: The Making and Unmaking of the World.* New York: Oxford University Press, 1985.

Schachtel, Ernest G. "On Memory and Childhood Amnesia" (1947). Reprinted in *Memory Observed: Remembering in Natural Contexts,* ed. Ulric Neisser, 189–200.

Schivelbusch, Wolfgang. *The Railway Journey: Trains and Travel in the 19th Century* (1977). Trans. Anselm Hollo. New York: Urizen, 1979.

Schor, Naomi, and Henry F. Majewski, eds. *Flaubert and Postmodernism.* Lincoln: University of Nebraska Press, 1984.

Selden, Daniel J. "'Dark Similitudes': Saint Augustine and *The Confessions of J. J. Rousseau.*" Typescript.

Shattuck, Roger. *Proust's Binoculars: A Study of Memory, Time, and Recognition in "A la recherche du temps perdu."* New York: Random House, 1963.

Shell, Marc. *The Economy of Literature.* Baltimore: Johns Hopkins University Press, 1978.

Sherover, Charles M. *The Human Perception of Time: The Development of Its Philosophic Meaning.* New York: New York University Press, 1975.

Shils, Edward. *Tradition.* Chicago: University of Chicago Press, 1981.

Simmel, Georg. *The Sociology of Georg Simmel.* Trans. Kurt H. Wolff. New York: Free Press, 1950.

——. *Soziologie: Untersuchungen über die Formen der Vergesellschaftung.* Leipzig: Duncker & Humblot, 1908.

Splitter, Randolph. *Proust's "Recherche": A Psychoanalytic Interpretation.* Boston: Routledge & Kegan Paul, 1981.

Starobinski, Jean. "The Idea of Nostalgia." *Diogenes* (English language) 54 (Summer 1966): 81–103.

La Statistique en France à l'époque napoléonienne: Journée d'étude, Paris, 14 février 1980. Brussels: Centre Guillaume Jacquemyns, Centre belge d'étude des sociétés contemporaines, 1981.

Stendhal. *Journal.* In *Oeuvres intimes,* new ed., ed. Vittorio Del Litto, 2 vols., 2:3–424. Paris: Gallimard-Pléiade, 1981–82.

——. *Souvenirs d'égotisme.* Ed. Henri Martineau. Paris: Le Divan, 1950.

Stewart, Susan. *Crimes of Writing: Problems in the Containment of Representation.* New York: Oxford University Press, 1991.

——. *On Longing: Narratives of the Miniature, the Gigantic, the Souvenir, the Collection.* Baltimore: Johns Hopkins University Press, 1984.

Sulloway, F. J. *Freud, Biologist of the Mind: Beyond the Psychoanalytic Legend.* New York: Basic Books, 1979.

Tanner, Tony. *Venice Desired.* Cambridge: Harvard University Press, 1992.

Taylor, Ronald, ed. *Aesthetics and Politics (Bloch, Lukács, Brecht, Benjamin, Adorno)*. London: NLB, 1977.

Terdiman, Richard. "Crise de mémoire: Pratiques mnémoniques et pratiques culturelles au 19e siècle." *Social Science Information/Information sur les Sciences sociales* 28, no. 1 (1989): 77–98.

——. "Deconstructing Memory: On Representing the Past and Theorizing Culture in France Since the Revolution." *Diacritics* 15 (Winter 1985): 13–36.

——. *The Dialectics of Isolation: Self and Society in the French Novel from the Realists to Proust*. New Haven: Yale University Press, 1976.

——. *Discourse/Counter-Discourse: The Theory and Practice of Symbolic Resistance in Nineteenth-Century France*. Ithaca: Cornell University Press, 1985.

——. "1848." In *Harvard History of French Literature*, ed. Denis Hollier, 705–10.

——. "1852." In *Harvard History of French Literature*, ed. Denis Hollier, 717–22.

——. "On the Dialectics of Postdialectical Thinking." In *Community at Loose Ends*, ed. James Creech, 111–20. Minneapolis: University of Minnesota Press, 1991.

Timpanaro, Sebastiano. *The Freudian Slip: Psychoanalysis and Textual Criticism* (1974). Trans. Kate Soper. London: NLB, 1976.

——. *On Materialism*. Trans. Lawrence Garner. London: NLB, 1975.

Tönnies, Ferdinand. *Community and Society* (1887). Trans. Charles P. Loomis. New York: Harper & Row, 1963.

Valéry, Paul. *Oeuvres*. Ed. Jean Hytier. 2 vols. Paris: Gallimard-Pléiade, 1957–60.

Van Tieghem, Philippe. *Les Grandes Doctrines littéraires en France*. Paris: Presses Universitaires de France, 1963.

Vernant, Jean-Pierre. "Aspects mythiques de la mémoire et du temps" (1959). In Vernant, *Mythe et pensée chez les grecs: Études de psychologie historique*, 1: 80–123. Paris: Maspéro, 1974.

Vigny, Alfred de. "Réflexions sur la vérité dans l'Art" [Preface to *Cinq-Mars*]. In *Critical Prefaces to the Nineteenth-Century French Novel*, ed. Herbert S. Gershman and Kernan B. Whitworth, Jr., 53–58. Columbia: University of Missouri Press, 1962.

Vološinov, V. N. *See* Bakhtin, M. M.

Weber, Eugen. *Peasants into Frenchmen: The Modernization of Rural France, 1870–1914*. Stanford: Stanford University Press, 1976.

Weber, Max. *Economy and Society: An Outline of Interpretive Sociology*. Ed. Guenther Roth and Claus Wittich. 2 vols. Berkeley and Los Angeles: University of California Press, 1978.

——. *From Max Weber: Essays in Sociology*. Ed. Hans Gerth and C. Wright Mills. New York: Oxford University Press, 1946.

Weiskel, Thomas. *The Romantic Sublime*. Baltimore: Johns Hopkins University Press, 1976.

Wellek, René. *Concepts of Criticism.* New Haven: Yale University Press, 1963.
——. *A History of Modern Criticism, 1750–1950.* 7 vols. New Haven: Yale University Press, 1955–91.
West, Rebecca. *The Court and the Castle: Some Treatments of a Recurrent Theme.* New Haven: Yale University Press, 1957.
White, Hayden. "The Burden of History." In White, *Tropics of Discourse: Essays in Cultural Criticism,* 27–50. Baltimore: Johns Hopkins University Press, 1978.
Whyte, Lancelot Law. *The Unconscious before Freud.* New York: Basic Books, 1960.
Williams, Raymond. *Culture and Society 1780–1950.* New York: Harper & Row, 1958.
Wilson, Edmund. *Axel's Castle: A Study in the Imaginative Literature of 1870–1930.* New York: Charles Scribner's Sons, 1931.
Wittgenstein, Ludwig. "Conversations on Freud; Excerpt from 1932–3 Lectures." In *Philosophical Essays on Freud,* ed. Richard Wollheim and James Hopkins, 1–11.
Wollheim, Richard. *Sigmund Freud.* New edition. Cambridge: Cambridge University Press, 1990.
Wollheim, Richard, and James Hopkins. *Philosophical Essays on Freud.* Cambridge: Cambridge University Press, 1982.
Woolf, Virginia. *A Writer's Diary.* Ed. Leonard Woolf. New York: Harvest, 1973.
Yates, Frances A. *The Art of Memory.* Chicago: University of Chicago Press, 1966.
Young, Robert M. *Mind, Brain, and Adaptation in the Nineteenth Century: Cerebral Localization and Its Biological Context from Gall to Ferrier.* Oxford: Clarendon Press, 1970.
Zonabend, Françoise. *La Mémoire longue: Temps et histoire au village.* Paris: Presses Universitaires de France, 1980. Trans. Anthony Forster, under the title *The Enduring Memory: Time and History in a French Village.* Manchester: Manchester University Press, 1985.

Index

Abstraction, 30, 37, 43, 45, 53, 325–26
Adorno, Theodor, 12–13, 30 n. 37, 65,
    290 n. 1
Althusser, Louis, 34 n. 1, 93 n. 13, 183
Amnesty, 36 n. 8, 107–8
Andromache, 256, 261. *See also* Bau-
    delaire, Charles: "Le Cygne"
Archive, 16, 30, 37, 273 n. 36, 344, 348–
    49
    in Freud, 219, 254, 273 n. 36, 284, 344
    in Proust, 194–95, 233–34, 238
    See also Freud, Sigmund: unconscious
    in; Memory: permanence of
Aristotle, 141 n. 60, 144 n. 67
Ars memoriae, Ars memorativa. See Art of
    memory
Art of memory, 16 n. 24, 33, 43 n. 18, 58,
    78, 287
    in Freud, 240–41, 271, 278, 292, 295
Art pour l'art, L', 134, 163
Augustine, Saint, 78 n. 4, 79, 278

Bakhtin, Mikhail M., 45–46, 67, 192
Balzac, Honoré de, 83–84, 136
    Cousine Bette, 115, 120 n. 34
Barbéris, Pierre, 80, 95
Bataille, Georges, 214
Baudelaire, Charles, vii, 17–18, 28, 37,
    39, 46–47, 161, 165, 170, 178
    aesthetics of, 133–35, 153
    formalism in, 111, 133–35, 146, 176.
        See also Baudelaire, Charles: aes-
        thetics of; Baudelaire, Charles: "Le
        Cygne," antiformalism of; Formal-
        ism
    and Gautier, 134, 141 n. 61, 153 n. 4,
        176 n. 30
    and "modernity," viii–ix, 111, 132–33,
        325–26

and Paris, 112–28, 261
preoccupation with memory, 109–10
self-plagiarism in, 141 n. 61
and working class, 116–18, 124
—Works:
    "Le Cygne," viii, 18, 106, 197, 207, 261,
        278, 297, 324 n. 26, 354
    Andromache in, 139–40, 143–46, 256,
        261
    antiformalism of, 133–35. *See also*
        Baudelaire, Charles: aesthetics of;
        Baudelaire, Charles: formalism in
    association in, 142–43, 297
    and the Bohème, 115–16
    and Carrousel quarter, 112, 115–17,
        121
    and class, 116–18
    displacement in, 138–39
    exiles in, 108, 127, 136, 138, 140–41,
        143 n. 64, 145, 207 n. 30
    and history, 106–7, 110–12, 121–22,
        134, 137, 140
    impropriety in, 140, 143
    and language, 107, 278
    Louvre in, 112, 114 n. 18, 120 n. 34,
        127–28
    and memory, 21, 106–9, 136, 142
    "mnemonics of dispossession" in, 106,
        108, 110, 112, 120, 124, 127, 133,
        136–37, 140, 143, 145–46
    opening of, 138–40
    organization of, 142–43
    and prostitution, 123
    references in, 144–45
    and Second Empire, 36, 106–7, 112,
        130–47
    "semiotic consciousness" in, 107, 130–
        31, 135–43
    "semiotics of bereavement" in, 136–
        40, 147

Library of Congress Cataloging-in-Publication Data

Terdiman, Richard.
    Present past : modernity and the memory crisis / Richard Terdiman.
        p. cm.
    Includes bibliographical references and index.
    ISBN 0-8014-2897-1 (alk. paper). ISBN 0-8014-8132-5 (pbk.)
        1. French literature—19th century—History and criticism—Theory,
etc.   2. French literature—20th century—History and criticism—
Theory, etc.   3. Proust, Marcel, 1871–1922.   A la recherche du
temps perdu.   4. Literature, Modern—History and criticism—
Theory, etc.   5. Freud, Sigmund, 1856–1939.   6. Modernism
(Literature).   7. Memory in literature.   I. Title.
PQ295.M63T47   1993
840.9′353—dc20   93-1183